MW01202094

AGGRESSION AND VIOLENCE

This book provides a broad and contemporary overview by some of the most internationally renowned researchers in the field of aggression and violence. It begins with an integrative theoretical understanding of aggression and shows how animal models shed light on human aggression and violence.

The volume then looks at the individual risk factors for aggression and violence from different research perspectives. First, there is a cognitive neuroscientific, neuropsychological, and psychophysiological study of the brain. It then explores the developmental psychological factors in aggressive behavior, incorporating work on gender and the family. Other perspectives include the role of testosterone, individual differences, and whether humans are innately wired for violence.

The following sections move from the individual to the contextual risk factors for aggression, including work on the effects of adverse events and ostracism, guns and other aggressive cues including violent media, and drugs and alcohol.

Targets of aggression and violence are covered in the next section, including violence against women and loved ones; aggression between social groups; and the two very contemporary issues of cyber bullying and terrorism.

The book concludes with work showing how we may make the world a more peaceful place by preventing and reducing aggression and violence.

The volume is essential reading for upper-level students and researchers of psychology and related disciplines interested in a rigorous and multi-perspective overview of work on aggression and violence.

Brad J. Bushman (Ph.D. 1989, University of Missouri) is a professor of communication and psychology at the Ohio State University, and a professor of communication science at the VU University Amsterdam. He holds the Rinehart Chair of Mass Communication. For over 25 years he has studied the causes, consequences, and solutions to the problem of human aggression and violence.

FRONTIERS OF SOCIAL PSYCHOLOGY

Series Editors:
Arie W. Kruglanski, *University of Maryland at College Park*
Joseph P. Forgas, *University of New South Wales*

Frontiers of Social Psychology is a series of domain-specific handbooks. Each volume provides readers with an overview of the most recent theoretical, methodological, and practical developments in a substantive area of social psychology, in greater depth than is possible in general social psychology handbooks. The editors and contributors are all internationally renowned scholars whose work is at the cutting edge of research.

Scholarly, yet accessible, the volumes in the *Frontiers* series are an essential resource for senior undergraduates, postgraduates, researchers, and practitioners and are suitable as texts in advanced courses in specific subareas of social psychology.

Published Titles

Aggression and Violence, Brad J. Bushman
Social Neuroscience, Harmon-Jones & Inzlicht
Addictions, Kopetz & Lejuez
Social Communication, Fiedler
Attitudes and Attitude Change, Crano
Negotiation Theory and Research, Thompson
The Self, Sedikides & Spencer
Social Psychology and the Unconscious, Bargh
Evolution and Social Psychology, Schaller, Simpson & Kenrick
The Science of Social Influence, Pratkanis
Close Relationships, Noller & Feeney
Affect in Social Thinking and Behavior, Forgas
Personality and Social Behavior, Rhodewalt
Stereotyping and Prejudice, Stangor & Crandall
Group Processes, Levine
Social Metacognition, Briñol & DeMarree
Goal-directed Behavior, Aarts & Elliot
Social Judgment and Decision Making, Krueger
Intergroup Conflicts and their Resolution, Bar-Tal
Social Motivation, Dunning
Social Cognition, Strack & Förster
Social Psychology of Consumer Behavior, Wänke

For continually updated information about published and forthcoming titles in the *Frontiers of Social Psychology* series, please visit: https://www.routledge.com/psychology/series/FSP

AGGRESSION AND VIOLENCE

A Social Psychological Perspective

Edited by Brad J. Bushman

Routledge
Taylor & Francis Group

NEW YORK AND LONDON

First published 2017
by Routledge
711 Third Avenue, New York, NY 10017

and by Routledge
2 Park Square, Milton Park, Abingdon, Oxon, OX14 4RN

Routledge is an imprint of the Taylor & Francis Group, an Informa business

© 2017 Taylor & Francis

The right of the editor to be identified as the author of the editorial material, and of the authors for their individual chapters, has been asserted in accordance with sections 77 and 78 of the Copyright, Designs and Patents Act 1988.

All rights reserved. No part of this book may be reprinted or reproduced or utilised in any form or by any electronic, mechanical, or other means, now known or hereafter invented, including photocopying and recording, or in any information storage or retrieval system, without permission in writing from the publishers. Printed in Canada.

Trademark notice: Product or corporate names may be trademarks or registered trademarks, and are used only for identification and explanation without intent to infringe.

Library of Congress Cataloging-in-Publication Data
Names: Bushman, Brad J., editor.
Title: Aggression and violence / edited by Brad J. Bushman.
Description: New York, NY : Routledge, 2016. | Includes bibliographical references and index.
Identifiers: LCCN 2016009088 | ISBN 9781138859883 (hb : alk. paper) | ISBN 9781138859890 (pb : alk. paper) | ISBN 9781315524696 (ebk)
Subjects: LCSH: Aggressiveness. | Violence.
Classification: LCC BF575.A3 A5125 2016 | DDC 155.2/32—dc23
LC record available at https://lccn.loc.gov/2016009088

ISBN: 978-1-138-85988-3 (hbk)
ISBN: 978-1-138-85989-0 (pbk)
ISBN: 978-1-315-52469-6 (ebk)

Typeset in Bembo
by Apex CoVantage, LLC

CONTENTS

CONTRIBUTORS

Craig A. Anderson, Iowa State University, USA
Farida Anwar, Åbo Akademi University, Finland
John Archer, University of Central Lancashire, UK
Bruce D. Bartholow, University of Missouri, USA
Brad J. Bushman, Ohio State University, USA, & VU University Amsterdam, The Netherlands
Justin M. Carré, Nipissing University, Canada
Wendy Cukier, Ryerson University, Canada
Sietse F. de Boer, University of Groningen, The Netherlands
Gwendoline Decat, Coalition for Gun Control, Canada
James Densley, Metropolitan State University, USA
C. Nathan DeWall, University of Kentucky, USA
Sarah Allen Eagen, Research and Social Practice, USA
Christopher I. Eckhardt, Purdue University, USA
Thomas Elbert, University of Konstanz, Germany
Douglas P. Fry, University of Alabama at Birmingham, USA
Ingrida Grigaitytė, Åbo Akademi University, Finland
Christopher L. Groves, Iowa State University, USA
L. Rowell Huesmann, University of Michigan, USA
Barbara Krahé, University of Potsdam, Germany
Arie W. Kruglanski, University of Maryland, USA
Daniel N. Jones, University of Texas at El Paso, USA
Madelyn H. Labella, University of Minnesota, USA
Jennifer E. Lansford, Duke University, USA
Kellie R. Lynch, University of Kentucky, USA
Ann S. Masten, University of Minnesota, USA

James Moran, University of Konstanz, Germany
Dan Olweus, University of Bergen, Norway
Dominic J. Parrott, Georgia State University, USA
Delroy L. Paulhus, University of British Columbia, Canada
Jillian Peterson, Hamline University, USA
Dongning Ren, Purdue University, USA
Claire M. Renzetti, University of Kentucky, USA
Maggie Schauer, University of Konstanz, Germany
David Webber, University of Maryland, USA
Eric D. Wesselmann, Illinois State University, USA
Kipling D. Williams, Purdue University, USA

PART I

Understanding the Roots of Aggression and Violence in Humans

1

AN INTEGRATIVE THEORETICAL UNDERSTANDING OF AGGRESSION

L. Rowell Huesmann

In this chapter I lay out the most important key principles for understanding the occurrence of aggressive behavior. These are principles that have emerged out of many decades of research on aggression but also draw on key findings from social, cognitive, and developmental psychology. Aggressive behavior is a social behavior, is influenced by peoples' cognitive processing, and changes over the developmental life course.

In the context of this chapter, aggressive behavior is any behavior intended to injure or irritate another person (Berkowitz, 1974, 1993; Eron et al., 1972). Psychologists have usually distinguished between the kind of aggressive behavior that is directed at the goal of obtaining a tangible reward for the aggressor (*instrumental or proactive aggression*) and the kind of aggressive behavior that is simply intended to hurt someone else (at different times denoted *hostile, angry, emotional, or reactive aggression*) (Berkowitz, 1993; Dodge & Coie, 1987, Feshbach, 1964). Nevertheless, an examination of the underlying cognitive processes involved (e.g., Dodge & Coie, 1987) has led to a realization that many of the same mechanisms are involved in both types of aggression (Bushman & Anderson, 2001); so many of the principles I describe in this chapter apply to both types. Finally, violent behavior is defined simply as an extreme form of aggressive behavior in which the target of the behavior is actually physically harmed, e.g., hit, punched, choked, beaten, bludgeoned, stabbed, shot.

Four Important Principles about the Occurrence of Aggressive Behavior

First, aggressive behavior, like other social behaviors, is always the product of personal predispositions and precipitating situational determinants. Personal predispositions are influenced over time by a variety of biological and environmental influences that lead to the development of characteristic emotional reactions, cognitions, and cognitive processing. Consequently, some people grow up to be more predisposed to behave more aggressively in almost any situation. Situational determinants then prime the cognitions and emotional reactions linked to the situation in associative memory (Bargh & Pietromonaco, 1982; Fiske & Taylor, 1984). Extreme situations can instigate almost anyone to behave aggressively.

Second, habitual aggressive behavior usually emerges early in life, and early aggressive behavior is very predictive of later aggressive behavior and even of aggressive behavior of offspring (Farrington, 1985; Huesmann et al., 1984; Olweus, 1979). Process models for aggressive behavior explain this continuity over time and across generations by the development of cognitive and emotional predispositions to aggression that last over time.

Third, predispositions to severe aggression are most often a product of multiple interacting social and biological factors (Huesmann, 1997), including genetic predispositions (Cloninger & Gottesman, 1987; Mednick et al., 1984), environment/ genetic interactions (Caspi et al., 2002; Lagerspetz & Lagersetz, 1971), central nervous system (CNS) trauma and neurophysiological abnormalities (Moyer, 1976), early temperament or attention difficulties (Kagan, 1988), arousal levels (Raine et al., 1990), hormonal levels (Olweus et al., 1988), family violence (Widom, 1989), cultural perspectives (Staub, 1996), poor parenting (Patterson, 1995), inappropriate punishment (Eron et al., 1971), environmental poverty and stress (Guerra et al., 1995), peer-group identification (Patterson et al., 1991), and other factors. No one causal factor by itself explains more than a small portion of individual differences in aggressiveness.

Fourth, early learning plays a key role in the development of a predisposition to habitually behave in an aggressive or nonaggressive manner. Most children need to be socialized out of the aggressive inclinations stimulated by the normal or abnormal personal factors mentioned above and taught self-control. Some children are never socialized out of aggression, and some children are socialized into more frequent and serious aggression. From a social cognitive perspective, the variety of predisposing factors discussed above may make the emergence of certain specific cognitive routines, scripts, and schemas more likely, but these cognitions are likely to be unlearned or more firmly learned through interactions of the child with the environment. Aggression is most likely to develop in children who grow up in environments that reinforce aggression, provide aggressive models, frustrate and victimize them, and teach them that aggression is acceptable.

Social Information Processing

In the past few decades it has become clear that to understand how, why, and when human aggressive and violent behavior occurs one has to understand how humans process social information in their brains. Building on the earlier theoretical formulations of Berkowitz (1974), Bandura (1973), and Eron (Eron et al., 1971), aggression researchers have established a number of principles of social information processing that explain much better than ever before both the processes by which predispositions to aggression are formed within a person, and the processes by which situations interact with these predispositions to instigate the individual to behave aggressively (e.g., Anderson & Bushman, 2002; Crick & Dodge, 1994; Dewall et al., 2011; Dodge, 1986; Huesmann, 1988, 1998; Huesmann & Kirwil, 2007).

The principles are best understood by viewing social interactions as a series of social problem-solving situations. The individual in any social situation has to decide how to behave—that is, how to solve the social problem. What has been discovered is that individuals—whether children or adults—go about this social problem solving rather systematically, even though they may be unaware of the information processing that they are doing. The process begins with evaluation of the social situation and ends with the decision to behave in a certain way, followed by a post hoc self-evaluation of the consequences of behaving that way. These processes may be automatic and out of awareness or they may be consciously controlled (Bargh & Pietromonaco, 1982; Schneider & Shiffrin, 1977; Shiffrin & Schneider, 1977). The sequence of processes based on the work of Anderson and Bushman (2002), Dodge (1980), and Huesmann (1988, 1998) is diagrammed in Figure 1.1.

These processes operate in human memory, which we now know can best be represented as a complex associative network of nodes representing cognitive concepts and emotions. There are many associative links between the nodes—some built in from birth and some established through learning experiences. Some links

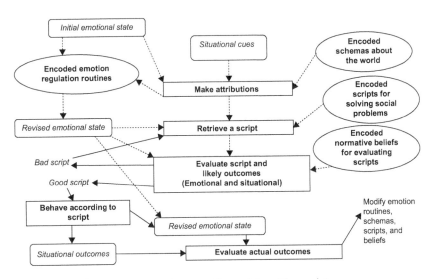

FIGURE 1.1 Information processing steps for social problem solving.

are stronger than others. When a node is activated by an external stimulus, activation "spreads out" from that node to linked nodes in proportion to how strong the links are. The activation of a node or a network of nodes at a particular time is determined by how many links to it have been activated, as well as the strength of the links. "Meaning" is only given to a node by its associations with other nodes. When the total activation of a node or set of nodes becomes above a certain "threshold," the "meaning" of the node is "experienced." Activation is cumulative, and when a node's activation level is increased but is still below threshold for "experiencing it," we say it has been "primed." Three particularly important knowledge structures relevant to social information processing are stored within a person's associative memory: 1) their schemas about the world and other people used to evaluate social situations, 2) their repertoire of social "scripts" that guide behavior, and 3) their self-schemas, including their normative beliefs about what are appropriate behaviors for them. A social script (Abelson, 1981) is a program of behaviors and expected responses by the environment designed to solve a social problem. The fourth important knowledge structure relevant to social information processing is the set of emotion regulation routines a person has encoded in memory.

We now know that there are four loci in the social problem-solving process at which individual differences in emotion regulation, schemas, scripts, and beliefs interact with situational variations to influence social information processing and thus social behavior including aggression: 1) the evaluation of the situation, 2) the retrieval of potential scripts for behavior, 3) the filtering of such scripts through the lens of effectiveness and appropriateness, and 4) the interpretation of the outcome of the behavior.

Evaluation of the Situation

To begin with, the objective situation primes cognitive structures in the brain and emotional reactions. However, which environmental cues are given most attention and how they are interpreted may vary from person to person and may depend on a person's neurophysiological predispositions, current mood state, and previous learning history. Negative affect (e.g., a bad mood) primes the interpretation of environmental events to be more negative. Very aversive situations and frustration will produce negative affect in almost everyone, but the intensity of the affect depends on the interpretation given to the situation. Environmental stimuli may directly trigger conditioned or unconditioned emotional reactions and may cue the retrieval from memory of cognitions that define the current emotional state. For example, the "sight of an enemy" or the "smell of a battlefield" may provoke both instantaneous physiological arousal and the recall of thoughts about the "enemy" that give meaning to the aroused state as anger. That emotional state may influence both what cues the person attends to and how those cues are evaluated. A highly aroused, angry person may focus on just a few highly salient cues and ignore others that convey equally important information about the social situation. Then the angry person's evaluation of these cues may be biased toward perceiving hostility when none is present. A person who finds hostile cues the most salient or who interprets ambiguous cues as hostile is said to have a "hostile attributional bias," and will be more likely to experience anger and activate schemas and scripts related to aggression.

Individuals who have greater characteristic tendencies to attribute hostility to even the benign actions of others tend to be more aggressive (Dodge, 1980). In fact, people who have such a "hostile attributional bias" are at high risk to be violent (Dodge et al., 1990). Furthermore, it is now known that this is a cross-cultural phenomenon. A higher tendency to make attributions of hostility about the benign actions of others is predictive of higher levels of aggression for individuals in many different societies (Dodge et al., 2015). More generally, attributions that a "bad" situation (a frustrating event or a failure to obtain an expected goal) is due to external causes, controllable by others, and due to unfair actions of others is a strong instigator to aggression for most people (Berkowitz, 1993). These attributions increase the likelihood of making a hostile attribution about the intentions of others and increase the priming of aggressive cognitions.

Retrieval of Potential Scripts for Behavior

After evaluating a social problem-solving situation, individuals then retrieve "scripts" that are associated in their memory with their evaluation of the situation. We know that more aggressive individuals have encoded in memory a more extensive, well-connected network of social scripts emphasizing aggressive problem solving. Therefore, such a script is more likely to be retrieved during any search. However, the likelihood of a particular script being retrieved is affected by one's interpretation of the social cues and attributions about the situation as well as one's mood state and arousal. If any of these prime the script, because they have been associated with the script in the past, the script is more likely to be retrieved. For example, bad moods, even in the absence of supporting cues, will make the retrieval of scripts previously associated with bad moods more likely. This leads to the principle: "When we feel bad, we act bad!" (Berkowitz, 1993). Similarly, the presence of a weapon, even in the absence of anger, will make the retrieval of scripts associated with weapons more likely (Berkowitz & LePage, 1967; Carlson et al., 1990), and the perception that another person has hostile intentions will activate scripts related to hostility. Finally, we know that angry, aroused people are less likely to engage in broad, time-consuming searches for a social script to follow and are more likely to focus on the first simple scripts that occur to them. Unfortunately, the first scripts that occur to them are likely to emphasize aggressive, retaliatory actions.

Filtering out Inappropriate Scripts

Before acting out a social script to try to solve a social problem, individuals have been shown to evaluate the script in light of internalized activated schemas and normative beliefs to determine if the suggested behaviors are socially appropriate and likely to achieve the desired goal. Normative beliefs are beliefs about what is "OK" or appropriate to do in a social situation (Guerra et al., 1994). Different people often evaluate the same script quite differently. Habitually aggressive people are known to hold normative beliefs condoning more aggression, and thus aggressive scripts are more likely to pass the filtering process for them than they are for habitually nonaggressive people. For example, if a man suddenly discovers that his wife has been unfaithful, he may experience rage, which primes the immediate retrieval of a script for physical retribution. However, whether or not the man executes that script will depend on his normative beliefs about the appropriateness of "hitting a female." Even within the same person, different normative beliefs may be activated in different situations and different mood states. The person who has just been to church may have activated quite different normative beliefs than the person who has just watched a fight in a hockey game on TV.

Although evaluation of the script on the basis of one's normative beliefs is probably the most important filtering process, two other evaluations also appear to play a role. Scripts include predictions about likely outcomes of behaviors, but people differ in their capacities to predict outcomes (e.g., positive or negative) accurately, and people discount future outcomes over current outcomes to different extents. More aggressive individuals tend to focus more on positive parts of the immediate outcome of using an aggressive script (e.g., an immediate tangible gain) and discount more future negative consequences or future positive outcomes of not behaving aggressively (i.e., they are less able to *delay gratification*).

This whole process of evaluating scripts against normative beliefs and desired goals and then deciding to follow or not follow a script is the essence of what most of us would call "self-control." An individual who has a high ability to reject scripts that will not achieve desired goals or that violate the individual's normative beliefs is an individual whom we say has high "self-control."

Interpreting the Outcome of Using the Script, and Modifying Cognitions and Mood

The fourth locus for individual differences in this model is a person's interpretation of society's responses to his or her behaviors and how that interpretation affects the person's schemas and mood. With some interpretations of society's responses, one may maintain aggressive scripts even in the face of strong negative responses from society. For example, a boy who is severely beaten for behaving aggressively may attribute the beating to being disliked by the punisher rather than to anything he did, so he will follow the same script again. Alternatively, he may mitigate society's negative reinforcements for his aggressive behavior by choosing environments in which aggression is more accepted; for example, the more aggressive adolescent male may spend more time interacting with other aggressive peers who accept his behaviors as a way of life and share normative beliefs accepting aggression.

The Role of Emotions

It would be a mistake to interpret the above social-cognitive processes as independent of emotional processes. Emotional states affect these processes, and these processes affect a person's emotional state. First, people in highly aroused states are generally poorer information processors who are more likely to go with the first solution to a social problem (i.e., the first script) that occurs to them (Anderson, 1980). If the dominant script in memory is aggressive, more aggressive behavior is the result. Similarly, hostile attributional bias is more likely under conditions of high emotional arousal (Dodge & Somberg, 1987). Second, some of the most serious aggressive acts (e.g., assaults, murders) are driven by angry emotions derived from attributions people make about the situation. A person's current emotional state is always one factor that primes the schema that is used to evaluate the situation and primes the scripts that might be used to solve a social problem. Thus, experiencing an aversive situation instigates anger and aggressive inclinations in many individuals. Although there is some disagreement about whether the aggressive inclination or experiencing the anger comes first (Berkowitz, 1993), retrieving an aggressive script is a likely outcome. Of course, such "aversively stimulated aggression" may be inhibited by the filtering process that evaluates scripts against self-schemas including normative beliefs. However, we know that "hurting" the other who is perceived as the cause of one's anger becomes a more palatable goal in its own right as anger increases. Research has shown that humans, who are seriously provoked, aggress against the provoker more if they know their aggression—for example, delivering electric shocks—is hurting the provoker than if it doesn't seem to hurt him or her (Baron, 1977; see also Berkowitz, 1993).

Excitation Transfer

A well-known phenomenon related to the occurrence of feelings of anger in any situation is known as excitation transfer (Bryant & Zillmann, 1979). Because emotions are a product of general arousal and cognitive interpretations of the cause of the arousal, a person who is already physically or emotionally aroused (e.g., by physical activity, competition, viewing an exciting film, etc.) will experience stronger feelings of any specific emotion that is stimulated shortly afterward because that person's general arousal is greater. Thus, a provocation will produce stronger feelings of anger if it follows other arousing stimuli, particularly if the person does not connect the emotional arousal with the prior event. This is excitation transfer.

"Feelings" Influence Script Choice

Still another important role that emotions play in the occurrence of aggression is in the filtering of retrieved scripts for behavior to decide whether the script is appropriate to use. If one retrieves a potential script that "feels bad" when one thinks about it, one is less likely to use it. If one "feels good" about an aggressive script, one is more likely to use it.

Because emotional reactions when one thinks about an aggressive script are important in determining whether a person will utilize an aggressive script, "desensitization to violence" (Bandura et al., 1967; McSweeney & Swindell, 2002) becomes important in affecting risk of aggression. While there are individual differences in young children's innate emotional reactions to violence, the dominant reaction is high arousal with negative valence. Seeing violence, blood, and gore is aversive for most young children. Emotional desensitization to violence, then, is defined as a decrease in both the physiological markers of the emotional arousal and a change in the cognitive interpretations of that arousal to make it less negative. Emotional desensitization to aggression and violence—a reduction in distress-related physiological reactivity to observations or thoughts of violence (Carnagey et al., 2007)—can be adaptive for people in certain situations, for example, war or disasters, where the repeated negative emotional reactions could be damaging to one's mental health. However, the unpleasant physiological arousal and negative emotional reactions normally associated with aggression have an inhibitory influence on thinking about aggression and following an aggressive script. Consequently, emotional desensitization to aggression and violence increases the likelihood of a person following an aggressive script.

Biological and Other Innate Influences on Aggression

As mentioned at the start of this chapter, a variety of biological factors predispose individuals behaving aggressively or nonaggressively. Some factors exert their influence at the moment a person is behaving; some factors exert their influence during the long period of development for humans; some factors exert their influence even before an individual is born; and some factors exert influence during all these periods. Many of these factors are discussed in other chapters in this book, so I will not discuss them here. However, there are two important points that need to be mentioned in this chapter on principles of aggressive behavior. First, all biological factors exert their influence on social behavior by affecting in some way the social and emotional information processing described above or the social cognitions (world schemas, scripts, normative beliefs) or emotion regulation routines stored in the brain and utilized in these processes. Second, most of the lasting influences on aggression of individual differences in biology are not deterministic effects but rather probabilistic effects. In fact, most factors only have an effect that is interactive with environmental factors. The classic example of such a "bio-social interaction" is the finding that having a genetic abnormality that causes lower brain monoamine oxidase only results in increased adult aggression when it is combined with growing up in a harsh parental environment (Caspi et al., 2002). It is unclear exactly how this interaction works, but somehow low MAO must exacerbate the effects of a harsh environment on socializing a child to grow up and utilize more aggressive scripts for social problem solving.

Some seemingly innate individual differences that predispose people to behave more or less aggressively are difficult to connect to any specific biological difference; yet we know they are important. These differences fall under the rubric of personality differences or, if they are apparent very early in life, temperament differences. Again, these differences operate by affecting the social cognitive or emotional processes described above for social problem solving. For example, toddlers whose temperament appears more fearless seem to grow up to be at more risk for aggression, probably because they experience less anxious arousal when they evaluate aggressive scripts. Similarly, adults who score high on callousness and unemotionality (psychopathy) are at higher risk for behaving aggressively, probably because they don't feel any negative consequences of aggression when they evaluate aggressive scripts. Also, adults who score high on narcissism (particularly on a sense of entitlement) behave more aggressively when threatened or provoked (Bushman & Baumeister, 1998), probably because they attribute the threat to them as more hostile because they have an inflated sense of self-entitlement.

Socialization (Learning) Processes Influencing Aggression

A major task for parents (and society) during any child's development from infancy to adulthood is socializing the child to behave appropriately. To most of us, that would mean, among other things, socializing the child to behave prosocially toward others and not to behave aggressively toward others. Most humans peak in physical aggression toward peers (e.g., hitting, shoving, etc.) when they are about two years old (Tremblay et al., 2004), probably because it yields tangible immediate rewards for them. Thus, socialization out of aggression is an important task. However, some parents desire to have their children behave aggressively in some situations, so they deliberately socialize them in that direction. Also, in many environments and families children are unintentionally socialized to behave aggressively. Formally, socialization is best viewed as the learning of new connections between social stimuli and social schemas, scripts, and normative beliefs on which social problem solving and social behaviors are based. Socialization occurs through either *enactive learning* or *observational learning* (Bandura, 1986).

Enactive Learning

Enactive learning encompasses both instrumental (operant) and classical conditioning. If the aggressive social scripts, hostile world schemas, or aggressive normative beliefs that a person utilizes result in a positively evaluated outcome, these cognitions become more accessible in memory and more likely to be used in the future. This is operant conditioning of nonaggression or aggression. Classical conditioning can also contribute to socialization into aggression. For example, if a child's unconditioned response to a situation is to see it as friendly, but the kind of situation repeatedly turns out to be hostile, the child will quickly learn it is hostile, which will promote the choice of aggressive scripts in that situation.

Fifty years ago or so, it was generally accepted that the most important socialization processes were the operant and classical conditioning of the child to behave appropriately by parents and society. However, we now know that an even more powerful socialization process is observational learning (Bandura, 1973; Bandura et al., 1961; Huesmann & Kirwil, 2007).

Observational Learning

In recent years indisputable evidence has accumulated that human and primate young have an innate tendency to imitate whomever they observe (Meltzoff, 2005; Meltzoff & Moore, 1977). They imitate expressions in early infancy and imitate behaviors by the time they can walk. Aggressive behaviors are no different from other observable motor behavior in this regard. Thus, the hitting, grabbing, pushing behaviors that young children see around them or in the mass media are generally immediately mimicked unless the child has been taught not to mimic them. Furthermore, there is good reason to believe that the automatic imitation of expressions on others' faces also leads to the automatic activation of the emotion that the other was experiencing, as expressions are innately linked to emotions (Zajonc, Murphy, & Inglehart, 1989).

This empirical evidence for automatic imitation in humans has been given added import by an explosion of neurophysiological findings (Iacoboni et al., 1999) and computational theorizing (Schaal, 1999) aimed at explaining how imitation works. Most recently this work has been connected directly with theorizing about social cognitions in adults and how they are acquired (Meltzoff & Decety, 2003). At the same time, the expanding work in artificial intelligence on learning by example (e.g., Schaal, 1999) has stimulated some developmentalists to think more broadly about the role of imitation and observation in creating the schemas, scripts, beliefs, and emotional dispositions we call the self.

The kind of mimicry of aggression that occurs immediately while the aggression is observed is a less complex kind of imitation that does not involve the need to form a lasting or abstracted cognitive representation of the observed act. More delayed replications of observed social behaviors and generalizations of the behavior to similar situations require a more complex cognitive process that is called "observational learning" (Bandura, 1973). Observational learning occurs when people encode schemas, scripts, or beliefs that they have observed others utilizing, and these encoded cognitions influence future behavior.

Humans begin imitating other humans at a very early age, and it quickly progresses to learning behavioral scripts that are emitted long after the observation. The innate neurophysiological processes that make imitation automatic allow the incorporation into the child's repertoire of simple social scripts at a very young age. Social interactions then hone these behaviors that children first acquire through observation of others, but observational learning of social cognitions and emotional reactions becomes an even more powerful mechanism for the acquisition of more complex social scripts as the toddler matures through childhood and adolescence. Normative beliefs and schemas about the world are acquired from inferences made about observed social behaviors. Children learn from whomever they observe—parents, siblings, peers, or media characters. Much of this learning takes place without an intention to learn and without an awareness that learning has occurred.

A variety of factors are known to affect the likelihood of observed social information being encoded, including the saliency of the stimuli, the schemas already active, and the interpretation given to the information. In addition, however, the likelihood that an individual will acquire an observed social script is increased when the model performing the script is similar to or attractive to the viewer, the viewer identifies with the model, the context is realistic, and the viewed behavior is followed by rewarding consequences (Bandura, 1977; Huesmann et al., 2003). The observer experiences *vicariously* the reinforcements and consequences that the observed model experiences, which, if positive, will also increase the likelihood of encoding. Thus, through observational learning and enactive conditioning, children develop habitual modes of behavior that persist over time and situations (e.g., Bandura, 1977, 1986; Huesmann, 1997).

It is important to understand that children not only learn specific behaviors from models, but they also learn more generalized, complex social scripts, world schemas, and normative beliefs. Once learned and encoded in the brain, these cognitions are strengthened and elaborated by being rehearsed (e.g., by fantasizing about them) and used with success. For example, from observing violent people in proximity to them or in the media, children learn that aggressive scripts can be used to try to solve interpersonal conflicts, that aggression is normative, and that the world is a hostile place. As a result of mental rehearsal (e.g., imagining this kind of scripted behavior) and repeated exposure, this kind of script for conflict resolution can become well established and easily retrieved from memory. Through inferences they make from repeated observations, children also develop beliefs about the world in general (e.g., is it hostile or benign) and about what kind of behavior is normative and acceptable. The result is firmly encoded cognitions that are difficult to change and that influence behavior for a long time—perhaps even a lifetime.

Observational learning is often thought of as a more conscious process than simple mimicry, but that need not be the case. Empirical studies have shown that some types of observational learning of simple scripts or emotional

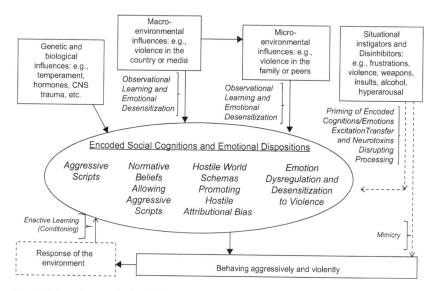

FIGURE 1.2 The psychological processes that promote aggressive behavior and the external inputs to the processes.

responses are very automatic and nonconscious (e.g., Bargh & Chartland, 1999; Neuman & Strack, 2000). Similarly, observational learning of complex scripts, world schemas, and normative beliefs can undoubtedly also occur outside of awareness.

These psychological processes that lead to the development of social cognitions and emotional dispositions that promote habitual aggression and the influence of situational factors that promote immediate aggression are summarized in Figure 1.2.

Environmental Influences

Given these principles of how social information processing influences social behavior and specifically aggression, of how the social cognitions and emotional dispositions promoting aggression are acquired and have lasting influence, and of how situational factors exert their influence, let us turn to a discussion of how and why some environmental factors influence aggression. To best understand the role that environmental variations play in this process, one must distinguish between *situational instigators* that may precipitate, motivate, or cue aggressive cognitions/responses (e.g., frustrations, moods, temperature) and those more lasting components of the child's *socializing environment* that mold the child's cognitions (schemas, scripts, normative beliefs) and therefore their behavior over time. A "mean" person who insults another is a situational instigator for aggressive behavior, but growing up in a "mean" general environment will socialize a child to believe that the world is "mean," which has more lasting influence on aggression. In this chapter, I am not going to discuss situational instigators in any detail, because they are covered in other chapters. Suffice it to say that any situation that primes cognitions or emotions connected to aggression influences social information processing and increases the risk of immediate aggression.

I will also discuss very few specific environmental factors that socialize youth into or out of aggression, because most are discussed more extensively in other chapters. In brief, an environment for a child that is rich with violence and that provides little monitoring, discipline, or exposure to prosocial behavior is one in which predispositions to aggressive behavior are socialized in children over time until they become habitual and resistant to change. On the other hand, an environment for a child that provides monitoring, appropriate contingent discipline, and exposures to prosocial behaviors, and that protects the child from exposures to violence, is one in which children are socialized out of aggression. Because once social cognitions supporting aggression are acquired and firmly encoded by youth in critical periods of development, they resist change, the more aggressive child generally grows up to be the more aggressive adult.

Exposure to Violence

I will focus on just one environmental socializing factor. Probably the most important environmental factor leading to lasting tendencies for a youth to behave aggressively or nonaggressively is the amount of their exposure to violent and aggressive behavior or prosocial behavior from birth to adolescence. The degree to which parents monitor and discipline children appropriately (Dishion & McMahon, 1998; Lansford et al., 2005) may moderate or exacerbate the effect of the children's exposure to aggression and violence, but exposure to aggression and violence (or in contrast, exposure to prosocial behavior) is the primary factor that socializes children into or out of aggression. Because of the pervasiveness of observational learning in the child's development, children who are exposed to violence anywhere in their environment—in their family, among their peers, in their neighborhood, in the mass media, in video games—tend to encode the aggressive scripts they see, tend to think the world is a more hostile place, and tend to adopt normative beliefs more approving of aggression. All these factors combine to increase the risk of future aggressive behavior. Thus, empirical studies have shown that youths' habitual exposure to neighborhood violence (e.g., Guerra et al., 2003), habitual exposure to family violence (Widom, 1989), habitual exposure to war violence (Boxer et al., 2013), and habitual exposure to media violence (Anderson et al., 2003; Anderson et al., 2010; Bushman & Huesmann, 2006; Huesmann et al., 2003; Huesmann & Taylor, 2006) all increase the likelihood of aggression and violence. Because of the economic and legal implications of concluding that violent media cause aggression, some researchers have disputed this conclusion. However, even review studies by skeptical researchers have found a positive link between exposure to violent media and aggressive behavior (e.g., Ferguson & Kilburn, 2009). Furthermore, recently a "blue-ribbon" task force of psychological scientists who do not conduct research in the area concluded unambiguously that "violent video game use has an effect on aggression" (APA, 2015).

Summary: The Contagion of Aggression and Violence

Perhaps the single most important summarizing integrative principle for understanding aggressive behavior to take away from this review is that violence is like a contagious disease. Violence begets violence in multiple domains. The contagion of violence occurs within families. The contagion of violence occurs within peer groups. The contagion of violence occurs within neighborhoods and communities. The contagion of violence occurs through the mass media. Contagion of violence even occurs between nations and cultures. And it is true across generations. Children catch violence from their parents, and parents can catch it from their children. The more violent people you are exposed to in any domain, the more likely you are to catch violence. Repeated exposures to even one infected person make it more likely that you will catch violence. Many individuals have characteristics that enhance their resistance to this disease, so they don't catch it despite repeated exposures. However, other people have characteristics that make them more susceptible to being infected.

The mode of transmission and infection with violence, however, is a little different from most diseases. You don't need to be near someone who is infected with violence to catch it. Of course, physical contact with a violent person in the form of violent victimization increases even more the risk of infection, but physical contact or victimization is not necessary. Violence is not only spread from the perpetrators of violence to the victims, it is spread to the onlookers and observers of violence. The victim of aggression (e.g., a child being beaten by a parent) is also an observer of the aggression and is learning a script that aggression is a normative way to achieve a desired goal. Violence can even be spread to faraway people who observe violence at a distance through the mass media. The boundaries of time and space that apply to most biological contagions do not apply to the contagion of violence. This contagion can become a downward spiral of violence begetting violence, as shown in Figure 1.3.

Violence is contagious because the social cognitions and social information processing systems that, as described in this chapter, control our social behavior, and thus our aggressive behavior, are exquisitely sensitive to being influenced by observational learning. The world schemas that affect attributions about situations, the repertoire of social scripts stored in memory, the normative beliefs used to filter out inappropriate scripts, and the emotional connections that influence evaluations of scripts and outcomes all are influenced by observational learning.

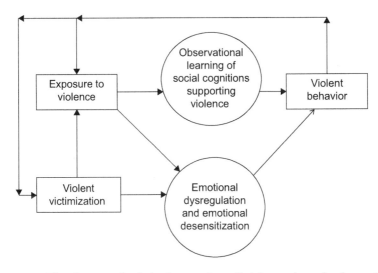

FIGURE 1.3 The downward spiral of contagion of violence through observational learning.

Of course, a positive consequence of our social behaviors being determined by a social information processing system that is so strongly influenced by observational learning is that habitual exposure to prosocial and nonaggressive behavior should result in the growth of social cognitions that promote nonaggressive behavior.

References

Abelson, R. P. (1981). The psychological status of the script concept. *American Psychologist, 36*, 715–729.

Anderson, C.A., Berkowitz, L., Donnerstein, E., Huesmann, L.R., Johnson, J., Linz, D., Malamuth, N., & Wartella, E. (2003). The influence of media violence on youth. *Psychological Science in the Public Interest, 4*(3), 81–110.

Anderson, C.A., & Bushman, B.J. (2002). Human aggression. *Annual Review of Psychology, 53*, 27–51.

Anderson, C.A., Shibuya, A., Ihori, N., Swing, E. L., Bushman, B.J., Sakamoto, A., & Saleem, M. (2010). Violent video game effects on aggression, empathy, and prosocial behavior in Eastern and Western countries. *Psychological Bulletin, 136*, 151–173.

Anderson, J. R. (1980). *Cognitive psychology*. San Francisco: Freeman.

APA (2015). American Psychological Association Task Force on Violent Media Technical Report on the Review of the Violent Video Game Literature. www.apa.org/news/press/releases/2015/08/technical-violent-games.pdf.

Bandura, A. (1973). *Aggression: A social learning analysis*. Englewood Cliffs, NJ: Prentice-Hall.

Bandura, A. (1977). *Social learning theory*. Englewood Cliffs, NJ: Prentice-Hall.

Bandura, A. (1986). *Social foundations of thought and action: A social-cognitive theory*. Englewood Cliffs, NJ: Prentice-Hall.

Bandura, A., Grusec, J. E., & Menlove, F. L. (1967). Vicarious extinction of avoidance behavior. *Journal of Personality and Social Psychology, 5,* 16–23.

Bandura, A., Ross, D., & Ross, D. A. (1961). Transmission of aggression through imitation of aggressive models. *Journal of Abnormal and Social Psychology, 63,* 575–582.

Bargh, J. A., & Chartland, T. L. (2000). The mind in the middle: A practical guide to priming and automaticity research. In H. T. Reis & C. M. Judd (Eds.), *Handbook of research methods in social and personality psychology* (pp. 253–285). New York: Cambridge University Press.

Bargh, J. A., & Pietromonaco, P. (1982). Automatic information processing and social perception: The influence of trait information presented outside of conscious awareness on impression formation. *Journal of Personality and Social Psychology, 43*(3), 437–449.

Baron, R. (1977). *Human aggression.* New York: Plenum.

Berkowitz, L. (1974). Some determinants of impulsive aggression: The role of mediated associations with reinforcements for aggression. *Psychological Review, 81,* 165–176.

Berkowitz, L. (1993). Pain and aggression: Some findings and implications. Special Issue: The pain system: A multilevel model for the study of motivation and emotion. *Motivation and Emotion, 17,* 277–293.

Berkowitz, L., & LePage, A. (1967). Weapons as aggression-eliciting stimuli. *Journal of Personality and Social Psychology, 7,* 202–207.

Boxer, P., Dubow, E. F., & Huesmann, L. R. (April 2011). The impact of exposure to ethno political violence on Middle-Eastern children's outcomes: Mediation by exposure to proximal violence. Society for Research on Child Development, Montreal, Canada.

Boxer, L. R., Huesmann, L. R., Dubow, E. F., Landau, S., Gvirsman, S., Shikaki, K., & Ginges, J. (2013). Exposure to violence across the social ecosystem and the development of aggression: A test of ecological theory in the Israeli-Palestinian conflict. *Child Development, 84*(1), 163–177.

Bryant, J., & Zillmann, D. (1979). Effect of intensification of annoyance through unrelated residual excitation on substantially delayed hostile behavior. *Journal of Experimental Social Psychology, 15,* 470–480.

Bushman, B. J., & Anderson, C. A. (2001). Is it time to pull the plug on the hostile versus instrumental aggression dichotomy? *Psychological Review, 108*(1), 273–279. DOI: 10.1037//0033–295X.108.1.273

Bushman, B. J., & Baumeister, R. F. (1998). Threatened egotism, narcissism, self-esteem, and direct and displaced aggression: Does self-love or self-hate lead to violence? *Journal of Personality and Social Psychology, 75*(1), 219–229. DOI: 10.1037/0022–3514.75.1.219

Bushman, B. J. & Huesmann, L. R. (2006). Short-term and long-term effects of violent media on aggression in children and adults. *Archives of Pediatrics and Adolescent Medicine, 160,* 348–352.

Carlson, M., Marcus-Newhall, A., & Miller, N. (1990). Effects of situational aggression cues: A quantitative review. *Journal of Personality and Social Psychology, 58,* 622–633.

Carnagey, N. L., Anderson, C. A., & Bushman, B. J. (2007). The effect of video game violence on physiological desensitization to real-life violence. *Journal of Experimental Social Psychology, 43,* 489–496.

Caspi, A., McClay, J., Moffitt, T. E., Mill, J., Martin, J., Craig, I. W., Taylor, A., & Poulton, R. (2002). Role of genotype in the cycle of violence in maltreated children. *Science, 297,* 851–854.

Cloninger, C. R., & Gottesman, A. (1987). Genetic and environmental factors in antisocial behavior disorders. In Mednick, S. A., Moffitt, T. E., & Stack, S. A. (Eds.), *The causes of crime: New biological approaches.* New York: Cambridge University Press.

Crick, N., & Dodge, K. (1994). A review and reformulation of social information processing mechanisms in children's adjustment. *Psychological Bulletin, 115*, 74–101.

Dewall, C. N., Anderson, C. A., & Bushman, B. J. (2011). The General Aggression Model: Theoretical extension to violence. *Psychology of Violence, 1*(3), 245–258.

Dishion, T. J., & McMahon, R. J. (1998). Parental monitoring and the prevention of child and adolescent problem behaviour: A conceptual and empirical formulation. *Clinical Child and Family Psychology, 1*, 61–75.

Dodge, K. A. (1980). Social cognition and children's aggressive behavior. *Child Development, 53*, 620-635.

Dodge, K. A. (1986). A social information processing model of social competence in children. In M. Perlmutter (Ed.), *The Minnesota symposium on child psychology* (pp. 77–125). Hillsdale, NJ: Erlbaum.

Dodge, K. A., & Coie, J. D. (1987). Social information-processing factors in reactive and proactive aggression in children's peer groups. *Journal of Personality and Social Psychology, 53*, 1146–1158.

Dodge, K. A., Price, J. M., Bachorowski, J. A., & Newman, J. P. (1990). Hostile attributional biases in severely aggressive adolescents. *Journal of Abnormal Psychology, 99*, 385–392.

Dodge, K. A., & Somberg, D. A. (1987). Hostile attributional biases among aggressive boys are exacerbated under conditions of threats to the self. *Child Development, 58*, 213-224.

Dodge, K. A., Malone, P. S., Lansford, J. E., Sorbring, E., Skinner, A. T., . . . & Pastorelli, C. (2015). Hostile attributional bias and aggressive behavior in global context. *Proceedings of the National Academy of Sciences, 112*(30), 9310–9315.

Dubow, E. F., Huesmann, L. R., & Boxer, P. (2009). A social-cognitive-ecological framework for understanding the impact of exposure to persistent ethnic-political violence on children's psychosocial adjustment. *Clinical Child and Family Psychology Review, 12*(2), 113–126.

Eron, L. D., Huesmann, L. R., Lefkowitz, M. M., & Walder, L. O. (1972). Does television violence cause aggression? *American Psychologist, 27*, 253–263.

Eron, L. D., Walder, L. O., & Lefkowitz, M. M. (1971). *The learning of aggression in children.* Boston: Little Brown.

Farrington, D. P. (1985). The development of offending and antisocial behavior from childhood: Key findings from the Cambridge study in delinquent development. *Journal of Child Psychology and Psychiatry, 36*, 1–36.

Ferguson, C. J., & Kilburn, J. (2009). The public health risks of media violence: A meta-analytic review. *Journal of Pediatrics, 154*, 759–763.

Feshbach, S. (1964). The function of aggression and the regulation of aggressive drive. *Psychological Review, 71*, 257–272.

Fiske, S. T., & Taylor, S. E. (1984). *Social cognition.* Reading, MA: Addison-Wesley.

Guerra, N. G., Huesmann, L. R., & Hanish, L. (1994). The role of normative beliefs in children's social behavior. In N. Eisenberg (Ed.), *Review of personality and social psychology, development and social psychology: The interface* (pp. 140–158). London: Sage.

Guerra, N. G., Huesmann, L. R., & Spindler, A. J. (2003). Community violence exposure, social cognition, and aggression among urban elementary school children. *Child Development, 74*(5), 1507–1522.

Guerra, N. G., Huesmann, L. R., Tolan, P. H., VanAcker, R. & Eron, L. D. (1995). Stressful events and individual beliefs as correlates of economic disadvantage and aggression among urban children. *Journal of Consulting and Clinical Psychology, 63*(4), 518–528.

Huesmann, L. R. (1988). An information processing model for the development of aggression. *Aggressive Behavior, 14*, 13–24.

Huesmann, L. R. (1997). Observational learning of violent behavior: Social and biosocial processes. In A. Raine, P. A. Brennen, D. P. Farrington, & S. A. Mednick (Eds.), *Biosocial bases of violence* (pp. 69–88). London: Plenum.

Huesmann, L. R. (1998). The role of social information processing and cognitive schema in the acquisition and maintenance of habitual aggressive behavior. In R. G. Geen & E. Donnerstein (Eds.), *Human aggression: Theories, research, and implications for policy* (pp. 73–109). New York: Academic Press.

Huesmann, L. R., Eron, L. D., Lefkowitz, M. M., & Walder, L. O. (1984). The stability of aggression over time and generations. *Developmental Psychology, 20*, 1120–1134.

Huesmann, L. R., & Kirwil, L. (2007). Why observing violence increases the risk of violent behavior in the observer. In D. J. Flannery, A. T. Vazsonyi, & I. D. Waldman (Eds.), *The Cambridge handbook of violent behavior and aggression* (pp. 545–570). Cambridge, UK: Cambridge University Press.

Huesmann, L. R., Moise-Titus, J., Podolski, C. P., & Eron, L. D. (2003). Longitudinal relations between childhood exposure to media violence and adult aggression and violence: 1977–1992. *Developmental Psychology, 39*, 201–221.

Huesmann, L. R., & Taylor, L. D. (2006). The role of the mass media in violent behavior. *Annual Review of Public Health, 26*, 1–23.

Iacoboni, M., Woods, R., Brass, M., Bekkering, H., Mazziotta, J., & Rizzolatti, G. (1999). Cortical mechanisms of human imitation. *Science, 286*, 2526–2528.

Kagan, J. (1988). Temperamental contributions to social behavior. *American Psychologist, 44*, 668–674.

Lansford, J. E., Chang, L., Dodge, K. A., Malone, P. S., Oburu, P., Palmérus, K., Bacchini, D., Pastorelli, C., Bombi, A. S., Zelli, A., Tapanya, S., Chaudhary, N., Deater-Deckard, K., Manke, B., & Quinn, N. (2005). Cultural normativeness as a moderator of the link between physical discipline and children's adjustment: A comparison of China, India, Italy, Kenya, Philippines, and Thailand. *Child Development, 76*, 1234–1246.

Lagerspetz, K., & Lagerspetz, K. M. J. (1971). Changes in aggressiveness of mice resulting from selective breeding, learning and social isolation. *Scandinavian Journal of Psychology, 12*, 241–278.

McSweeney, F. K., & Swindell, S. (2002). Common processes may contribute to extinction and habituation. *Journal of General Psychology, 129*, 364–400.

Mednick, S. A., Gabrielli, W. F., & Hutchings, B. (1984). Genetic influences in criminal convictions: Evidence from an adoption cohort. *Science, 224*, 891–894.

Meltzoff, A., & Decety, J. (2003). What imitation tells us about social cognition: A rapprochement between developmental psychology and cognitive neuroscience. (Available at www.royalsoc.ac.uk/).

Meltzoff, A. N. (2005). Imitation and other minds: The "Like Me" hypothesis. In S. Hurley & N. Chater (Eds.), *Perspectives on imitation: From mirror neurons to memes* (Vol. 2, pp. 55–78). Cambridge, MA: MIT Press.

Meltzoff, A. N., & Moore, K. M. (1977). Imitation of facial and manual gestures by human neonates. *Science, 109*, 77–78.

Moyer, K. E. (1976). *The psychobiology of aggression*. New York: Harper & Row.

Neuman, R., & Strack, F. (2000). "Mood contagion": The automatic transfer of mood between persons. *Journal of Personality and Social Psychology, 79*, 211–223.

Olweus, D. (1979). The stability of aggressive reaction patterns in males: A review. *Psychological Bulletin, 86*, 852–875.

Olweus, D., Mattsson, A., Schalling, D., & Low, H. (1988). Circulating testosterone levels and aggression in adolescent males: A causal analysis. *Psychosomatic Medicine, 50*, 261–273.

Patterson, G. R. (1995). Coercion—a basis for early age of onset for arrest. In J. McCord (Ed.), *Coercion and punishment in long-term perspective* (pp. 81–105). New York: Cambridge University Press.

Patterson, G. R., Capaldi, D. M., & Bank, L. (1991). An early starter model for predicting delinquency. In D. J. Pepler & K. H. Rubin (Eds.), *Systems and development: Symposia on child psychology* (pp. 139–168). Hillsdale, NJ: Lawrence Erlbaum.

Raine, A., Venables, P. H., & Williams, M. (1990). Relationships between central and autonomic measures of arousal at age 15 and criminality at age 24 years. *Archives of General Psychiatry, 47*, 1003–1007.

Schaal, S. (1999). Is imitation learning the route to humanoid robots? *Trends in Cognitive Science, 3*, 233–242.

Schneider, W., & Shiffrin, R. M. (1977). Controlled and automatic human information processing: I. Detection, search, and attention. *Psychological Review, 84*, 1-66.

Shiffrin, R. M., & Schneider, W. (1977). Controlled and automatic human information processing: II. Perceptual learning, automatic attending, and general theory. *Psychological Review, 84*, 127–190.

Staub, E. (1996). Cultural-societal roots of violence: The examples of genocidal violence and of contemporary youth violence in the United States. *American Psychologist, 51*, 117–132.

Tremblay, R. E., Nagin, D. S., Seguin, J. R., Zoccolillo, M., Zelazo, P., Boivin, M., Perusse, D., & Japel, C. (2004). Physical aggression during early childhood: Trajectories and predictors. *Pediatrics, 114*(1), e43–e50.

Widom, C. S. (1989). Does violence beget violence? A critical examination of the literature. *Psychological Bulletin, 106*(1), 3–28.

Zajonc, R. B., Murphy, S. T., & Inglehart, M. (1989). Feeling and facial efference: Implications of the vascular theory of emotion. *Psychological Review, 96*, 395–416.

2

ANIMAL MODELS

Implications for Human Aggression and Violence

Sietse F. de Boer

The human capacity for uncontrolled aggressiveness and violence inflicts an awful and costly burden on society. Unfortunately, the current intervention strategies and treatment options for curbing aggression and violence are largely inadequate. Hence, a more fundamental knowledge about the social and neurobiological determinants of aggression is desperately needed. In particular, the interaction between environmental factors and the neurochemical substrates that causally underlies the shift from aggression to violence is in great need to be unraveled. Novel experimental laboratory models of violent-like aggression in rodents combined with newly emerging technologies for mapping and manipulating neuronal activity with anatomical, genetic, and temporal precision are indispensable to obtain this goal. This chapter presents some of the most significant developments made during the last decade in this preclinical animal research field that promise to significantly advance our understanding of the etiology, brain mechanisms, and potential therapeutic interventions of aggression and violence in humans.

It is commonly accepted in biology that, throughout the animal kingdom, aggression is one of the most widespread and functional forms of social behavior that ultimately contributes to fitness (procreation) and survival of individuals. Clearly, aggression is the behavioral weapon of choice for both animals and humans to defend themselves and their offspring, secure food and mates, compete for limited resources, and maintain social status/hierarchies. Although most individuals engage in social conflicts with appropriate and well-controlled (functional) forms of aggressive behavior, a relatively small fraction of individuals can become violent. However, this small percentage of violent individuals is a major source of death and injury, and they constitute one of the most significant problems for public health, medical institutions, and criminal justice systems. Violent individuals inflict a terrible burden on human societies. These violent, hostile, and presumably less adaptive forms of aggression observed in our human society and clinically, comorbid across a wide spectrum of DSM-defined psychiatric and neurological disorders, have motivated much of the scientific interest in aggressive behavior in animals. In particular, there is a need to understand these problematic behaviors in terms of their underlying causal mechanisms and modulating factors. In general, animal models are essential to obtain experimental support of the causal nature of physiological and environmental factors. As a matter of fact, a considerable part of our current knowledge on the ethology, etiology, neurobiology, genetics, and pharmacology of this behavior is based on experimental and laboratory studies of aggressive behaviors in a wide variety of animals (e.g., fruit flies, honeybees, ants, crickets, zebra fish, songbirds, mice, rats, hamsters, prairie voles, dogs, cats, monkeys).

Most neurobehavioral and pharmacological studies of aggressive behavior in the laboratory setting are performed in rodent species (rats, voles, and mice) that can show high levels of territorial aggression characteristic of their generally dispersive social structure under low population densities in their natural habitats. Therefore, much of the preclinical aggression research is conducted in territorial male resident rats/mice confronting an intruder of the same species (called a "conspecific"). This so-called resident-intruder paradigm allows the spontaneous and natural expression of both offensive aggression and defensive behavior in laboratory rodents in a semi-natural laboratory setting. By recording the frequencies, durations, latencies, and temporal and sequential patterns of all the observed behavioral acts and postures in the combatants during these confrontations, a detailed quantitative picture (ethogram) of offensive (resident) and defensive (intruder) aggression is obtained. The resident-intruder paradigm brings this natural form of behavior into the laboratory, allowing controlled studies of both the resident aggressor and the intruder victim (Koolhaas et al., 2013). The paradigm is strongly based on the fact that an adult male rat will establish a territory when given sufficient living space. Territoriality is significantly enhanced in the presence of females and/or sexual experiences. As a consequence of territoriality, the resident will attack unfamiliar males intruding in its home cage. The intruder in turn will show defensive behavior in response to the offensive attack by the resident. Although typical patterns of aggressive behavior differ between species, there are several concordances in the ethology and neurobiology of aggression among rodents, primates, and humans.

Aggressive Behavior: Different Forms in Both Animals and Humans

The existence of different kinds of aggression has long been recognized mainly on the basis of animal research (Adams, 2006; Blanchard & Blanchard, 1981; Brain, 1979). There are generally two types of attacks in both males and females: offensive and defensive. These differ in motor patterns, bite/attack targets, ultimate functional consequences, and proximate neurobiological control mechanisms. *Offensive aggression* can be defined as a form of social communication aimed at the (pro)active control of the social environment. The motor patterns for offensive aggression are chase, offensive upright posture, offensive sideways posture, attacks (simple bites or bite and kick), piloerection (bristling) of the fur, and teeth chattering (mainly in rats) or tail rattling (mostly in mice). In the minutes leading up to intense attack bites, the resident rat emits brief pulses of ultrasonic vocalizations in the 50 kHz range that may reflect high excitement. The bite targets are primarily the hindquarters of the flanks, back, and base of the tail (less vulnerable body regions). The function is to obtain and retain resources such as space, food, and mates. *Defensive aggression* can be defined as a set of social behaviors performed in defense to an attack by a conspecific or a potential predator. The motor patterns for defensive aggression are flight, defensive upright posture, defensive sideways posture (keep-away), and attacks (lunge and bite). These defensive motor acts are usually accompanied with urination/defecation and emittance of 22 kHz ultrasonic vocalizations. The bite targets are primarily the face (snout), neck, and belly (vulnerable body regions). Defensive aggressive behavior differs from offensive aggression in that bite attacks are not signaled in advance by threats. The function is to defend one's self, mates, and progeny from attacks of another animal of the same or different species. For example, a dominant resident against an unfamiliar male conspecific intruder of the home territory displays offensive behavior (territorial aggression). The offense-defense distinction plays a prominent role in understanding the biology and physiology of animal aggression.

Besides this distinction in offense and defense, additional forms of aggressive behavior in animal research can be distinguished, such as infant-directed aggression or *infanticide, predatory aggression, play-fighting* (in juvenile animals), and *maternal aggression.* The latter can be observed in females during the late stages of pregnancy and the early stages of nursing. Predatory aggression is known as the quiet-biting attack observed in cats killing their prey and as the swift killing of a mouse or a cricket by a rat.

Different forms of aggression are also recognized in humans, and the offensive pattern of aggression in animals generally relates to the "hot-tempered" *hostile aggression* subtype in humans (also called *reactive, emotional, affective,* and *impulsive* aggression). The most basic acts of aggression in humans are hitting, kicking, biting, pushing, grabbing, pulling, shoving, beating, twisting, and choking. Threatening (vocal) and using objects (weapons) to aggress are also included in this definition (Tremblay & Szyf, 2010). This form of aggression has its strong initiative engagement and autonomic/neuroendocrine arousal in common with offensive aggression in animals. Moreover, both in animals and humans, this form of aggressive behavior is usually initiated in response to a perceived threat, such as the intrusion of an unfamiliar conspecific into the territory or in response to fear and frustration (omission of expected rewards). In contrast, "cold-blooded" *instrumental aggression* (also called *premeditated* and *proactive* aggression) is callous-unemotional aggression that seems to resemble more the quiet-biting attack or predatory forms of aggressive behavior in rodents.

Although both male and female rodents perform offensive aggression, there is a clear gender difference in the frequency and intensity of aggression, similar to what is generally observed in humans. Males may perform frequent and fierce offensive aggression in a territorial and socio-sexual context. Females show defensive aggression mostly in a maternal context, but low to medium levels of offensive aggression can certainly be observed in all female groups in relation to competition within the social hierarchy (De Jong et al., 2014).

Finally, it should be noted that aggression in both animals and humans has to be conceptualized into two components: trait-like aggressiveness and state-like aggressive behavior. Whereas *trait-like aggressiveness* refers to an individual's predisposition to act persistently aggressive in various different contexts, *state-like aggression* refers to the actual execution of aggressive behaviors. This distinction appears to be of crucial importance when linking certain physiological or neurobiological parameters to aggression.

Violence Is the Pathology of Functional Aggressive Behavior

From a biological point of view, aggressive behavior can be considered as a highly functional form of social communication leading to active control of resources and the social environment. It is characterized by a ritualized set of species-typical behaviors performed in close interaction with a conspecific opponent. Overt aggression and physical conflicts are potentially harmful not only for the victim but for the aggressor as well. Therefore, strong inhibitory control mechanisms have developed to minimize and control physical aggression in order to prevent its potentially adverse (i.e., injury or death) consequences. Such mechanisms include, for example, threatening behavior that often predicts aggressive arousal and intent and may thereby prevent actual physical attacks. Other mechanisms to keep aggression in control are taboos, ritualization, submission, reconciliation, and appeasement. For animals, this holds in particular for offensive aggression. For humans, this holds where social norms and rules set the boundaries between appropriate aggressive intentions and inappropriate aggressive displays in the form of violence. Because historically much of the scientific and public interest in aggression has been motivated by the more violent, hostile, and presumably less adaptive forms of exaggerated aggression, most definitions of (human) aggression are broadly formulated around the principal goal of inflicting harm or injury to another living being, that is, "any form of behavior that inflicts harm or injury or threatens to do so" (Berkowitz, 1993). Hence, these types of definitions seem more appropriate for escalated or pathological aggression, that is, violence.

Although violence is a controversial term in animal ethology and often considered exclusively a human proclivity, several recent studies in wildlife primate species as well as in laboratory rodents under particular experimental conditions show that extreme forms of physical aggression can be provoked in some but not all animals (for review, see de Boer et al., 2009; Miczek et al., 2013; Natarajan & Caramaschi, 2010). Escalated levels of aggression that exceed species-normative forms, its indiscriminative nature, and the complete absence of any introductory social behavior characterize maladaptive and more violent-like aggressive behavior in rodents. Violent-like rats and mice attack any kind of opponent, including anesthetized ones or even females, target their bites at vulnerable body parts, and do not show social exploration and threatening behavior preceding an overt attack. In this view, *violence* can be defined as an extreme and pathological form of physical aggression that is not subjected to inhibitory control mechanisms and that has lost its function in social communication (i.e., aggression out of control and out of context). The relationship between the functional and maladaptive extremes of the offensive aggression spectrum is still far from clear and forms a major obstacle in the integration of animal research with data on human aggression. Unfortunately, the current animal literature often does not make a clear distinction between aggression and violence as defined above.

Development of Pathological or Deviant Forms of Resident-Intruder Aggression

Until approximately a decade ago, most animal studies of aggression were concerned with the ultimate and proximate mechanisms of normal adaptive aggressive behavior, while clinically the focus was predominantly on violent individuals and excessive or inappropriate forms of human aggression. Besides several political, ethical, funding, and translational constraints, the lack of biologically relevant and valid animal models for these pathological forms of aggressive behavior is one important reason for the gap in our knowledge about the neurobiological roots and molecular genetic mechanisms of violence in humans. Therefore, new experimental models in preclinical research are being developed that focus more on provoking escalated and uncontrolled forms of aggressive behavior in order to capture the problematic clinical phenotype. Ideally, such models should demonstrate excessive, injurious, and impulsive physical aggression that exceeds and/or deviates from normal species-typical levels or patterns (see de Boer et al., 2009; Miczek et al., 2007, 2013). However, most laboratory rodent strains are very placid and docile compared to their wild ancestors. In virtually all commercially available laboratory mouse and rat strains today, the aggressive behavioral traits, including the putatively underlying molecular genetic components, are dramatically compromised in terms of absolute level and variation. Most likely, this is the result of artificial selection for tame and tractable behavior during the century-long domestication process of this wild-caught animal being kept, reared, and bred in captivity (de Boer et al., 2003). A classic example of this is the maintenance of docile characteristics long after selection for tameness in wild silver foxes even though the behavioral selection criteria are no longer applied, indicating that alleles that predispose to aggression have been removed from the population (Belyaev, 1979).

Consequently, to obtain appreciable levels of offensive aggression in these constitutionally docile laboratory strains, several procedural (often rather artificial) manipulations have been employed to promote and/or enhance the tendency to display offensive aggressive behavior (see de Boer et al., 2009; Natarajan & Caramaschi, 2010 for review). Obviously, some of these procedures have been adopted with the intent to mimic the conditions under which violent behavior in humans occurs (e.g., frustration, stress, instigation, alcohol, anabolic/androgenic steroid use). Although these experimentally heightened forms of aggressive behavior may to some extent resemble more intense forms when compared to their already low species-typical rates of aggression, they may still fall into the normative range when compared to the patterns and levels of their wild ancestors. Indeed, higher levels and wider ranges of spontaneous intraspecific aggression are encountered in feral (wild-derived) or semi-natural populations of rats and mice as compared to their laboratory-bred conspecifics (de Boer & Koolhaas, 2003; see Figure 2.1).

Therefore, an increase in solely the frequency and duration of aggressive acts is only one component of pathological aggressive behavior. More productive and relevant animal models of excessive and abnormal forms of aggression should demonstrate intense and/or injurious physical aggression that exceeds normal species-typical levels and patterns. In other words, a form of aggressive behavior that is not subject to inhibitory control anymore and has lost its function in social communication. Hence, this loss of the social communicative nature of the aggressive interaction in the currently available animal models of escalated aggressive behavior is operationally defined by: (a) low provocation threshold, short latency to initiate attack; (b) high rate and intensity, leading to significant tissue damage; (c) disregard of appeasement signals; and (d) lack of species-normative behavioral structure (i.e., attacks are deficient in conveying signaling intention, and lack of context in that critical features of the opponent such as age, sex, or situation are misjudged) (De Boer et al., 2009; Haller & Kruk, 2006; Miczek et al., 2013, 2015; Nelson & Trainor 2007). Several of these signs and symptoms of violent-like aggressive display are validly and reliably engendered in the following animal models.

Escalated Aggressive Behavior in Unselected Feral Animals and Selective Breeding for Escalated Aggression

Feral or semi-natural populations of rats and mice display much higher levels and a broader range of innate and normal adaptive offensive aggression compared to their highly domesticated laboratory-bred conspecifics (see Figure 2.1). More interestingly however, clear escalated aggressive and violent characteristics, as defined above, can be engendered in approximately 10%–15% of these constitutionally medium- to high-aggressive rats that experience repeated victorious

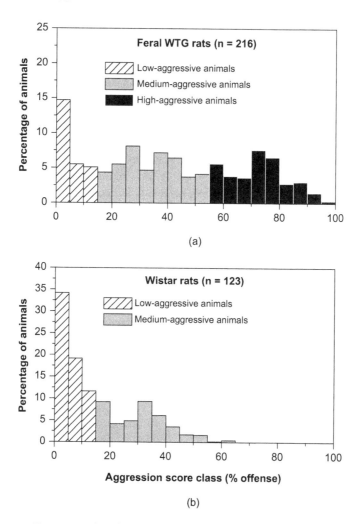

(a)

(b)

FIGURE 2.1   Frequency distribution of offensive resident-intruder aggression in a population of unselected feral Wild-Type Groningen (A) and domesticated laboratory Wistar (B) rat strains. Rats are categorized according to their level of aggressive behavior, expressed as percentage of time in the RI test. Note that the highly aggressive (> 55% aggressive behavior) phenotype is virtually absent in the domesticated rat strain (de Boer et al. 2003).

episodes of social conflict (i.e., by permitting them to physically dominate other conspecifics more than 10 times) (see Figure 2.2). Like humans, most individual rats respond to these repetitive social conflicts with appropriate and well-controlled functional forms of aggressive behavior, while only a small fraction demonstrate escalated aggression and become violent and destructive. Enhanced

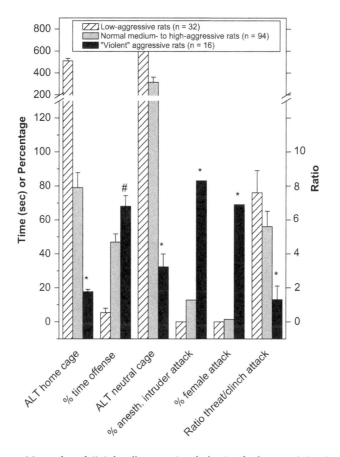

FIGURE 2.2 Normal and "violent" aggressive behavioral characteristics in a small fraction (10%–15%) of resident wild-derived WTG rats before and after multiple (> 10) victorious experiences. Asterisk (★) indicates significantly (p < 0.05; student t-test) different from untrained and trained normal aggressive groups.

levels of offensive aggression and an increased probability of winning an aggressive encounter following previous victories (the so-called "trained fighter" or "winner" effect) was originally already described by Ginsburg and Allee in 1942, and since then has been demonstrated frequently in a wide variety of animal species (see Hsu et al., 2005, for review). Similarly, male wild-derived house mice that were artificially selected for short-attack latencies (i.e., high-aggressive SAL mice) show virtually all of the above-mentioned signs of violent aggressive behavior already after three to five repeated winning experiences (Caramaschi et al., 2008; Natarajan & Caramaschi, 2010).

Thus, upon positive reinforcing or "pleasurable" victorious social experiences, a small group of constitutionally aggressive rats and artificially selected aggressive mice are very prone to show a breakdown of the aggressive behavioral inhibition mechanisms, and transform their initial functional adaptive aggressive behavior into a more violent-like and pathological behavior.

Numerous studies in a wide variety of animal species have convincingly demonstrated that, in addition to securing access to resources, the most intriguing consequence of winning an aggressive conflict is the self-reinforcing or rewarding effect of this type of behavior. Actually, individuals seek out the opportunity to fight and engage in aggressive behavior as a source of pleasure. The most convincing evidence that aggression is rewarding to animals is that the opportunity to engage in aggressive behavior can reinforce operant responding, that is, animals are willing to work (e.g., bar pressing, nose poking) for aggression as a source of reward and satisfaction (see Miczek et al., 2004 for review). Not surprisingly, just like other positive reinforcers such as food, drugs, or sex, the mesocorticolimbic dopamine system is associated with the incentive salience of the rewarding properties of winning fights: Nucleus accumbens (NAcc) dopamine is strongly released during (anticipation of) aggressive episodes (Ferrari et al., 2003), and pharmacological antagonism of dopamine D1/D2 receptors in the NAcc diminishes the seeking of the opportunity to fight (Couppis & Kennedy, 2008). This animal model translates well to impulsive aggressive and violent behavior in humans, and in particular affords the opportunity to identify the plastic neuromolecular changes in the "aggression" control systems that are hypothesized to underlie a shift of normal adaptive aggression into more violent forms (de Boer et al., 2009; Sluyter et al., 2003). For example, in mice that have won territorial disputes repeatedly, a selective enhancement of androgen sensitivity in neural pathways related to motivation (VTS and NAcc) and social aggression (BNST) was observed (Fuxjager et al., 2010). In addition, profound functional changes in the key regulatory sites ($5\text{-HT}_{1A/B}$ autoreceptors and reuptake transporters) that control the (re)activity of serotonergic neurons were found to be causally related to the transition into excessive forms of aggression (de Boer et al., 2015).

Alcohol-Heightened Aggression

Among all psychoactive substances, alcohol is the most potent agent for eliciting aggression and reduction of behavioral control in a subset of human individuals (Heinz et al., 2011; also see Parrott & Eckhardt in Chapter 13 of this volume). Over half of all incidences of violence involve alcohol consumption, either by the perpetrator or the victim. Acute low doses of alcohol, as well as withdrawal from long-term alcohol use, may lead to escalated aggressive behavior in a significant subgroup (approximately one-third) of individual mice, rats, and monkeys (Miczek et al., 2015). Emerging pharmacological evidence from these alcohol animal models points to major individual differences in the brain serotonergic and/or dopaminergic systems that play an important part in the biological vulnerability to increased alcohol-related aggressiveness. For example, trait-like reductions in frontal cortical serotonin functioning seem to mediate the increased propensity for alcohol-induced aggression. Furthermore, there is growing support for the hypothesis that the neural mechanism mediating alcohol's reinforcing effects overlaps or closely interacts with those that are responsible for aggressive and violent acts, which in themselves function as reinforcers.

Excessive Aggression in the Hypoglucocorticoid Rat

The development of the hypoglucocorticoid model was prompted by the discovery that violence in patients with antisocial personality disorder and conduct disorder is accompanied by a marked hypoarousal in terms of glucocorticoid production, heart rate, and skin conductance (Raine, 1996; Van Goozen & Fairchild, 2006). Glucocorticoid deficiency, induced by adrenalectomy with low-dose glucocorticoid replacement, considerably increases attacks aimed at vulnerable targets, diminishes intention signaling, disturbs social behavior, and reduces autonomic activation (Haller & Kruk, 2006). Intriguingly, the abnormal aggression in this model is associated with the marked activation of predation-related brain structures (Tulogdi et al., 2010). Thus, this animal model seems to capture the callous-unemotional hallmarks of antisocial personality and conduct disordered patients.

Early-Life Social Isolation Enhanced Aggressiveness

Another interesting set of animal models has recently been developed to capture the cardinal features of early-life adversity (i.e., emotional neglect, loss of parents, child abuse) induced hyperaggressiveness and antisocial behavior in humans by studying the underlying neuromolecular and (epi)genetic mechanisms (Sandi & Haller, 2015;Veenema et al., 2009). Generally, early-life stress in animals enhances adult anxiety-like behaviors and has a major impact on social and aggressive behaviors. In particular, post-weaning social isolation models early social neglect by eliminating social contacts with conspecifics from weaning into early adulthood. Rodents submitted to this paradigm show strong signs of social incompetence as adults and display abnormally high levels of aggression, attacks on vulnerable body parts, sudden attacks, and ambivalence between offensive and defensive behavior (Toth et al., 2008). Like humans, rats show exacerbated autonomic arousal and glucocorticoid stress responses in this model. Early-life stress and maltreatment is an important model to study the neuromolecular and epigenetic mechanisms that underlie the development of excessive aggressive behaviors.

Neurobiological Correlates of Aggression and Violence

For over a century, neuroscientists have sought to understand the neural basis of aggression and violence by perturbing and monitoring brain activity through a variety of methods and in a wide variety of animals such as monkeys, dogs, cats, rats, mice, voles, and hamsters. By employing numerous increasingly sophisticated tools of functional neuroanatomy (i.e., from the classic electric/chemical lesion and stimulation techniques to neurochemical mapping and manipulations), many important strides have been made in understanding the functional brain circuit organization of different social (aggression, sex, parental care) behaviors, that is, the structurally and functionally highly interconnected "social behavior neural network" (SBN) (Newman, 1999).

A Highly Interconnected Network of Brain Regions Controls Aggression

To more comprehensively identify this SBN, and particularly the specific neural circuitry involved in aggressive behaviors, determining the pattern of activation of immediate early gene expression has been employed successfully within the last two decades. Fos is the protein product of an immediate early gene (IEG), *c-fos*, which is expressed in neurons shortly after their depolarization (activation) and then induces expression of downstream genes. Fos-expression can be visualized using immuno-histochemical staining techniques, and the number of Fos-positive neurons in each brain area is used to quantify the activation the area. Application of this technique in offensive aggression paradigms in rats, mice, and hamsters reveals a neuronal network that includes (but is not limited to) the intimately interconnected forebrain (limbic) structures like cortical and medial amygdala (CoA and MeA), bed nucleus of the stria terminalis (BNST), lateral septal area (LS), mediodorsal and anterior thalamus, several hypothalamic nuclei including the anterior hypothalamus (AHA), ventromedial hypothalamus (VMH), lateral hypothalamus (LH), the paraventricular nucleus (PVN), the medial prefrontal cortex (mPFC), the midbrain periaqueductal gray (PAG), dorsal raphe nucleus (DRN), locus coeruleus (LC), and ventral tegmental area (VTA) (see Figure 2.3 and de Boer et al., 2015 for a more detailed review on the neurobiology of offensive aggression). Comparative research indicates that this highly interconnected neuronal network for offensive aggression is remarkably similar in many vertebrate species including humans, indicating that it is evolutionarily ancient and very well conserved (Goodson, 2005; O'Connell & Hofmann, 2012). Indeed, this interconnected brain aggression circuitry is generally confirmed in humans by modern brain imaging techniques such as functional magnetic resonance imaging (fMRI) and positron emission tomography (PET) that allow the *in vivo* analysis of entire neuronal networks involved in certain types of aggressive behavior. However, it is quite surprising that in most of the human neuroimaging studies, the hypothalamic limbic brain structures involved in the direct control of animal fighting and attack usually do not show up in their region of interest analyses. Rather, these studies predominantly focus on the higher cortical (i.e., prefrontal, cingulate) and temporal lobe (amygdala) brain structures.

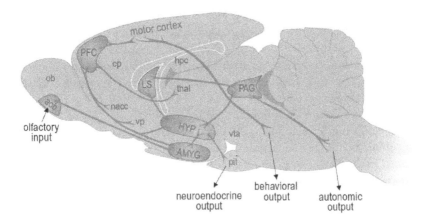

FIGURE 2.3 A scheme of the neuronal network in rodents involved in aggressive behavior and the organization of the accompanying neuroendocrine and autonomic activation (aob = accessory olfactory bulb; AMYG = amygdala; cp = caudate putamen; HYP = hypothalamus; hpc = hippocampus; LS = lateral septum; nacc = nucleus accumbens; ob = olfactory bulb; PAG = Periaqueductal gray; PFC = Prefrontal cortex; pit = pituitary; thal = thalamus; vp = ventral pallidum; vta = ventral tegmental area).

The function of the "SBN" brain areas in the expression and control of aggressive behavior ranges from sensory processing and perception up to the generation of somatomotor output patterns, the autonomic and neuroendocrine support of behavior, and all organizational processes in between. However, although the neural circuitry of aggressive social behavior is mapped relatively well in terms of brain (sub)nuclei and their interconnections, it still remains a challenging task to decipher how the activity of distinct sets of neurons within the various nodes of this basic SBN circuitry give rise to different phases (initiation, execution, and termination), levels, and/or forms of aggressive behavior.

The Hypothalamus as a Critical Brain Region for Offensive Attack

Of all the areas in the brain, the hypothalamus is by far the best-studied region in relation to aggression, ever since seminal lesion experiments found suppression of raging aggressive acts in cats (Bard, 1928) and intracranial stimulation experiments induced this behavior (Hess & Bruegger, 1943). With the development of appropriate stereotaxic instruments, an extensive series of groundbreaking lesion and electric stimulation studies defined the attack area in the hypothalamus, hence called the hypothalamic attack area (HAA). This HAA consists of an area extending between the LH and the VMH rostrally alongside the anterior hypothalamic nucleus (see Kruk, 2014, for detailed review). Electrical stimulation of parts of the HAA has been reported to induce fierce attack behavior in a variety of animals (e.g., rats, cats, monkeys). This hypothalamically induced attack behavior can be directed against male, female, anesthetized, or even dead rats, and is directed toward vulnerable body parts. Hence, this form of induced aggression is clearly abnormal and violent-like.

However, despite their anatomical precision, electrodes still affect a rather ill-defined population of neurons and fibers of passage that do not allow definite conclusions on the precise neuronal and circuit-level mechanisms underlying offensive attack. The brain packs roughly 100,000 neurons and a billion synaptic connections in every cubic millimeter of tissue, and electrically stimulating or lesioning even a tiny location in the brain will excite/silence a very large number of intermeshed cells of different kinds. Recently, newly emerging techniques for mapping, measuring, and manipulating neural activity based on genetic targeting of specific neuron subtypes has solved many of these problems. In particular, optogenetics and pharmacogenetics have recently made it possible to rapidly and reversibly activate or inhibit small molecularly distinct populations of neurons (anatomical and genetic precision) at any moment in time (temporal precision) (Anderson, 2012; Deisseroth, 2014). These revolutionary techniques offer the ability to selectively manipulate individual neural circuit elements that underlie aggression-relevant behaviors. The first experiments investigating the role of the hypothalamus in the regulation of aggression using optogenetic stimulation focused on the ventrolateral subdivision of the VMH. Following virally delivered expression of the light-sensitive protein channelrhodopsin-2 (ChR2) in this VMHvl region of mice, light pulses delivered through an implanted optic fiber produced robust offensive attacks directed toward male mice, castrated male mice, female mice, and inanimate objects (Lin et al., 2011). Accordingly, inhibiting these neurons using virally expressed *C. elegans* ivermectin-gated chloride channel, which prevents the initiation of action potentials by hyperpolarizing the neurons upon ligand binding (i.e., a pharmacogenetic approach), suppressed normal attacks. Subsequent studies have capitalized on the fact that the neurons of the VMHvl are primarily glutaminergic and are enriched with estrogen receptors of the alpha subtype (Er_α). Both Er_α-knockout mice and RNAi knockdown of Er_α in the VMHvl resulted in a dramatic decrease of natural inter-male aggression (Sano et al., 2013). Most recently, optogenetic stimulation of Er_α VMHvl neurons triggered attack behavior whereas optogenetic inhibition suppressed fighting, suggesting that Er_α neurons in this small hypothalamic area are necessary and sufficient to initiate and terminate bouts of aggression (Lee et al., 2014). Beside Er_α, neurons in the VMHvl also express a variety of other neuromodulator receptors, including serotonin 1A, 2A, 2C, muscarinic acetylcholinergic, and oxytocin receptors. Since many neuromodulators such as serotonin, dopamine, and oxytocin change their levels dynamically during the course of aggressive behaviors, they may influence VMHvl neuron excitability and hence aggressive attack. Similar types of opto/pharmacogenetic interrogations and viral vector-based approaches in rodent models of aggression are recently being performed in various other nodes of the brain social aggression circuitry, that is, amygdala (Hong et al., 2014), prefrontal cortex (Takahashi et al., 2014) and VTA (Yu et al., 2014), and illuminate the precise neuromolecular determinants of aggressive behavior in both its normal and excessive forms.

Neurochemical Modulation of the Aggressive Neural Network

Obviously, the functional activity of this entire social behavior neural network, and thereby the selection of the appropriate behavioral response to social challenges and opportunities, is determined by a wide variety of molecular substrates (i.e., neurotransmitters, hormones, cytokines, and their respective metabolic enzymes, receptors, and intraneuronal signaling molecules). Undisputedly, among the neurochemical systems that are considered key signaling molecules in this neurocircuitry controlling aggression are the monoamines serotonin (5-HT) and dopamine (DA), the "social" neuropeptides oxytocin (OXT) and vasopressin (AVP), the "stress" neuropeptide corticotropin-releasing factor (CRF), the "stress" HPA-axis and "sex" HPG-axis's steroid hormones (corticosterone, testosterone, estrogen), and their cognate receptors. Indeed, several studies in wild-type rats and artificially selected short attack latency (SAL) and long attack latency (LAL) mice show a widespread central nervous differentiation between the high- and low-aggressive extremes, for example at the level of the oxytocinergic modulation of the central nucleus of the amygdala (Calcagnoli et al., 2015), the vasopressin-ergic neurons in the bed nucleus of the stria terminalis and its innervation (density) of the lateral septum (de Boer et al., 2015), and the auto-inhibitory control mechanisms of serotonin neurotransmission (see next section). However, the exact functional role of these neurobiological systems in the generation of a particular behavior and/or their behavioral specificity is still far from clear. Moreover, with the notable exception of serotonin signaling components, the causal involvement of these neurobiological substrates in determining aggressive behavior requires further experimental evidence employing the novel opto- and pharmacogenetic manipulation techniques.

Serotonin Is the Main Molecular Orchestrator

All nodes in the neuronal network for offensive aggression are substantially innervated by serotonergic (5-HT) neurons originating in the dorsal and median raphe nuclei in the brain stem (see Figure 2.4). More than any other neurochemical system, this evolutionarily ancient and extremely well-conserved neurotransmitter system is generally considered the primary molecular orchestrator of aggressive behavioral traits in virtually every animal species, including human beings (Nelson & Trainor, 2007; Siever, 2008). However, the direction and exact causal

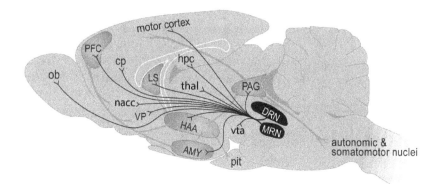

FIGURE 2.4A Serotonergic control of the social behavior neuronal network. See legend of Figure 2.3. DRN = dorsal raphe nucleus; MRN = medial raphe nucleus.

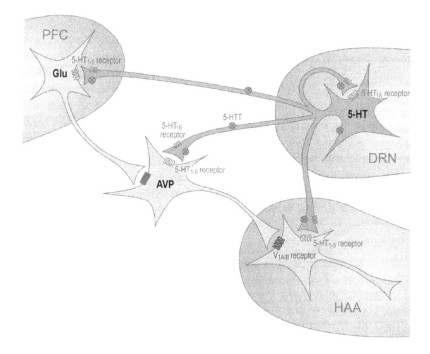

FIGURE 2.4B More detailed neuromolecular characteristics of part of the DRN-prefrontal-HAA microcircuitry involved in the control of aggressive behavior. Glu = glutamate; AVP = arginine vasopressin; 5-HT = serotonin; 5-HTT = serotonin transporter.

linkage of this association is very complex, and it has proven notoriously difficult to unravel the precise role of this amine (and every facet of its synthetic and metabolic pathways, uptake and storage processes, and dynamic receptor signaling mechanisms) in the predisposition for and execution of aggressive behavior in both its normal and pathological forms. For decades, high levels of aggressive behavior have been believed to be associated with low brain 5-HT neurotransmission activity. This frequently reiterated serotonin deficiency hypothesis seems consistent with the fact that serotonergic receptor agonists, used to mimic higher serotonergic activity, generally reduce aggressive behavior. However, recent studies of the functional status of the 5-HT system before, during, and after the execution of normal adaptive and abnormal pathological forms of aggression have led to a somewhat different view. Display of normal adaptive offensive aggressive behavior aimed at territorial control and social dominance is associated with a higher 5-HT neuronal activity (see de Boer et al., 2015 for relevant references). A negative correlation between aggression and 5-HT as captured in the deficiency hypothesis seems to be a trait-like characteristic of pathological forms of aggression (e.g., violence). For example, a clear positive correlation was found between the level of normal adaptive expressions of offensive aggression and basal cerebrospinal fluid (CSF) concentrations of 5-HT and/or its metabolite 5-HIAA. A significant negative correlation between aggression and 5-HT levels was found only upon inclusion of samples from abnormally and excessively aggressive trained fighter animals. A critical evaluation of the CSF 5-HIAA data in aggressive humans confirms this idea that the serotonergic deficiency appears to hold in particular for specific groups of individuals who persistently engage in more aberrant, impulsive, and violent forms of aggressive behavior rather than in individuals with instrumental (functional) forms of offensive aggression.

Treatment with 5-HT_{1A} or 5-HT_{1B} receptor agonists is one of the most potent pharmacological methods to selectively suppress aggressive behavior in a variety of animal species and experimental paradigms (de Boer & Koolhaas, 2005). Apart from acting on receptors at postsynaptic sites, these two receptor agonists also affect the two main serotonergic autoreceptors involved in the negative feedback control of the 5-HT neuron at the level of the synapse (5-HT_{1B}) and at the level of the cell soma (5-HT_{1A}) (see Figure 2.4). Hence, activation of these receptors by agonists will potently activate the negative feedback and thereby reduce 5-HT firing and neurotransmission. It appears that the potent anti-aggressive effects of these compounds are largely expressed via their action on these inhibitory autoreceptors located at the cell soma and the nerve terminal, by attenuating intruder-activated 5-HT neurotransmission (de Boer et al., 2015).

Interestingly, highly aggressive animals are characterized by upregulated somatodendritic 5-HT_{1A} and terminal 5-HT_{1B} autoreceptor functionality. This considerably (approximately 20-fold) enhanced tonic inhibitory control of serotonergic neurons in aggressive males may explain the negative correlation between baseline levels of 5-HT and escalated aggression found in many species. Furthermore, to signify the causality of this correlation, 5-HT$_{1A}$ autoreceptor sensitivity increased or decreased upon enhancing (by repeated victorious experiences) or attenuating (by repeated defeat experiences) aggressiveness, respectively. Notably, animals that escalated their aggressiveness and started to engage in violent-like aggressive behavior demonstrated 5-HT$_{1A}$ autoreceptor super-sensitivity. More persuasively, recent molecular genetic studies have shown that transgenic mice with conditional (at adult age) overexpression of somatodendritic 5-HT$_{1A}$ autoreceptors demonstrate suppressed 5-HT neural firing that was associated with a profound hyperaggressive behavioral phenotype (Audero et al., 2013). These data confirm the causal role of tonic 5-HT activity in setting a trait-like threshold for executing overt aggressive behavior.

Vasopressin and Oxytocin as Important Neuropeptidergic Modulators of the Social Behavior Network

Besides their important peripheral physiological functions as neurohypophysial-released hormones, the neuropeptides arginine vasopressin (AVP) and oxytocin (OXT) are also implicated in inter-neuronal communication within various nodes of the social brain network to modulate emotional and social behavioral and physiological responding (Lee et al., 2009a). AVP is generally known to increase anxiety-like behaviors, stress, and aggressiveness, whereas OXT has the opposite effects and facilitates social attachment, care, and affiliation (Heinrichs et al., 2009). Existing data from early pioneering work on these neuropeptides convincingly demonstrated opposite roles for AVP and OXT in fear-learning processes (Bohus & de Wied, 1998). More recent studies in our wild-type rats and/or artificially selected aggressive (SAL) and nonaggressive (LAL) house mice have demonstrated that high-aggressive animals exhibit higher levels of AVP release when compared to their nonaggressive counterparts (Koolhaas et al., 2010). In addition, there is abundant experimental evidence to support a causal function of vasopressin in proactive aggressive behavior and OXT in passive affiliative behavior. Direct micro-infusion of AVP or OXT into the cerebral ventricles or in selected brain regions facilitates or suppresses, respectively, offensive aggression (Calcagnoli et al., 2015). In addition, a positive correlation between levels of CSF vasopressin and life history of general aggression as well as aggression toward individuals (Lee et al., 2009a) has been reported, whereas impaired brain OXTergic signaling has been implicated in several human neuropsychiatric disorders associated with social deficits, impulsivity, and excessive aggression (Lee et al., 2009b). Furthermore, mutant mice with the vasopressin receptor V1A/B gene deleted showed virtually no offensive aggressive behavior anymore, whereas elevated aggressiveness was found in mice with deletions of the OXT receptor gene. Consistent with the aggression-promoting of brain AVP, systemic as well as intra-hypothalamic administration of AVP V1A/B receptor antagonists effectively block offensive aggressive behavior in male hamsters and WTG rats (Blanchard et al.,

2005; Koolhaas et al., 2010). Basically, an opposite picture seems to emerge for brain OXT signaling. Recent ethopharmacological studies have clearly demonstrated that enhancement of brain OXTergic function, using both intraventricular, intra-amygdalar, and even intranasal administration routes, produced marked anti-aggressive and pro-social affiliative effects that are dose-dependent, behavior- and receptor-selective, and long-lasting (Calcagnoli et al., 2013, 2015).

Based on the findings outlined above, it can be hypothesized that an endogenous balance between vasopressin and oxytocin signaling within (components of) the social behavioral neural circuit may gate the expression of either aggressive or affiliative responses to salient social stimuli.

Summary

A large body of animal neurobehavioral research convincingly demonstrates that abnormal expressions of aggressive behavior principally find their origin in a dysregulation of the deeply rooted neuronal circuits and/or neurochemical pathways in the brain that mediate normal social affective-aggressive behaviors. This highly conserved neural and gene expression brain network encompasses neurons in the mesencephalon projecting to hypothalamic areas, amygdaloid, septal, prefrontal, and hippocampal forebrain regions, striatal and thalamic loops with the frontal and prefrontal cortex, as well as important feedback loops to limbic and mesencephalic nuclei. The structural and functional properties of this social behavior brain network are established and constantly shaped by a dynamic interplay of genetic and environmental factors (stress, maltreatment, vicarious experiences, substance abuse), in particular during certain sensitive (i.e., perinatal and adolescent) developmental periods. Undisputedly, among the neurochemical systems that are considered key signaling molecules in this neurocircuitry controlling aggression are the canonical monoamines serotonin and dopamine, the "social" neuropeptides oxytocin and vasopressin, the "stress" neuropeptide CRF, the "stress" HPA-axis and "sex" HPG-axis's steroid hormones (corticosterone, testosterone, estrogen), and their cognate receptors. Genetic studies in both humans and animals have demonstrated that polymorphisms or mutations in a number of genes regulating the functional activity of these important signaling molecules may confer risk factors, sometimes alone but usually in co-action with (early) adverse and stressful life conditions, for development of antisocial aggressive traits. Particularly, from the viewpoint of targeting novel molecular sites for intervention, the intrinsic 5-HT autoregulatory mechanisms (i.e., the presynaptic $5-HT_{1A/B}$ autoreceptors and 5-HT reuptake transporter), and extrinsic neuropeptidergic (i.e., OXT, AVP, and CRF) and steroid receptor (i.e., mineralo-/glucocorticoid receptor [MR/GR] and androgen receptor [AR]) modulatory influences of 5-HT signaling are emerging as important molecular determinants of (escalated) aggression regulation. Although early efforts during the 1950s and 1960s to translate preclinical neurobiological aggression research findings into clinical use have a sordid history, the current circuit-level knowledge of the neuromolecular underpinnings of escalated aggression has great potential to guide the rational development of therapeutic interventions for pathological social and aggressive behavior in humans.

References

Adams, D. B. (2006). Brain mechanisms of aggressive behavior: An updated review. *Neuroscience & Biobehavioral Reviews, 30,* 304–318.

Anderson, D. J. (2012). Optogenetics, sex, and violence in the brain: Implications for psychiatry. *Biological Psychiatry, 71,* 1081–1089.

Audero, E., Mlinar, B., Baccini, G., Skachokova, Z. K., Coradetti, R., & Gross, C. (2013). Suppression of serotonin neuron firing increases aggression in mice. *Journal of Neuroscience, 33*(20), 8678–8688.

Bard, P. (1928). A diencephalic mechanism for the expression of rage with special reference to the sympathetic nervous system. *American Journal of Physiology, 84,* 490–515.

Belyaev, D. K. (1979). The Wilhelmine E. Key 1978 invitational lecture. Destabilizing selection as a factor in domestication. *Journal of Heredity, 70,* 301–308.

Berkowitz, L. (1993). *Aggression: Its causes, consequences and control.* Philadelphia: Temple University Press.

Blanchard, R. J., & Blanchard, D. C. (1981). The organization and modeling of animal aggression. In P. F. Brain & D. Benton (Eds.), *The biology of aggression* (pp. 529–563). Alphen aan den Rijn: Sijthoff et Noordhoff.

Blanchard, R. J., Griebel, G., Farrokhi, C., Markham, C., Yang, M., & Blanchard D. C. (2005). AVP V1b selective antagonist SSR149415 blocks aggressive behaviors in hamsters. *Pharmacology Biochemistry & Behavior, 80*(1), 189–194.

Bohus, B., & de Wied, D. (1998). The vasopressin deficient Brattleboro rats: A natural knockout model used in the search for CNS effects of vasopressin. *Progress in Brain Research, 119,* 555–573.

Brain, P. F. (1979). Differentiating types of attack and defense in rodents. In P. F. Brain & D. Benton (Eds.), *Multidisciplinary approaches to aggression research* (pp. 53–77). Amsterdam: Elsevier.

Calcagnoli, F., de Boer, S. F., Althaus, M., den Boer, J. A., & Koolhaas, J. M. (2013). Antiaggressive activity of central oxytocin in male rats. *Psychopharmacology, 229,* 639–651.

Calcagnoli, F., Stubbendorff, C., Meyer, N., de Boer, S. F., Althaus, M., & Koolhaas, J. M. (2015). Oxytocin microinjected into the central amygdaloid nuclei exerts anti-aggressive effects in male rats. *Neuropharmacology, 90,* 74–81.

Caramaschi, D., de Boer, S. F., Vries, H. D., & Koolhaas, J. M. (2008). Development of violence in mice through repeated victory along with changes in prefrontal cortex neurochemistry. *Behavioural Brain Research, 189,* 263–272.

Couppis, M. H., & Kennedy, C. H. (2008). The rewarding effect of aggression is reduced by nucleus accumbens dopamine receptor antagonism in mice. *Psychopharmacology, 197,* 449–456.

De Boer, S. F., Caramaschi, D., Natarajan, D., & Koolhaas, J. M. (2009). The vicious cycle towards violence: Focus on the negative feedback mechanisms of brain serotonin neurotransmission. *Frontiers in Behavioral Neuroscience, 3,* 1–6.

De Boer, S. F., & Koolhaas, J. M. (2005). 5-HT1A and 5-HT1B receptor agonists and aggression: A pharmacological challenge of the serotonin deficiency hypothesis. *European Journal of Pharmacology, 526*(1–3), 125–139.

De Boer, S. F., Olivier, B., Veening, J., & Koolhaas, J. M. (2015). The neurobiology of aggression: Revealing a modular view. *Physiology & Behavior, 146*, 111–127.

De Boer, S. F., van der Vegt, B. J., & Koolhaas, J. M. (2003). Individual variation in aggression of feral rodent strains: A standard for the genetics of aggression and violence? *Behavioural Genetics, 33*(5), 481–497.

Deisseroth, K. (2014). Circuit dynamics of adaptive and maladaptive behavior. *Nature, 505*(7483), 309–317.

De Jong, T. R., Beiderbeck, D. I., & Neumann, I. D. (2014). Measuring virgin female aggression in the female intruder test (FIT): Effects of oxytocin, estrous cycle, and anxiety. *PLoS One, 9*(3), e91701.

Ferrari, P. F., van Erp, A. M. M., Tornatzky, W., & Miczek, K. A. (2003). Accumbal dopamine and serotonin in anticipation of the next aggressive episode in rats. *European Journal of Neuroscience, 17*, 371–378.

Fuxjager, M. J., Forbes-Lorman, R. M., Coss, D. J., Auger, C. J., Auger, A. P., & Marler, C. A. (2010). Winning territorial disputes selectively enhances androgen sensitivity in neural pathways related to motivation and social aggression. *Proceedings of the National Academy of Sciences, 107*(27), 12393–12398.

Ginsburg, B., & Allee, W. C. (1942). Some effects of conditioning on social dominance and subordination in inbred strains of mice. *Physiological Zoology, 15*, 485–506.

Goodson, J. L. (2005), The vertebrate social behavior network: Evolutionary themes and variations. *Hormones and Behavior, 48*, 11–22.

Haller, J., & Kruk, M. R. (2006). Normal and abnormal aggression: Human disorders and novel laboratory models. *Neuroscience & Biobehavioral Reviews, 30*(3), 292–303.

Heinrichs, M., von Dawans, B., & Domes, G. (2009). Oxytocin, vasopressin, and human social behavior. *Frontiers in Neuroendocrinology, 30*(4), 548–557.

Heinz, A. J., Beck, A., Meyer-Lindenberg, A., Sterzer, P., & Heinz, A. (2011). Cognitive and neurobiological mechanisms of alcohol-related aggression. *Nature Reviews Neuroscience, 12*(7), 400–413.

Hess, W. R., & Bruegger, M. (1943). Das subkortikale Zentrum der affectiven Abwehrreaktion. *Helv. Physiol. Acta, 1*, 33.

Hong, W., Kim, D. W., & Anderson, D. J. (2014). Antagonistic control of social versus repetitive self-grooming behaviors by separable amygdala neuronal subsets. *Cell, 158*, 1348–1361.

Hsu, Y., Earley, R. L., & Wolf, L. L. (2005). Modulation of aggressive behavior by fighting experience: mechanisms and contest outcomes. *Biological Reviews of the Cambridge Philosophical Society, 81*, 33–74.

Koolhaas, J. M., Coppens, C. M., de Boer, S. F., Buwalda, B., Meerlo, P., & Timmermans, P. J. A. (2013). The resident-intruder paradigm: A standardized test for aggression, violence and social stress. *Journal of Visualized Experiments, 4*, 77.

Koolhaas, J. M., de Boer, S. F., & Buwalda, B. (2010). Neuroendocrinology of coping styles: Towards understanding the biology of individual variation. *Frontiers in Neuroendocrinology, 31*(3), 307–321.

Kruk, M. (2014). Hypothalamic attack: A wonderful artifact or a useful perspective on escalation and pathology of aggression? A viewpoint. *Current Topics in Behavioral Neurosciences, 17*, 143–188.

Lee, H. J., Macbeth, A. H., Pagani, J. H., & Young, W. S. (2009a). Oxytocin: The great facilitator of life. *Progress in Neurobiology, 88*, 127–151.

Lee, H., Kim, D. W., Remedios, R., Anthony, T. E., Chang, A., Madisen, L., Zeng, H., Anderson, D. J. (2014). Scalable control of mounting and attack by Esr1+ neurons in the ventromedial hypothalamus. *Nature, 509*, 627–632.

Lee, R., Ferris, C., Van de Kar, L. D., & Coccaro, E. F., (2009b). Cerebrospinal fluid oxytocin, life history of aggression, and personality disorder. *Psychoneuroendocrinology, 34*, 1567–1573.

Lin, D., Boyle, M. P., Dollar, P., Lee, H., Lein, E. S., Perona, P., & Anderson, D. J. (2011) Functional identification of an aggression locus in the mouse hypothalamus. *Nature, 470*, 221–226.

Miczek, K. A., de Almeida, R. M., Kravitz, E. A., Rissman, E. F., de Boer, S. F., & Raine, A. (2007). Neurobiology of escalated aggression and violence. *J Neuroscience, 27*(44), 11803–11806.

Miczek, K. A., de Boer, S. F., & Haller, J. (2013). Excessive aggression as model of violence: A critical evaluation of current preclinical methods. *Psychopharmacology, 226*, 445–458.

Miczek, K. A., DeBold, J. F., Hwa, L. S., Newman, E. L., & de Almeida, R. M. (2015). Alcohol and violence: Neuropeptidergic modulation of monoamine systems. *Annals of the New York Academy of Sciences*, 2015 August 18.

Miczek, K.A., Faccidomo, S., De Almeida, R.M., Bannai, M., Fish, E.W., Debold, J.F. (2004). Escalated aggressive behavior: New pharmacotherapeutic approaches and opportunities. *Annals of the New York Academy of Sciences, 1036*, 336–355.

Miczek, K.A., Takahashi, A., Gobrogge, K. L., Hwa, L. S., & de Almeida, R. M. (2015). Escalated aggression in animal models: Shedding new light on mesocorticolimbic circuits. *Current Opinion in Behavioral Sciences, 1*(3), 90–95.

Natarajan, D., & Caramaschi, D. (2010). Animal violence demystified. *Frontiers in Behavioral Neuroscience, 4*, 9.

Nelson, R. J., & Trainor, B. C. (2007). Neural mechanisms of aggression. *Nature Reviews Neuroscience, 8*, 536–546.

Newman, S. W. (1999). The medial extended amygdala in male reproductive behavior. A node in the mammalian social behavior network. *Annals of the New York Academy of Sciences, 877*, 242–57.

O'Connell, L. A., & Hofmann, H. A. (2012). Evolution of a vertebrate social decision-making network. *Science, 336*(6085), 1154–1157.

Raine, A. (1996). Autonomic nervous system factors underlying disinhibited, antisocial, and violent behavior. Biosocial perspectives and treatment implications. *Annals of the New York Academy of Sciences, 94*, 46–59.

Sandi, C., & Haller, J. (2015). Stress and the social brain: Behavioural effects and neurobiological mechanisms. *Nature Reviews Neuroscience, 16*(5), 290–304.

Sano, K., Tsuda, M. C., Musatov, S., Sakamoto, T., & Ogawa, S. (2013). Differential effects of site-specific knockdown of estrogen receptor alpha in the medial amygdala, medial pre-optic area, and ventromedial nucleus of the hypothalamus on sexual and aggressive behavior of male mice. *European Journal of Neuroscience, 37*, 1308–19.

Siever, L. J. (2008). Neurobiology of aggression and violence. *American Journal of Psychiatry, 165*, 429–442.

Sluyter, F., Arseneault, L., Moffitt, T. E., Veenema, A. H., de Boer, S. F., & Koolhaas, J. M. (2003). Toward an animal model for antisocial behavior: Parallels between mice and humans. *Behavior Genetics, 33*, 563–574.

Takahashi, A., & Miczek, K. A. (2014). Neurogenetics of aggressive behavior: Studies in rodents. *Current Topics in Behavioral Neurosciences, 17*, 3–44.

Toth, M., Halasz, J., Mikics, E., Barsy, B., & Haller, J. (2008). Early social deprivation induces disturbed social communication and violent aggression in adulthood. *Behavioral Neuroscience, 122*, 849–854.

Tremblay, R. E., & Szyf, M. (2010). Developmental origins of chronic physical aggression and epigenetics. *Epigenomics, 2*, 495–499.

Tulogdi, A., Toth, M., Halasz, J., Mikics, E., Fuzesi, T., & Haller, J. (2010). Brain mechanisms involved in predatory aggression are activated in a laboratory model of violent intra-specific aggression. *European Journal of Neuroscience, 32*, 1744–1753.

Van Goozen, S. H., & Fairchild, G. (2006). Neuroendocrine and neurotransmitter correlates in children with antisocial behavior. *Hormones and Behavior, 50*(4), 647–654.

Veenema, A. H. (2009). Early life stress, the development of aggression and neuroendocrine and neurobiological correlates: What can we learn from animal models? *Frontiers in Neuroendocrinology, 30*(4), 497–518.

Yu, Q., Teixeira, C. M., Mahadevia, D., Huang, Y., Balsam, D., Mann, J. J., Gingrich, J. A, & Ansorge, M. S. (2014). Optogenetic stimulation of DAergic VTA neurons increases aggression. *Molecular Psychiatry, 19*(6), 688–698.

PART II
Individual Risk Factors for Aggression and Violence

3

THE AGGRESSIVE BRAIN

Bruce D. Bartholow

Aggression is a complex, multifaceted behavior often caused by numerous factors and expressed in innumerable ways. Like all complex behaviors, aggression ultimately has its roots in the brain. Although this might sound obvious, discovering the specific neural circuits and neurophysiological processes responsible for engendering aggressive responses has proven anything but simple. The purpose of this chapter is to provide a brief overview of discoveries in both human cognitive neuroscience and animal behavioral neuroscience that have begun to shed light—literally in some cases—on the heretofore mysterious neural processes and connections responsible for producing aggressive behavioral responses.

Basic Principles

Aggressive behavior is nearly ubiquitous across species (see Briffa, 2010). From fruit flies to fish and lower vertebrates to nonhuman primates to humans, virtually all animals display aggression both within their own species and, at times, directed at members of other species. Although the term "aggression" is often (mis)applied in referring to behaviors that are better captured by terms like "assertive" (as in commanding someone's attention), "persistent" (as in a diligent salesperson), or "energetic" (as in a competitive athlete), in psychological terms aggression is defined as any behavior that is intended to harm (or threaten harm to) another individual (e.g., Baron & Richardson, 1994). Aggression by this definition involves a real social exchange, involving at least two individuals (not an imagined interaction); aggression is an observable behavior, not merely a thought or angry feeling; and aggression is intentional, not an accidental injury or social faux pas (see Bushman & Bartholow, 2010). A behavior does not have to result in actual harm to qualify as aggressive; throwing a punch that misses its target is still an aggressive act.

Within modern human societies, aggression is nearly always seen as a maladaptive response, something that should be controlled and that can bring nearly as much harm to the perpetrator (e.g., through societal scorn or retaliatory responses) as to the intended victim. In nonhuman animals, however, the vast majority of aggressive behavior is functional and adaptive. Animals routinely must stake out and defend territories, fend off mating competitors, and protect themselves and their offspring from various threats. With the exception of the actions carnivores must take to secure prey, these types of *functional aggression* in nonhuman animal species rarely result in lasting harm, particularly within species. In contrast, *escalated aggression* often does produce harm, involving more extreme forms of behavior that elevate normal or functional aggression to abnormal and destructive violence.

Human analogues of functional aggression are not difficult to find (e.g., a shoving match between two people over the affections of a third), and though arguably human aggression often involves (or can involve) more high-level thinking compared to that of our nonhuman cousins, the neural bases of aggression appear to be strikingly similar across species. Thus, considerable research has been devoted to understanding the neurophysiological and neurochemical mechanisms responsible for aggression in animals, one aim of which is to apply this knowledge to better understanding human aggression (also see Chapter 2 of this volume). It is important to point out that although specific expressions of aggression (i.e., phenotypes) often differ across species (e.g., between humans and other animals), the organization and function of relevant brain structures is often highly similar. In particular, despite some important differences in gene expression, the neuronal organization of limbic structures in rat and mouse brains is known to be very comparable to that of human brains (see Huber & Kravitz, 2010; Nelson & Trainor, 2007). Also, considerable evidence (for a review, see Nelson & Trainor, 2007) points to the conclusion that multiple neurochemical systems that regulate species-specific aggressive behaviors have co-evolved in humans and mice (for example), making animal models very useful analogues of human neural function in this context (see Cheng et al., 2014). The next section provides a brief review of what scientists have discovered concerning those neural processes.

Neuroanatomy of Aggression

It goes without saying that the brains of virtually all species are extremely complex systems, which scientists have only just begun to understand in any detail. In attempting to understand the brain basis for the kinds of behaviors that support aggression, researchers face a very daunting challenge. A basic premise of understanding brain-behavior dynamics is that as behaviors become more complex their neural substrates likewise become more complicated and multifaceted. This makes the problem of identifying specific neural structures or circuits responsible for complex behaviors like aggression very difficult.

Investigating the neural substrates of aggression in humans is especially challenging. Historically, knowledge on this topic came largely from case studies of individuals who suffered lesions to various neural structures as the result of disease or injury. For example, the famous case of Phineas Gage, the nineteenth-century railroad worker who survived a horrific accident in which an iron tamping rod, measuring nearly four feet in length (1.2 meters) and weighing over 13 pounds (5.9 kg), was blasted through his left cheek and out the top of his skull, provided some of the first clues about the role of specific cortical areas in shaping interpersonal responses, including aggressiveness. It was initially considered something of a miracle that Gage had not died from his massive head wound, particularly because the iron rod had "[broken] up considerable portions of brain" (Harlow, 1848, p. 389). Subsequent to his initial recovery, his apparent retention of his mental faculties—"he has memory as perfect as ever" (Harlow, 1848, p. 392)—seemed to indicate an extreme plasticity in the functions of brain areas.

Later, however, those close to him began to notice dramatic changes in Gage's temperament. In reporting on his case, J.M. Harlow, the physician who treated and subsequently observed him for many years, remarked, "Previous to his injury, though untrained in the schools, he possessed a well-balanced mind, and was looked upon by those who knew him as a shrewd, smart business man, very energetic and persistent in executing all his plans of operation. In this regard his mind was radically changed [following the injury], so decidedly that his friends and acquaintances said he was 'no longer Gage'" (Harlow, 1868, p. 338). Gage was described as fitful and irreverent, "indulging at times in the grossest profanity (which was not previously his custom)," and "at times pertinaciously obstinate" (p. 338).

Prefrontal Cortex

Because some of Gage's mental abilities were spared (e.g., his memory; basic functions like walking and talking), whereas his personality and social behaviors were drastically altered, his case represents an early example of discoveries related to neural specialization. More specifically, the location of Gage's injury provided some of the first clues concerning the importance of frontal lobe structures, particularly the portion generally termed *prefrontal cortex* (PFC), in regulating emotions including anger and social behaviors including aggression (see Blair, 2004; Damasio et al., 1994). While somewhat difficult to rigidly define, the PFC is generally said to consist of the most anterior parts of the frontal lobe, especially regions directly behind the forehead and the eyes, encompassing Brodmann areas 8–11 and 44–47 (see Garey, 2006). The PFC is primarily associated with high-level cognition and executive functioning (see Fuster et al., 2000; Goldman-Rakic, 1996; Roberts et al., 1998), suggesting that aggressive actions often result from a failure of self-regulatory control (see Giancola, 2000; Giancola et al., 1998; Seguin & Zelazo, 2005).

A large body of research has confirmed that PFC structures play an important role in regulating aggression. For example, one study found that men who performed poorly on at least some cognitive tests thought to rely on PFC functioning behaved more aggressively after being provoked in a laboratory setting relative to their peers who performed better on the cognitive tests (Giancola & Zeichner, 1994). Another study linked increased aggression in humans to poor functioning in the orbital prefrontal cortex (Giancola, 1995), an area severely damaged in Gage's accident, confirming earlier reports of increased aggression in rats following orbital prefrontal lesions (de Bruin et al., 1983). Other studies have used lesion (e.g., Anderson et al., 1999; Grafman et al., 1996) and brain imaging methodologies (e.g., Yang et al., 2010) to document the negative association between prefrontal functioning and aggression.

Social Behavior Network

Of course, the PFC is not the only patch of neural real estate involved in the generation and regulation of aggression. Moreover, the areas of the brain that appear to control aggression are not specialized for this purpose, leading some to suggest that aggression is an emergent property of a larger neural network involved in the regulation of numerous social behaviors (Newman, 1999). This proposed network includes several structures often considered part of the limbic system, including the anterior hypothalamic nucleus (AHN), ventromedial hypothalamus (VMH), medial amygdala (MA), bilateral septum (BLS), periaqueductal gray (PAG), and the bed nucleus of the stria terminalis (BNST). PFC structures are thought to interact with the structures of the social behavior network, largely functioning to inhibit or modulate their activation (see Nelson & Trainor, 2007). Evidence supporting this interpretation has come from studies with rats showing that lesions of the BLS, BNST, AHN, and MA tend to reduce aggression between males (Kruk, 1991), whereas lesions of the orbitofrontal cortex tend to enhance aggression (de Bruin et al., 1983).

Of the structures in this social behavior network, the hypothalamus appears to have particular significance for aggression. Early lesion studies with cats established the hypothalamus as important for the control of rage-related behavior (Bard, 1928). More recently, focused electrical stimulation of the AHN has been shown to increase aggression in both rats (Bermond et al., 1982; Kruk et al., 1984) and cats (see Siegel et al., 1999), whereas micro-injection of a vasopressin-receptor antagonist into the AHN reduces aggression in hamsters (Ferris & Potegal, 1988). Studies with nonhuman primates appear to confirm the key role of the hypothalamus in aggressive responding. For example, electrical stimulation of the AHN in rhesus monkeys and the VHA in marmosets increases aggressive displays and attacks on subordinate males (see Nelson & Trainor, 2007). Research with humans likewise points to an important role for the hypothalamus in triggering escalated, abnormal levels of aggression (see Haller, 2013).

Shedding Light on Neural Function

Such electrical and chemical stimulation studies represent a major advance over earlier "knife cut" lesion studies (e.g., Bard, 1928) or other neural ablation techniques, which often afford little precision in targeting specific structures or groups of neurons for study. Still, even these more advanced stimulation techniques can be problematic because the current (in the case of electrical stimulation) activates both the neurons of interest and the fibers connecting them with other cells and structures, making it difficult to know whether observed behavioral effects result only from stimulation of the area of interest. This problem is particularly acute when using mouse or insect models, whose neural structures are tiny in comparison with other model organisms like cats or primates. A very recent development from genetic research, known as *optogenetics*, provides a solution to this problem. With optogenetics, scientists engineer neurons in a given location to be activated by specific frequencies of light. This is accomplished by delivering a gene that encodes light-sensitive protein onto the cells of interest. Those cells can then be activated with high temporal and spatial precision using light delivered via an implanted optic fiber aimed at the region of interest (see Boyden et al., 2005). Unlike with electrical current delivered through an implanted electrode, the photons that inadvertently shine on nearby cells that have not been genetically altered will have no effect on their activation.

Using this optogenetic technique, recent studies have shown that very specific neurons in the ventrolateral portion of the VMH (VMHvl) in mice, a microscopic area comprised of only around 10,000 cells, control male attack behaviors. One study found that attack responses—but not males' social investigation behavior—are strongly suppressed by VMHvl inhibition, and that aggression returns to normal levels when VMHvl activity is restored (Lin et al., 2011). A more recent study provided perhaps the strongest evidence yet that aggression is an emergent property of a neural network subserving a range of social behaviors (Lee et al., 2014). By adjusting the intensity of the light delivered to VMHvl neurons, researchers could reliably control whether mice engaged in sexual mounting behaviors (low-intensity light) or attack behaviors (high-intensity light); intermediate intensity of the light prompted a mixture of attacking and mounting behaviors. These data show not only the exquisite sensitivity of VMHvl neurons to varying levels of stimulation (mimicking changing levels of neurochemical signaling that might occur in response to changing environmental circumstances), but also that the functional significance of their activation ranges dramatically, from the highly prosocial to the extremely antisocial. Such findings represent an important step away from a so-called "brain mapping" approach, in which particular behaviors are mapped onto specific neural structures, and toward a more nuanced understanding of multidimensional neural systems governing whole classes of behavioral responding.

Neurochemistry of Aggression

Even within a circumscribed cluster of cells like VMHvl, there is variation with respect to the presence of receptors for differing neurotransmitters. This means that not all cells within a given structure are responsive to the same kind of neurochemical signaling and, ultimately, are probably not all responsible for regulating the same kinds of behaviors. This property of neurochemical heterogeneity among physically proximal neurons proved to be very important in the optogenetic study just described (Lee et al., 2014). Specifically, it was a relatively small subset of VMHvl neurons, distinguished by the presence of a receptor for the hormone estrogen, that were responsible for the scalable mounting-to-attacking behaviors elicited by the optical stimulation.

Research involving other populations of neurons in other structures also underscores the critical role of specific neurotransmitters in regulating aggressive and other social behaviors. One study found that optogenetically modified neurons in the medial amygdala with receptors for gamma-aminobutyric acid (GABA) promote aggression when stimulated with high-intensity light, social grooming when stimulated with moderate-intensity light, and sex-related mounting when stimulated with low-intensity light (Hong et al., 2014). A different group of medial amygdalar neurons with receptors for glutamate (but not GABA) promote asocial repetitive self-grooming when activated using the optogenetic technique. Moreover, the two groups of neurons appear to prompt mutually inhibitory responses, in that activation of the GABAergic neurons suppresses self-grooming, whereas activation of the glutamatergic neurons reduces social responses (aggression and mounting). These findings underscore that even within individual brain structures or groups of neurons, neural function is not homogeneous.

Other neurotransmitters linked to aggression include monoamines such as dopamine (DA) and serotonin (see de Almeida et al., 2005). In addition to mice, *Drosophila melanogaster*—the common fruit fly—provides an excellent laboratory model for the study of aggression (see Chen et al., 2002). Male fruit flies routinely fight when confronted with other males, particularly when food or a mating opportunity is at stake. Their relatively simple brains, consisting of only around 100,000 neurons, offer an opportunity to understand the role of specific monoaminergic neurons in modulating aggression. DA is particularly tricky in this regard because it is implicated in so many different kinds of behaviors (Huber & Kravitz, 2010). However, researchers were able to identify two pairs of DA neurons in the fruit fly that modulate aggression but have no significant impact on other behaviors, providing some of the first direct evidence of a specialized role for DA in aggression (Alekseyenko et al., 2013).

Considerable research implicates serotonin in regulating aggressive responses. In humans, serotonin appears to be particularly implicated in the kinds of responses often associated with reactive, angry aggression. Serotonin appears to play an important role in regulating affective responses. In very simple terms, too little serotonin can make people irritable and less able to control anger, and therefore can indirectly lead to aggression. In correlational studies, brain serotonin levels have been negatively related to violence in both human epidemiological (Moffitt et al., 1998) and clinical samples (Goveas et al., 2004), as well as in nonhuman primates (see Higley et al., 1992; Westergaard et al., 1999).

More direct support for the role of serotonin in aggression comes from experimental laboratory studies showing that short-term reduction in serotonin levels, achieved by decreasing dietary tryptophan, increases aggressive responding, whereas increasing serotonin levels via dietary supplements of tryptophan decreases aggressive responding (e.g., Cleare & Bond, 1995; Marsh et al., 2002; Pihl et al., 1995). Brain imaging studies show a potential mechanism for this effect. For example, one study found that tryptophan-depleted participants showed weaker co-activation of limbic (amygdala) and prefrontal cortical structures during viewing of angry faces compared to non-depleted participants, suggesting that prefrontal regulation of anger-related responses is more difficult when serotonin levels are low (Passamonti et al., 2012). This hypothesis is consistent with the idea that factors that increase aggression by reducing inhibitory control (e.g., alcohol consumption) have their effects through decreases in serotonin levels (see McCloskey et al., 2009). Drug studies similarly have shown that acutely increasing serotonin levels—for example, using drugs like fenfluramine (see Cherek & Lane, 2001) and paroxetine (Berman et al., 2009)—reduces aggression in the short term, and prolonged exposure to medications that increase serotonin levels chronically reduce impulsive aggression in patients with personality disorders (e.g., Coccaro & Kavoussi, 1997; Salzman et al., 1995).

But the link between serotonin and aggression is more complicated than it might seem. A recent review summarized and integrated laboratory findings in cats, rodents, and humans and concluded that serotonergic neurotransmission in the hypothalamus, among other mechanisms, distinguishes reactive/emotional aggression from proactive/low-arousal aggression (Haller, 2013). Specifically, reactive, high-arousal aggression is associated with increased activation in the mediobasal portion of the hypothalamus, which is accompanied by increased vasopressinergic and decreased serotonergic neurotransmission. In aggression models associated with low arousal (unemotional/proactive aggression), the lateral but not the mediobasal hypothalamus is over-activated and the link between aggression and serotonergic neurotransmission is lost. This conclusion accords with previous findings showing that serotonin influences impulsive (but not planned) aggression (see Berman et al., 1997).

Neural Responses Associated with Aggression

Thus far, the current chapter has focused primarily on evidence of the neural foundations of aggression from studies in which neural structure and function have been manipulated, either naturally (i.e., via injury) or in laboratory lesion and neural activation studies. Another class of studies from cognitive and behavioral neuroscience involves measuring naturally occurring neural responses either as aggressive behaviors are enacted or as environmental cues associated with aggression are processed. Work of this type is important for establishing links between aggression-related triggers in the environment and the neural processes that give rise to overt behavioral expression of aggression. This section provides a brief review of some of that research.

A considerable amount of human aggression research is concerned with factors in the external environment (e.g., perceiving hostility in others; witnessing others' aggressive acts; seeing others in pain) that are believed to elicit aggressive or anti-aggressive (i.e., empathic or prosocial) behavioral responses. Studies of this type often involve participants being asked to view violence-related stimuli while their brain activity is measured. For example, one correlational study found that repeated viewing of violence in the media is associated with reduced neural responding to depictions of real-life violence, seen as attenuated amplitude of the P3 (or P300) component of the event-related brain potential (ERP) when violent images are shown (Bartholow et al., 2006). An experimental study showed that, among participants who typically do not expose themselves to large amounts of media violence, playing a violent video game (versus a nonviolent game) in the lab for 25 minutes also reduced the P3 response to images of violence (Engelhardt et al., 2011). ERPs represent electrical responses generated by the postsynaptic firing of (primarily cortical) neurons during information processing (see Fabiani et al., 2007). The P3 is a voltage deflection occurring roughly 300–700 ms following the onset of a stimulus (e.g., an image of violence), which has been associated with the activation of approach and avoidance motivational systems in response to positive and negative images (e.g., Hilgard et al., 2014; Schupp et al., 2000; Weingberg & Hajcak, 2010). Thus, the findings reported by Bartholow and colleagues (2006; Engelhardt et al., 2011) suggest that exposure to virtual violence can lead to desensitization of avoidance motivational responses to real-life violence (also see Bailey et al., 2011).

As mentioned in the previous section, functional magnetic resonance imaging (fMRI) also has been used to study the specific neural structures involved in processing violence and in regulating aggressive responding (e.g., Passamonti et al., 2012). In a nutshell, fMRI involves the measurement of blood flow to specific brain areas in response to specific stimuli or events, which can be used to infer that those areas were activated by those stimuli or events (see Huettel et al., 2014). In one study, researchers used fMRI to investigate neural structures that increase and decrease in activation during violent video game play (Weber et al.,

2006). These researchers found a negative linear relation between the potential for violence in a game scene and the fMRI signal change in the rostral anterior cingulate cortex (rACC), amygdala, and orbitofrontal cortex, structures implicated in affect/emotion-related processing and self-regulation. More recently, researchers compared neural activity during video game play between individuals with mostly violent or mostly nonviolent game experience (Gentile et al., 2014). ACC and amygdala activity during violent games (compared to nonviolent games) was higher in individuals with predominantly nonviolent game experience, suggesting that these individuals were more emotionally reactive to the violence in the game than were individuals with considerable violent gaming experience. These results complement those using ERPs (Engelhardt et al., 2011), providing validation of the desensitization hypothesis using a different technique.

Other brain imaging studies also point to areas in the prefrontal cortex as important for regulating anger and aggression. These data are consistent with the neuropsychological data reviewed previously. For example, participants in one study were insulted and induced to ruminate while in the fMRI scanner (Denson et al., 2009). The results showed that activity in areas of the PFC was positively related to self-reported feelings of anger and to individual differences in self-reported aggression, suggesting less efficient PFC engagement is associated with more difficulty regulating angry feelings. In another study, women received injections of testosterone while viewing slides depicting angry and happy faces (Hermans et al., 2008). The results showed consistent activation to angry versus happy faces in brain areas known to be involved in reactive aggression, such as the amygdala and hypothalamus.

Integration

This chapter has presented a lot of information concerning the neural foundations of aggression, while at the same time not providing much in the way of an explanation for how various neurochemical and neurophysiological processes give rise to aggression. One scholar reviewed the genetic and brain imaging literatures related to violent and antisocial behavior and proposed a model in which specific genes produce structural and functional brain alterations that predispose certain individuals to behave in an aggressive manner (Raine, 2008). Based in large part on research in psychopathy, this model proposes a key role for the prefrontal cortex (as well as limbic structures, such as the amygdala) in regulating aggression and violence. Critically, however, the model goes beyond mere biology by incorporating the influence of environmental factors that may alter gene expression in these areas, "to trigger the cascade of events that translate genes into antisocial behavior" (Raine, 2008, p. 323). For example, a common polymorphism (i.e., an individual difference in the form or expression of a biological process) in the monoamine oxidase A (MAOA) gene, which produces an enzyme important for breaking down neurotransmitters such as serotonin and dopamine, has been associated with both antisocial behavior (Moffitt et al., 2002) and reduced volume of brain structures, such as the amygdala and orbitofrontal cortex, important for emotion and self-regulation. Future treatments for violent, antisocial behavior could therefore include drug therapy to regulate levels of MAOA activity.

In summary, the available biochemical, neuropsychological, and brain imaging data all indicate areas of the prefrontal cortex and a social behavior network (mainly comprised of limbic structures) as important for regulating aggressive behavior across species. In particular, both human and animal models point to a critical role for hypothalamic neurons in a range of social behaviors, including aggression. Moreover, serotonergic neurotransmission in the hypothalamus appears critical for angry, reactive (or escalated) forms of aggression, but not for low-arousal, proactive or functional forms.

Although both humans and other species engage in both of these forms of aggression, this distinction appears to be much larger in modern human aggression than in either animal or even historical human forms of the behavior. In recent history, humans have become much more adept at escalated forms of aggression and violence than have other animals, and have developed much more sophisticated and deadly ways of behaving aggressively. From arrows and rifles to drones and warships to cyberattacks, modern weapons allow humans to inflict massive amounts of harm from long distances, often without directly confronting or even seeing their victims. This more detached form of escalated aggression differs dramatically from the aggression perpetrated by nonhuman animals and even our relatively recent human ancestors, in several ways. For one, this kind of aggression often occurs in the absence of an instigating emotional response, such as anger, and diverts subsequent emotional responses that often arise following an aggressive act, such as empathy for others' pain and suffering, which can help to inhibit future aggression (see Funk et al., 2004). Additionally, being physically removed from the location of an aggressive action, as in the case of launching a missile attack from hundreds of miles away, allows us to avoid the potential for being harmed ourselves (at least in the short term). In the not-too-distant past, causing physical harm to another person meant engaging in hand-to-hand combat, in which the perpetrator risked being injured as much as the victim. It seems likely that the quantum leap in humans' ability to aggress in more detached and emotionless ways represents a decoupling of aggressive actions from the neurochemical and neurophysiological processes that evolved to support functional aggression.

The aim of this chapter was to provide a brief overview of recent advances in behavioral and cognitive neuroscience research investigating the neural foundations of aggressive behavior. Although in many cases these approaches are complementary, representing the essence of translational research across levels of analysis, the preceding discussion highlights some important ways in which human and animal aggression have diverged. Given such distinctions, it would seem that understanding uniquely human forms of aggression and violence, such as mass shootings and acts of war, likely will be achieved primarily through human behavioral, neuropsychological, and psychophysiological research.

References

Alekseyenko, O.V., Chan, Y.-B., Li, R., & Kravitz, E.A. (2013). Single dopaminergic neurons that modulate aggression in Drosophila. *Proceedings of the National Academy of Sciences, 110*, 6151–6156.

Anderson, S.W., Bechara, A., Damasio, H., Tranel, D., & Damasio, A. R. (1999). Impairment of social and moral behavior related to early damage in human prefrontal cortex. *Nature Neuroscience, 2*, 1032–1037.

Bailey, K., West, R., & Anderson, C. A. (2011). The association between chronic exposure to video game violence and affective picture processing: An ERP study. *Cognitive, Affective, & Behavioral Neuroscience, 11*, 259–276.

Bard, P. (1928). A diencephalic mechanism for the expression of rage with special reference to the sympathetic nervous system. *American Journal of Physiology, 84*, 490–515.

Baron, R. A., & Richardson, D. R. (1994). *Human aggression* (2nd ed.). New York: Plenum.

Bartholow, B. D., Bushman, B. J., & Sestir, M. A. (2006). Chronic violent video game exposure and desensitization: Behavioral and event-related brain potential data. *Journal of Experimental Social Psychology, 42*, 532–539.

Berman, M.E., McCloskey, M.S., Fanning, J.R., Schumacher, J.A., & Coccaro, E.F. (2009). Serotonin augmentation reduces response to attack in aggressive individuals. *Psychological Science, 20*, 714–720.

Berman, M. E., Tracy, J. I., & Coccaro, E. F. (1997). The serotonin hypothesis of aggression revisited. *Clinical Psychology Review, 17*, 651–665.

Bermond, B., Mos, J., Meelis, W., van der Poel, A. M., & Kruk, M. R. (1982). Aggression induced by stimulation of the hypothalamus: Effects of androgens. *Pharmacology Biochemistry and Behavior, 16*, 41–45.

Blair, R. (2004). The roles of orbital frontal cortex in the modulation of antisocial behavior. *Brain and Cognition, 55*, 198–208.

Boyden, E. S., Zhang, F., Bamberg, E., Nagel, G., & Deisseroth, K. (2005). Millisecond-timescale, genetically targeted optical control of neural activity. *Nature Neuroscience, 8*, 1263–1268.

Briffa, M. (2010). Territoriality and aggression. *Nature Education Knowledge, 3*, 81.

Bushman, B. J., & Bartholow, B. D. (2010). Aggression. In R. F. Baumeister & E. J. Finkel (Eds.), *Advanced social psychology* (pp. 303–340). New York: Oxford University Press.

Chen, S., Lee, A.Y., Bowens, N. M., Huber, R., & Kravitz, E. A. (2002). Fighting fruit flies: A model system for the study of aggression. *Proceedings of the National Academy of Sciences of the USA, 99*(8), 5664–5668.

Cheng, Y., Ma, Z., Kim, B-H., Wu, W., Cayting, P., Boyle, A.P., Sundaram, V., Xing, X., Dogan, N., Li, J., Euskirchen, G., Lin, S., Lin, Y., Visel, A., Kawli, T., Yang, X., Patacsil, D., Keller, C.A., Giardine, B., the Mouse ENCODE Consortium, Kundaje, A., Wang, T., Pennacchio, L.A., Weng, Z., Hardison, R.C., & Snyder, M.P. (2014). Principles of regulatory information conservation between mouse and human. *Nature, 515*(7527), 371–375.

Cherek, D. R., & Lane, S. D. (2001). Acute effects of D-fenfluramine on simultaneous measures of aggressive escape and impulsive responses of adult males with and without a history of conduct disorder. *Psychopharmacology (Berlin), 157*, 221–227.

Cleare, A. J., & Bond, A. J. (1995). The effect of tryptophan depletion and enhancement on subjective and behavioural aggression in normal male subjects. *Psychopharmacology, 118*, 72–81.

Coccaro, E. F., & Kavoussi, R. J. (1997). Fluoxetine and impulsive aggressive behavior in personality-disordered subjects. *Archives of General Psychiatry, 54*, 1081–1088.

Damasio, H., Grabowski, T., Frank, R., Galaburda, A.M., & Damasio, A.R. (1994). The return of Phineas Gage: Clues about the brain from the skull of a famous patient. *Science, 264*(5162), 1102–1105.

de Almeida, R. M., Ferrari, P. F., Parmigiani, S., & Miczek, K.A. (2005). Escalated aggressive behavior: Dopamine, serotonin and GABA. *European Journal of Pharmacology, 526*, 51–64.

de Bruin, J. P., van Oyen, H. G., & Van de Poll, N. (1983). Behavioural changes following lesions of the orbital prefrontal cortex in male rats. *Behavioral Brain Research, 10*, 209–232.

Denson, T. F., Pedersen, W. C., Ronquillo, J., & Nandy, A. S. (2009). The angry brain: Neural correlates of anger, angry rumination, and aggressive personality. *Journal of Cognitive Neuroscience, 21*, 734–444.

Engelhardt, C. R., Bartholow, B. D., Kerr, G. T. & Bushman, B. J. (2011). This is your brain on violent video games: Neural desensitization to violence predicts increased aggression following violent video game exposure. *Journal of Experimental Social Psychology, 47*, 1033–1036.

Fabiani, M., Gratton, G., & Federmeier, K. D. (2007). Event-related brain potentials: Methods, theory, and applications. In J. T. Cacioppo, L. G. Tassinary, & G. Berntson (Eds.), *Handbook of psychophysiology* (3rd ed., pp. 85–119). New York: Cambridge University Press.

Ferris, C. F., & Potegal, M. (1988). Vasopressin receptor blockade in the anterior hypothalamus suppresses aggression in hamsters. *Physiology and Behavior, 44*, 235–239.

Funk, J. B., Bechtoldt-Baldacci, H., Pasold, T., & Baumgartner, J. (2004). Violence exposure in real-life, video games, television, movies, and the Internet: Is there desensitization? *Journal of Adolescence, 27*, 23–39.

Fuster, J. M., Bodner, M., & Kroger, J. K. (2000). Cross-modal and cross-temporal association in neurons of frontal cortex. *Nature, 405*, 347–351.

Garey, L. J. (2006). *Brodmann's localisation in the cerebral cortex*. New York: Springer.

Gentile, D. A., Swing, E. L., Anderson, C. A., Rinker, D., & Thomas, K. M. (2014). Differential neural recruitment during violent game play in violent- and nonviolent-game players. *Psychology of Popular Media Culture*. Advance online publication. http://dx.doi.org/10.1037/ppm0000009

Giancola, P. R. (1995). Evidence for dorsolateral and orbital prefrontal cortical involvement in the expression of aggressive behavior. *Aggressive Behavior, 21*, 431–450.

Giancola, P. R. (2000). Executive functioning: A conceptual framework for alcohol-related aggression. *Experimental and Clinical Psychopharmacology, 8*, 576–597.

Giancola, P. R., Mezzich, A. C., & Tarter, R. E. (1998). Executive cognitive functioning, temperament, and antisocial behavior in conduct-disordered adolescent females. *Journal of Abnormal Psychology, 107*, 629–641.

Giancola, P. R., & Zeichner, A. (1994). Neuropsychological performance on tests of frontal-lobe functioning and aggressive behavior in men. *Journal of Abnormal Psychology, 103*, 832–835.

Goldman-Rakic, P. S. (October 1996). The prefrontal landscape: Implications of functional architecture for understanding human mentation and the central executive. *Philosophical Transactions of the Royal Society of London. Series B, Biological Sciences, 351*, 1445–1453.

Goveas, J. S., Csernansky, J. G., & Coccaro, E. F. (2004). Platelet serotonin content correlates inversely with life history of aggression in personality-disordered subjects. *Psychiatry Research, 126*, 23–32.

Grafman, J., Schwab, K., Warden, D., Pridgen, A., Brown, H. R., & Salazar, A. M. (1996). Frontal lobe injuries, violence, and aggression: A report of the Vietnam Head Injury Study. *Neurology, 46*, 1231–1238.

Haller, J. (2013). The neurobiology of abnormal manifestations of aggression—A review of hypothalamic mechanisms in cats, rodents, and humans. *Brain Research Bulletin, 93*, 97–109.

Harlow, J. M. (1848). Passage of an iron rod through the head. *Boston Medical and Surgical Journal, 39*(20), 389–393.

Harlow, J. M. (1868). Recovery after severe injury to the head. *Publications of the Massachusetts Medical Society, 2*(3), 324–347.

Hermans, E., Ramsey, N., & van Honk, J. (2008). Exogenous testosterone enhances responsiveness to social threat in the neural circuitry of social aggression in humans. *Biological Psychiatry, 63*, 263–270.

Higley, J.D., Mehlman, P.T., Taub, D.M., Higley, S.B., Suomi, S.J., Linnoila, M., & Vickers, J.H. (1992). Cerebrospinal fluid monoamine and adrenal correlates of aggression in free-ranging rhesus monkeys. *Archives of General Psychiatry, 49*, 436–441.

Hilgard, J., Weinberg, A., Hajcak Proudfit, G., & Bartholow, B. D. (2014). The negativity bias in affective picture processing depends on top-down and bottom-up motivational significance. *Emotion, 14*, 940–949.

Hong, W., Kim, D-W., & Anderson, D. J. (2014). Antagonistic control of social versus repetitive self-grooming behaviors by separable amygdala neuronal subsets. *Cell, 158* (6), 1348–1361.

Huber, R. H., & Kravitz, E. A. (2010). Aggression: Towards an integration of gene, brain and behavior. In T. Szekely, A. J. Moore, & J. Komdeur (Eds.), *Social behavior: Genes, ecology and evolution* (pp. 165–180). Cambridge, UK: Cambridge University Press.

Huettel, S. A., Song, A.W., & McCarthy, G. (2014). *Functional magnetic resonance imaging* (3rd ed.). Sunderland, MA: Sinauer Associates.

Kruk, M. R. (1991). Ethology and pharmacology of hypothalamic aggression in the rat. *Neuroscience and Biobehavioral Reviews, 15*, 527–538.

Kruk, M. R., Van der Laan, C. E., Mos, J., Van der Poel, A. M., Meelis, W., & Olivier, B. (1984). Comparison of aggressive behaviour induced by electrical stimulation in the hypothalamus of male and female rats. *Progress in Brain Research, 61*, 303–314.

Lee, H., Kim, D.W., Remedios, R., Anthony, T.E., Chang, A., Madisen, L., Zeng, H., & Anderson, D.J. (2014). Scalable control of mounting and attack by Esr1+ neurons in the ventromedial hypothalamus. *Nature, 509*, 627–632.

Lin, D., Boyle, M.P., Dollar, P., Lee, H., Lein, E.S., Perona, P., & Anderson, D. J. (2011). Functional identification of an aggression locus in the mouse hypothalamus. *Nature, 470*, 221–226.

McCloskey, M. S., Berman, M. E., Echevarria, D. J., & Coccaro, E. F. (2009). Effects of acute alcohol intoxication and paroxetine on aggression in men. *Alcoholism: Clinical and Experimental Research, 33*, 581–590.

Marsh, D. M., Dougherty, D. M., Moeller, F. G., Swann, A. C., & Spiga, R. (2002). Laboratory-measured aggressive behavior of women: Acute tryptophan depletion and augmentation. *Neuropsychopharmacology, 26*, 660–71.

Moffitt, T., Brammer, G., Caspi, A., Fawcett, J., Raleigh, M., Yuwiler, A., & Silva, P. (1998). Whole blood serotonin relates to violence in an epidemiological study. *Biological Psychiatry, 43*, 446–457.

Moffitt, T. E., Caspi, A., Harrington, H., & Milne, B. J. (2002). Males on the life-course-persistent and adolescence-limited antisocial pathways: Follow-up at age 26 years. *Development and Psychopathology, 14, 179–207.*

Nelson, R.J., & Trainor, B.C. (2007). Neural mechanisms of aggression. *Nature Reviews Neuroscience, 8,* 536–546.

Newman, S. (1999). The medial extended amygdala in male reproductive behavior. A node in the mammalian social behavior network. *Annals of the New York Academy of Sciences, 877,* 242–257.

Passamonti, L., Crockett, M. J., Apergis-Schoute, A. M., Clark, L., Rowe, J. B. Calder, A. J., & Robbins, T. W. (2012). Effects of acute tryptophan depletion on prefrontal-amygdala connectivity while viewing facial signals of aggression. *Biological Psychiatry, 71,* 36–43.

Pihl, R. O., Young, S. N., Harden, P., Plotnick, S., Chamberlain, B., & Ervin, F. R. (1995). Acute effect of altered tryptophan levels and alcohol on aggression in normal human males. *Psychopharmacology, 119,* 353–360.

Raine, A. (2008). From genes to brain to antisocial behavior. *Current Directions in Psychological Science, 17,* 323–328.

Roberts, A., Robbins, T.W., & Weiskrantz, L. (Eds.). (1998). *The prefrontal cortex: Executive and cognitive functions.* New York: Oxford University Press.

Salzman, C., Wolfson, A.N., Schatzberg, A., Looper, J., Henke, R., Albanese, M., Schwartz, J., & Edison, M. (1995). Effect of fluoxetine on anger in symptomatic volunteers with borderline personality disorder. *Journal of Clinical Psychopharmacology, 15,* 23–29.

Schupp, H. T., Cuthbert, B. N., Bradley, M. M., Cacioppo, J. T., Ito, T., & Lang, P. J. (2000). Affective picture processing: The late positive potential is modulated by motivational relevance. *Psychophysiology, 37,* 257–261.

Seguin, J.R., & Zelazo, P.D. (2005). Executive function in early physical aggression. In R.E. Tremblay, W.W. Hartup, & J. Archer (Eds.), *Developmental origins of aggression* (pp. 307–329). New York: Guilford Press.

Siegel, A., Roeling, T. A. P., Gregg, T. R., & Kruk, M. R. (1999). Neuropharmacology of brain-stimulation-evoked aggression. *Neuroscience and Biobehavioral Reviews, 23,* 359–389.

Weber, R., Ritterfield, U., & Mathiak, K. (2006). Does playing violent video games induce aggression? Empirical evidence of a functional magnetic resonance imaging study. *Media Psychology, 8,* 39–60.

Weinberg, A., & Hajcak, G. (2010). Beyond good and evil: The timecourse of neural activity elicited by specific picture content. *Emotion, 10,* 767–782.

Westergaard, G. C., Mehlman, P. T., Suomi, S. J., & Higley, J. D. (1999). CSF 5-HIAA and aggression in female macaque monkeys: Species and interindividual differences. *Psychopharmacology, 146,* 440–446.

Yang, Y., Raine, A., Colletti, P., Toga, A. W., & Narr, K. L. (2010). Morphological alterations in the prefrontal cortex and the amygdala in unsuccessful psychopaths. *Journal of Abnormal Psychology, 119,* 546–554.

4

DEVELOPMENT OF AGGRESSION IN MALES AND FEMALES

Jennifer E. Lansford

Aggressive behaviors, as well as biological and social risk factors for aggression, are highly stable over time. In a 22-year longitudinal study, the individuals who were most aggressive at the age of 8 years continued to be the most aggressive at the age of 30; stability of aggression was .50 for boys and .35 for girls over this 22-year period (Huesmann et al., 1984). However, there is some evidence that a number of environmental factors can affect the stability of aggression. For example, aggression is more stable from childhood to adulthood in the United States than in Finland (Kokko et al., 2014), perhaps in part because of macro-environmental features of Finland that make it easier for individuals to break out of aggressive trajectories (e.g., free access to higher education in Finland but not in the United States). Thus, it is important to understand factors that promote stability versus change in the development of aggression.

This chapter begins with a consideration of different types of aggression and mean differences between males and females in these different types of aggression. The bulk of the chapter focuses on developmental trajectories of aggression, risk factors for aggression, and developmental sequelae of aggression; gender differences and similarities in trajectories, risk factors, and developmental sequelae are discussed. The chapter concludes with a description of interventions that have been demonstrated to prevent or reduce aggression, along with a description of gender-based considerations that might influence the effectiveness of particular interventions for males and females.

Conceptualizations of aggression often hinge on distinctions among sub-types of aggression that vary in form and function (e.g., Vitaro et al., 2006). The form of aggression involves particular behavioral manifestations such as physical aggression or direct verbal aggression (Little et al., 2003), on the one hand, in contrast to indirect aggression (e.g., Bjorkqvist et al., 1992), relational aggression (e.g., Crick & Grotpeter, 1995), and social aggression (e.g., Galen & Underwood, 1997) on the other. Key distinctions among these forms of aggression involve the means through which harm is imparted (physically, through verbal insults, or through the manipulation or sabotage of social relationships such as by spreading rumors or excluding a peer). In contrast, the function of aggression involves the motivation underlying the behavior. The most frequently distinguished functions are between reactive aggression (an angry, retaliatory response to provocation) and proactive aggression (an instrumental behavior that seeks to obtain some desired outcome; Dodge & Coie, 1987). Different forms and functions of aggression may develop similarly or in unique ways, and males and females may differ in their expression of different forms and functions of aggression.

Mean Differences between Males and Females

A meta-analytic review of 78 studies revealed a robust difference in mean levels of physical aggression with males, on average, being more physically aggressive than females (Archer, 2004). This difference held regardless of age, cultural background, or even species. Likewise, males had higher mean levels of verbal aggression than females. Gender differences in indirect aggression were less consistent. Averaged across age, females exhibit more indirect aggression than males when assessed using some methods (e.g., observations, peer ratings, teacher reports) but not others (e.g., peer nominations, self-reports); effect sizes for these gender differences were small to medium. Disaggregating by age, the higher mean levels of indirect aggression by females held only in late childhood and adolescence.

Likewise, in a meta-analysis of 107 studies, moderate effect sizes were found for gender differences in direct aggression (Card et al., 2008). Larger effect sizes for gender differences were found with peer and teacher reports of aggression than for self-reports or observations. Effect sizes were smaller in samples that included a higher proportion of ethnic minorities. Child age and the country in which the study was conducted were not related to the magnitude of the gender differences. Gender differences were more pronounced for physical than verbal forms of direct aggression. Gender differences in mean levels of other forms of aggression were less consistent. Small gender differences in indirect aggression were characterized as trivial (Card et al., 2008); the magnitude of effects did not vary by child age, country, or proportion of ethnic minorities in the sample. Aside from gender differences in mean levels of aggression, direct and indirect aggression were more strongly correlated for boys than girls (Card et al., 2008).

A note about possible cohort effects is warranted. Early research on the development of aggression often included only males because of the preponderance of males who exhibited extreme forms of aggression resulting in arrests for assault, homicide, and other violent crimes. The historical gap between men's and women's violent crime has been narrowing over time (Heimer, 2000), but males still greatly outnumber females in arrests, particularly for violent crimes (e.g., males comprise more than 70% of all arrests and nearly 80% of arrests for violent crimes in the United States; U.S. Department of Justice, 2014). It is possible that seemingly robust gender differences even in a domain such as physical aggression will become less pronounced over time.

Developmental Trajectories of Aggression for Males and Females

Two of the most influential theories regarding the development of aggression and other antisocial behaviors focus on timing of onset and offset of aggressive behavior as well as risk factors predicting the trajectories (Moffitt, 1993; Patterson et al., 1991). One model describes a life course-persistent versus adolescence-limited developmental taxonomy (Moffitt, 1993). The life course-persistent trajectory is, as the name suggests, characterized by antisocial behavior that begins in early childhood, continues through adolescence, and persists into adulthood. In contrast, the adolescence-limited trajectory begins and ends in adolescence, without the continuity across development that characterizes the life course-persistent trajectory. Individuals who follow a life course-persistent trajectory have a number of risk factors during early childhood, including neuropsychological deficits that lead to impulsivity, poor executive functioning, and verbal delays, all of which make these children more difficult to parent. Compounding the neuropsychological problems, if these children are reared in adverse environments, they enter school at risk of academic and social failure, which further contributes to an escalating pattern of antisocial behavior. In contrast, individuals on an adolescence-limited trajectory typically do not experience these risk factors during childhood. Instead, they increase in antisocial behavior during adolescence as they encounter a maturity gap between their desire for independence and privileges of adulthood and the limitations imposed by parents and society in engaging in those behaviors. As adolescents witness peers engaging in adultlike behaviors (e.g., drinking, smoking, becoming sexually active), they might begin experimenting with risky behaviors as a way to assert independence from adult authority. However, once these adolescents become adults with attendant privileges, they no longer seek to make themselves appear more mature by engaging in antisocial behavior but instead engage in more socially accepted adult roles. Because they do not have the early neuropsychological or environmental risks associated with the life course-persistent pattern, they have the resources to switch to a less risky trajectory.

Like the life course-persistent versus adolescence-limited developmental taxonomy, the early versus late starter model also distinguishes between antisocial trajectories that begin early versus later in life (Patterson et al., 1991). Early starters, like life course-persistent offenders, are more likely to engage in antisocial behavior that extends through adolescence into adulthood. However, the early versus late starter model emphasizes a different set of risk factors, and does not posit that late starters have as benign a trajectory as is described in the life course-persistent versus adolescence-limited developmental taxonomy. According to the early versus late starter model, poor parental management of children's early noncompliant behavior sets the stage for early starters' antisocial behavior. In a prototypical exchange, the child would make a request of the parent (e.g., candy in a store checkout lane), and the parent would respond by denying the request. The child would then escalate the request (e.g., start to whine), and the parent would escalate the refusal (e.g., angrily tell the child to stop). Further cycles would continue to escalate in negativity (e.g., temper tantrums, corporal punishment) until the parent gives up (reinforcing the child's aversive behavior) or the child gives up (reinforcing the parent's harshness). As this coercive cycle is repeated over time, children come to learn that they get what they want through aversive behavior. When such behaviors are extended to peer settings, they often lead to rejection by the peer group, which exacerbates the risk of early starting aggression to lead to chronic trajectories of antisocial behavior over time. As with early starters, poor parenting in adolescence sets the stage for late starters to begin engaging in antisocial behavior. Often in response to a psychosocial stressor (e.g., divorce, unemployment), parents become overwhelmed by stress and less effective at monitoring and setting appropriate limits for adolescents, who are then more susceptible to influence by deviant peers, who provide training in antisocial behavior. However, because these late starters' early development has not been characterized by risk and adversity, they have developed better social and academic skills that help them desist from antisocial behavior when environmental contingencies make other options more appealing.

These prominent developmental models of aggression differ in the extent to which they focus on potential gender differences in trajectories of aggression. The early versus late starter model was originally formulated based on a sample of boys. A review of the literature on the development of antisocial behavior in girls concluded that the distinction between childhood and adolescent onset antisocial behavior that has been a central aspect of developmental models of aggression for boys may not apply as well to girls (Silverthorn & Frick, 1999). In particular, a delayed onset pathway for girls was characterized by onset of antisocial behavior during adolescence, despite the presence of many of the same neuropsychological and family problems that posed risk for boys' onset of antisocial behavior during childhood (Silverthorn & Frick, 1999). Furthermore, these researchers posited that an adolescent-onset pathway with only relatively benign consequences (as in the life course-persistent versus adolescence-limited developmental taxonomy) does not apply to girls. Some empirical support has been found for this model. For example, in a sample of adjudicated youth in a secure detention center, boys were approximately evenly split between childhood and adolescent onset of their serious antisocial behavior, but serious antisocial behavior began during adolescence rather than during childhood for more of the girls (Silverthorn et al., 2001).

Nevertheless, other studies have found more similarities than differences between girls' and boys' developmental trajectories. For example, in a sample of urban African Americans, boys and girls were equally as likely to have had police contact by age 13 (evidence for early onset offending for both genders), and correlates and future criminal history of early versus later onset offenders were similar for boys and girls (White & Piquero, 2004). Although boys and girls are differentially represented in childhood-onset (male-to-female ratio of 10 to 1) versus adolescent-onset pathways (male-to-female ratio of 1.5 to 1), the predictors of membership in these trajectory groups are similar for boys and girls (Moffitt & Caspi, 2001). That is, both males and females in the childhood-onset pathway had neurocognitive deficits, difficult temperaments, and a history of problematic parenting, whereas males and females on the adolescent-onset pathway did not. Several other studies also have found that although the ratio of males to females is markedly larger for the early-onset/life-course persistent pattern than the adolescence-limited pattern, the risk factors predicting these two typologies are similar (Fergusson et al., 2000; Mazerolle et al., 2000). These findings suggest that girls are less at risk than boys for early onset trajectories because girls are less likely to have neuropsychological deficits, temperamental risk, hyperactivity, learning disabilities, motor delays, and other risk factors that predict early onset antisocial behavior (Moffitt & Caspi, 2001).

One aspect of these models that deserves further attention is whether they apply specifically to the development of aggression or to the development of antisocial behavior more broadly construed. Some theories differentiate between overt (e.g., physical aggression) and covert (e.g., theft) antisocial pathways and provide evidence that some individuals specialize in different types of crimes (Loeber & Stouthamer-Loeber, 1998). In contrast, other models largely blur distinctions between aggression and other forms of antisocial behavior. Indeed, some models are described by explicitly noting that the form of antisocial behavior may change over time: "biting and hitting at age 4, shoplifting and truancy at age 10, selling drugs and stealing cars at age 16, robbery and rape at age 22, and fraud and child abuse at age 30" (Moffitt, 1993, p. 679).

Developmental Precursors of Aggression for Males and Females

To an extent, examination of gender differences in developmental trajectories of aggression touches on differences and similarities in precursors of aggression for males and females. Apart from consideration of the leading theoretical models of the development of aggression, a large body of literature documents a wide array of developmental precursors of aggressive behavior including individual, familial, peer, community, and even historical risk factors (see Dodge et al., 2006, for a review). Some studies have investigated the extent to which gender moderates associations between risk factors and aggressive behavior or between aggressive behavior and other constructs. Meta-analysis revealed that gender did not moderate the association between aggression and other forms of maladaptation (e.g., internalizing problems, peer rejection, emotion dysregulation; Card et al., 2008).

At the individual level, neuropsychological difficulties, difficult temperament, impulsivity, and social information processing biases all increase the likelihood of subsequent aggression. Several biological factors have been investigated as predictors of aggression at the individual level. Some of these factors, such as gender differences in levels of testosterone, have been used to explain higher levels of aggression for males than females. Others appear to operate as biological risk factors without gender moderation. For example, resting heart rate, heart rate variability, and the stress hormone cortisol all have been demonstrated to be risk factors for aggressive behavior for girls and boys (e.g., Kibler et al., 2004; McBurnett et al., 2000; Susman, 2006). However, the specific ways in which these biological risks operate may differ by gender. Greater cardiac reactivity during provocation has been related to more relational aggression for girls, but less cardiac reactivity has been related to more physical aggression for boys (Murray-Close & Crick, 2007).

Within families, harsh and inconsistent parenting, exposure to interparental conflict, and poverty all function as risk factors for children's aggression. Many of these socialization factors have been demonstrated to predict aggression for both boys and girls. However, having a warm, supportive mother appears to be more protective against aggression for females than for males (Blitstein et al., 2005). Similarly, estranged mother-child relationships present more risk for daughters' than sons' aggressive behavior (Serbin et al., 2004).

Peer rejection (Dodge et al., 2003) and affiliating with antisocial peers (Dishion & Patterson, 2006) are risk factors for both males' and females' aggression, although there is some evidence that girls may be more susceptible than boys to deviant peer influence (O'Donnell et al., 2012). A risk factor that has been noted particularly for females is having an older, antisocial boyfriend (Young & d'Arcy, 2005). One mechanism through which peer influence operates is via deviancy training (Dishion et al., 1996), when peers reinforce aggressive behavior by laughing or demonstrating approval when an individual describes or engages in antisocial behavior, increasing the likelihood that peers in the group will engage in such behaviors in the future.

At the community level, children who live in dangerous neighborhoods or societies that value and endorse violence are more likely to behave aggressively. According to the cultural spillover theory of violence, violence in one domain tends to generalize, or spill over, into other domains (Baron & Straus, 1989). In certain cultural groups, gender differences in aggression may be augmented by norms and expectations that men will behave in a way that defends honor (e.g., machismo in Latin America, Arciniega et al., 2008). For example, males in the Southern United States, compared to males in the Northern United States, are more likely to interpret interpersonal slights as threats to their honor and to react aggressively when so provoked (Nisbett & Cohen, 1996). Thus, community-level norms and values become internalized in a way that can increase risk for aggressive behavior.

Historically, aggression increases during times characterized by economic turmoil and recession. This applies both to parents' aggression toward children and to children's aggression toward others. For example, housing insecurity is associated with child maltreatment, with rates of child abuse requiring hospital admission and of traumatic brain injury allegedly caused by child abuse increasing along with 90-day mortgage delinquency rates between 2000 and 2009 in the United States (Wood et al., 2012). Children's externalizing problems (including aggression) have been found to increase during economic recession, in part because recession leads to more economic pressure within families, which in turn decreases parents' mental health, marital quality, and parenting quality (Solantaus et al., 2004).

Exposure to violent media deserves attention as a risk factor for the development of aggression apart from other levels of risk factors because it extends across several. In a meta-analysis of 381 effects from studies involving over 130,000 participants, exposure to violent video games increased aggressive behavior, aggressive cognition, and aggressive affect equally for males and females (Anderson et al., 2010). These results are consistent with a large literature demonstrating similar effects of viewing violent television programs and movies on aggression, effects that are nearly as large in magnitude as the link between smoking and the development of lung cancer and larger than many other widely accepted links in public health (e.g., using condoms and reduced risk of HIV infection; Bushman & Anderson, 2001). Exposure to violent media increases risk for aggressive behavior by increasing aggressive thoughts (which then increase hostile attributions in the face of ambiguous social situations), aggressive affect (such as anger), arousal (such as heart rate), and imitation of aggressive behaviors (Anderson & Bushman, 2001).

In contrast to the body of research examining individual risk factors for the development of aggression, other studies have examined multiple risk factors simultaneously. When boys and girls experience few cumulative risks, there are no gender differences in aggressive behavior (Ribeaud & Eisner, 2010). However, with exposure to more risk factors, the relation between cumulative risk and aggressive behavior becomes steeper for boys than for girls (Ribeaud & Eisner, 2010). In the face of multiple risk factors, girls appear to be more resilient than boys, at least in terms of not behaving aggressively.

Although all of these individual, family, and community risk factors are important predictors of aggressive behavior, individuals' cognitive processing patterns are a more proximal mechanism accounting for aggression in the moment. Dodge and colleagues (Crick & Dodge, 1994; Dodge et al., 1990) have proposed a model that includes several social-cognitive steps through which an individual takes in information from the social environment and (subconsciously) processes the information before enacting a response. In the first step, individuals encode, or take in, social information. Individuals who encode only partial information are more likely to behave aggressively than individuals who fully and accurately encode social situations. In the second step, individuals make attributions about the intentions of other people in social situations. Compared to individuals who make benign attributions, individuals who make hostile attributions are more likely to behave aggressively. In the third step, individuals generate possible responses. Individuals who ultimately behave aggressively generate fewer possible responses overall and a larger proportion of aggressive responses than do individuals who do not behave aggressively. In the fourth step, individuals evaluate possible responses, taking into account how readily they could engage in the response, how others would react if they responded that way, and how likely the response would be to lead to their intended goal. Individuals who more positively evaluate aggressive responses are more likely to behave aggressively. Finally, individuals select and enact a response.

This social information processing model shares similarities with other models of aggression such as the General Aggression Model (GAM; Anderson & Bushman, 2002). The GAM incorporates three stages including person and situation inputs; current internal states involving cognition, affect, and arousal; and outcomes of appraisal and decision-making processes. One of the key premises of the GAM is that knowledge structures that develop through experience in different settings shape the way that individuals perceive, interpret, make decisions about, and behave in relation to stimuli in new situations. In a given situation, knowledge structures may be activated that trigger affective (e.g., anger) and behavioral (e.g., retaliation) scripts that increase the likelihood that individuals will behave aggressively.

Developmental Sequelae of Aggression for Males and Females

Aggressive girls and boys, compared to nonaggressive girls and boys, are more likely to be rejected by peers, struggle academically, drop out of school, use drugs, and have a number of other psychological and behavioral adjustment problems (Cairns & Cairns, 1994; Moffitt et al., 2001). Subsequent risky behaviors and depression are associated not only with physical aggression but also with relational aggression (see Kamper & Ostrov, 2013). Disentangling causes of aggression from consequences of aggression can be difficult, but longitudinal studies have made progress in addressing temporal ordering of aggression in relation to other risks and behaviors. Reciprocal and transactional models best characterize how risk factors lead to aggressive behavior, which then leads to further maladaptation.

Peer relationships have been proposed as one mechanism through which aggression might affect subsequent functioning. Early research found that aggression was a robust predictor of subsequent rejection by peers, when rejection was assessed by asking peers to nominate which classmates they like and do not like (Coie et al., 1990). Peer rejection then further increases subsequent aggression, even after taking into account initial levels of aggression (Dodge et al., 2003). However, in research that has examined peer nominations of perceived popularity rather than liking, the relation between aggression and status in the peer group appears more complex. Rodkin et al. (2000) found two types of popular boys in adolescent peer groups. The "model" type was characterized by being friendly, outgoing, academically oriented, and athletic, but the "tough" type was characterized by high levels of aggression, along with being cool and athletic. Both the model and tough boys were classroom leaders. However, the majority of aggressive children are not nominated as being popular (Rodkin et al., 2006). For adolescent girls, there is evidence that the relation between use of relational aggression and perceived popularity is bidirectional over time (Rose et al., 2004). That is, girls who are popular may have enough social power to use social relationships to manipulate peers, and girls who use their social status in a relationally aggressive way also increase their popularity over time. For boys, perceived popularity predicted an increase in relational aggression over the course of six months, but the use of relational aggression was not predictive of an increase in perceived popularity (Rose et al., 2004). Thus, taken together, the research suggests both direct and indirect (e.g., via peer relationships) effects of aggression on future development.

Interventions to Prevent or Reduce Males' and Females' Aggression

The most promising interventions to prevent or reduce aggression have been highlighted in Blueprints for Healthy Youth Development (www.blueprintsprograms. com). For example, Promoting Alternative Thinking Strategies (PATHS) has been rated as a model program effective as a universal prevention program administered in elementary schools that reduces aggression by promoting self-control, emotional understanding, positive self-esteem, relationships, and interpersonal problem-solving skills (e.g., Greenberg et al., 1995). As an intervention for at-risk youth, Functional Family Therapy has been rated as a model program that can reduce aggression by changing dysfunctional family relationships (Barton et al., 1985). Other effective interventions depend on factors such as the level of risk (e.g., community sample vs. incarcerated youth) and age of the target participants (e.g., childhood vs. adolescence).

There is some controversy over whether mixed-sex or same-sex interventions are equally effective for girls and boys. Some studies show no gender differences in the effectiveness of mixed-sex treatment groups (Beauchaine et al., 2005; Hipwell & Loeber, 2006), but gender differences may be difficult to detect because boys typically far outnumber girls in these groups. Some interventions have explicitly attempted to address issues related to gender. For example, Pepler et al. (2010) tailored the Stop Now and Plan (SNAP) intervention to make it sensitive to girls' risk and protective factors (e.g., improving the quality of girls' relationships with their mothers). Girls in the intervention group improved significantly with respect to externalizing behaviors and social problems compared to girls in a waiting list control group, moderate effects that held at the six-month follow-up. Likewise, the Preventing Relational Aggression in Schools Everyday (PRAISE) Program was designed as an intervention for relationally aggressive girls in urban settings that could be adapted for use as a universal prevention program (Leff et al., 2010). The intervention involved 20 sessions that were co-led by the classroom teachers and therapists. Results indicated that the intervention was effective for girls but not for boys. For example, girls randomly assigned to intervention classrooms had more knowledge about social information processing and anger management techniques as well as lower levels of relational aggression after the intervention than did girls in no-intervention control classrooms. Boys in the intervention versus control classrooms did not differ from one another on most of the measures, suggesting that adaptations or a different approach would be needed to reduce boys' relational aggression. Taken together, evaluations of interventions designed to prevent or reduce aggression indicate that similar intervention targets are important for both boys and girls but that programs that address gender may have additional benefits.

Conclusions

Theoretical models of the development of aggression focus on the timing of onset of aggressive behavior (childhood vs. adolescence) as well as different risk factors predicting timing of onset. Important risk factors for the development of aggression include neuropsychological problems, harsh or coercive parenting, peer rejection, exposure to violent media, and poverty. Aggression predicts future negative outcomes including both further externalizing problems as well as internalizing, academic, and social difficulties. Universal and targeted interventions have shown promise in reducing aggressive behavior.

References

Anderson, C. A., & Bushman, B. J. (2001). Effects of violent video games on aggressive behavior, aggressive cognition, aggressive affect, physiological arousal, and prosocial behavior: A meta-analytic review of the scientific literature. *Psychological Science, 12*, 353–359.

Anderson, C. A., & Bushman, B. J. (2002). Human aggression. *Annual Review of Psychology, 53*, 27–51.

Anderson, C. A., Shibuya, A., Ihori, N., Swing, E. L., Bushman, B. J., Sakamoto, A., Rothstein, H. R., & Saleem, M. (2010). Violent video game effects on aggression, empathy, and prosocial behavior in Eastern and Western countries: A meta-analytic review. *Psychological Bulletin, 136*, 151–173.

Archer, J. (2004). Sex differences in aggression in real-world settings: A meta-analytic review. *Review of General Psychology, 8*, 291–322.

Arciniega, G. M., Anderson, T. C., Tovar-Blank, Z. G., & Tracey, T. J. G. (2008). Toward a fuller conception of machismo: Development of a traditional machismo and caballerismo scale. *Journal of Counseling Psychology, 55*, 19–33.

Baron, L., & Straus, M. A. (1989). *Four theories of rape in American society. A state-level analysis.* New Haven, CT: Yale University Press.

Barton, C., Alexander, J. F., Waldron, H., Turner, C. W., & Warburton, J. (1985). Generalizing treatment effects of Functional Family Therapy: Three replications. *The American Journal of Family Therapy, 13,* 16–26.

Beauchaine, T. P., Webster-Stratton, C., & Reid, M. J. (2005). Mediators, moderators, and predictors of 1-year outcomes among children treated for early-onset conduct problems: A latent growth curve analysis. *Journal of Consulting and Clinical Psychology, 73,* 371–388.

Bjorkqvist, K., Lagerspetz, K. M. J., & Kaukiainen, A. (1992). Do girls manipulate and boys fight? Developmental trends in regard to direct and indirect aggression. *Aggressive Behavior, 18,* 117–127.

Blitstein, J. L., Murray, D. M., Lytle, L. A., Birnbaum, A. S., & Perry, C. L. (2005). Predictors of violent behavior in an early adolescent cohort: Similarities and differences across genders. *Health Education and Behavior, 32,* 175–194.

Bushman, B. J., & Anderson, C. A. (2001). Media violence and the American public: Scientific facts versus media misinformation. *American Psychologist, 56,* 477–489.

Cairns, R., & Cairns, B. (1994). *Lifelines and risks: Pathways of youth in our time.* New York: Cambridge University Press.

Card, N. A., Stucky, B. D., Sawalani, G. M., & Little, T. D. (2008). Direct and indirect aggression during childhood and adolescence: A meta-analytic review of gender differences, intercorrelations, and relations to maladjustment. *Child Development, 79,* 1185–1229.

Coie, J. D., Dodge, K. A., & Kupersmidt, J. (1990). Peer group behavior and social status. In S. R. Asher & J. D. Coie (Eds.), *Peer rejection in childhood* (pp. 17–59). New York: Cambridge University Press.

Crick, N. R., & Dodge, K. A. (1994). A review and reformulation of social information-processing mechanisms in children's social adjustment. *Psychological Bulletin, 115,* 74–101.

Crick, N. R., & Grotpeter, J. K. (1995). Relational aggression, gender, and social-psychological adjustment. *Child Development, 66,* 710–722.

Dishion, T. J., & Patterson, G. R. (2006). The development and ecology of antisocial behavior in children and adolescents. In D. Cicchetti & D. J Cohen (Eds.), *Developmental psychopathology* (2nd ed., pp. 503–541). New York: Wiley.

Dishion, T. J., Spracklen, K. M., Andrews, D. W., & Patterson, G. R. (1996). Deviancy training in male adolescent friendships. *Behavior Therapy, 27,* 373–390.

Dodge, K. A., Bates, J. E., & Pettit, G. S. (1990). Mechanisms in the cycle of violence. *Science, 250,* 1678–1683.

Dodge, K. A., & Coie, J. D. (1987). Social-information-processing factors in reactive and proactive aggression in children's peer groups. *Journal of Personality and Social Psychology, 53,* 1146–1158.

Dodge, K. A., Coie, J. D., & Lynam, D. (2006). Aggression and antisocial behavior in youth. In W. Damon (Series Ed.) & N. Eisenberg (Vol. Ed.), *Handbook of child psychology: Vol. 3. Social, emotional, and personality development* (6th ed., pp. 719–788). New York: Wiley.

Dodge, K. A., Lansford, J. E., Burks, V. S., Bates, J. E., Pettit, G. S., Fontaine, R., & Price, J. M. (2003). Peer rejection and social information-processing factors in the development of aggressive behavior problems in children. *Child Development, 74,* 374–393.

Fergusson, D., Horwood, L., & Nagin, D. (2000). Offending trajectories in a New Zealand birth cohort. *Criminology, 38,* 525–552.

Galen, B. R., & Underwood, M. K. (1997). A developmental investigation of social aggression among children. *Developmental Psychology, 33,* 589–600.

Greenberg, M. T., Kusche, C. A., Cook, E. T., & Quamma, J. P. (1995). Promoting emotional competence in school-aged children: The effects of the PATHS curriculum. *Development and Psychopathology, 7*, 117–136.

Heimer, K. (2000). Changes in the gender gap in crime and women's economic marginalization. *Criminal Justice 2000, 1*, 427–483.

Hipwell, A. E., & Loeber, R. (2006). Do we know which interventions are effective for disruptive and delinquent girls? *Clinical Child and Family Psychology Review, 9*, 221–225.

Huesmann, L. R., Eron, L. D., Lefkowitz, M. M., & Walder, L. O. (1984). Stability of aggression over time and generations. *Developmental Psychology, 20*, 1120–1134.

Kamper, K. E., & Ostrov, J. M. (2013). Relational aggression in middle childhood predicting adolescent adjustment outcomes: The role of friendship quality. *Journal of Clinical Child and Adolescent Psychology, 42*, 855–862.

Kibler, J. L., Prosser, V. L., & Ma, M. (2004). Cardiovascular correlates of misconduct in children and adolescents. *Journal of Psychophysiology, 18*, 184–189.

Kokko, K., Simonton, S., Dubow, E., Lansford, J. E., Olson, S. L., Huesmann, L. R., Boxer, P., Pulkkinen, L., Bates, J. E., Dodge, K. A., & Pettit, G. S. (2014). Country, sex, and parent occupational status: Moderators of the continuity of aggression from childhood to adulthood. *Aggressive Behavior, 40*, 552–567.

Leff, S. S., Waasdorp, T. E., Paskewich, B., Gullan, R. L., Jawad, A., MacEvoy, J. P., Feinberg, B. E., & Power, T. J. (2010). The Preventing Relational Aggression in Schools Everyday (PRAISE) program: A preliminary evaluation of acceptability and impact. *School Psychology Review, 39*, 569–587.

Little, T. D., Henrich, C. C., Jones, S. M., & Hawley, P. H. (2003). Disentangling the 'whys' from the 'whats' of aggressive behavior. *International Journal of Behavioral Development, 27*, 122–133.

Loeber, R., & Stouthamer-Loeber, M. (1998). Development of juvenile aggression and violence: Some common misconceptions and controversies. *American Psychologist, 53*, 242–259.

McBurnett, K., Lahey, B. B., Rathouz, P. J., & Loeber, R. (2000). Low salivary cortisol and persistent aggression in boys referred for disruptive behavior. *Archives of General Psychiatry, 57*, 38–43.

Mazerolle, P., Brame, R., Paternoster, R., Piquero, A., & Dean, C. (2000). Onset, age, persistence, and offending versatility: Comparisons across gender. *Criminology, 38*, 1143–1172.

Moffitt, T. E. (1993). Adolescence-limited and life-course-persistent antisocial behavior: A developmental taxonomy. *Psychological Review, 100*, 674–701.

Moffitt, T. E., & Caspi, A. (2001). Childhood predictors differentiate life-course persistent and adolescence-limited antisocial pathways among males and females. *Development and Psychopathology, 13*, 355–375.

Moffitt, T. E., Caspi, A., Rutter, M., & Silva, P. A. (2001). *Sex differences in antisocial behavior.* Cambridge, MA: Cambridge University Press.

Murray-Close, D., & Crick, N. R. (2007). Gender differences in the association between cardiovascular reactivity and aggressive conduct. *International Journal of Psychophysiology, 65*, 103–113.

Nisbett, R. E., & Cohen, D. (1996). *Culture of honor: The psychology of violence in the South.* Boulder, CO: Westview Press.

O'Donnell, P., Richards, M., Pearce, S., & Romero, E. (2012). Deviant peers as predictors of delinquent behavior among low-income urban African American youth. *Journal of Early Adolescence, 32*, 431–459.

Patterson, G. R., Capaldi, D., & Bank, L. (1991). An early starter model for predicting delinquency. In D. J. Pepler & K. H. Rubin (Eds.), *The development and treatment of childhood aggression* (pp. 139–168). Hillsdale, NJ: Erlbaum.

Pepler, D., Walsh, M., Yuile, A., Levene, K., Jiang, D., Vaughan, A., & Webber, J. (2010). Bridging the gap: Interventions with aggressive girls and their parents. *Prevention Science, 11,* 229–238.

Ribeaud, D., & Eisner, M. (2010). Risk factors for aggression in pre-adolescence: Risk domains, cumulative risk and gender differences—Results from a prospective longitudinal study in a multi-ethnic urban sample. *European Journal of Criminology, 7,* 460–498.

Rodkin, P. C., Farmer, T. W., Pearl, R., & Van Acker, R. (2000). Heterogeneity of popular boys: Antisocial and prosocial configurations. *Developmental Psychology, 36,* 14–24.

Rodkin, P. C., Farmer, T. W., Pearl, R., & Van Acker, R. (2006). They're cool: Social status and peer group supports for aggressive boys and girls. *Social Development, 15,* 175–204.

Rose, A. J., Swenson, L. P., & Waller, E. M. (2004). Overt and relational aggression and perceived popularity: Developmental differences in concurrent and prospective relations. *Developmental Psychology, 40,* 378–387.

Serbin, L. A., Stack, D. M., De Genna, N., Grunzeweig, N., Temcheff, C. E., Schwartzman, A. E., & Ledingham, J. (2004). When aggressive girls become mothers. In M. Putallaz & K. L. Bierman (Eds.), *Aggression, antisocial behavior and violence among girls* (pp. 262–285). New York: Guilford Press.

Silverthorn, P., & Frick, P. J. (1999). Developmental pathways to antisocial behavior: The delayed-onset pathway. *Development and Psychopathology, 11,* 101–126.

Silverthorn, P., Frick, P. J., & Reynolds, R. (2001). Timing of onset and correlates of severe conduct problems in adjudicated girls and boys. *Journal of Psychopathology and Behavioral Assessment, 23,* 171–181.

Solantaus, T., Leinonen, J., & Punamäki, R.-L. (2004). Children's mental health in times of economic recession: Replication and extension of the family economic stress model in Finland. *Developmental Psychology, 40,* 412–429.

Susman, E. J. (2006). Psychobiology of persistent antisocial behavior: Stress, early vulnerabilities and the attenuation hypothesis. *Neuroscience and Biobehavioral Reviews, 30,* 376–389.

U.S. Department of Justice. (2014). *Crime in the United States, 2013.* Washington, DC: U.S. Department of Justice.

Vitaro, F., Brendgen, M., & Barker, E. D. (2006). Subtypes of aggressive behaviors: A developmental perspective. *International Journal of Behavioral Development, 30,* 12–19.

White, N. A., & Piquero, A. R. (2004). A preliminary empirical test of Silverthorn and Frick's delayed-onset pathway in girls using an urban, African-American, US-based sample. *Criminal Behaviour and Mental Health, 14,* 291–309.

Wood, J. N., Medina, S. P., Feudtner, C., Luan, X., Localio, R., Fieldston, E. S., & Rubin, D. M. (2012). Local macroeconomic trends and hospital admissions for child abuse, 2000–2009. *Pediatrics, 130,* e358–e364.

Young, A. M., & d'Arcy, H. (2005). Older boyfriends of adolescent girls: The cause or a sign of the problem? *Journal of Adolescent Health, 36,* 410–419.

5

FAMILY INFLUENCES ON AGGRESSION AND VIOLENCE

Madelyn H. Labella and Ann S. Masten

A large body of research implicates families in the development and prevention of aggressive and violent behavior. This research is consistent with broader theoretical perspectives emphasizing family as a critical context of child development. Developmental systems theory sees individual development as the product of many interactions across system levels, including *inter*-personal as well as *intra*-personal (i.e., biological, cognitive, affective) processes. Developmental processes extend beyond the individual to include interactions with social systems, including the local community, peer group, and perhaps most proximally, the family (Gottlieb, 2007; Masten, 2014).

The bioecological model, a contemporary extension of ecological systems theory, situates the individual at the center of concentric circles of contextual influence (Bronfenbrenner & Morris, 2006). These circles of influence interact reciprocally with the individual's developmental history and the broader sociohistorical context to shape later functioning (Bronfenbrenner & Morris, 2006). The most proximate circle, called the microsystem, contains the contexts and people that interact directly with the target child, including neighbors, classmates, and the immediate family. Interactions between a child's microsystems, such as parent-teacher interactions, comprise the "mesosystem." Other, more distal and macro-level influences, including a parent's work situation, cultural values, community norms, or economic trends are theorized to influence individual development largely through their effects on more proximal interactions within the microsystem. For example, disrupted parenting has been widely implicated as a key mediator of the effects of socioeconomic status or economic downturns on child development (e.g., Conger & Donnellan, 2007).

Given the empirical and theoretical significance of family socialization for child development, it is not surprising that many of the best-established risk factors for the emergence of violent behavior reside in the family system. Family-based risks include sociodemographic and experiential factors, such as low social status, poverty, and exposure to chronic stress (Bradley & Corwyn, 2002; Farrington et al., 2012; Loeber & Farrington, 1998). Such contextual risks affect development beginning in utero, with both direct and indirect influences on child adjustment (Conger & Donnellan, 2007; Dodge & Pettit, 2003). Effects of poverty on behavioral development are mediated in part by their influence on family ecology (e.g., household chaos, interparental conflict, divorce), parental adjustment (e.g., mental illness, substance abuse, criminal behavior), and parenting quality (e.g., harshness, inconsistent discipline, low monitoring) (Dodge et al., 2006; Farrington et al., 2012). Aggression in children is predicted by direct exposure to family violence, including domestic violence and child maltreatment (Cicchetti & Toth, 2015; Van Horn & Lieberman, 2012). Furthermore, parents are responsible for facilitating interactions with extra-familial contexts of development, providing opportunities for peer socialization and selecting neighborhoods, school systems, and community groups. Parents thus have an indirect influence on antisocial development by shaping exposure to broader "aggressogenic" influences, including deviant peers, neighborhoods characterized by poverty and crime, and community violence (Dodge et al., 2006; Margolin & Gordis, 2000).

Parents serve as the agent and gatekeeper of multiple risks associated with violent behavior. However, families also play a key role in protecting their children from effects of risk on behavioral development. Broader research on risk and resilience has repeatedly identified aspects of parenting as protective in the context of a diverse range of risks, including those associated with violence (Masten, 2014; Masten & Labella, in press). Well-organized families with established routines, good supervision, and consistent discipline promote adaptive behavioral development (Loeber et al., 2009; Masten & Monn, 2015). Within the parent-child relationship, parental warmth and close attachment bonds predict lower levels of violent behavior in children (Dodge et al., 2006; Sroufe et al., 2005). Parental values, including disapproval of violence and value of education, also predict lower child aggression despite substantial adversity (Herrenkohl et al., 2005; Lösel & Farrington, 2012).

Overall, families can serve as both a source of risk and a powerful adaptive system, jeopardizing or optimizing children's behavioral development. This chapter examines specific risks and protective factors located in the family system, and then describes how these influences cascade outward from the family unit to affect children's functioning at school, with friends, and in the community. Interventions to prevent or eliminate violent behavior by targeting family processes are highlighted, and future directions for multilevel research and targeted interventions are discussed.

Risk Factors in the Family System

Prenatal Risks

Family-based risks for violence begin before a child is born. In addition to potentially sharing genetic risks, parents influence behavioral development prenatally through the uterine environment. Fetal exposure to environmental toxins (e.g., lead poisoning) has been linked to offspring aggressive and antisocial behavior, as has maternal use of alcohol, cocaine, opiates, marijuana, and nicotine during pregnancy (Dodge & Pettit, 2003). The family's psychosocial environment also has powerful effects on fetal development. The hypothalamic-pituitary axis produces the stress hormone cortisol in response to internal (e.g., sepsis) or external (e.g., public speaking) challenges. Maternal levels of cortisol rise during pregnancy, and 10% to 20% of this hormone passes through the placental barrier to affect the developing fetus (Reynolds, 2013). Although maternal cortisol is important for fetal development, extreme or chronic stress simultaneously increases stress hormones beyond normative levels and down-regulates barrier enzymes in the placenta, resulting in atypically high fetal exposure to cortisol (Sandman & Davis, 2012). In animals and humans, prenatal cortisol exposure is associated with higher cardiovascular reactivity and higher infant cortisol (at birth and during minor stressors, such as blood draws), as well as lower birth weight, reduced insulin sensitivity, and increased production of glucose and fat (Meaney et al., 2007; Sandman & Davis, 2012). In humans, alterations in stress reactivity are evident even in utero: high maternal stress, anxiety, and depression during pregnancy have been linked to higher fetal activity and reactivity to mild stressors (Monk et al., 2012). Accumulating evidence with animals and humans suggests that prenatal stress shapes development epigenetically—that is, by altering the way stress-relevant genes are expressed (Meaney et al., 2007; Monk et al., 2012). Through epigenetic modifications, environmental risk embeds itself in the biology of the developing fetus.

Taken together, these findings suggest that maternal stress exposure during pregnancy (including experiences of violence, mental illness, economic hardship, and natural disaster) helps program the developing stress response system, increasing its reactivity in preparation for a stressful postnatal environment (Meaney et al., 2007; Sandman & Davis, 2012). Resulting alterations in biology and behavior can be seen as adaptive trade-offs, increasing the likelihood of survival at the cost of long-term decrements in social, psychological, and physical health—including increased propensity to violence (Del Giudice et al., 2011; Margolin & Gordis, 2000; Repetti et al., 2011). Chronic activation of a hyper-responsive stress system can lead to an eventual down-regulation of hypothalamic-pituitary axis reactivity, resulting in later failure to mobilize an adaptive stress response. Both hyper- and hypo-activation of the stress response system have been linked to poorer developmental outcomes, including violent and antisocial behavior (van Goozen et al., 2007).

Behaviorally, prenatal exposure to cortisol has been linked to difficult temperament during infancy, as well as verbal deficits, poor problem solving, and behavior problems later in life (Monk et al., 2012; Reynolds, 2013; Sandman & Davis, 2012).

Early Postnatal Risks

The effects of prenatal stress are often compounded by ongoing adversity in the postnatal period. Prenatal stressors including maternal psychopathology often carry forward into the postnatal period, fine-tuning the reactivity of the developing stress response system (Monk et al., 2012). As with prenatal adversity, effects are mediated largely through caregivers. In both animals and humans, maternal separation, low nurturance, rejection, and abuse are linked to epigenetic changes in genes that regulate the hypothalamic-pituitary axis, often with the effect of increasing stress sensitivity (Gunnar & Quevedo, 2007).

The effects of prenatal and postnatal stress on neurobehavioral development have major implications for the role of individual differences in predicting violent behavior. Several models of antisocial development highlight individual differences in biology, temperament, and cognitive ability as risk factors for later aggression (Dodge & Pettit, 2003; Moffitt, 1993; van Goozen et al., 2007). One influential model differentiates childhood-onset antisocial behavior from adolescent-onset offending and identifies deficits in verbal intelligence and executive functions (including attention and impulse control) as prominent risks for a stable pattern of antisocial behavior beginning in early childhood (Moffitt, 1993). Similarly, difficult temperament has been theoretically and empirically linked to externalizing behavior in early and middle childhood (Dodge & Pettit, 2003). Though initially conceived as child-driven effects, these individual vulnerabilities are affected by stress in the family environment. They should not be interpreted as purely genetic risks, but instead as outcomes of genetic and environmental influences co-acting to shape development.

Early Childhood Risks

Whatever their origin, individual differences in stress biology, cognitive ability, and temperament serve as vulnerabilities for the development of violence. The expression of these vulnerabilities is strongly influenced by the family environment, but unfortunately, high-risk offspring tend to experience risky rearing environments. Families affected by shared genetic risk and/or ongoing contextual stress are more likely to provide pathogenic care (Repetti et al., 2002; van Goozen et al., 2007). Furthermore, irritable, impulsive, and dysregulated infants and toddlers are more likely to elicit parental frustration, low warmth, and harsh or inconsistent discipline (Dodge & Pettit, 2003; Moffitt, 1993). The resulting transactions between a difficult child and an unsupportive environment compound and escalate individual

risks: evidence suggests that child risk factors and family adversity act synergistically to increase the likelihood of antisocial behavior (Dodge et al., 2006).

Several features of the family environment have been identified as risk factors
for offspring aggression. The daily strains of economic hardship may have direct
and indirect effects on child outcomes, exerting effects through repeated activation of the child's stress response system and/or through effects on parents and
families. In terms of family ecology, household chaos (including disorganization,
excessive noise, and crowding) has been linked to physiological stress, low self-
regulation, and aggressive behavior in children (Evans & English, 2002). Similarly,
exposure to hostility, interparental conflict, and marital separation is associated
with children's antisocial behavior, perhaps mediated through alterations in stress
reactivity (Dodge et al., 2006; Repetti et al., 2002).

Parental adjustment variables, such as mental illness, substance abuse, and
criminality, are also associated offspring violent behavior. These likely serve as
markers of genetic risk, models of antisocial behavior, and predictors of disrupted
parenting (Dodge et al., 2006; Farrington et al., 2012). Several aspects of parenting, including high parental negativity and low warmth, have been implicated
in the development of child aggression (Dodge & Pettit, 2003; Repetti et al.,
2002). Emotionally unsupportive environments may heighten children's distress
without facilitating regulatory development, undermining children's attempts to
effectively express and recover from negative emotions. A lack of predictable caregiving relationships undermines the development of secure attachment bonds.
Without the co-regulatory functions of secure caregiving relationships, young
children—especially those at high sociodemographic or temperamental risk—
may struggle to develop self-regulatory skill (Sroufe et al., 2005).

Harsh and inconsistent discipline has also received substantial empirical support as a predictor of antisocial development (Dodge & Pettit, 2003). According
to the social interaction learning model, when parents do not consistently enforce
expectations, they inadvertently contribute to the consolidation of behavior
problems by rewarding aggression and noncompliance. Intermittent harshness in
response to misbehavior involves parents and children in a series of conflictual
exchanges, called "coercive cycles," that maintain and escalate child aggression
(Patterson et al., 1992). Harshness may take verbal or physical form: evidence suggests that non-abusive physical punishment predicts later externalizing behavior,
although this association may be attenuated in the context of cultural normativity
and/or parental warmth (Dodge et al., 2006).

When harsh punishment crosses the line into abuse, effects may be even more
devastating. Physical abuse has been consistently identified as a powerful predictor in the development of violence. Longitudinal and genetically informed
research demonstrates robust associations between physical abuse and antisocial
behavior, including child aggression (Cicchetti & Toth, 2015; Dodge et al., 2006).
Studies have identified genetic variations associated with greater vulnerability to
antisocial behavior following physical abuse, although importantly, maltreatment

operates as a risk factor regardless of genotype (Caspi et al., 2002; Cicchetti et al., 2012; Jaffee et al., 2005; Kim-Cohen et al., 2006). Other forms of maltreatment (e.g., neglect, sexual abuse) have also been linked to the development of violence, although effects are somewhat weaker (Cicchetti et al., 2012; Dodge et al., 2006; Margolin & Gordis, 2000).

Child maltreatment frequently co-occurs with exposure to interparental violence, which independently predicts aggressive and antisocial behavior (Margolin, 2005). From an organizational perspective, experiencing violence undermines children's basic sense of security and jeopardizes trust in the caregiving relationship, which may be seen as threatening, unpredictable, or inadequate in the face of danger (Margolin & Gordis, 2000). This would be expected to generate negative arousal and disrupt the normative achievements of early childhood, including trust, attachment, and positive expectations for social relationships (Sroufe et al., 2005). Furthermore, according to social learning theory, modeling violent behavior promotes imitation and internalization of aggression as acceptable in the context of close relationships. Indeed, acceptance of aggression may mediate the association between interparental violence exposure and later perpetration of intimate partner violence (Temple et al., 2013). In addition, accumulating evidence suggests that experiencing violence (as a recipient or witness) is associated with alterations in stress biology, with long-term consequences for physical and behavioral health (Moffitt & the Klaus-Grawe 2012 Think Tank, 2013).

Neighborhood factors, including concentrated poverty, disorganization, and community violence, also predict conduct problems (Dodge et al., 2006; Margolin & Gordis, 2000; Van Horn & Lieberman, 2012). Multiple longitudinal studies document prospective links between community violence exposure and increased aggressive behavior, similar to the effects of domestic violence (Margolin & Gordis, 2000). Because parents select young children's environments, exposure to violence in the broader community represents an indirect family influence on children's behavioral development, undermining self-regulation, shaping appraisals, and modeling aggressive behavior.

Risks in Middle Childhood and Adolescence

Family-based risk factors for aggression accumulate and interact over the course of early development. As children get older, dysfunctional behavior patterns acquired in the family can spread to other domains in a process called a "developmental cascade." The "dual failure" model proposes that incipient behavior problems at school entry contribute to academic failure and peer rejection, which in turn predict increased antisocial behavior and internalizing distress (Dodge & Pettit, 2003; Patterson et al., 1992). Children who have been rejected by mainstream peers are more likely to affiliate with deviant peers who engage in aggressive behavior. This occurs spontaneously as well as systematically: antisocial children are often diverted into low-achieving classrooms and the juvenile justice system, which may have the unintended effect of promoting deviant group norms. In response to peer modeling, children may internalize aggression as an acceptable strategy and engage in violence themselves (Dodge et al., 2006).

Parents play a critical role in structuring peer socialization, both by fostering prosocial interactions (e.g., through extracurricular activities) and by minimizing antisocial interactions. Parental knowledge of children's whereabouts, activities, and companions can limit involvement with deviant peers. Parental monitoring is also invaluable in promoting school engagement, ensuring firearm safety, and encouraging safe media use (Dodge et al., 2006; Bushman et al., 2016). Unfortunately, early behavioral problems predict lower levels of parental monitoring in adolescence, perhaps because parents respond to the stress of chronic conflict by disengaging. Low parental monitoring predicts even greater adolescent delinquency, with cascading effects on violent behavior (Dodge et al., 2006; Hoeve et al., 2009).

In addition to shaping peer interactions, families continue to influence behavioral development through the quality of parent-child interactions. Inconsistent discipline, unclear expectations, and uncontrolled anger continue to predict antisocial behavior in middle childhood and adolescence (Dodge et al., 2006). Similarly, psychological control strategies such as guilt and coercion have been found to accelerate behavior problems (Hoeve et al., 2009). Youth aggression can thus escalate through reciprocal interactions with peer and family environments.

Family-Based Risks throughout Childhood and Adolescence

Family-based risk factors begin in utero and continue through adolescence and beyond. Risks tend to cluster together and exacerbate each other: shared genes may underlie both harsh parenting and an infant's difficult temperament. Prenatal risks may contribute to a child's cognitive deficits, which may in turn elicit parenting stress and inconsistent discipline. Prenatal stress portends postnatal stress, and child vulnerability interacts with an unsupportive environment to predict the growth of behavior problems. Parents may respond to aggression by relaxing expectations, lashing out harshly, or withdrawing supervision, all of which confer further risk for youth violence. Risk factors interact reciprocally over time, amplifying initial differences in aggressive behavior in a developmental cascade toward youth violence (Dodge et al., 2008). Importantly, however, many children break this cycle, avoiding or desisting from violence. This resilience, defined as successful adaptation in the context of adversity, suggests that positive influences on behavioral development can compensate or mitigate the effects of risk (Masten, 2014).

Protective and Promotive Factors in the Family System

Decades of resilience research have converged on a common list of factors and processes associated with adaptive development (Masten, 2014). Factors that have generally positive effects (regardless of level of risk) are often referred to as promotive factors. With regard to the development of violence, promotive factors would be expected to reduce the likelihood of aggressive behavior across the entire community, offsetting risk factors where they exist. In contrast to this "main effects" model, protective factors interact with level of risk, predicting functioning most powerfully when adversity is high. For example, close attachment bonds are generally good for development but serve special functions in emergencies (Masten 2014; Masten & Labella, in press).

Research suggests that several powerful yet common adaptive systems promote and protect behavioral adjustment, accounting for much of children's resilience. Several of these factors are located within the family, including consistent structure, stable routines, and close attachment bonds between parents and children. Other promotive/protective factors involve child characteristics (e.g., self-regulation, intelligence, self-efficacy), and others are found in the broader community (e.g., effective school systems, cohesive neighborhoods). Several have been specifically implicated in preventing the development of aggression.

Many of the most powerful adaptive processes occur in a family context. For example, parental warmth and nurturance have been found to predict lower levels of aggression and antisocial behavior in children. Among an ethnically diverse, low-income sample, observed positive parenting at age two predicted lower levels of aggression at age five (Vanderbilt-Adriance et al., 2015). Similarly, maternal and partner warmth has been found to buffer effects of intimate partner violence on children's externalizing behavior problems, consistent with a protective effect (Skopp et al., 2007). Some research suggests that mothers may attempt to compensate for their children's exposure to domestic violence by becoming more effective and responsive parents; however, this is not successful for mothers suffering from mental illness, suggesting that parents' emotional health may be integral to supporting vulnerable children (Levendosky et al., 2003). By providing a model of constructive coping, parents may set the stage for positive behavioral development in the context of risk (Howell, 2011).

Warm and responsive caregiving is expected to promote secure parent-child attachment, which has in turn been linked to lower behavior problems (Fearon et al., 2010). Notably, secure attachment is more consistently predictive of child behavior in low-income versus middle-income samples, suggesting that attachment exercises particular influence in the context of adversity (Dodge et al., 2006). Positive parent-child attachment has also been found to buffer against negative outcomes among children exposed to violence (Howell, 2011). The attachment relationship theoretically serves as a "secure base," providing emotional security and supporting efforts to process distressing events (Sroufe et al., 2005).

Effective parents also provide structure, including routines, supervision, and consistent discipline (Masten & Monn, 2015). These organizational factors have a powerful influence on behavioral outcomes, particularly as children grow older. In the Pittsburgh Youth Study, intensive supervision, consistent discipline, and child involvement in family activities predicted lower levels of youth violence (Loeber et al., 2008).

High parental monitoring has been consistently linked to lower levels of antisocial behavior, especially for children at heightened risk of behavior problems due to behavioral history and/or dangerous environments (Dodge et al., 2006). A balance of structure and warmth may be the optimal parenting style for supporting prosocial development. According to the nurturance hypothesis, the combination of positive attention, emotional investment, and behavioral management promotes resilient behavior among children at risk for violence (Dishion & Bullock, 2002).

Parental values also predict lower engagement in violent behavior despite the presence of substantial adversity (Lösel & Farrington, 2012). Among participants of the Lehigh Longitudinal Study, parent and peer disapproval of violence predicted lower levels of self-reported violence and delinquency in adolescence, regardless of maltreatment history (Herrenkohl et al., 2005). Parental values regarding the child's education also protect against antisocial behavior, perhaps by supporting children's achievement, motivation, and engagement with school (Herrenkohl et al., 2005; Resnick et al., 2004).

Family influences operate both directly and indirectly, through child-level and community-level promotive/protective processes. Many individual predictors of resilient functioning, such as cognitive skills, self-regulation, hopeful attitude, and motivation, are shaped by family influences. Just as low-investment parenting tends to promote reactivity to stress, nurturing and responsive parenting may mitigate such reactivity, increasing the likelihood of adaptable temperamental styles or personality traits (Shiner et al., 2012). Personalities characterized by good emotion regulation (low neuroticism), agreeableness, and a drive for mastery or openness to experience are associated with competent functioning in a wide range of environments, including following exposure to violence (Howell, 2011; Shiner & Masten, 2012). Parents also have a strong influence on their children's emerging cognitive skills, in part by providing cognitively stimulating environments (Lösel & Farrington, 2012). Family organization, consistent routines, and responsive parenting are associated with the development of cognitive control skills, which in turn predict positive development (Blair & Raver, 2012; Vanderbilt-Adriance et al., 2015). Research with homeless families suggests that the effects of high-quality parenting on child adjustment are mediated through children's self-regulatory and attentional development (Herbers et al., 2011).

Families also shape community-level predictors of positive behavioral development. By selecting houses, neighborhoods, and school systems, parents indirectly influence their children's behavioral development. Just as low-organization, high-conflict neighborhoods increase risk for youth violence, high neighborhood quality (i.e., high cohesion and control, low crime and conflict) protects against the development of conduct problems in low-income children (Jaffee et al., 2007; Vanderbilt-Adriance et al., 2015). Living in a high-quality neighborhood may be particularly beneficial for children at behavioral risk due to high impulsivity (Dodge et al., 2006). Parents also influence behavioral development through high-quality housing and religious affiliation, both associated with lower youth violence (Herrenkohl et al., 2005; Resnick et al., 2004). Encouragingly, these family processes are malleable rather than fixed in the individual, making them plausible targets for intervention.

Family-Focused Intervention Programs

Interventions for youth violence and conduct problems often focus on family functioning, most notably parent behavior. A prime example is Parent Management Training: Oregon model, which emerges from a social interaction learning perspective. This model seeks to replace coercive cycles of parent-child interaction with positive involvement and consistent mild consequences for misbehavior. Parent Management Training: Oregon model has been used as both an intervention and a prevention program for families living in high-crime neighborhoods and/or coping with marital separation (Weisz & Kazdin, 2010). Evidence from randomized control trials suggests that the intervention generates a positive developmental cascade, with changes in one family member spreading to others. Specifically, Parent Management Training: Oregon model reduces coercive parenting practices and increases positive parenting, which in turn leads to lower child aggression and antisocial behavior (Patterson et al., 2010).

Other prevention programs begin even earlier, targeting families during critical prenatal and early childhood years. The Nurse-Family Partnership sends nurse practitioners to the homes of high-risk mothers beginning in pregnancy until the child is aged three (Olds, 2006). Visiting nurses provide psychoeducation and support regarding child development, parenting, and financial security. Although Nurse-Family Partnership was not found to reduce conduct problems in elementary school, it had beneficial effects on later antisocial and criminal behavior in adolescence and early adulthood (Olds, 2006). Other early childhood programs targeting parenting behavior and the parent-child relationship (e.g., Triple-P Parenting Program, Healthy Families America) have had positive effects on family processes and children's behaviors (Loeber & Farrington, 1998; Sanders, 2008).

Other prevention programs take a multidimensional approach, simultaneously targeting processes in the child, home, and/or community. The Perry Preschool Project and Child-Parent Center are rigorously tested prevention programs combining preschool curriculums with family support in the form of home visits and job assistance. A randomized control trial of the Perry Preschool Project linked the intervention to lower aggression in elementary school and fewer arrests in adolescence and adulthood (Schweinhart et al., 1993). Similarly, preschoolers who attend Child-Parent Centers have fewer arrests in adulthood (Reynolds et al., 2011). The Incredible Years program has shown similar benefits using a combination of child coaching, parenting training, and teacher skills training targeting classroom management and parent involvement (Weisz & Kazdin, 2010).

Similar results have been found in middle childhood and adolescent samples. Several multimodal prevention programs have demonstrated positive effects on aggression and antisocial behavior among high-risk youth using a combination of parent management training, teacher training, and direct coaching of children's social skills and self-regulation (Dodge et al., 2006; Loeber & Farrington, 1998). Interventions teaching skills in peer groups need to be aware of the potential for deviancy training: when youth with conduct problems are brought together in groups, social reinforcement for aggressive behavior may outweigh treatment benefits (Burke et al., 2002). With this caveat, multimodal prevention programs targeting child, family, and community-based processes are well situated to miti-gate aggressive behavior through comprehensive environmental support.

Multimodal interventions can also be used to treat behavior problems that have already arisen. Multidimensional treatment foster care has been shown to reduce antisocial and aggressive behavior among youth involved in the child welfare sys-tem (Weisz & Kazdin, 2010). Multidimensional treatment foster care components include behavioral parent training and support for foster parents (who are specially recruited for this treatment), family therapy for biological parents, skills training and supportive therapy for youth, and school-based behavioral and academic sup-port. Intervention benefits are mediated through consistent supervision, effec-tive discipline, adult mentoring, and separation from deviant peers. Outside of the foster care system, multisystemic therapy provides similarly intensive support to chronically violent adolescents at risk for out-of-home placement (Hengge-ler et al., 1998). Treatment is individualized to family needs and aims to help youth make good decisions about peer groups and support families in monitoring youth behavior. Multisystemic therapy has demonstrated short- and long-term effects on violent and nonviolent offending in youth and young adults (Loeber & Farrington, 1998). Given the intensive nature of these programs, it is noteworthy that the therapeutic benefits of both multisystemic therapy and multidimensional treatment foster care have been found to outweigh their costs (Burke et al., 2002).

A growing body of research suggests that some youth are more responsive to interventions than others. Some of the same genetic variants that confer risk in the context of adversity are associated with increased treatment response, sug-gesting that these youth are generally more sensitive to environmental influences, good *or* bad (Brody et al., 2013). This is consistent with the theory of differential susceptibility, which proposes genetically based variation in environmental sensi-tivity, and raises the possibility of genetically personalized interventions (Belsky & Pluess, 2009).

Conclusions and Future Research Directions

Although much progress has been made in understanding family-based influences on youth violence, a great deal is unknown. Further research is needed on the early experiences in shaping neurobehavioral development, including the effects of pre- and postnatal stress on the developing hypothalamic-pituitary axis and cognitive control skills. A better understanding of the biological embedding of early experience would clarify how aggressive behavior is transferred from one generation to the next and identify opportunities to intervene.

In terms of intervention, we need more information on the best strategies for reducing stress in pregnant mothers, helping families prepare their children for kindergarten, and educating parents about developmentally appropriate monitoring of their older children and adolescents. These efforts would be greatly aided by public policies designed to reduce family stress and support positive development (for example, by improving the quality of foster care, providing high-quality early childhood education, and increasing access to affordable housing). A multi-pronged approach may help to shift the balance of risk and promotive/protective processes, initiating positive cascades in the lives of vulnerable youth.

Information is also needed about who benefits from a given intervention. As noted previously, research on differential susceptibility suggests that some individuals may be more genetically sensitive to environmental influences (including behavioral interventions) than others. Individuals with less sensitive genetic variants may require more intensive services to produce behavioral change. Meanwhile, individuals who are highly sensitive may be particularly vulnerable to relapse if their pathogenic environment has not changed. Genetic, structural, and social factors may make one family an excellent candidate for the Parent Management Training: Oregon model, while another would benefit more from a youth-focused approach. Little is known about how to predict such variations in treatment response and personalize intervention accordingly.

Much is known about family influences on the development of aggression and violence, but much remains to be learned. The future of the field requires rigorous research incorporating biological and behavioral levels of analysis, as well as longitudinal designs tracking developmental trajectories through the life span and across generations. Intervention research is needed to refine strategies, clarify optimal developmental timing, and tailor interventions to families' specific needs. This translational work will combat child aggression and violence by harnessing one of the most powerful adaptive systems in a child's life: the family.

References

Belsky, J., & Pluess, M. (2009). Beyond diathesis: Differential susceptibility to environmental influences. *Psychological Bulletin, 135*, 885–908.

Blair, C., & Raver, C. C. (2012). Child development in the context of adversity: Experiential canalization of brain and behavior. *American Psychologist, 67*(4), 309–18.

Bradley, R. H., & Corwyn, R. F. (2002). Socioeconomic status and child development. *Annual Review of Psychology, 53*, 371–399.

Brody, G. H., Chen, Y. F., & Beach, S. R. (2013). Differential susceptibility to prevention: GABAergic, dopaminergic, and multilocus effects. *Journal of Child Psychology and Psychiatry, 54*, 863–871.

Bronfenbrenner, U., & Morris, P. A. (2006). The bioecological model of human development. In W. Damon & R. M. Lerner (Eds.), *Handbook of child* psychology (6th ed., Vol. 1, pp. 793–828). New Jersey: Wiley.

Burke, J. D., Loeber, R., & Birmaher, B. (2002). Oppositional defiant disorder and conduct disorder: A review of the past 10 years. *Journal of the American Academy of Child and Adolescent Psychiatry, 41*, 1275–1293.

Bushman, B.J., Newman, K., Calvert, S.L., Downey, G., Dredze, M., Gottfredson, M., Jablonski, N.G., Masten, A., Morrill, C., Neill, D.B., Romer, D., & Webster, D. (2016). Youth violence: What we know and what we need to know. *American Psychologist, 71*(1), 17–39. doi: 10.1037/a0039687.

Caspi, A., McClay, J., Moffitt, T. E., Mill, J., Martin, J., Craig, I. W., Taylor, A., & Poulton, R. (2002). Role of genotype in the cycle of violence in maltreated children. *Science, 297*, 851–853.

Cicchetti, D., Rogosch, F. A., & Thibodeau, E. L. (2012). The effects of child maltreatment on early signs of antisocial behavior: Genetic moderation by tryptophan hydroxylase, serotonin transporter, and monoamine oxidase A genes. *Development and Psychopathology, 24*, 907–928.

Cicchetti, D., & Toth, S. L. (2015). Child maltreatment. In R. M. Lerner (Ed.), *Handbook of child psychology and developmental science* (7th ed., Vol. 4, pp. 1–51.) New Jersey: Wiley.

Conger, R. D., & Donnellan, M. B. (2007). An interactionist perspective on the socioeconomic context of human development. *Annual Review of Psychology, 58*, 175–199.

Del Giudice, M., Ellis, B. J., & Shirtcliff (2011). The adaptive calibration model of stress responsivity. *Neuroscience and Biobehavioral Reviews, 35*, 1562–1592.

Dishion, T. J., & Bullock, B. M. (2002). Parenting and adolescent problem behavior: An ecological analysis of the nurturance hypothesis. In J. G. Borkowski, S. L. Ramey, & M. Bristol-Power (Eds.), *Parenting and the child's world: Influences on academic, intellectual, and social emotional development* (pp. 231–249). New Jersey: Lawrence Erlbaum Associates.

Dodge, K. A., Coie, J. D., & Lynam, D. (2006). Aggression and antisocial behavior in youth. In W. Damon & R. M. Lerner (Eds.), *Handbook of child psychology* (6th ed., Vol. 3, pp. 719–788). New Jersey: Wiley.

Dodge, K. A., Greenberg, M. T., Malone, P. S., and the Conduct Problems Prevention Research Group. (2008). An idealized dynamic cascade model of the development of serious violence in adolescence. *Child Development, 79*, 1907–1927.

Dodge, K.A. & Pettit, G. S. (2003). A biopsychosocial model of the development of chronic conduct problems in adolescence. *Developmental Psychology, 39*, 349–371.

Evans, G. W., & English, K. (2002). The environment of poverty: Multiple stressor exposure, psychophysiological stress, and socioemotional adjustment. *Child Development, 73*, 1238–1248.

Farrington, D. P., Loeber, R., & Ttofi, M. M. (2012). Risk and protective factors for offending. In B.C. Welsh & D. P. Farrington (Eds.), *The Oxford handbook of crime prevention* (pp. 46–69). New York: Oxford University Press.

Fearon, R. P., Bakermans-Kranenburg, M. J., van IJzendoorn, M. H., Lapsley, A. M., & Roisman, G. I. (2010). The significance of insecure attachment and disorganization in the development of children's externalizing behavior. *Child Development, 81*, 435–456.

Gottlieb, G. (2007). Probabilistic epigenesis. *Developmental Science, 10*, 1–11.

Gunnar, M. R., & Quevedo, K. (2007). The neurobiology of stress and development. *Annual Review of Psychology, 58*, 145–173.

Henggeler, S.W., Schoenwald, S. K., Borduin, C. M., Rowland, M. D., & Cunningham, P. B. (1998). *Multisystemic treatment of antisocial behavior in children and adolescents.* New York: Guilford Press.

Herbers, J. E., Cutuli, J. J., Lafavor, T. L., Vrieze, D., Leibel, C., Obradović, J., & Masten, A. S. (2011). Direct and indirect effects of parenting on academic functioning of young homeless children. *Early Education and Development, 22*, 77–104.

Herrenkohl, T. I., Tajima, E. A., Whitney, S. D., & Huang, B. (2005). Protection against antisocial behavior in children exposed to physically abusive discipline. *Journal of Adolescent Health, 36*, 457–465.

Hoeve, M., Dubas, J. S., Eichelsheim, V. I., van der Laan, P. H., Smeenk, W., & Gerris, J. R. M. (2009). The relationship between parenting and delinquency: A meta-analysis. *Journal of Abnormal Child Psychology, 37*, 749–775.

Howell, K. H. (2011). Resilience and psychopathology in children exposed to family violence. *Aggression and Violent Behavior, 16*, 562–569.

Jaffee, S. R., Caspi, A., Moffitt, T. E., Dodge, K. A., Rutter, M., Taylor, A., & Tully, L. A. (2005). Nature x nurture: Genetic vulnerabilities interact with physical maltreatment to promote conduct problems. *Development and Psychopathology, 17*, 67–84.

Jaffee, S. R., Caspi, A., Moffitt, T. E., Polo-Tomas, M., & Taylor, A. (2007). Individual, family, and neighborhood factors distinguish resilient from non-resilient maltreated children. Child *Abuse and Neglect, 31*, 231–253.

Kim-Cohen, J., Caspi, A., Taylor, A., Williams, A., Newcombe, R., Craig, I. W., & Moffitt, T. E. (2006). MAOA, maltreatment, and gene-environment interaction predicting children's mental health: New evidence and a meta-analysis. *Molecular Psychiatry, 11*, 903–913.

Levendosky, A. A., Huth-Bocks, A. C., Shapiro, D. L., & Semel, M. A. (2003). The impact of domestic violence on the maternal-child relationship and preschool-age children's functioning. *Journal of Family Psychology, 17*, 275–287.

Loeber, R., Burke, J. D., & Pardini, D. A. (2009). Development and etiology of disruptive and delinquent behavior. *Annual Review of Clinical Psychology, 5*, 291–310.

Loeber, R., & Farrington, D. P. (Eds.). (1998). *Serious and violent Juvenile offenders: Risk factors and successful interventions.* Thousand Oaks, CA: Sage.

Loeber, R., Farrington, D. P., Stouthamer-Loeber, M., & White, H. R. (Eds.). (2008). *Violence and serious theft: Development and prediction from childhood to adulthood.* New York: Taylor & Francis Group.

Lösel, F., & Farrington, D. P. (2012). Direct protective and buffering protective factors and in the development of youth violence. *American Journal of Preventive Medicine, 43*, S8–S23.

Margolin, G. (2005). Children's exposure to violence: Exploring developmental pathways to diverse outcomes. *Journal of Interpersonal Violence, 20*, 72–81.

Margolin, G., and Gordis, E. B. (2000). The effects of family and community violence on children. *Annual Review of Psychology, 51*, 445–479.

Masten, A. S. (2014). *Ordinary magic: Resilience in development.* New York: Guilford.

Masten, A. S., & Labella, M. H. (in press). Risk and resilience in child development. In L. Balter & C. S. Tamis-LeMonda (Eds.), *Child psychology: A handbook of contemporary issues.*

Masten, A. S., & Monn, A. R. (2015). Child and family resilience: A call for integrated science, practice, and professional training. *Family Relations, 64*, 5–21.

Meaney, M. J., Szyf, M., & Seckl, J. R. (2007). Epigenetic mechanisms of perinatal programming of hypothalamic-pituitary-adrenal function and health. *Trends in Molecular Medicine, 13*, 269–277.

Moffitt, T. E. (1993). Adolescence-limited and life-course-persistent antisocial behavior: A developmental taxonomy. *Psychological Review, 100*, 674–701.

Moffitt, T. E., & the Klaus-Grawe 2012 Think Tank. (2013). Childhood exposure to violence and lifelong health: Clinical intervention science and stress-biology research join forces. *Development and Psychopathology, 25*, 1619–1634.

Monk, C. Spicer, J., & Champagne, F. A. (2012). Linking prenatal maternal adversity to developmental outcomes in infants: The role of epigenetic pathways. *Development and Psychopathology, 24*, 13–61–1376.

Olds, D. L. (2006). The nurse-family partnership: An evidence-based preventive intervention. *Infant Mental Health Journal, 27*, 5–25.

Patterson, G. R., Forgatch, M. S., & DeGarmo, D. S. (2010). Cascading effects following intervention. *Developmental Psychopathology, 22*, 941–970.

Patterson, G. R., Reid, J. B., & Dishion, T. J. (1992). *Antisocial boys*. Eugene, OR: Castalia.

Repetti, R. L., Robles, T. F., & Reynolds, B. (2011). Allostatic processes in the family. *Development and Psychopathology, 23*, 921–938.

Repetti, R. L., Taylor, S. E., & Seeman, T. E. (2002). Risky families: Family social environments and the mental and physical health of offspring. *Psychological Bulletin, 128*, 330–366.

Resnick, M. D., Ireland, M., & Borowsky, I. (2004). Youth violence perpetration: What protects? What predicts? *Journal of Adolescent Health, 35*(424), e1–424.e10.

Reynolds, A. J., Temple, J. A., White, B. A., Ou, S-R., & Roberston, D. L. (2011). Age-26 cost-benefit analysis of the Child-Parent Center early education program. *Child Development, 82*, 379–404.

Reynolds, R. M. (2013). Glucocorticoid excess and the developmental origins of disease: Two decades of testing the hypothesis. *Psychoneuroendocrinology, 38*, 1–11.

Sanders, M. R. (2008). Triple P-Positive parenting program as a public health approach to strengthening parenting. *Journal of Family Psychology, 22*, 506–517.

Sandman, C. A., & Davis, E. P. (2012). Neurobehavioral risk is associated with gestational exposure to stress hormones. *Expert Reviews of Endocrinology and Metabolism, 7*, 445–459.

Schweinhart, L. J., Barnes, H. V., & Weikart, D. P. (1993). *Significant benefits: The High Scope Perry preschool study through age 27*. Ypsilanti: HighScope Press.

Shiner, R. L., Buss, K. A., McClowry, S. G., Putnam, S. P., Saudino, K. J., & Zentner, M. (2012). What is temperament now? *Child Development Perspectives, 6*, 436–444.

Shiner, R., & Masten, A. S. (2012). Childhood personality traits as a harbinger of competence and resilience in adulthood. *Development and Psychopathology, 24*, 507–528.

Skopp, N. A., McDonald, R., Jouriles, E. N., & Rosenfield, D. (2007). Partner aggression and children's externalizing problems: Maternal and partner warmth as protective factors. *Journal of Family Psychology, 21*, 459–467.

Sroufe, L. A., Egeland, B., Carlson, E. A., & Collins, W. A. (2005). *The development of the person: The Minnesota study of risk and adaptation from birth to adulthood*. New York: Guildford Press.

Temple, J. R., Shorey, R. C., & Tortolero, S. R., Wolfe, D. A., & Stuart, G. L. (2013). Importance of gender and attitudes about violence in the relationship between exposure to interparental violence and the perpetration of teen dating violence. *Child Abuse & Neglect, 37*, 343–352.

Vanderbilt-Adriance, E., Shaw, D. S., Brennan, L. M., Dishion, T. J., Gardner, F., & Wilson, M. N. (2015). Child, family, and community protective factors in the development of children's early conduct problems. *Family Relations, 64*, 64–79.

Van Goozen, S. H. M., Fairchild, G., Snoek, H., & Harold, G. T. (2007). The evidence for a neurobiological model of childhood antisocial behavior. *Psychological Bulletin, 133,* 149–182.

Van Horn, P., & Lieberman, A. F. (2012). Early exposure to trauma: Domestic and community violence. In L. C. Mayes, & M. Lewis (Eds.), *The Cambridge handbook of environment in human development* (pp. 466–479). New York: Cambridge University Press.

Weisz, J. R. & Kazdin, A. E. (Eds.) (2010). *Evidence-based psychotherapies for children and adolescents.* New York: Guilford Press.

6

TESTOSTERONE AND AGGRESSION

John Archer and Justin M. Carré

Introduction: The Mouse Model

It is well known that testosterone facilitates aggressive behavior in a wide range of birds and mammals. Bulls are viewed as dangerous, whereas their castrated counterparts are not. Experimental studies have demonstrated, using the ablation-replacement method, that testosterone is responsible for territorial aggression in house mice (Beeman, 1947). Such laboratory studies were often used as "models" for human behavior, that is, the controlled procedure provides a simplified version of the more complex human case.

It was with this "mouse model" in mind that studies began on the association between testosterone and aggression in humans—not, of course, involving castration and replacement, as with the experimental animals. Instead, correlational studies were undertaken to establish whether there was any association between blood plasma (and later salivary) levels of testosterone and aggressive behavior, typically measured by self-report questionnaires. The first of these found an association between testosterone production rate and measures of hostility in a small sample of young men (Persky et al., 1971). Since then, a range of other correlational studies have been reported, leading to the overall conclusion that there is a small association ($r = .08$ over 42 studies) between testosterone levels and measures of aggression (Archer et al., 2005). The associations were strongest for young men and for offenders. Although there are fewer studies, there are also associations for women and for pre-pubertal boys (Archer, 2006).

In all of these studies, the evidence is for a link between testosterone and aggression: we cannot infer that there is, as in the case of other animals, a causal connection. There are three problems with using the data in this way. First, there is some evidence that being successful in aggressive competition can lead to an increase in testosterone levels, which could accumulate over time to produce higher levels in aggressive individuals. Second, the evidence from the few studies involving controlled trials of testosterone on measures of mood and aggression produced only a few isolated positive findings (Archer, 2006, Table 2). Third, a large-sample study of testosterone and aggression in boys going through puberty found no association between testosterone levels and aggression (Halpern et al., 1994).

These reservations about a causal link have not stopped both psychologists and journalists believing that there is one. For example, one research group concluded: "The above information suggests that the rise in testosterone and thus aggressive behavior at puberty coincides with a time of intense competition for mates and/or status" (Book et al., 2001). Another research group concluded: "The male sex hormone testosterone contributes to high levels of violence in both sexes" (Stillman et al., 2010). In this chapter, we argue that these statements are not wholly incorrect, but they do oversimplify a complex situation, which is better appreciated if we consider testosterone-aggression associations from an evolutionary perspective.

An Evolutionary Framework for Testosterone and Aggression

The evolutionary basis of the mouse model is usually implicit. Steroid hormones, including testosterone, are found throughout vertebrates, and are therefore likely to be of ancient origin (Baker, 1997). This ancient origin has led to a degree of consistency in the hormone-behavior relations throughout the vertebrates; in particular, testosterone and related hormones (androgens) control the reproductive physiology and behavior of males in most vertebrate species. Since competition between males is necessary for successful breeding, the control of territorial and dominance-related aggression between males by testosterone provides a contextual link between success in aggressive encounters and in reproduction. Thus in a wide range of species, from all vertebrate groups (fish, amphibians, reptiles, birds, and mammals), testosterone facilitates male aggression (Archer, 1988).

There are, however, many cases where this statement does not apply, and the neuroendocrine control of aggression is different in a number of the species that have been studied. It was against this background that the "Challenge Hypothesis" was first proposed to explain interspecific variations in the hormonal regulation of behavior in birds (Wingfield, 1984; Wingfield et al., 1990). It is based on the following evolutionary rationale: Continued high levels of testosterone are maladaptive, because they are associated with suppression of immune function and risky behavior. This hypothesis leads to two alternative adaptive solutions. The first is to incur these costs, which will be adaptive where the potential benefits of high testosterone are also great (i.e., when inter-male competition is high and success is necessary for mating opportunities). The second alternative is to maintain a lower level of testosterone that is sufficient for reproductive physiology and behavior, and to respond to challenges in reproductive contexts with a temporary increase in testosterone, which in turn supports inter-male competitive aggression in the short term. This second alternative is typically, but not exclusively, found in species (such as most birds) where a considerable degree of paternal care is necessary for offspring survival.

The Challenge Hypothesis provides a more subtle and complex description of the association between testosterone and aggression than a model that assumes a straightforward causal relationship between testosterone and aggression. The Challenge Hypothesis does not rule out a causal link, but holds that it occurs in two circumstances: (1) in highly competitive, polygynous species; and (2) in species with paternal care, during those phases of the life history when males are competing for females or for status and/or resources necessary for reproduction.

Thus the restrictions of the original Challenge Hypothesis are that it applies primarily to monogamous and biparental species, and not to polygynous and non-parental species. In polygynous and non-parental species, levels of adult male testosterone are maintained at a high level, as inter-male competition is high. Generally, there is support for the Challenge Hypothesis throughout the vertebrates, but not necessarily for the specific predictions that link it to biparental and monogamous species only (Hirschenhauser & Oliveira, 2006). Humans have been characterized as mildly polygynous or as monogamous. Studies of the relative variance in reproductive success of the two sexes, and the presence of sexually selected attributes in humans (Archer, 2009), provide evidence for mild polygyny. Yet humans also have a considerable, but variable, degree of paternal care (Geary, 2000). This background, together with evidence supporting aspects of the Challenge Hypothesis in chimpanzees (Muller & Wrangham, 2004), which are neither biparental nor monogamous, make it worthwhile examining whether the Challenge Hypothesis applies to humans.

Assessing the Challenge Hypothesis in Humans

The Challenge Hypothesis involves five predictions: (1) high testosterone levels will be associated with maladaptive attributes, both physical and behavioral; (2) there will be no increase in aggression as a function of the increased testosterone in males at puberty; (3) adult males will respond to sexual and competitive situations with a transient increase in testosterone; (4) this testosterone surge will increase competitive aggression; and (5) pair-bonding and paternal care will lead to a decrease in testosterone levels. Two additional predictions can be derived from the Challenge Hypothesis, although they are not part of the original hypothesis: (1) individual differences in testosterone levels will be associated with differences in the relative emphasis the person places on mating versus parental effort; and (2) many of the associations predicted for men will also be found in women.

In a review of studies involving testosterone and human behavior, evidence for most if not all of these predictions was found (Archer, 2006). Since then, a large number of additional relevant studies have been published. Here we concentrate on those that are concerned with testosterone and aggression, first that competitive situations will lead to increased testosterone, especially in the winners, and second that these relatively transient increases in testosterone will produce an increase in competitive and aggressive behavior.

Does Competitive Behavior Increase Testosterone Levels?

A central aspect of the Challenge Hypothesis is that there will be a testosterone increase as a consequence of competition in young men for women or for status. Although they were not aimed at testing this prediction, a number of previous studies have measured testosterone levels following inter-male competition in the form of sports activities, since these are likely to be equivalent to a challenge situation, particularly when they involve bodily contact (Archer 2006, p. 325). The findings were actually rather similar for physical and non-physical sports, and somewhat different to those for lab-based competitive situations (Archer, 2006).

A small increase in testosterone was found in anticipation of a sports competition ($d = 0.30$; six studies), although there was no appreciable increase in three other studies involving lab-based tasks with arbitrary winners and losers.[1] During the competition itself, testosterone levels increased in the studies involving sports, to a moderate extent ($d = 0.37$; 12 studies), but there was little or no increase for the lab-based tasks. In apparent contrast to these findings, there was little or no difference between winners and losers in sports competitions (there were substantial increases during the competition), whereas there were larger increases in winners than losers in the other tasks, which generally involved contrived winners and losers ($d = 0.38$; seven studies). One caution about these conclusions is that the studies typically involved small samples, and there was variability between studies. To seek to explain such variability, a number of studies have investigated possible mediators or moderators of the effects of winning on testosterone levels, in the form of personality variables. We consider the role of personality on the link between testosterone and aggression in a later section.

Do Increased Testosterone Levels Increase Aggression?

A crucial part of the original Challenge Hypothesis is that an increase in testosterone following competition will produce a transient increase in the willingness to respond to a challenge with aggression. In practice it is difficult to separate increased aggressiveness due to testosterone and that due to another cause and also occurring following a competitive encounter.

Studies of judo competitors found that increases in testosterone from before to after the bout were greater in competitors who looked angry and were more violent in their bouts, as judged by coaches (Suay et al., 1996). A follow-up study involving observations of participants' behavior found that initial testosterone levels were correlated with more attack, fighting, and threat, as coded by two judo specialists (Salvador et al., 1999). If the initial testosterone levels represent an anticipatory rise in testosterone, as in other studies (Archer, 2006), this finding would fit the expectations of the Challenge Hypothesis. Alternatively, the pre-contest levels may reflect long-term circulating levels, and represent a stable individual difference in aggression that is associated with these circulating levels.

More recent laboratory-based studies have examined the extent to which competition-induced fluctuations in testosterone modulate subsequent competitive and aggressive behavior. In the first study (Mehta & Josephs, 2006), men competed in dyads on a number-tracing task in which the outcome of the competition was rigged so that one person was assigned to experience a series of victories, whereas the other was assigned to experience a series of defeats. Saliva samples were collected before and after the competition. After the competition, participants were given the opportunity to pick the next task to be performed from two alternatives: either to compete against the same person on the same task; or to complete a questionnaire on entertainment preferences. A rise in testosterone predicted greater willingness to choose the competitive option, whereas a decrease in testosterone predicted a greater willingness to choose the noncompetitive option. Notably, this effect was most robust among losers of a competitive interaction. Thus, losers whose testosterone increased during the competition were more likely than those whose testosterone decreased to choose the competitive option.

In another experiment, male participants performed the Point Subtraction Aggression Paradigm (PSAP) and provided saliva samples before and after the competition (Carré & McCormick, 2008). The PSAP is a well-validated behavioral measure that assesses reactive aggression in a controlled laboratory setting (Cherek et al., 2006). After performing the PSAP, participants were given the opportunity to compete on a puzzle-solving task with the same person with whom they were paired on the PSAP (which was actually a computer program) or complete a questionnaire on music and food preferences. There was a positive correlation between aggressive behavior and changes in testosterone during the PSAP. Moreover, men showing a rise in testosterone during the PSAP were more likely to choose a subsequent competitive task than were men who showed a decrease in testosterone (Carré & McCormick, 2008).

Although these findings indicate a positive correlation between competition-induced testosterone reactivity and aggressive behavior on the PSAP, the design of the study makes it difficult to draw strong conclusions regarding the direction of the effect. Although it is possible that a rise in testosterone during the PSAP promoted heightened aggressive behavior, it is equally possible that increased aggressive behavior on the PSAP promoted a robust increase in testosterone.

To address this limitation, subsequent studies were designed to carefully assess aggressive behavior *after* a change in testosterone is detected.

In the first of these experiments, 99 participants each competed with a same-sex opponent on a number-tracing task. Saliva samples were collected before and after the competition. Next, participants performed the PSAP with the same opponent. Changes in testosterone in response to the number-tracing task were positively correlated with subsequent aggressive behavior for men, but not women (Carré et al., 2009). In a subsequent study, with a larger sample ($n = 237$), participants played a video game competition (volleyball or boxing) in which they were randomly assigned to experience a string of victories or defeats (Carré et al., 2013). Again, saliva samples were collected before and after the competition. Next, participants performed the PSAP against a same-sex opponent again (a computer program). Male (but not female) winners showed a larger increase in testosterone and were more aggressive than were losers. Notably, the association between winning and subsequent aggressive behavior was statistically mediated by changes in testosterone for men, but not for women.

A third study investigated whether an intensive intervention program designed to curtail antisocial behavior reduced aggression through its modulation of neuroendocrine function (Carré et al., 2014). At six years of age, at-risk children were randomly assigned to either a control group that received no specific program, or to an intervention group that received a comprehensive training program designed to increase their social competencies, including peer mentoring, cognitive-behavioral training, and study skills. Participants from the intervention group showed a range of benefits compared to the control group (e.g., higher academic achievement, higher social competence, and lower antisocial behavior, such as crime and drug-taking). However, the mechanisms through which the intervention reduced antisocial behavior were not clear. To investigate this, a subsample of men from the larger study were investigated at 26 years of age, to assess the extent to which the early intervention affected later aggressive behavior through different testosterone responses to social provocation (Carré et al., 2014). Participants provided saliva samples before, during, and after performing three 10-minute blocks of the PSAP. The control and intervention groups did not differ in baseline testosterone concentrations or in aggressive behavior during the first block of the PSAP. However, the intervention group showed a decrease in testosterone after the first block of the PSAP and also a decrease in aggressive behavior in blocks 2 and 3 of the PSAP. In contrast, the control group showed an *increase* in testosterone after the first block of the PSAP and also an *increase* in aggressive behavior in blocks 2 and 3 of the PSAP. The decreased aggressive behavior in the intervention group was statistically mediated by dampened testosterone reactivity to the PSAP. This suggests that one (or more) components of the intervention program modulated the way the hypothalamic-pituitary-gonadal axis responded to social provocation.

The findings reported in this section provide some support for the view that acute fluctuations in testosterone during competitive interactions may serve to fine-tune ongoing and/or future competitive and aggressive behavior. However, a major limitation of the evidence is that it is correlational. Thus, it is not possible to make strong causal claims concerning the role of testosterone in the modulation of human aggression. Research in animal models and recent pharmacological challenge probes designed for use in humans enable us to get one step closer toward understanding the neuroendocrine mechanisms underlying variability in aggression.

Acute Testosterone Dynamics and Aggression in Animal Models

A number of animal studies have investigated the extent to which competition-induced changes in testosterone play a causal role in the modulation of future aggressive and competitive behavior. In one study, a group of castrated male mice were randomly assigned to receive a single injection of testosterone or placebo after winning a competitive interaction (Trainor et al., 2004). The testosterone injection produced a very acute response, with testosterone concentrations rising rapidly, and then returning to baseline 45 minutes later. The next day, the mice engaged in another competitive interaction with a novel male. Those mice that received testosterone after winning a fight were more aggressive on the second (and third) day of testing. In a second study, the role of testosterone in mediating the "winner" and "loser" effects in male tilapia was examined (Oliveira et al., 2009). Winners of a first aggressive interaction were more likely to win a subsequent aggressive interaction (88% won a second fight), whereas losers were more likely to lose subsequent interactions (87% lost a second fight). However, winners treated with an anti-androgen drug, which prevented the normal increase in testosterone that occurs after winning a competition, were much less likely to win a subsequent aggressive interaction (44% won a second fight). In contrast, losers treated with an androgen (11-ketotestosterone, the primary metabolite of T in fish) were not more likely to win a subsequent aggressive interaction (71% lost a second fight). These findings indicate that the "winner effect" (but not the "loser effect") depends critically on acute fluctuations in testosterone concentrations. Collectively, these results provide compelling support for the idea that competition-induced fluctuations in testosterone may enable organisms to adaptively fine-tune their social behavior according to their social context.

Studies of Exogenously Administered Testosterone

Based on the Challenge Hypothesis, we would not necessarily expect long-term administration of testosterone to increase aggressiveness in men, and the null results in a number of studies is consistent with this expectation, as is the lack of evidence for a testosterone-induced increase in aggression at puberty (Archer, 2006). However, we might expect that testosterone administration would affect responses connected with aggressive responding in the short term.

In a series of studies, an oral preparation of testosterone was administered to young female volunteers and their responses on a number of laboratory tasks were measured while their levels of testosterone were transiently increased to those typical of young men. Testosterone was found to alter a range of responses, some of which were directly related to aggression, and others to attributes associated with aggression. The first study found increases in the cardiac defense reflex to subliminally presented angry faces (van Honk et al., 2001), the second study found increased eye gaze to angry faces (Terburg et al., 2012), and the third study found decreased avoidance of angry faces when these were presented in a series of reaction-time tests involving approach or avoidance to happy, angry, or neutral faces (Enter et al., 2014). The findings from all three studies seem to indicate greater reactivity to briefly presented angry faces and that the effects are specific to anger rather than to other emotional expressions.

Other studies have found that testosterone administration induces a decrease in cognitive empathy (Hermans et al., 2006) and in the unconscious vigilant response to fearful faces (van Honk et al., 2005). Both empathy and fear are attributes that are inversely related to aggression. Testosterone also produced lesser sensitivity to punishment (van Honk et al., 2004), which is associated with greater impulsiveness. Testosterone was also found to affect activity in brain regions associated with aggression: it led to increased amygdala and hypothalamic reactivity to angry faces (Hermans et al., 2008; van Wingen et al., 2008), and decreased amygdala-orbitofrontal cortex connectivity (van Wingen et al., 2011).

These studies demonstrate that a wide range of measures that are directly or indirectly associated with aggression can be altered by short-term administration of testosterone. Nevertheless, there are two aspects of the methods used that may limit their applicability to situations where there is a transient rise in endogenous testosterone in men. First, the doses involved are clearly higher than those that young women would experience from endogenous testosterone. Second, women rather than men were involved in the studies (for the good reason that the physiological protocol for the hormone administration was only available for women).

To overcome these possible limitations, there are now novel pharmacological challenge paradigms that investigate the extent to which a single administration of testosterone modulates neural and behavioral processes in healthy young men (e.g., Eisenegger et al., 2013; Goetz et al., 2014; Zak et al., 2009). One study examined the role of testosterone in modulating threat-related neural function (Goetz et al., 2014). Male participants were first given a gonadotropin-releasing hormone-antagonist (GnRH-ant), which temporarily suppressed testosterone concentrations and reduced variability in basal testosterone levels. After achieving testosterone suppression, participants were given a single dose of testosterone (100 mg AndroGel) to acutely elevate testosterone concentrations. Next, participants performed an emotion face-matching task during functional magnetic resonance imaging (fMRI). Within 90 minutes, testosterone rapidly increased amygdala, hypothalamic, and periaqueductal gray reactivity to angry, but not fearful or surprised, faces. Notably, these same regions of the brain are rich in androgen receptors (Newman, 1999; Wood & Newman, 1999) and also play a key role in modulating reactive aggression in animals (Blair, 2010). It should be noted that individuals at risk for engaging in reactive aggression also show heightened amygdala reactivity to angry facial expressions (Carré et al., 2012; Coccaro et al., 2007).

The evidence presented in this section complements the studies of the link between competition-induced testosterone surges and aggression and competitive behavior, by indicating that exogenously administered testosterone produces both behavioral and neurological changes that may predispose individuals toward aggressive behavior in the context of competitive and/or threat-related situations. Together, these two lines of research seem to have produced the evidence needed to fill the gap in the Challenge Hypothesis (Archer, 2006). This does not mean that there is nothing left to investigate, since novel techniques provide the start of a series of further studies to cover other possible measures that might be influenced by testosterone (Goetz et al., 2014). In addition, there are a number of individual differences that are likely to complicate the existing findings. Some of these are discussed in the next two sections.

The Influence of Personality

A number of studies indicate that individual differences moderate the relationship between testosterone reactivity and aggressive behavior. An earlier study found that having a high level of a form of power motivation that involved using direct domination of others in face-to-face interactions was associated with larger post-competition increases in testosterone for both winners and losers of a contrived laboratory task, but especially for the winners (Schultheiss et al., 1999). The attribute identified in this study, seeking to dominate others in a direct and forceful way, is consistent with the Challenge Hypothesis, as it would have been adaptive in direct competitive encounters between young men.

More recently, researchers have shown that a rise in testosterone among winners positively predicted subsequent aggression, but only among men scoring relatively high on trait dominance (Carré et al., 2009). Similarly, exogenous testosterone administration increases competitive motivation, but only among winners scoring relatively high in trait dominance (Mehta et al., in press). In two other studies (Norman et al., 2015), a rise in testosterone during competition was associated with heightened aggressive behavior, but only among men (not women) scoring relatively low in trait anxiety (see Figure 6.1). These findings are notable in the light of animal research showing that trait anxiety modulates

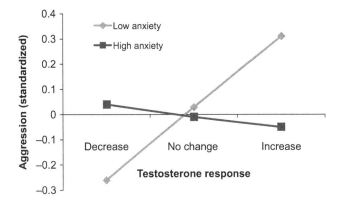

FIGURE 6.1 Trait anxiety moderates the relationship between competition-induced testosterone reactivity and aggressive behavior in men.

Note: This figure is redrawn based on the findings of Norman et al. (2015). Simple slopes are depicting response at low versus high anxiety scores (i.e., anxiety scores at −1/+1 SD from the mean). Results indicate a strong positive correlation between testosterone reactivity during competition and subsequent aggression among men scoring low in trait anxiety ($B = .29, SE = .12, p = .01$), but not high in trait anxiety ($B = −.06, SE = .12, p = .62$).

neuroendocrine function and aggression. Specifically, male rats selectively bred for low anxiety showed a heightened testosterone response to social threat and aggressive behavior relative to male rats bred for high anxiety (Veenema et al., 2007).

Dual Hormone Effects on Aggressive Behavior

The research reviewed in this chapter suggests that competition-induced *changes* in testosterone may in part modulate ongoing and/or subsequent competitive and aggressive behavior. As indicated earlier, there is evidence for a weak association between trait-like testosterone (i.e., baseline levels) and aggressive behavior. A growing body of evidence suggests that this association may be more robust when one considers variability in cortisol concentrations. Cortisol is a steroid hormone secreted by the adrenal glands during periods of physical and psychological stress (Dickerson & Kemeny, 2004). Research in adolescent males found that testosterone concentrations were positively correlated with physical aggression, but only among individuals with relatively low cortisol concentrations (Dabbs et al., 1991; Popma et al., 2007). More recent research has discovered this pattern of findings for various measures that share conceptual and empirical overlap with aggression (e.g., risk-taking, dominance; see Mehta & Prasad, 2015). However, other studies have not found this dual hormone effect (e.g., Mazur & Booth, 2014), and others have found that testosterone is positively correlated with reactive aggression and psychopathic traits, but only among individuals with *high* cortisol concentrations (Denson et al., 2013; Welker et al., 2014). Clearly, more research will be required to determine if (and under what circumstances) testosterone and cortisol interact to predict variability in aggression and related constructs, and how this might be related to testosterone reactivity to competition.

Conclusions

In this chapter we have shown that the role of testosterone in modulation of aggression and related behavior is more complex than the simple cause-and-effect model originally derived from selective animal studies. A broader evolutionarily based theory (the "Challenge Hypothesis") provided the basis for considering research that now dates back over 40 years, ranging from the initial correlational studies to recent studies that involve sophisticated manipulation of testosterone levels, laboratory procedures rooted in experimental social psychology, and brain imaging. Taken together, the emerging evidence shows that competitive behavior influences testosterone levels, which in turn influence aggressive behavior, in a complex way that is moderated by individual differences in personality.

Note

1 These *d* values refer to standardized differences between two groups or the same group at different times. In general terms, $d = 0$ to 0.10 is a negligible difference, $d = 0.11$ to 0.35 is a small difference, $d = 0.36$ to 0.65 is a moderate, and $d = 0.66$ to 1.00 is large. Thus the differences discussed here are in the small to moderate range. This classification is taken from Hyde (2005), and is based on the earlier values offered by Cohen (1988): "small" $d = 0.20$, "medium" $d = 0.50$, and "large" $d = 0.80$.

References

Archer, J. (1988). *The behavioural biology of aggression*. Cambridge, UK: Cambridge University Press.

Archer, J. (2006). Testosterone and human aggression: An evaluation of the challenge hypothesis. *Neuroscience and Biobehavioral Reviews, 30*, 319–335. http://dx.doi.org/10.1016/j.neubiorev.2004.12.007

Archer, J. (2009). Does sexual selection explain human sex differences in aggression? *Behavioral and Brain Sciences, 32*, 249–311. http://dx.doi.org/10.1017/S0140525X09990951

Archer, J., Graham-Kevan, N., & Davies, M. (2005). Testosterone and aggression: A reanalysis of Book, Starzyk, and Quinsey's (2001) study. *Aggression and Violent Behavior, 10*, 241–261. http://dx.doi.org/10.1016/j.avb.2004.01.001

Baker, M. E. (1997). Steroid receptor phylogyny and vertebrate origins. *Molecular and Cellular Endocrinology, 135*, 101–107. http://dx.doi.org/10.1016/S0303-7207(97)00207-4

Beeman, A. E. (1947). The effect of male hormone on aggressive behavior in male mice. *Physiological Zoology, 20*, 373–405.

Blair, R. J. R. (2010). Neuroimaging of psychopathy and antisocial behavior: A targeted review. *Current Psychiatry Reports, 12*, 76–82. http://dx.doi:10.1007/s11920–009–0086-x

Book, A. S., Starzyk, K. B., & Quinsey, V. L. (2001). The relationship between testosterone and aggression: A meta-analysis. *Aggression and Violent Behavior: A Review Journal, 6*, 579–599. http://dx.doi.org/10.1016/S1359–1789(00)00032-X

Carré, J. M., Campbell, J. A., Lozoya, E., Goetz, S. M. M., & Welker, K. M. (2013). Changes in testosterone mediate the effect of winning on subsequent aggressive behaviour. *Psychoneuroendocrinology, 38*, 2034–2041. http://dx.doi.org/10.1016/j.psyneuen.2013.03.008

Carré, J. M., Fisher, P. M., Manuck, S. B., & Hariri, A. R. (2012). Interaction between trait anxiety and trait anger predict amygdale reactivity to angry facial expressions in men but not women. *Social Cognitive and Affective Neuroscience, 7*, 213–221. http://dx.doi.org:10.1093/scan/nsq101

Carré, J. M., Iselin, A-M. R., Welker, K. M., Hariri, A. R., & Dodge, K. A. (2014). Testosterone reactivity to provocation mediates the effect of early intervention on aggressive behavior. *Psychological Science, 25*, 1140–1146. http://dx.doi.org/10.1177/0956797614525642

Carré, J. M., & McCormick, C. M. (2008). Aggressive behavior and change in salivary testosterone predict willingness to engage in a competitive task. *Hormones and Behavior, 54*, 403–409. http://dx.doi.org/10.1016/j.yhbeh.2008.04.008

Carré, J. M., Putman, S. K., & McCormick, C. M. (2009). Testosterone responses to competition predict future aggressive behaviour at a cost to reward in men. *Psychoneuroendocrinology, 34*, 561–570. http://dx.doi.org/10.1016/j.psyneuen.2008.10.018

Cherek, D. R., Tcheremissine, O. V., & Lane, S. D. (2006). Psychopharmacology of human aggression: Laboratory and clinical studies. In R. J. Nelson (Ed.), *Biology of aggression* (pp. 424–446). New York: Oxford University Press.

Coccaro, E. F., McCloskey, M. S., Fitzgerald, D. A., & Phan, K. L. (2007). Amygdala and orbitofrontal reactivity to social threat in individuals with impulsive aggression. *Biological Psychiatry, 62*, 168–178. http://dx.doi.org/10.1016/j.biopsych.2006.08.024

Cohen, J. (1988). *Statistical power analysis for the behavioral sciences* (2nd ed.). New York: Academic Press.

Dabbs, J. M. Jr., Jurkovic, G. J., & Frady, R. L. (1991). Salivary testosterone and cortisol among late adolescent male offenders. *Journal of Abnormal Clinical Psychology, 19*, 469–478. http://dx.doi.org/10.1007/BF00919089

Denson, T. F., Mehta, P. H., & Ho Tan, D. (2013). Endogenous testosterone and cortisol jointly influence reactive aggression in women. *Psychoneuroendocrinology, 38*, 416–424. http://dx.doi.org/10.1016/j.psyneuen.2012.07.003

Dickerson, S. S., & Kemeny, M. E. (2004). Acute stressors and cortisol responses: A theoretical integration and synthesis of laboratory research. *Psychological Bulletin, 130*, 355–391. http://dx.doi.org/10.1037/0033–2909.130.3.355

Eisenegger, C., von Eckardstein, A., Fehr, E., & von Eckardstein, S. (2013). Pharmokinetics of testosterone and estradiol gel preparations in healthy young men. *Psychoneuroendocrinology, 38*, 171–178. http://dx.doi.org/10.1016/j.psyneuen.2012.05.018

Enter, D., Spinhoven, P., & Roelofs, K. (2014). Alleviating social avoidance: Effects of single dose testosterone administration on approach-avoidance action. *Hormones and Behavior, 65*, 351–354. http://dx.doi.org/10.1016/j.ybeh.2014.02.001

Geary, D. C. (2000). Evolution and proximate expression of human paternal investment. *Psychological Bulletin, 126*, 55–77. http://dx.doi.org/10.1037/0033–2909.126.1.55

Goetz, S. M. M, Tang, L., Thomason, M. E., Diamond, M. P., Hariri, A. R., & Carré, J. M. (2014). Testosterone rapidly increases neural reactivity to threat in healthy men: A novel two-step pharmacological challenge paradigm. *Biological Psychiatry, 76*, 324–331. http://dx.doi.org/10.1016/j.biopsych.2014.01.016

Halpern, C. T., Udry, J. R., Campbell, B., & Suchindran, C. (1994). Relationships between aggression and pubertal increases in testosterone: A panel analysis of adolescent males. *Social Biology, 40*, 8–24.

Hermans, E. J., Putman, P., & van Honk, J. (2006). Testosterone administration reduces empathic behavior: A facial mimicry study. *Psychoneuroendocrinology, 31*, 859–866. http://dx.doi.org/10.1016/j.psyneuen.2006.04.002

Hermans, E. J., Ramsay, N. F., & van Honk, J. (2008). Exogenous testosterone enhances responsiveness to social threat in the neural circuitry of social aggression in humans. *Biological Psychiatry, 63*, 263–270. http://dx.doi.org/10.1016/j.biopsych.2007.05.013

Hirschenhauser, K., & Oliveira, R. F. (2006). Social modulation of androgens in male vertebrates: Meta-analysis of the challenge hypothesis. *Animal Behaviour, 71*, 265–277. http://dx.doi.org/10.1016/j.anbehav.2005.04.014

Hyde, J. S. (2005). The gender similarities hypothesis. *American Psychologist, 61*, 581–592. http://dx.doi.org/10.1037/0003–066X.60.6.581

Mazur, A., & Booth, A. (2014). Testosterone is related to deviance in male army veterans, but relationships are not moderated by cortisol. *Biological Psychology, 96*, 72–76. http://dx.doi.org/10.1016/j.biopsycho.2013.11.015

Mehta, P. H. & Josephs, R. A. (2006). Testosterone change after losing predicts the decision to compete again. *Hormones and Behavior, 50*, 684–692. http://dx.doi.org/10.1016/j.yhbeh.2006.07.001

Mehta, P. H., & Prasad, S. (2015). The dual-hormone hypothesis: A brief review and future research agenda. *Current Opinion in Behavioral Sciences, 3*, 163–168. http://dx.doi.org/10.1016/j.cobeha.2015.04.008

Mehta, P. H., van Son, V., Welker, K. M., Prasad, S., Sanfey, A. G., Smidts, A., & Roelofs, K. (in press). Exogenous testosterone in women enhances and inhibits competitive decision-making depending on victory-defeat experience and trait dominance. *Psychoneuroendocrinology*. http://dx.doi.org/10.1016/j.psyneuen.2015.07.004

Muller, M. N., & Wrangham, R. W. (2004). Dominance, aggression and testosterone in wild chimpanzees: A test of the 'challenge' hypothesis. *Animal Behaviour, 67*, 113–123. http://dx.doi.org/10.1016/j.anbehav.2003.03.013

Newman, S. (1999). The medial extended amygdala in male reproductive behavior. A node in the mammalian social behavior network. *Annals of the New York Academy of Sciences, 877*, 242–257. http://dx.doi.org/10.1111/j.1749–6632.1999.tb09271.x

Norman, R. E., Moreau, B. J. P, Welker, K. M., & Carré, J. M. (2015). Trait anxiety moderates the relationship between testosterone responses to competition and aggressive behavior. *Adaptive Human Behavior and Physiology, 1*, 312–324. http://dx.doi.org/10.1007/s40750–014–0016–y

Oliveira, R. F., Silva, A., & Canario, A. V. (2009). Why do winners keep winning? Androgen mediation of winner but not loser effects in cichlid fish. *Proceedings of the Royal Society of London: Biological Sciences, 276*, 2249–2256. http://dx.doi.org/10.1098/rspb.2009.0132.

Persky, H., Smith, K. D., & Basu, G. K. (1971). Relation of psychological measures of aggression and hostility to testosterone production in man. *Psychosomatic Medicine, 33*, 265–277. http://dx.doi.org/10.1097/00006842–197105000–00007

Popma, A., Vermeiren, R., Geluk, C. A., Rinne, T., van den Brink, W., Knol, D. L., . . . Doreleijers, T. A. H. (2007). Cortisol moderates the relationship between testosterone and aggression in delinquent male adolescents. *Biological Psychiatry, 61*, 405–411. http://dx.doi.org/10.1016/j.biopsych.2006.06.006

Salvador, A., Suay, F., Martinez-Sanchis, S., Simon, V. M., & Brain, P. F. (1999). Correlating testosterone and fighting in male participants in judo contests. *Physiology and Behavior, 68,* 205–209. http://dx.doi.org/10.1016/S0031–9384(99)00168–7

Schultheiss, O. C., Campbell, K. L., & McClelland, D. C. (1999). Implicit power motivation moderates men's testosterone response to imagined and real dominance success. *Hormones and Behavior, 36,* 234–241. http://dx.doi.org/10.1006/hbeh.1999.1542

Stillman, T. F., Maner, J. K., & Baumeister, R. F. (2010). A thin slice of violence: Distinguishing violent from nonviolent sex offenders at a glance. *Evolution and Human Behavior, 31,* 298–303. http://dx.doi.org/10.1016/j.evolhumbehav.2009.12.001

Stanton, S. J., Wirth, M. M., Waugh, C. E., & Schultheiss, O. C. (2009). Endogenous testosterone levels are associated with amygdale and ventromedial prefrontal cortex responses to anger faces in men but not women. *Biological Psychology, 81,* 118–122. http://dx.doi.org/10.1016/j.biopsycho.2009.03.004

Suay, F., Salvador, A., González-Bono, E., Sanchis, C., Simon, V. M., & Montoro, J. B. (1996). Testosterona y evaluacion de la conducta adresiva en jovenes judokas. *Revista de Psicologia del Deporte [Journal of Sport Psychology], 9/10,* 79–91.

Terburg, D., Aarts, H., & van Honk, J. (2012). Testosterone affects gaze aversion from angry faces outside of conscious awareness. *Psychological Science, 23,* 459–463. http://dx.doi.org/10.1177/0956797611433336

Trainor, B. C., Bird, I. M., & Marler, C. A. (2004). Opposing hormonal mechanisms of aggression revealed through short-lived testosterone manipulations and multiple winning experiences. *Hormones and Behavior, 45,* 115–121. http://dx.doi.org/10.1016/j.yhbeh.2003.09.006

van Honk, J., Peper, J. S., & Schutter, D. J. L. G. (2005). Testosterone reduces unconscious fear but not consciously experienced anxiety: Implications for the disorders of fear and anxiety. *Biological Psychiatry, 58,* 218–225. http://dx.doi.org/10.1016/j.biopsych.2005.04.003

van Honk, J., Schutter, D. J. L. G., Hermans, E. J., Putman, P., & Koppeschaar, H. (2004). Testosterone shifts the balance between sensitivity for punishment and reward in healthy young women. *Psychoneuroendocrinology, 29,* 937–943. http://dx.doi.org/10.1016/j.psyneuren.2003.08.007

van Honk, J., Tuiten, A., Hermans, E. J., Putman, P., Koppeschaar, H. Thijssen, J., . . . van Dooren, L. (2001). A single administration of testosterone induces cardiac acceleration response to angry faces in healthy young women. *Behavioral Neuroscience, 115,* 238–242. http://dx.doi.org/10.1037/0735–7044.115.1.238

van Wingen, G. A., Ossewaarde, L., Backstrom, T., Hermans, E. J., & Fernandez, G. (2011). Gonadal hormone regulation of the emotion circuitry in humans. *Neuroscience, 191,* 38–45. http://dx.doi.org/10.1016/j.neuroscience.2011.04.042

van Wingen, G. A., Zylicz, A., Pieters, S., Mattern, C., Verkes, R. J., & Buitelaar, J. K., (2008). Testosterone increases amygdala reactivity in middle-aged women to a young adulthood level. *Neuropsychopharmacology, 34,* 539–547. http://dx.doi.org/10.1038/sj.npp.2008.2

Veenema, A. H., Torner, L., Blume, A., Beiderbeck, D. L., & Neumann, I. D. (2007). Low inborn anxiety correlates with high intermale aggression: Link to ACTH response and neuronal activation of the hypothalamic paraventricular nucleus. *Hormones and Behavior, 51,* 11–19. http://dx.doi.org/10.1016/j.yhbeh.2006.07.004

Welker, K. M., Lozoya, E., Campbell, J. A., Neumann, C. S., & Carré, J. M. (2014). Testosterone cortisol, and psychopathic traits in men and women. *Hormones and Behavior, 129,* 230–236. http://dx.doi.org/0.1016/j.physbeh.2014.02.057

Wingfield, J. C. (1984). Androgens and mating systems: Testosterone-induced polygyny in a normally monogamous bird. *The Auk, 4*, 665–671. http://dx.doi.org/10.2307/4086893

Wingfield, J. C., Hegner, R. E., Dufty Jr., A. M., & Ball, G. F. (1990). The 'challenge hypothesis': Theoretical implications for patterns of testosterone secretion, mating systems, and breeding strategies. *American Naturalist, 136*, 829–846. http://dx.doi.org/10.1086/285134

Wood, R., & Newman, S. W. (1999). Androgen receptor immunoreactivity in the male and female Syrian hamster brain. *Journal of Neurobiology, 39*, 359–370. http://dx.doi.org/10.1002/(SICI)1097–4695(19990605)39:3<359::AID-NEU3>3.0.CO;2-W

Zak, P. J., Kurzban, R., Ahmadi, S., Swerdloff, R. S., Park, J., Efremidze, L., . . . Matzner, W. (2009). Testosterone administration decreases generosity in the ultimatum game. *PLoS ONE, 4*, e8330. http://dx.doi:10.1371/journal.pone.0008330

7

INDIVIDUAL DIFFERENCES IN AGGRESSION

The Role of Dark Personalities

Delroy L. Paulhus and Daniel N. Jones

Introduction

Is aggression a trait? Specifically, do individual differences in aggression form a coherent and stable continuum along which all of us can be arrayed? That is the assumption behind the development of the Buss-Perry Aggression Questionnaire (BPAQ) (1992), often considered the gold standard for dispositional aggression.[1] This notion is supported by a number of empirical findings. First, scores on the BPAQ show large variance and substantial temporal stability (Becker, 2007). BPAQ scores also map onto other personality variables in a consistent fashion (Egan, 2009; Miller et al., 2012).

Arguments against a trait perspective include the following. The BPAQ content is starkly heterogeneous: The current version and its predecessors have included such diverse elements as hostility, assault, suspicion, verbal aggression, irritability, resentment, and general negativity (Becker, 2007). Rather than aggression per se, most of these elements appear to capture a stage in several possible psychological sequences leading to aggression (e.g., hostility—> aggression and irritability—> aggression). With hostility as a central element, the measure is unlikely to tap any colder forms of aggression.

The assumed importance of aggression as a trait is also belied by the fact that it does not appear in major structural models of personality such as the Five Factor or HEXACO models. Because those models were derived from comprehensive personality item pools, it is surprising that an aggression factor never emerged.[2] The BPAQ does cut across the Big Five space, but the links are complex (Barlett & Anderson, 2012). Disagreeableness is the strongest correlate, but aggression also overlaps with two other traits orthogonal to agreeableness (Egan, 2009).

The trait notion of aggression is also inconsistent with another important structural model, the Interpersonal Circumplex. The latter is organized around the axes of Agency and Communion (Bakan, 1966). But low scores on Communion represent indifference (lack of communion) rather than aggression per se (Horowitz & Strack, 2009). Finally, all the BPAQ subscales are contaminated with socially desirable responding (Becker, 2007). As Becker points out, however, the uniformity of contamination leaves unchanged the correlations among the BPAQ subscales.

The complex placement of aggression in standard personality models likely ensues from its interaction with situational factors (Bettencourt et al., 2006; Bushman & Anderson, 1998). Indeed, aggression triggers tend to be idiosyncratic (Lawrence, 2006). Consider the unique form of aggression provoked by ostracism (Williams, 2007) or the culture of honor in southern U.S. states (Nisbett & Cohen, 1996). Another unique example is the aggression triggered in minority communities by the sense of being disrespected (Miller, 2001). The latter may also explain the violence triggered in those sensitive to rejection (Downey et al., 2001). In sum, a diversity of traits (including some that are orthogonal) may predispose individuals to aggression.

Consistent with the interaction perspective, we will argue that much aggressive behavior can be traced to a small set of already-established traits and a set of situational provocations (Bushman & Anderson, 1998; Lawrence, 2006). The trait set in focus here has been labeled the *Dark Triad* (Paulhus & Williams, 2002), recently updated to the *Dark Tetrad* (Buckels et al., 2013). The Dark Tetrad members each interact differently with situational provocations to generate aggressive responses. To set the stage, we begin this essay with a review of these dark personalities.

The Dark Triad: Background

In attempting to organize work on aversive (but subclinical) personalities, Paulhus and Williams (2002) concluded that narcissism, Machiavellianism, and psychopathy dominated the literature. Because they were found to overlap both theoretically and psychometrically, these three variables came to be known as a constellation called the "Dark Triad." The most thorough review was published by Furnham et al. (2013). A review including a fourth member, *everyday sadism*, appeared more recently (Paulhus, 2014). Because the Dark Triad framework has the most solid research base, we begin by updating those three literatures.

Machiavellianism

In introducing the construct into the personality literature, Christie and Geis (1970) drew largely from the writings of political strategist Niccolò Machiavelli. In a recent update, Jones and Paulhus (2011b) added elements drawn from a neglected predecessor, namely, the first century military strategist-philosopher

Sun Tzu (translated 1998). Along with themes similar to Machiavelli's, Sun Tzu added planning, coalition-formation, and reputation-building. The latter qualities turn out to be important in distinguishing among the Dark Triad constructs. Whereas psychopaths pay little attention to their reputations (Hare & Neumann, 2008), Machiavellians plan ahead, build alliances, and try to maintain a positive reputation. By integrating Machiavelli's precepts with those of Sun-Tzu, Jones and Paulhus concluded that three elements best define Machiavellianism as a trait: (a) manipulative tendencies, (b) callous affect, and (c) strategic inhibition. Ignoring this last element has led some writers to confuse Machiavellianism with psychopathy.

Christie and Geis (1970) also developed the first questionnaire measures of Machiavellianism. The most influential of these, the Mach IV, continues to be regarded as the gold standard. It includes subscales capturing themes such as cynical worldview, lack of morality, and a manipulative nature (for a full review, see Jones & Paulhus, 2009). Alternative measures were reviewed by Jones and Paulhus (2014).

Psychopathy

Modern conceptions of psychopathy originated in the work of Cleckley (1941). He postulated a self-control deficit that, along with callousness, has remained central to criminal conceptions (Hare & Neumann, 2008) as well as non-criminal conceptions of psychopathy (Hall & Benning, 2006; Lebreton et al., 2006). Though no more empathic than Machiavellians, psychopaths manifest their callousness in a reckless fashion (Jones & Paulhus, 2011b). When extreme, this combination of callous manipulation and other short-term tendencies (i.e., erratic lifestyle, thrill seeking) eventuates in relentless criminal behavior (Hare & Neumann, 2008).

Non-criminal research has been facilitated by the availability of self-report measures of psychopathy: These include the Levenson Self Report Psychopathy scale (Levenson et al., 1995), the Psychopathic Personality Inventory (Lilienfeld & Andrews, 2006), and the Self Report Psychopathy (SRP) scale (Paulhus et al., 2016). These measures have been compared and contrasted by Hicklin and Widiger (2005).

Narcissism

Theoretical conceptions of narcissism are anchored in the writings of Kohut and Kernberg (see review by Jones & Paulhus, 2011a). The characteristic grandiosity and attention seeking of narcissists was traditionally explained by a conflict between a superior self-presentation and underlying insecurity: in short, a compensatory self-promotion. This maladaptive version remains the concern for modern clinicians dealing with pathological cases of narcissism (see Cain et al., 2008).

The advent of the Narcissistic Personality Inventory (NPI) (Raskin & Hall, 1979) redirected much research energy toward subclinical narcissism (e.g., Emmons, 1987). The key element in the NPI operationalization is grandiosity, that is, an exaggerated sense of self-importance (Miller & Campbell, 2008). Note that the interpersonal difficulties created by grandiosity (Morf & Rhodewalt, 2001) do not necessarily translate into personal maladjustment (Campbell & Foster, 2007).

Subsequent research has confirmed that the subclinical conception tapped by the NPI shows remarkable parallels with clinical conceptions of narcissism (Miller & Campbell, 2008). In both cases, for example, grandiosity leads narcissistic individuals on a never-ending quest for ego-reinforcement (Morf & Rhodewalt, 2001), often resulting in self-destructive behaviors (Vazire & Funder, 2006).

It is this grandiose aspect of narcissism that is most relevant to the Dark Triad. Whereas psychopaths and Machiavellians are motivated by instrumental gain, ego-reinforcement is the all-consuming motive behind narcissistic behavior (Jones & Paulhus, 2011b).

Dark Triad as a Constellation

The original rationale for grouping the three Dark Triad members was the disturbing contrast between their theoretical distinctiveness and their empirical overlap (Paulhus & Williams, 2002). We have argued that the reason for their empirical overlap is a common element, namely, interpersonal callousness (Jones & Figueredo, 2013; Jones & Paulhus, 2011a). This callousness (i.e., lack of empathy) leads inevitably to the tendency to manipulate others (Jones & Paulhus, 2011a). Hence the three triad members often exhibit similar malevolent behavior.

In other cases, the Dark Triad members exhibit markedly different behavior: Ego-promoting outcomes (e.g., bragging) are best predicted by narcissism; those involving reckless antisocial behavior (e.g., criminality) are best predicted by psychopathy; and long-term schemes (e.g., elaborate frauds) are best predicted by Machiavellianism (Furnham et al., 2013). In sum, the literature suggests that (a) ego-identity goals drive narcissistic behavior, whereas instrumental goals drive Machiavellian and psychopathic behavior, (b) Machiavellianism differs from psychopathy with respect to impulsivity, and (c) all three have a callous core that engenders manipulation of others (Jones & Paulhus, 2011a).

The recent burst of research on the Dark Triad (Veselka & Vernon, 2014) can be attributed to the availability of two brief inventories designed to capture three or more of them. One is the "Dirty Dozen" published by Jonason and Webster (2010). The other is the Short Dark Triad (SD3) published by Jones and Paulhus (2014).

Sadistic Personality

Sadism is the enjoyment of hurting others. Historical examples suggest that sadistic behavior and the vicarious enjoyment of observing it has been prevalent throughout human history (Paulhus & Dutton, 2016; Pinker, 2011).[3] Although traditionally associated with serial killers or sado-masochistic sexuality, recent work has demonstrated that sadistic behavior is not uncommon among regular folks. In contemporary society, one only has to consider (a) the regular reports of sadistic behavior among terrorist groups, military, and so forth and (b) the widespread enjoyment of extreme violence in sports, films, and video games. Such examples implicate an appetite for cruelty that far exceeds instrumental benefits and illustrates what we have dubbed "everyday sadism" (Paulhus & Dutton, 2016).

Research on everyday sadism did not become viable until the recent development of questionnaire measures (Chabrol et al., 2009; O'Meara et al., 2011; Paulhus et al., 2011). These measures have now been used in large surveys as well as laboratory studies.

Our laboratory conducted extensive work on the questionnaire labeled the Varieties of Sadistic Tendencies (VAST; available in Paulhus & Jones, 2015). It includes separate subscales for direct and vicarious forms of sadism. Although structural analyses revealed separate factors for direct and vicarious sadism, they were highly correlated. Hence, the same people who claim enjoyment of hurting others also like to watch others being hurt. Men tend to score higher than women on both subscales (Paulhus & Jones, 2015).

An extended version of the questionnaire, entitled the Comprehensive Assessment of Sadistic Tendencies (CAST; Buckels & Paulhus, 2013), comprises three subscales tapping vicarious, physical, and verbal forms of sadism. Total scores for both the CAST and the VAST have shown moderate positive correlations with the members of the Dark Triad. Together, the four variables have been labeled the *Dark Tetrad* (Buckels et al., 2013; Chabrol et al., 2009; Paulhus, 2014).

Note that our conception of everyday sadism shares the same interpersonal callousness as members of the triad. In distinction from the other members, however, the everyday sadist has an appetite for hurting others (Paulhus, 2014).

Summary

Because of the overlap in their standard measures, it is difficult to be sure which one is responsible for any given empirical finding. Therefore, we have strongly recommended that the Dark Triad not be used alone as predictors, but concurrently in a constellation of predictors. Depending on which one of the triad is responsible, the interpretation of any external link will differ dramatically. Lumping them together in a single measure simply hides this differentiation.

Empirical Links with Aggression

Despite the recent appearance of the Dark Tetrad publications, research on aggression has already received attention. These studies include large surveys mostly using the Buss-Perry measure as well as behavioral measures collected in laboratory studies.

Correlations with Buss-Perry Aggression Questionnaire

At the self-report level, a small number of studies have addressed the links between the Dark Triad and dispositional aggression as operationalized with the Buss-Perry scale (BPAQ). Jonason and Webster (2010), for example, argued that the Dark Triad members are equally predictive of aggression. However, these conclusions were based on their use of the Dirty Dozen, a measure of the Dark Triad that has been called into question (Maples et al., 2014; Miller et al., 2012).

A recent comparison using more established measures of the Dark Triad was provided by Jones and Neria (2015). They extracted the common core as well as the unique contributions of the triad members. Hence, their results were able to reveal a more complex pattern. The common core showed a strong overall association with the Buss-Perry total score ($r = +.62$). That link is not surprising given that most specialists argue that the common core includes callousness (Jakobwitz & Egan, 2006; Jones & Figueredo, 2013; Jones & Paulhus, 2011a). However, the results showed additional links that could not be explained by the common core. These additional associations suggested that each Dark Triad trait is uniquely related to different aspects of aggression. For example, psychopathy was positively associated with physical aggression, Machiavellianism was positively associated with hostility, and narcissism was negatively associated with hostility.

Because they used multifaceted assessments of the Dark Triad, Jones and Neria (2015) were able to show further the specific links with the facet scores of each Dark Triad scale. For example, the interpersonal manipulation facet of psychopathy was not associated with aggression, whereas the other three facets of psychopathy were. This finding supports a recent article by Mokros et al. (2015) arguing that psychopaths tend to show one of three distinct latent profiles: manipulative, aggressive, and sociopathic. Those in the aggressive group are moderate in manipulation but high on the other three factors, a profile that maximizes aggressive behavior. In contrast, the manipulative psychopath is noticeably low on antisocial behavior but appreciably high in interpersonal manipulation.

Similar patterns have been found in other studies. For example, Hamel et al. (2015) examined the inter-correlations among the Short Dark Triad, Buss-Perry aggression, and domestic conflict in a large sample of adults. The overall findings were similar to that of Jones and Neria (2015), whether aggression was measured with the BPAQ or domestic violence reports. In particular, psychopathy was a strong and consistent predictor of all measures and facet scores related to direct aggression. This consistency did not hold for Machiavellianism or narcissism: Among men, Machiavellianism had little association with domestic aggression or any of its sub-factors; among women, however, Machiavellianism was associated with all BPAQ facets and most facets of domestic violence.

Narcissism, however, showed the reverse pattern with respect to gender and aggression (Hamel et al., 2015). Whereas most correlations between narcissism and aggression were significant in men, those same correlations were near zero among women. These findings suggest that gender may have an important role to play in how the Dark Triad traits are expressed with respect to aggression. Machiavellian men may better anticipate the long-term outcomes that would result from domestic aggression. Similarly, the behavioral tactics associated with female narcissism do not seem to include direct physical aggression. According to Hamel and colleagues, these findings may be explained by gender-based roles (narcissism) and gender-based strategies for long-term success (Machiavellianism).

In short, at the questionnaire level, the pattern of associations of the Dark Triad with aggressive dispositions exemplifies their complexity. In fact, each of the Dark Triad members manifests aggression in a qualitatively different fashion.

Behavioral Studies

Narcissistic Aggression

The aggressive behavior of those with positive self-evaluations was documented in a series of studies by Bushman and Baumeister (Baumeister et al., 2000; Bushman & Baumeister, 1998). Follow-up research showed that when two forms of self-evaluation, self-esteem and narcissism, were pitted against each other, the latter appeared most responsible for antisocial outcomes (Paulhus et al., 2004). Among such personalities, the situational trigger for aggression appeared to be ego-threat (Bushman & Baumeister, 1998).

However, no allowance was made for the overlap of narcissism with other dark personalities. A follow-up study, which did include measures of the Dark Triad, confirmed the Bushman-Baumeister findings. Jones and Paulhus (2010) included all three triad measures and compared participants' reactions to ego-threat versus physical provocation. Using the white noise paradigm developed by Taylor (1967), the researchers gave participants the opportunity to aggress with a white noise blast against an ostensible partner who had provoked them. Results replicated the Bushman-Baumeister finding that narcissists aggress in response to ego-threat provocation (a personal insult), even when overlap with psychopathy is controlled.

Psychopathic Aggression

The association of psychopathy with aggression is well established at the criminal level (Hare & Neumann, 2008; Porter & Woodworth, 2006). At the non-criminal subclinical level, such associations have also been well confirmed (Patrick, 2006; Westhead & Egan, 2015).

In our own laboratory research, psychopathy emerged as the unique predictor of aggression (Jones & Paulhus, 2010). As opposed to ego-threat, it was physical provocation that triggered aggression (a gratuitous blast of loud white noise). The results point to qualitatively different aggression mechanisms underlying narcissistic and psychopathic aggression.

Machiavellian Aggression

Based on their sketchy morality, Machiavellians should not object to aggression as a means to reaching their goals (Christie & Geis, 1970). But their cautious and strategic nature places limits on overt antisocial behavior (at least, compared to psychopaths). Therefore, research on Machiavellian aggression is more challenging: It is likely to be characterized by inconsistency and complexity (Jones & Paulhus, 2009). In particular, direct aggression is inconsistent with their strategic nature. It is rarely in their long-term self-interest. Instead, Machiavellians should be more likely to entertain the idea of instrumental rather than reactive aggression.[4]

Nonetheless, violence such as bullying can sometimes represent the most efficient path for achieving long-term goals (Jones & Paulhus, 2009). Indeed, some data have emerged to support this assertion. For example, in research on children, those highest in Machiavellianism were most likely to engage in aggression designed to establish dominance over other children (Hawley, 2003; Kerig & Stellwagen, 2010). In contrast, other traits predicted hostile or direct aggression. With respect to sexually aggressive behavior, Jones and Olderbak (2014) found that Machiavellianism, unlike psychopathy and narcissism, had no fixed association with sexual coaxing or coercion across a variety of circumstances.

Overall, the cases where aggression would profit Machiavellians should be limited to: (a) consequence-free situations where their reputation may not be damaged, or (b) situations where short-term profit significantly outweighs potential long-term costs. Using this logic, it stands to reason that Machiavellian individuals should avoid harming loved ones or those perceived as useful in the future. Indeed, some research has suggested that Machiavellian individuals are reluctant to harm family members (Barber, 1994).

Note that a more recent paper by Krupp and colleagues (2013) made a similar argument about psychopathic individuals. A closer inspection of the paper reveals that they drew this conclusion based on only Factor 1 (callous manipulation) of the Psychopathy Checklist-Revised (PCL-R; Hare, 2003). Research has found that psychopathy Factor 1 is represented in all three Dark Triad traits (Jones & Figueredo, 2013). Thus, the findings of Barber (1994) and Krupp and colleagues (2012) may be significant for research on Machiavellianism, psychopathy, or both.

If one cardinal tenet can capture the Machiavellian mentality, it is that "the end justifies the means" (Christie & Geis, 1970). This policy of aggression for a "good" cause seems reasonable to most human beings and self-evident to some. A return to this original tenet opens up new directions for understanding Machiavellian aggression research. One is the notion of "moral Machiavellianism": Not all Machiavellian goals need be selfish ones. Many folks believe strongly enough in pro-social goals that cutting corners on more trivial issues (lying, cheating, and even aggression) seems more than reasonable, indeed necessary. An example of one such goal is the protection of so-called sacred values (Atran, et al., 2007). Machiavellians should be willing to harm others to gain what they see as overriding moral benefits (e.g., religion, national identity). By this token, violent terrorists may be moral Machiavellians.

Not unrelated is the notion of value manipulation. The notion follows from a potent advantage of the Machiavellian personality noted by Christie and Geis (1970): They stay cool and use other people's emotions to their advantage. In a paper with contemporary implications, Jones detailed how Machiavellians exploit other people's sacred values to instigate intergroup conflicts (see Jones, 2016).

Sadistic Aggression

Given its definition as the enjoyment of hurting others, sadism would appear to be inherently aggressive. However, the repercussions of overtly sadistic behavior can be severe—unless one is in a position of power. Hence, empirical research on the topic is severely constrained (Buckels et al., 2013). Criminal forms are rare (Mokros et al., 2012) and sado-masochism is difficult to research for ethical and privacy reasons (Sagarin et al., 2009). It is only in the last five years that researchers have found ways of verifying the construct of sadistic behavior as a personality variable.

A key development was the appearance of several new questionnaires developed for use in empirical research. These include the Short Sadistic Impulse Scale (SSIS) (O'Meara et al., 2011), the Varieties of Sadistic Tendencies (VAST) (Paulhus & Jones, 2015), and the Comprehensive Assessment of Sadistic Tendencies (CAST) (Buckels & Paulhus, 2014). The latter subdivides sadistic personality into three facets: physical sadism, verbal sadism, and vicarious sadism. The astonishing frankness and variance in responses to these questionnaires motivated us to confirm behaviorally what respondents are willing to admit on these self-report measures.

Laboratory Research

The nature of so-called everyday sadism has been demonstrated empirically in several recent papers (Buckels et al., 2013; Buckels et al., 2014; Chabrol et al., 2009). In all these studies, the Dark Triad were controlled: Hence, sadism made an incremental contribution to aggressive outcomes.

As noted earlier, the verification of sadism in the modern (ethically sensitive) laboratory setting is clearly a challenge. Two unique approaches were devised by Buckels and colleagues (2013). One featured a bug-killing paradigm. As expected, those scoring high on the CAST measure of sadistic personality volunteered to kill bugs at greater rates than did non-sadists.

The second laboratory approach followed up a demonstration that certain college students seem to enjoy indiscriminate harming of others (Reidy et al., 2010): Those scoring high on sadism purposely blasted innocent others with loud white noise. Buckels and colleagues (2013) then verified that the motivation for such sadism was appetitive in nature. When aggression was made easy, sadism and Dark

Triad measures all predicted unprovoked aggression. However, only sadists were willing to work for the opportunity. Those scoring high on the CAST chose to do a boring task just so they could blast the innocent partner. Such results indicate that hurting others is a rewarding experience for some individuals.

In both studies, sadism emerged as an independent predictor of behavior reflecting an appetite for cruelty (see Elbert Moran, and Schauer, this volume). Together, these findings support the construct validity of everyday sadism and its incorporation into a new "Dark Tetrad" of personality (Buckels et al., 2013; Chabrol et al., 2009).

Online Research

A more recent paper by Buckels et al. (2014) showed the role of modern technology (namely, the Internet) in opening up new opportunities for those predisposed to cruelty. In two studies, Buckels and colleagues asked respondents to complete personality inventories and a survey of their Internet commenting styles. Overall, strong positive associations emerged between online commenting frequency, trolling enjoyment, and troll identity, pointing to a common construct underlying the measures. Of all personality measures, the CAST measure of everyday sadism showed the most robust associations with trolling and, importantly, the relationship was specific to trolling behavior. Enjoyment of other online activities, such as chatting and debating, was unrelated to sadism. Thus cyber-trolling appears to be an Internet manifestation of everyday sadism.

Conclusions

Individual differences in aggression may not easily be construed as a trait, that is, a stable and coherent dimension of personality. Instead, aggressive behavior may be intrinsically interactional, that is, provoked by different triggers in different personality traits. In our view, the underlying traits are not captured by measures such as the BPAQ. Instead, members of the Dark Tetrad of personality contribute in different ways to aggression and have unique provocations. Of course, the Dark Tetrad members may not be the only traits that, when provoked appropriately, lead to aggressive responses. In sum, we suggest that our interactional approach may prove more profitable than assuming that aggression can be construed as a single dimension.

Notes

1 Because of its predominance among aggression measures, we will focus only on the BPAQ.
2 One exception is the ZKPQ developed by Zuckerman et al. (1993). However, the aggression component is restricted to hostile aggression.
3 Arguably, the historical trend has been toward less sadism across time (Pinker, 2011).
4 However, Bushman and Anderson (2001) note that most aggressive behaviors involve a combination of hostile and instrumental motivations.

References

Atran, S., Axelrod, R., & Davis, R. (2007). Sacred barriers to conflict resolution. *Science, 317*, 1039–1040.

Bakan, D. (1966). *The duality of human existence: Isolation and communion in Western man.* Boston: Beacon Press.

Barber, N. (1994). Machiavellianism and altruism: effect of relatedness of target person on Machiavellian and helping attitudes. *Psychological Reports, 75*, 403–422.

Barlett, C. P., & Anderson, C. A. (2012). Direct and indirect relations between the Big Five personality traits and aggressive and violent behavior. *Personality and Individual Differences, 52*, 870–890.

Baumeister, R. F., Bushman, B. J., & Campbell, W. K. (2000). Self-esteem, narcissism, and aggression: Does violence result from low self-esteem or from threatened egotism? *Current Directions in Psychological Science, 9*, 26–29.

Becker, G. (2007). The Buss-Perry aggression questionnaire: Some unfinished business. *Journal of Research in Personality, 41*, 434–452.

Bettencourt, B. A., Talley, A., Benjamin, A. J., & Valentine, J. (2006). Personality and aggression under provoking and neutral conditions: A meta-analytic review. *Psychological Bulletin, 132*, 751–777.

Buckels, E. E., Jones, D. N., & Paulhus, D. L. (2013). Behavioral confirmation of everyday sadism. *Psychological Science, 24*, 2201–2209.

Buckels, E.E., & Paulhus, D.L. (2014). *The Comprehensive Assessment of Sadistic Tendencies* (CAST). Unpublished instrument, University of British Columbia, Vancouver, Canada.

Buckels, E. E., Trapnell, P. D., & Paulhus, D. L. (2014). Trolls just want to have fun. *Personality and Individual Differences, 67*, 97–102.

Bushman, B. J., & Anderson, C. A. (1998). Methodology in the study of aggression: Integrating experimental and nonexperimental findings. In R. G. Geen & E. I. Donnerstein (Eds.), *Aggression: Theoretical and empirical views* (Vol. 1, pp. 23–48). New York: Academic Press.

Bushman, B. J., & Anderson, C. A. (2001). Is it time to pull the plug on hostile versus instrumental aggression dichotomy? *Psychological Review, 108*, 273–279.

Bushman, B. J., & Baumeister, R. F. (1998). Threatened egotism, narcissism, self-esteem and direct vs. displaced aggression: Does self-love or self-hate lead to violence? *Journal of Personality and Social Psychology, 75*, 219–229.

Buss, A., & Perry, M. (1992). The aggression questionnaire. *Journal of Personality and Social Psychology, 63*, 452–459.

Cain, N. M., Pincus, A. L., & Ansell, E. B. (2008). Narcissism at the crossroads. *Clinical Psychology Review, 28*, 638–656.

Campbell, W.K., & Foster, J.D. (2007). The narcissistic self: Background, an extended agency model, and ongoing controversies. In C. Sedikides & S.J. Spencer (Eds.), *The self: Frontiers of social psychology* (pp. 115–138). New York: Psychology Press.

Chabrol, H., Leeuwen, N.V., Rodgers, R., & Séjourne, N. (2009). Contributions of psychopathic, narcissistic, Machiavellian, and sadistic personality traits to juvenile delinquency. *Personality and Individual Differences, 47*, 734–739.

Christie, R., & Geis, F. (1970). *Studies in Machiavellianism.* New York: Academic Press.

Cleckley, H. (1941). *The mask of sanity.* Oxford, England: Mosby.

Downey, G., Feldman, S., & Ayduk, O. (2001). Rejection sensitivity and male violence in romantic relationships. *Personal Relationships, 7*, 45–61.

Egan, V. (2009). The Big Five: Neuroticism, extraversion, openness, agreeableness, and conscientiousness as an organisational scheme for thinking about aggression and violence.

In M. McMurran & R. C. Howard (Eds.), *Personality disorder and violence* (pp. 63–84). New York: Wiley & Sons.

Emmons, R. A. (1987). Narcissism: Theory and measurement. *Journal of Personality and Social Psychology, 52*, 11–17.

Furnham, A., Richards, S.C., & Paulhus, D.L. (2013). The Dark Triad of personality: A 10 year review. *Social and Personality Psychology Compass, 7*, 199–216.

Hall, J. R., & Benning, S. D. (2006). The "successful" psychopath: Adaptive and subclinical manifestations of psychopathy in the general population. In C. J. Patrick (Ed.), *Handbook of psychopathy* (pp. 459–478). New York: Guilford.

Hamel, J., Jones, D. N., Dutton, D. G., & Graham-Kevan, N. (2015). The CAT: A gender-inclusive measure of controlling and abusive tactics. *Violence & Victims, 30*, 574–580.

Hare, R. D. (2003). *Manual for the revised psychopathy checklist* (2nd ed.). Toronto, ON: Multi-Health Systems.

Hare, R. D., & Neumann, C. S. (2008). Psychopathy as a clinical and empirical construct. *Annual Review of Psychology, 4*, 217–246.

Hawley, P.H. (2003). Prosocial and coercive configurations of resource control in early adolescence: A case for the well-adapted Machiavellian. *Merrill-Palmer Quarterly, 49*, 279–309.

Hicklin, J., & Widiger, T. A. (2005). Similarities and differences among antisocial and psychopathic self-report inventories from the perspective of general personality functioning. *European Journal of Personality, 19*, 325–342.

Jakobwitz, S., & Egan, V. (2006). The dark triad and normal personality. *Personality and Individual Differences, 40*, 331–339.

Jonason, P. K., & Webster, G. D. (2010). The Dirty Dozen: A concise measure of the Dark Triad. *Psychological Assessment, 22*, 420–432.

Jones, D. N. (2016). Moral conflicts and dark resolutions. In D. T. Kong & D. R. Forsyth (Eds.), *Leading through conflict: Into the fray* (pp. 1–21). New York: Palgrave MacMillan.

Jones, D. N., & Figueredo, A. J. (2013). The core of darkness: Uncovering the heart of the Dark Triad. *European Journal of Personality, 27*, 521–531.

Jones, D. N., & Neria, A. L. (2015). The Dark Triad and dispositional aggression. *Personality and Individual Differences, 86*, 360–364.

Jones, D. N., & Olderbak, S. G. (2014). The associations among dark personalities and sexual tactics across different scenarios. *Journal of Interpersonal Violence, 29*, 1050–1070.

Jones, D. N., & Paulhus, D. L. (2009). Machiavellianism. In M. R. Leary & R. H. Hoyle (Eds.), *Handbook of individual differences in social behavior* (pp. 93–108). New York: Guilford.

Jones, D. N., & Paulhus, D. L. (2010). Different provocations provoke aggression in psychopaths and narcissists. *Social Psychological and Personality Science, 1*, 12–18.

Jones, D.N., & Paulhus, D.L. (2011a). Differentiating the Dark Triad within the interpersonal circumplex. In L.M. Horowitz & S.N. Strack (Eds.), *Handbook of interpersonal psychology: Theory, research, assessment, and therapeutic interventions* (pp. 249–268). New York: Wiley.

Jones, D.N., & Paulhus, D.L. (2011b). The role of impulsivity in the Dark Triad of personality. *Personality and Individual Differences, 51*, 670–682.

Jones, D. N., & Paulhus, D. L. (2014). Introducing the Short Dark Triad (SD3): A brief measure of dark personality traits. *Assessment, 21*, 28–41.

Kerig, P. K., & Stellwagen, K. K. (2010). Roles of callous-unemotional traits, narcissism, and Machiavellianism in childhood aggression. *Journal of Psychopathology and Behavioral Assessment, 32*, 343–352.

Krupp, D. B., Sewall, L. A., Lalumière, M. L., Sheriff, C., & Harris, G. T. (2012). Nepotistic patterns of violent psychopathy: Evidence for adaptation? *Frontiers in Psychology: Evolutionary Psychology, 3*, 305–312.

Krupp, D.B., Sewall, L.A., Lalumière, M.L., Sheriff, C., & Harris, G.T. (2013). Psychopathy, adaptation, and disorder. *Frontiers in Psychology, 4,* 139.

Lawrence, C. (2006). Measuring individual responses to aggression-triggering events: Development of the situational triggers of aggressive responses (STAR) scale. *Aggressive Behavior, 32,* 241–252.

Lebreton, J. M., Binning, J. F., & Adorno, A. J. (2006). Subclinical psychopaths. In J. C. Thomas & D. Segal (Eds.), *Comprehensive handbook of personality and psychopathology* (Vol.1, pp. 388–411). New York: Wiley.

Levenson, M. R., Kiehl, K. A., & Fitzpatrick, C. M. (1995). Assessing psychopathic attributes in a noninstitutionalized population. *Journal of Personality and Social Psychology, 68,* 151–158.

Lilienfeld, S. O., & Andrews, B. P. (1996). Development and preliminary validation of a self-report measure of psychopathic personality traits in noncriminal populations. *Journal of Personality Assessment, 66,* 488–524.

Maples, J. L., Lamkin, J., & Miller, J. D. (2014). A test of two brief measures of the dark triad: The dirty dozen and short dark triad. *Psychological Assessment, 26,* 326–331.

Miller, D.T. (2001). Disrespect and the experience of injustice. *Annual Review of Psychology, 52,* 527–553.

Miller, J.D., & Campbell, W.K. (2008). Comparing clinical and social-personality conceptualizations of narcissism. *Journal of Personality, 76,* 449–476.

Miller, J.D., Few, L.R., Seibert, L.A., Watts, A., Zeichner, A., & Lynam, D.R. (2012). An examination of the Dirty Dozen measure of psychopathy: A cautionary tale about the costs of brief measures. *Psychological Assessment, 24,* 1048–1053.

Mokros, A., Hare, R. D., Neumann, C. S., & Santtila, P. (2015). Variants of psychopathy in adult male offenders: A latent profile analysis. *Journal of Abnormal Psychology, 124,* 372–386.

Mokros, A., Schilling, F., Eher, R., & Nitschke, J. (2012). The Severe Sexual Sadism Scale: Cross-validation and scale properties. *Psychological Assessment, 24,* 764–769.

Morf, C. C., & Rhodewalt, F. (2001). Unraveling the paradoxes of narcissism: A dynamic self-regulatory processing model. *Psychological Inquiry, 12,* 177–196.

Nisbett, R. E., & Cohen, D. (1996). *Culture of honor: The psychology of violence in the South.* Boulder, CO: Westview Press.

O'Meara, A., Davies, J., & Hammond, S. (2011). The psychometric properties and utility of the short sadistic impulse scale (SSIS). *Psychological Assessment, 23,* 523–531.

Patrick, C.J. (Ed.) (2006). *Handbook of psychopathy.* New York: Guilford.

Paulhus, D. L. (2014). Toward a taxonomy of dark personalities. *Current Directions in Psychological Science, 23,* 421–426.

Paulhus, D. L., & Dutton, D. G. (2016). Everyday sadism. In V. Zeigler-Hill & D. Marcus (Eds.), *The dark side of personality* (pp. 109–120). Washington, DC: American Psychological Association.

Paulhus, D. L., & Jones, D. N. (2015). Measures of dark personalities. In G. J. Boyle, D. H. Saklofske, & G. Matthews (Eds.), *Measures of personality and social psychological constructs* (pp. 562–594). San Diego: Academic Press.

Paulhus, D. L., Neumann, C. S., & Hare, R. D. (2016). *Manual for the Self-Report Psychopathy (SRP) scales.* Toronto: Multi-Health Systems.

Paulhus, D. L., & Williams, K. M. (2002). The Dark Triad of personality: Narcissism, Machiavellianism, and psychopathy. *Journal of Research in Personality, 36,* 556–563.

Pinker, S. (2011). *The better angels of our nature: Why violence has declined.* New York: Viking.

Porter, S., & Woodworth, M. (2006). Psychopathy and aggression. In C.J. Patrick (Ed.), *Handbook of psychopathy* (pp. 481–494). New York: Guilford.

Raskin, R.N., & Hall, C.S. (1979). A narcissistic personality inventory. *Psychological Reports, 45*, 590.

Reidy, D.E., Foster, J.D., & Zeichner, A. (2010). Narcissism and unprovoked aggression. *Aggressive Behavior, 36*, 414–422.

Sagarin, B. J., Cutler, B., Cutler, N., Lawler-Sagarin, K. A., & Matuszewich, L. (2009). Hormonal changes and couple bonding in consensual sadomasochistic activity. *Archives of Sexual Behavior*, 38, 186–200.

Taylor, S. P. (1967). Aggressive behavior and physiological arousal as a function of provocation and the tendency to inhibit aggression. *Journal of Personality, 35*, 297–310.

Vazire, S., & Funder, D.C. (2006). Impulsivity and the self-defeating behavior of narcissists. *Personality and Social Psychology Review, 10*, 154–165.

Veselka, L., & Vernon, P.A. (Eds.). (2014). The Dark Triad of personality [special issue]. *Personality and Individual Differences, 67*(4).

Westhead, J., & Egan, V. (2015). Untangling the concurrent influences of Dark Triad, personality and mating effort on violence. *Personality and Individual Differences, 86*, 222–225.

Williams, K. D. (2007). Ostracism. *Annual Review of Psychology, 58*, 425–452.

Zuckerman, M., Kuhlman, D. M., Joireman, J., Teta, P., & Kraft, M. (1993). A comparison of three structural models for personality: The Big Three, the Big Five, and the Alternative Five. *Journal of Personality and Social Psychology, 65*, 757–768.

8

APPETITIVE AGGRESSION

Thomas Elbert, James Moran, and Maggie Schauer

Thus speaks the red judge: "Why did this criminal kill? He wanted to rob." But I say to you: his soul wanted blood, not robbery. He thirsted for the bliss of the knife!

But his poor reason did not comprehend this madness and it persuaded him. "What does blood matter?" it said. "Don't you at least want to commit robbery in the process? Take revenge?"

And so he listened to his poor reason, like lead its speech lay upon him—and he robbed as he murdered. He did not want to be ashamed of his madness.

Friedrich Nietzsche, *Thus Spoke Zarathustra*

Current Concepts of Aggression

Theories of aggression frequently divide it into two forms (Fontaine, 2007; McEllistrem, 2004; Meloy, 2006; Weinshenker & Siegel, 2002): *Reactive aggression* is a defensive survival response against threat, typically associated with a bodily alarm response (fight-flight), and thus negative emotions like fear, anger, rage and hostility. When the threat is conquered, the negative arousal subsides and the reactive response will be rewarded as a relief from aversive conditions. *Instrumental aggression*, in contrast, is predatory, proactive and controlled. Its goal is to achieve a gain, which could be either materialistic, like seizing prey, or social, like dominance or increased opportunity to reproduce. Instrumental aggression is deliberate and requires planning. The usefulness of this dichotomy has been questioned, as in the real world, aggressive acts are always a mixture of both a defensive response and the goal-directed action (Bushman & Anderson, 2001). Where aggression is perpetrated just for the enjoyment of an act in its own right ("his soul wanted blood, not robbery"), it has mostly been viewed as psychopathological and thought to be restricted to individuals with *antisocial personality disorder* or *psychopaths* (Blair, 2013; Meloy, 2006; Yang & Raine, 2009; see Chapter 7 in this volume). Violence is defined as an extreme act of aggression, intended to cause physical injury or death (e.g., Bushman & Anderson, 2001).

In most humans, aggression can be driven by the pleasure of attacking and fighting ("thirst for the bliss of the knife"), by the thrill of hunting someone down, by the desire to hear the sound of a screaming victim, or even by the smell of blood. We have called this *appetitive aggression* (Elbert et al., 2010; Weierstall & Elbert, 2011), and it is this form of aggression that this chapter concerns itself with. Our study of appetitive aggression had its genesis in observations of fighters in conflict regions. In many scenarios of modern warfare, the vast majority of ordinary combatants report that with some habituation and repetition they enjoy violent aggression, including killing, mutilation and torture, and finally seek out opportunities to perpetrate it. The phenomenon manifests itself in other non-combat contexts as well. Clinical interviews with gang members in townships of South Africa showed very high levels of appetitive aggression (Weierstall et al., 2013). Observations in many different settings apply to the population as a whole and are not limited to a small fraction with clinical psychological disorders. We argue that this predisposition is an intrinsic, universal part of human psychobiology and that situational circumstances of continuous violence and war enable it to manifest itself. Therefore, any culture has to morally and legally regulate this form of aggression, as it does for sexual behavior and drug use, the other major drivers of the reward system, which, in vicious cycles, can spiral out of control. For the general population in a peaceful society, pleasure in aggressive behavior is restricted to socially sanctioned activities, such as contact sports or violent computer games. Evidence about the nature of the observed violence stems from wartime and can be examined in empirical work on its relation to other psychological constructs, particularly responses to trauma.

Aggression and Killing during War in Combatants and Former Combatants

Table 8.1 presents statements from fighters that describe the essential nature of appetitive aggression. Although such statements are not new, quantitative investigations of the phenomenon required the development of a corresponding instrument—the *Appetitive Aggression Scale* (Weierstall & Elbert, 2011), which is a reliable and valid 15-item scale (four more items address reactive aggression). According to Weierstall and Elbert (2011), analyzing the scores from 1,632 former combatants from three different continents, the items with about equally high scores in combatants are: • *Do you know what it is like to feel the hunger/thirst to fight?* • *Once fighting has started, do you get carried away by the violence?* • *Do you feel powerful when you go to a fight?* • *Is defeating the opponent more fun for you, when you see them*

TABLE 8.1 Example of Statements from Hooligans and Combatants

Football hooligan Danny Brown in *Villains*	"Now, the passion to fight for your club and the adrenaline rush that comes with it was unbelievable. But I don't think that this addiction can be understood."
Football hooligan and policeman in Stefan Schubert (2010), *Violence Is the Solution*, [authors' translation]	"At this point it seemed as if the adrenaline had been pushed aside by endorphins. The tension fell away—and I had to smile. As I continued to hit him, I had this fey grin on my face."
From Jack Thompson, "Hidden Enemies," quoted in Lt. Col. Dave Grossmann (1996), *On Killing, the Psychological Cost of Learning to Kill in War and Society* (p. 234)	"This combat high is like getting an injection of morphine—you float around, laughing, joking, having a great time, totally oblivious to the dangers around you. The experience is very intense if you live to tell about it. Problems arise when you begin to want another fix of combat, and another, and another."
German WWII soldier, in Neitzel & Welzer (2011), p. 87 [authors' translation]	"I would say well, on the first day it was terrible. Then I said: Shit, orders are orders. On the second and third day I said: I don't care one way or another, and on the fourth day, I started to have fun with it."
Vietnam veteran in De Vries & Petit (2001)	"That first moment, your first kill . . . it's . . . strange. Because it's something you've never done before. But after that, well, with me—it started getting good. The killing started getting good. Well, you know . . . something is wrong here. Something is wrong in this picture."
Maggie Schauer (2011) Interviews with combatants of Eastern DRCongo (in Elbert et al., 2013)	"We were sitting together, my uncle and me, we were talking about our glorious fights and then the need for fighting, the urge came up in us. It could be even at 7 o'clock at night, when it was already dark, that we took the guns then and went to kill."
Tobias Hecker (2011) Interviews with combatants of Eastern DRCongo (in Elbert et al., 2013)	"For a man fighting is everything. If I hear the sounds of bullets I wish I could be fighting. This thirst to fight is in me. It is like the thirst of a person who likes Coca Cola. The thirst will not be satisfied until the person drinks a Coke."
Jean Hatzfeld (2005) in *Machete Season* (Interviews with perpetrators of the genocide in Rwanda)	"The more we killed, the more motivated we were to keep doing it. When you can act on your desires without consequence, then it never lets you go. You could recognize us by our dead eyes. . . . It was an unexpected collective pleasure."
Neitzel and Welzer (2011), *Soldaten: On Fighting, Killing and Dying: The Secret Second World War Tapes of German POWs*	"A desire to throw bombs grew within me. That sensation was intense, a fine feeling. It is just as enjoyable as shooting someone."

bleed? Using this instrument, it became quickly apparent that the development of high levels of appetitive aggression are common in the vast majority of those people involved in bloody fights. The descriptions presented in Table 8.1 are not an exception but rather the dominant response in humans.

From our studies in war-torn regions and gang violence, we derive the following seven statements as characteristic in relation to appetitive aggression supported by empirical evidence:

1. Appetitive aggression is different from reactive aggression: Human aggressive behavior emerges not only as a response to a threat imposed upon one ("reactive"), but may be activated through a biologically prepared reward circuitry, which reinforces a lust for attacking and fighting. If this is not adequately controlled (e.g., by moral restraints or social laws), it can potentially lead to violence and destruction. An example is the teenager playing violent computer games, who kills in virtual reality despite negative feedback from his parents. Another example is the football hooligan who seeks to justify bloody fights with a quite irrational solidarity with his club. We know that reactive aggression aims to reduce arousal with a negative valence; appetitive aggression seeks to enhance arousal with a positive valence (Weierstall & Elbert, 2012). In some violent situations, for example combat, a person can switch quickly between these extremes.
2. Appetitive aggression is a physiologically distinct biological preparedness: Because appetitive aggression is in its behavioral and functional aspects in opposition to reactive aggression, it is reasonable to posit that it is physiologically distinct from reactive aggression. In fact, the first human studies indicate that neural circuitries associated with reactive and with appetitive aggression differ from each other, that is, the two forms relate to different biologically prepared response modes (Moran et al., 2014). Evidence for the different neurophysiological natures of both aggressive modes is presented Figure 8.1.
3. Appetitive aggression is similar to hunting behavior: The act of "hunting" represents the archetypical form of appetitive aggression, encompassing the tracking and pursuit of animals with the intention of killing. Though hunting is no longer an everyday practice in modern societies, its outlines are nevertheless visible in a variety of activities. Competitive sport or combat in any form can call this passion for the hunt into play. It is unlikely that people could be collectively roused to commit genocide without an intrinsic desire to hunt. Studies in violent scenarios like the genocide against the Tutsi (Schaal et al., 2012, 2015), or war (Weierstall & Elbert, 2011) or criminal gangs (Weierstall et al., 2013), indicate that people can be drawn into frequent violence with all the qualities of a hunt, including cruel humiliation and killing of others.
4. Appetitive aggression needs regulatory measures in all human communities: In order to prevent this apparently addictive compulsion to ever more violent

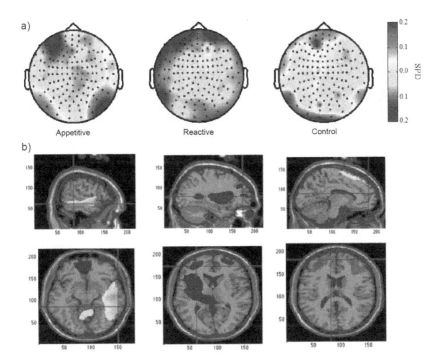

FIGURE 8.1   In an experimental study of male student participants by Moran and colleagues, different aggression states were induced via an imaginary role-playing task, in which people took on the role of murderer. Although the story itself was exactly the same across conditions, it was primed by different motives—either a reactive rage, or an appetitive lust to kill. Differences in low-frequency delta brain oscillatory activity, measured with magnetoencephalography, were found in right temporal/parietal regions, which are involved with the theory of mind aspect of empathy with others (Decety & Lamm, 2007), and are in fact associated with testosterone-modulated variations in gray matter density in the region in men (Lombardo et al., 2012). These results suggest the possibility of a site in the brain where sex hormone–modulated brain development has a direct influence on a stereotypically masculine aggression behavior. a) Maps of power of delta oscillations in appetitive (left), reactive (middle), and control conditions; b) thresholds of power projected onto MRI model (data from Moran et al., 2014).

acts, cultures regulate aggression through moral and legal rules. Violent scenarios may prevent development of proper inhibition, especially during vulnerable early stages of human development (Köbach & Elbert, 2015), that is, when children are raised in violent settings. This can be observed wherever the state monopoly of power has been abolished. In scenarios where boys are raised by armed groups or criminal gangs, when no male role model/father is available, a cycle of violence leads to ever greater cruelness and brutality (Elbert et al., 2006, 2013).

5. Both genders are biologically attracted to appetitive aggression—although not every individual: Men and also women who have been involved in deadly bloody killings may report the experience of combat high and a murderous bloodlust (see Figure 8.2). A first study investigating blood scent indicates that blood may be a biologically prepared stimulus that in a context-dependent manner for both sexes may serve as a powerful cue (Moran et al., 2015). More studies are needed to test this hypothesis though.

6. Appetitive aggression is a protective factor for sanity: Those who have learned to overcome their moral inhibition (often with the use of drugs), and thereby display greater appetitive aggression scores, seem to be less vulnerable to mental disorders (evidence summarized below).

7. Continuous and childhood trauma perpetuates appetitive aggression: People who have learned to enjoy cruelty have typically experienced physical violence and neglect during upbringing and were frequently socialized by gangs of violent peers rather than within a socially intact community.

Appetitive Aggression—Not Only a Male Domain

Women with significant combat experience show similar psychological profiles to male fighters, with elevated appetitive aggression scores equal to their male counterparts, illustrated in Figure 8.2. It is possible that these women may only represent a small, self-selected minority of extreme cases joining up with militias. Nevertheless, the fact that a group of women have been shown capable of perpetrating extreme physical violence on the same scale as men presents a challenge to the assumption holding women to be less violent than men.

The Protective Effect of Appetitive Aggression

The greater the cumulative exposure to traumatic and life-threatening events, the greater the likelihood of developing post-traumatic stress disorder (PTSD) and depression (Schauer et al., 2003; Wilker et al., 2015). But not all individuals are equally prone to trauma-related mental illness. In fact, those who report high values of appetitive aggression seem to be less vulnerable to the development of trauma-related disorders, including PTSD and depression: a number of studies confirm this protective effect of appetitive aggression in scenarios such as the war-torn regions of the Democratic Republic of Congo (Hecker et al., 2013b; Köbach et al., 2014), Uganda (Weierstall et al., 2012a; Wilker et al. 2015), or the armed clashes in Colombia (Weierstall et al., 2013). Even for the generally drug-dependent members of criminal gangs in South Africa's townships, a higher level of functioning in this context is associated with a greater intrinsic motivation

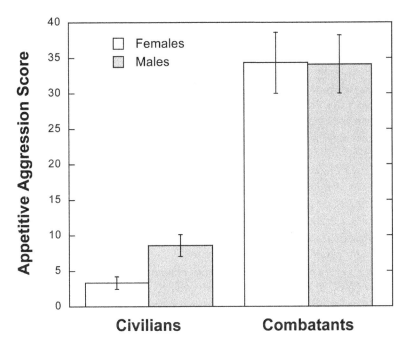

FIGURE 8.2   For civilians, men present with higher levels of appetitive aggression than women. However, combat experience (in this case in the Burundian civil war) boosts these values to extreme levels (data from Meyer-Parlapanis et al., 2016).

to fight with others (Weierstall et al., 2013). This resilience effect seems to be maintained across the entire life span, as indicated by the investigations of elderly German war veterans (Weierstall et al., 2012b).

How can we explain this effect? PTSD develops slowly with the accretion of traumatic events as a dysfunction of memory (Elbert & Schauer, 2014; Elbert et al., 2015; Schauer & Elbert, 2010a). The intensity of traumatic events means that anything reminiscent of these events is avoided. Consequently, memory consolidation is disrupted, leading to a failure of threatening cues to be properly contextualized in memory. Free-floating association of memory chunks then manifest themselves as intrusions and nightmares (Elbert & Schauer, 2002; Elbert & Schauer, 2014). Thus a war veteran may have a traumatic response to any noises reminiscent of combat—for example, fireworks, or a car tire bursting. This chain of associations is called the fear or trauma network. Appetitive aggression disrupts this process, as violence-related stimuli are perceived with an appetitive rather than aversive valence, that is, approach rather than avoidance. Consequently, during the event, the individual doesn't feel horrified and helpless in panic, reaching an *alarm response*, but instead is able to gain conscious control over the situation, as soon as aggression kicks in. Victims of trauma typically suffer from so-called "peritraumatic dissociation," a defensive fright state of immobility in which anger and acting out is suppressed (see Schauer & Elbert, 2010a). Peritraumatic dissociation has been described as a major risk factor for subsequent post-traumatic stress disorder. Feeling powerful and being able to fight the opponent counteracts the risky dissociative states and allows for action. There is no need to fear trauma memory in the aftermath of an appetitive aggression event. Investigations could show that maladaptive control strategies including avoidance behavior (e.g., avoiding unfamiliar places or situations), cognitive avoidance (e.g., trying to distract oneself from distressing thoughts), safety seeking (e.g., carrying a weapon) and ruminative attempts to erase or 'undo' assault memories (e.g., imagining ways one could have defended oneself) of victims leads to chronification of symptoms (Dunmore et al., 2001). Positive associations between avoidance strategies and post-trauma psychopathology have been found across different types of trauma. Overcoming avoidance allows contextualization and memory consolidation. The cues of violent experiences may be associated with appetitive responses to violent stimuli, that is, a positively valent associative memory, the "hunting network" competes with the fear network for connectivity to cues (Elbert et al., 2010). It is possible that for people in a crisis region, a motivation to actively cultivate an enjoyment of aggression functions is a coping mechanism; that people are drawn towards violence as a means of attaining power and safety, rather than being helpless (Crombach & Elbert, 2014; Hart et al., 2007)

Evolutionary Aspects of Appetitive Aggression

The examples in Table 8.1 exemplify people's experiences of learning to kill. Killing another person is often at first committed under duress, for example, from a military commander (child soldiers are routinely punished with violent death for disobeying commands [Schauer & Elbert, 2010b]), which quickly becomes routine, and then finally intensely enjoyable. How can one explain the origins of this behavior?

Aggression has evolved independently in different animal groups. The genetic mechanisms underlying it are therefore not homologous across species. Inborn programs involve motor patterns, innate releasing mechanisms, releasers, motivating mechanisms and learning dispositions specific for the species. Innateness in humans is suggested by the observation that certain behaviors, like the cutting of lips or ears, are universal across cultures (Elbert et al., 2010). Motor patterns and cues underlying aggression can even be found in deaf- and blind-born people (Eibl-Eibesfeldt, 1977). Strong selection pressures must be responsible for its development along analogous lines. Its most obvious functions are in competition for mates, natural resources and territories, and in the preservation of group identity. On the side of evolutionary theory, killing rivals could have an (inclusive) fitness value: this eliminates intrasexual competitors, enables greater access to reproductive partners, provides preventative effects of having a fearsome

FIGURE 8.3   In a defensive mode, the cat shows piloerection, loud hissing, arching of the back, striking with the front paws, and pupil dilation; in contrast, hunting behavior is characterized by quiet and controlled stalking of the prey, which is killed by biting it on the back of its neck (Siegel et al., 2007).

reputation for violence, and eliminates people who divert resources from genetic progeny (Duntley & Buss, 2011). Studies of chimpanzees suggest commonalities in the violence of both humans and chimpanzees, which are driven by a combination of social organization and environmental pressure (Wrangham, 1999). Hunting behavior and coalitionary killing could be related to each other, though it is not known which begat the other. An evolutionary cycle of bodily adaptation, like a shorter gut and greater brain capacity, required a diet with more animal protein, which could have driven earlier hominids to the necessity to hunt. This is a difficult task, for which the ultimate reward for the stone-age hunter may have been days away. Only those people who learned to enjoy the associated proximal stimuli—tracking, chasing the prey, the death struggle, the scent of blood—had an advantage (Nell, 2006). Although the two forms of aggression—reactive and appetitive—clearly exist in predatory animals (see Figure 8.3), the active killing conducted by humans and chimpanzees is not like the hunting behavior of any other carnivore, which is characterized by low arousal and a quick discreet kill. Humans and chimpanzees show high arousal, piloerection and ambivalence towards the victim (Wrangham, 1999). They experience the thrill of chasing the prey and bringing it down, and fear as it strikes back; they also form coalitions; "sophisticated assessment of power differentials" (Wrangham, 1999, p. 22). One recent study found that the number of killings per year for each community of chimpanzees (but not bonobos) was correlated with the number of males in the community, whereby they would frequently hunt down, kill and eventually feed on other monkeys in groups (Wilson et al., 2014).

The true prevalence of war in human prehistory is intensely debated, with scholars arguing at both extremes that organized fighting was either a rare exception or an elemental part of human behavior. Even without any evolutionary force, violence is one of the currencies of power, manifest in ordinary children's behavior, who in spite of admonitions from adults, will frequently resort to violence—be it appetitive, predatory or reactive. Many traditionally masculine virtues, such as courage, endurance, loyalty, heroic recklessness and self-sacrifice, are bound with the expression of aggression. Although often pathologized, a large proportion of gang members are often free of clinical disturbances, and are otherwise functional in their communities (Kröber, 2012). Congolese child soldiers with the highest levels of appetitive aggression were those recruited around the age of 16–17 years (Köbach & Elbert, 2015); in this transitional period from boyhood to manhood, the imperative to demonstrate these violence-related virtues is at its peak (Kröber, 2012).

Neurobiology of Appetitive Aggression

Understanding the individual from an evolutionary perspective necessitates a more focused biological picture of aggression, rather than the simpler calculus of the inclusive fitness outcomes of particular violent behaviors. Many different structures in the brain work together to determine the expression of aggression. The various forms of aggression are initiated and coordinated over many structures of the brain, from the vegetative centers regulating muscular and respiratory systems for fighting, to the highest cognitive structures, making sophisticated social judgments of a specific threat. Based on animal models, this is relatively well understood in reactive aggression (Blair, 2004; Panksepp, 1998; Weiger & Bear, 1988; see Chapter 2 of this volume). The lower structures include the hypothalamus, periaqueductal gray and pituitary gland, which directly prepare the body for stress responses. It is modulated by superior structures in the brain, like the nuclei of the amygdalae, which receive motivationally relevant sensory input and are associated with fear conditioning. Reactive aggression, as a defensive response, is part of the defense cascade, the sequence of stereotyped behavioral, emotional, physiological and cognitive responses to threat, where the organism is readied to escape before giving way to a parasympathetically dominated fright/faint response, which is a harm minimization strategy (Schauer & Elbert, 2010a).

Many animal studies show a distinction between stereotyped predatory and defensive aggression. These include both carnivores, such as cats, and omnivores, such as rats, mice and hamsters. The differences in forms of aggression are clearly demonstrated in the cat (Figure 8.3), where hunting behavior can be induced by stimulating different nuclei of the hypothalamus: the lateral hypothalamus potentiates predatory aggression, and the medial produces defensive aggression. The medial and lateral nuclei of the hypothalamus play analogous roles in other animals, including rats, mice, hamsters and primates (see Haller, 2013, for review).

It is unlikely that animal models in rodents or cats are directly transferable to appetitive aggressive response and reward system in humans or other primates. Humans do not have this apparent hypothalamic switch, although hypothalamic abnormalities have been shown in clinically aggressive populations (Koch et al., 2007; Kuhlmann et al., 2013). Just as reactive aggression is the culmination of different neural structures, appetitive aggression is likely to be governed by a similar mixture of flexible higher cortical structures (Moran et al., 2014) and more automatic visceral structures. Since appetitive aggression is per definition rewarding, one could infer that reward-related structures are a part of this. The motivational elements of human behavior likely separate into fundamental motivational elements, with appetitive systems belonging to approach-related reward systems, and reactive aggression belonging to a defensive withdrawal system.

The Problem of Empathy

If we were to look for another essential component of mind that is modulated through appetitive aggression apart from reward-related structures, then empathy is an obvious candidate. There is an intuitive link between empathy and violence, in postulating that overcoming an inhibition to kill requires a lowering of a moral threshold. Forensic perpetrators are often seen as psychopaths, that is, as emotionless, cold killers with no sense of empathy. However, correlations of empathy with violence, measured as personality traits, are weak (Vachon et al., 2014). Rather, perpetration means the regulation of empathy: the dehumanization of the prospective victim, for example by seeing the enemy as a "monkey" or "rat" (Grossman, 1996; Staub, 2006) is a typical example of how to turn off empathy. Similarly, when gang members target a victim, it does not matter who that is, so long as the victim is a member of an enemy group, an out-group individual (Eibl-Eibesfeldt, 1977), someone fundamentally "other"—for example, homosexual, rival gang member, or other ethnic group (Kröber, 2012). This echoes the intraspecies violence carried out by chimpanzees, which is focused upon individuals that are outside of the group (Wrangham, 1999).

The dynamic relation between traumatization and appetitive aggression can be theoretically explained by differences in modulating empathy. Although one's autonomic defensive reactions are supposed to maximize one's own chance of survival, they can also be primed by the suffering of others. People who actually kill others may also suffer from PTSD, even if they take on the predatory role rather than the prey role (Hecker et al., 2013a; Hermenau et al., 2013; MacNair, 2001; Weierstall et al., 2012a, b). A higher level of appetitive aggression might reduce the traumatic implications of killing by blunting empathy with the victims: child soldiers who voluntarily joined the militias have been compared to conscripts and found to have higher appetitive aggression scores. Although they showed trauma symptoms, these were only in association with danger experienced by themselves, not with their own perpetrated acts of violence (Hecker et al., 2013a, b).

Relation to Psychopathology

Many of the above observations of appetitive aggression match with the symptoms of psychopathy (Hare & Neumann, 2008), particularly the capacity to be cruel to another person without empathy. People with this diagnosis have apparent alterations in reward-related structures of the brain (Buckholtz et al., 2010; Carre et al., 2013), as well as emotional empathy-related regions (Blair, 2005, 2013; Marsh et al., 2013). However, it may also be possible that psychopaths do not lack the ability for empathy but rather are masters of switching empathic mirroring on and off. In this case, children raised in a violent environment may learn this response, which in turn would also alter their brain structure and organization as a consequence of brain plasticity (Elbert et al., 2006). At present, however, the connection between psychopathology and appetitive aggression remains to be researched. Psychopathy conceived as a dimensional construct (Hare & Neumann, 2008) would imply that people diagnosed as such in a peaceful society are merely those who are least sensitive to aggression-inhibiting effects of upbringing and morality or simply never are offered the possibility to learn morality in as much as they grow up in a violent family with no adequate role models. This assumption is supported by the observations that criminals in peaceful societies consistently report that they had to endure harsh and violent environments during their upbringing, typically with the father as a role model for violent behavior, a situation that we consistently observe in the adolescent gangsters of South Africa's townships.

Conclusion

Appetitive aggression has been shown to make a distinct and potentially dominant element of human aggressive behavior. It arises from the thrill of the hunt and can arouse intense excitement. Because access to the reward system via the appetitive aggression system is exploited by armed groups, many individuals in conflict lands may show elevated levels, affecting the large-scale stability of a society. Although contrary to more humanistic views of "human nature," appetitive aggression appears to be commonplace enough in the ordinary population to suggest that it is an innately prepared part of the behavioral repertoire of human beings, rather than a psychopathological aberration. Though it is facilitated by particular social conditions, appetitive aggression arises on the basis of certain genetically guided psychological qualities, shaped over the course of human evolution. Culture is what then constrains us from wanton violence by delineating who is friend and who is foe. Or as Albert Einstein has expressed it:

> . . . man has within him a lust for hatred and destruction. In normal times this passion exists in a latent state, it emerges only in unusual circumstances, but it is a comparatively easy task to call it into play and raise it to the power of a collective psychosis.
>
> (Einstein, 1932, according to Nathan & Nordan, 1963)

References

Blair, R. J. (2004). The roles of orbital frontal cortex in the modulation of antisocial behavior. *Brain and Cognition, 55*(1), 198–208.

Blair, R. J. (2005). Responding to the emotions of others: Dissociating forms of empathy through the study of typical and psychiatric populations. *Consciousness and Cognition, 14*(4), 698–718.

Blair, R. J. (2013). The neurobiology of psychopathic traits in youths. *Nature Reviews Neuroscience, 14*(11), 786–799.

Buckholtz, J. W., Treadway, M. T., Cowan, R. L., Woodward, N. D., Benning, S. D., Li, R., . . . Shelby, E. S. (2010). Mesolimbic dopamine reward system hypersensitivity in individuals with psychopathic traits. *Nature Neuroscience, 13*(4), 419–421.

Bushman, B. J., & Anderson, C. A. (2001). Is it time to pull the plug on hostile versus instrumental aggression dichotomy? *Psychological Review, 108*(1), 273.

Carre, J. M., Hyde, L. W., Neumann, C. S., Viding, E., & Hariri, A. R. (2013). The neural signatures of distinct psychopathic traits. *Society for Neuroscience, 8*(2), 122–135.

Crombach, A., & Elbert, T. (2014). Controlling offensive behavior using narrative exposure therapy a randomized controlled trial of former street children. *Clinical Psychological Science, 3*(2), 270–282.

Decety, J., & Lamm, C. (2007). The role of the right temporoparietal junction in social interaction: How low-level computational processes contribute to meta-cognition. *The Neuroscientist, 13*(6), 580–593.

De Vries, J., & Petit, L. (Producers), & Schrijber, C. (Director). (2001). *First kill* [Documentary]. Netherlands: Lemmer Film.

Dunmore, E., Clark, D. M., & Ehlers, A. (2001). A prospective investigation of the role of cognitive factors in persistent posttraumatic stress disorder (PTSD) after physical or sexual assault. *Behaviour Research and Therapy, 39*(9), 1063–1084.

Duntley, J. D., & Buss, D. M. (2011). Homicide adaptations. *Aggression and Violent Behavior, 16*, 399–410.

Eibl-Eibesfeldt, L. (1977). Evolution of destructive aggression. *Aggressive Behavior, 3*(2), 127–144.

Elbert, T., Rockstroh, B., Kolassa, I. T., Schauer, M., & Neuner, F. (2006). The influence of organized violence and terror on brain and mind: A co-constructive perspective. In N. P. Baltes, P. Reuter-Lorenz, & F. Rösler (Eds.), *Lifespan development and the brain: The perspective of biocultural co-constructivism* (pp. 326–349). New York: Cambridge University Press.

Elbert, T., & Schauer, M. (2002). Psychological trauma: Burnt into memory. *Nature, 419*(6910), 883–883.

Elbert, T., & Schauer, M. (2014). Epigenetic, neural and cognitive memories of traumatic stress and violence. In S. Cooper & K. Ratele (Eds.), *Psychology serving humanity: Proceedings of the 30th international congress of psychology: Volume 2: Western psychology* (pp. 215–227). East Sussex, NY: Psychology Press.

Elbert, T., Schauer, M., Hinkel, H., Riedke, H., Maedl, A., Winkler, N., . . . Hecker, T. (2013). *Sexual and gender-based violence in the Kivu provinces of the DRC.* Washington, DC: The International Bank for Reconstruction and Development/The World Bank.

Elbert, T., Schauer, M., & Neuner, F. (2015). Narrative Exposure Therapy (NET)— Reorganizing memories of traumatic stress, fear and violence. In U. Schnyder & M. Cloitre (Eds.), *Evidence based treatments for trauma-related psychological disorders* (pp. 229–253). Berlin, Heidelberg, New York, Tokio: Springer.

Elbert, T., Weierstall, R., & Schauer, M. (2010). Fascination violence: On mind and brain of man hunters. *European Archives of Psychiatry and Clinical Neuroscience, 260 Suppl 2,* S100–105.

Fontaine, R. G. (2007). Disentangling the psychology and law of instrumental and reactive subtypes of aggression. *Psychology, Public Policy, and Law, 13*(2), 143–165.

Grossman, D. (1996). *On killing: The psychological cost of learning to kill in war and society.* New York: Little Brown and Company.

Haller, J. (2013). The neurobiology of abnormal manifestations of aggression—a review of hypothalamic mechanisms in cats, rodents, and humans. *Brain Research Bulletin, 93,* 97–109.

Hare, R. D., & Neumann, C. S. (2008). Psychopathy as a clinical and empirical construct. *Annual Review of Clinical Psychology, 4*, 217–246.

Hart, J. L., O'Toole, S. K., Price-Sharps, J. L., & Shaffer, T. W. (2007). The risk and protective factors of violent juvenile offending an examination of gender differences. *Youth Violence and Juvenile Justice, 5*(4), 367–384.

Hatzfeld, J. (2005). *Machete season: The killers in Rwanda speak* (L. Coverdale, trans.). New York: Farrar, Straus and Giroux.

Hecker, T., Hermenau, K., Maedl, A., Hinkel, H., Schauer, M., & Elbert, T. (2013a). Does perpetrating violence damage mental health? Differences between forcibly recruited and voluntary combatants in DR Congo. *Journal of Traumatic Stress, 26*(1), 142–148. doi: 10.1002/jts.21770

Hecker, T., Hermenau, K., Maedl, A., Schauer, M., & Elbert, T. (2013b). Aggression inoculates against PTSD symptom severity-insights from armed groups in the eastern DR Congo. *European Journal of Psychotraumatology, 4*. doi:http://dx.doi.org/10.3402/ejpt.v4i0.20070

Hermenau, K., Hecker, T., Maedl, A., Schauer, M., & Elbert, T. (2013). Growing up in armed groups: Trauma and aggression among child soldiers in DR Congo. *European Journal of Psychotraumatology, 4.* doi:http://dx.doi.org/10.3402/ejpt.v4i0.21408

Köbach, A., & Elbert, T. (2015). Sensitive period for developing a robust trait of appetitive aggression. *Frontiers in Psychiatry, 6,* 144. doi:http://doi.org/10.3389/fpsyt.2015.00144

Köbach, A., Schaal, S., & Elbert, T. (2014). Combat high or traumatic stress: Violent offending is associated with appetitive aggression but not with symptoms of traumatic stress. *Frontiers in Psychology, 5,* 1518. doi: http://doi.org/10.3389/fpsyg.2014.01518

Koch, W., Schaaff, N., Pöpperl, G., Mulert, C., Juckel, G., Reicherzer, M., . . . Tatsch, K. (2007). [I-123] ADAM and SPECT in patients with borderline personality disorder and healthy control subjects. *Journal of Psychiatry & Neuroscience, 32*(4), 234.

Kröber, H.-L. (2012). Zusammen kämpfen, zusammen schlagen? *Forensische Psychiatrie, Psychologie, Kriminologie, 6*(3), 166–176.

Kuhlmann, A., Bertsch, K., Schmidinger, I., Thomann, P. A., & Herpertz, S. C. (2013). Morphometric differences in central stress-regulating structures between women with and without borderline personality disorder. *Journal of Psychiatry & Neuroscience, 38*(2), 129–137.

Lombardo, M. V., Ashwin, E., Auyeung, B., Chakrabarti, B., Taylor, K., Hackett, G., . . . Baron-Cohen, S. (2012). Fetal testosterone influences sexually dimorphic gray matter in the human brain. *The Journal of Neuroscience, 32*(2), 674–680.

McEllistrem, J. E. (2004). Affective and predatory violence: A bimodal classification system of human aggression and violence. *Aggression and Violent Behavior, 10,* 1–30.

MacNair, R. (2001). Psychological reverberations for the killers: Preliminary historical evidence for perpetration-induced traumatic stress. *Journal of Genocide Research, 3*(2), 273–282.

Marsh, A. A., Finger, E. C., Fowler, K. A., Adalio, C. J., Jurkowitz, I. T., Schechter, J. C., . . . Blair, R. J. (2013). Empathic responsiveness in amygdala and anterior cingulate cortex in youths with psychopathic traits. *Journal of Child Psychology and Psychiatry, 54*(8), 900–910. doi: 10.1111/jcpp.12063

Meloy, J. R. (2006). Empirical basis and forensic application of affective and predatory violence. *Australian and New Zealand Journal of Psychiatry, 40,* 539–547.

Meyer-Parlapanis, D., Weierstall, R., Nandi, C., Bambonyé, M., Elbert, T., & Crombach, A. (2015). Appetitive aggression in women: Comparing male and female war combatants. *Frontiers in Psychology, 6.* doi:http://dx.doi.org/10.3389/fpsyg.2015.01972

Moran, J. K., Dietrich, D. R., Elbert, T., Pause, B. M., Kübler, L., & Weierstall, R. (2015). The scent of blood: A driver of human behavior? *PLoS ONE, 10*(9): e0137777. doi:10.1371/journal.pone.0137777

Moran, J. K., Weierstall, R., & Elbert, T. (2014). Differences in brain circuitry for appetitive and reactive aggression as revealed by realistic auditory scripts. *Frontiers in Behavioral Neuroscience, 8,* 425. doi: http://dx.doi.org/10.3389/fnbeh.2014.00425

Nathan, O., & Nordan, H. (1963). *Einstein on peace.* London: Methuen.

Neitzel, S., & Welzer, H. (2011). *Soldaten: Protokolle vom Kämpfen, Töten und Sterben* [Soldiers: German POWs on fighting, killing, and dying]. Frankfurt am Main: S. Fischer Verlag.

Nell, V. (2006). Cruelty's rewards: The gratifications of perpetrators and spectators. *Behavioral and Brain Sciences, 29,* 211–257.

Nietzsche, F. (2006). *Thus Spoke Zarathustra* (A. Del Caro & R. Pippin Eds.). Cambridge, UK: Cambridge University Press.

Panksepp, J. (1998). *Affective neuroscience: The foundations of human and animal emotions.* New York: Oxford University Press.

Schaal, S., Heim, L., & Elbert, T. (2014). Posttraumatic stress disorder and appetitive aggression in Rwandan genocide perpetrators. *Journal of Aggression, Maltreatment & Trauma, 23*(9), 930–945.

Schaal, S., Weierstall, R., Dusingizemungu, J.P., & Elbert, T. (2012). Mental health 15 years after the killings in Rwanda: Imprisoned perpetrators of the genocide against the Tutsi versus a community sample of survivors. *Journal of Traumatic Stress, 25*(4), 446–453.

Schauer, M., & Elbert, T. (2010a). Dissociation following traumatic stress. *Zeitschrift für Psychologie/Journal of Psychology, 218*(2), 109–127.

Schauer, E., & Elbert, T. (2010b). The psychological impact of child soldiering. In E. Martz (Ed.), *Trauma rehabilitation after war and conflict: Community and individual perspectives* (pp. 311–360). New York: Springer.

Schauer, M., Neuner, F., Karunakara, U., Klaschik, C., Robert, C., & Elbert, T. (2003). PTSD and the "building block" effect of psychological trauma among West Nile Africans. ESTSS (European Society for Traumatic Stress Studies). *Bulletin, 10*(2), 5–6.

Schubert, S. (2010). *Gewalt ist eine Lösung: Morgens Polizist, abends Hooligan—mein geheimes Doppelleben* [Violence is a solution—my secret double life]. München: Riva Verlag.

Siegel, A., Bhatt, S., Bhatt, R., & Zalcman, S. S. (2007). The neurobiological bases for development of pharmacological treatments of aggressive disorders. *Current Neuropharmacology, 5*, 135–147.

Staub, E. (2006). Reconciliation after genocide, mass killing, or intractable conflict: Understanding the roots of violence, psychological recovery, and steps toward a general theory. *Political Psychology, 27*(6), 867–894.

Vachon, D. D., Lynam, D. R., & Johnson, J. A. (2014). The (non) relation between empathy and aggression: Surprising results from a meta-analysis. *Psychological Bulletin, 140*(3), 751.

Weierstall, R., & Elbert, T. (2011). The Appetitive Aggression Scale-development of an instrument for the assessment of human's attraction to violence. *European Journal of Psychotraumatology, 2*. doi: 10.3402/ejpt.v2i0.8430

Weierstall, R., & Elbert, T. (2012). Formen und Klassifikation menschlicher Aggression. In J. Endrass, A. Rossegger & B. Borchard (Eds.), *Interventionen bei Gewalt- und Sexualstraftätern. Risk-Management, Methoden und Konzepte der forensischen Therapie* (pp. 3–14). Berlin: MWV Medizinisch-Wissenschaftliche Verlagsgesellschaft.

Weierstall, R., Hinsberger, M., Kaminer, D., Holtzhausen, L., Madikane, S., & Elbert, T. (2013). Appetitive aggression and adaptation to a violent environment among youth offenders. *Peace and Conflict: Journal of Peace Psychology, 19*(2), 138.

Weierstall, R., Huth, S., Knecht, J., Nandi, C., & Elbert, T. (2012b). Appetitive aggression as a resilience factor against Trauma disorders: Appetitive aggression and PTSD in German World War II veterans. *PLoS One, 7*(12), 1–6.

Weierstall, R., Schalinski, I., Crombach, A., Hecker, T., & Elbert, T. (2012a). When combat prevents PTSD symptoms—results from a survey with former child soldiers in Northern Uganda. *BMC Psychiatry, 12*, 41.

Weiger, W. A., & Bear, D. M. (1988). An approach to the neurology of aggression. *Journal of Psychiatric Research, 22*(2), 85–98.

Weinshenker, N. J., & Siegel, A. (2002). Bimodal classification of aggression: Affective defense and predatory attack. *Aggression and Violent Behavior, 7*, 237–250.

Wilker, S., Pfeiffer, A., Kolassa, S., Koslowski, D., Elbert, T., & Kolassa, I. (2015). How to quantify exposure to traumatic stressors? Reliability and validity of measures for cumulative trauma exposure in a post-conflict population. *European Journal of Psychotraumatology, 6*. doi: http://dx.doi.org/10.3402/ejpt.v6.28306

Wilson, M.L., Boesch, C., Fruth, B., Furuichi, T., Gilby, I.C., Hashimoto, C., . . . & Lloyd, J.N. (2014). Lethal aggression in *Pan* is better explained by adaptive strategies than human impacts. *Nature, 513*(7518), 414–417.

Wrangham, R. W. (1999). Evolution of coalitionary killing. *American Journal of Physical Anthropology, 110*(29), 1–30.

Yang, Y., & Raine, A. (2009). Prefrontal structural and functional brain imaging findings in antisocial, violent, and psychopathic individuals: A meta-analysis. *Psychiatry Research, 174*(2), 81–88.

PART III

Contextual Risk Factors for Aggression and Violence

9

AVERSIVE EVENTS AND AGGRESSION

Christopher L. Groves and Craig A. Anderson

The experience of unpleasant or aversive events is an integral component of human life. Much of human motivation and action is designed specifically for avoiding aversive experiences (and seeking pleasant experiences) either in the immediate or distant future. Yet, despite these efforts, we often fail to deter or avoid the onset of an aversive event. At a broad level, work that seeks to understand the effects of these events serves as an important contributor to the study of aggression. As has been noted elsewhere in this volume (see Chapter 5), a useful tool for under-standing aggressive and violent behavior is through risk and resilience models of aggression (Anderson et al., 2007; Gentile & Bushman, 2012). Many risk factors for aggression are not inherently aversive (e.g., playing a violent video game, the acti-vation of goals that might be attained via aggressive acts, the depletion of cognitive resources, the learning of aggressive scripts). Yet, many aggression risk factors are inherently aversive, and therefore a full picture of aggression requires a thorough examination of the role of aversive experience in understanding aggressive acts.

We begin with a historical account of the main theoretical approaches advanced to explain why and how aversive experience often leads to aggression. Next, we examine some specific aversive risk factors for aggression. Space limita-tions preclude an in-depth discussion of all relevant topics, so our primary goal is to present a broad picture of the impact of aversive events and to emphasize the value of understanding such effects in the study of aggression-related phenomena.

Theoretical Processes

Frustration-Aggression Hypothesis

Perhaps the most prominent historical theoretical account regarding the influ-ence of aversive experience on aggression comes from the book *Frustration and*

Aggression, which presents the frustration-aggression hypothesis (Dollard et al., 1939). In a simplified form, the hypothesis states that "people are driven to attack others when they are frustrated: when they are unable to reach their goals, or they do not obtain the rewards they expect" (Berkowitz, 1993a, p. 30).

Before detailing the hypothesis further, it is important to discuss definitional issues surrounding the term "frustration." *Frustration* can be and has been defined in many ways. One approach is to think of a frustration as any external barrier to a goal. Alternatively, frustration can be thought of as an internal state triggered by failure to obtain an expected reward, an emotional reaction that often results from external circumstance (e.g., the thwarting of a goal). According to the original frustration-aggression hypothesis, the "external barrier" version serves as the operational definition, but emphasis was placed on the barrier as preventing one from obtaining an expected reward.

This definitional rationale provides some interesting nuance to predicting the effects of some apparent barriers to goal attainment. For instance, poverty most certainly leads to a limiting of opportunities and material possessions. However, whereas poverty is a well-known risk factor for aggression (e.g., Guerra et al., 1995), the effects of poverty, according to the frustration-aggression hypothesis, should be limited as a function of the degree to which impoverished individuals desire and seek out possessions, opportunities, etc. . . . that are *unattainable* or *difficult to attain*. In other words, thwarted expectations serve as the "key ingredient" in understanding when frustration is likely to occur (and thus, aggression to ensue).

The original frustration-aggression hypothesis posited that *all* forms of aggression are due, in some way, to the experience of frustration. Although this strong version of the hypothesis led to many valuable insights into aggression-related phenomena, it has some clear limitations. For instance, it is difficult for the frustration-aggression hypothesis to explain some instrumental forms of aggression (e.g., a contract killer paid to murder someone). It has even greater difficulty explaining the more subtle effects of aggressive priming tasks (e.g., the weapons effect; Bartholow et al., 2005; see Chapter 12) or the effects of automatically activated aggressive scripts. Further, aggression scholars responded to the frustration-aggression hypothesis by noting that only specific types of frustrations increase the likelihood of aggressive response. For example, early work suggested that aggression was most likely to ensue when a frustrating event was viewed as illegitimate, unjustified, or arbitrary (Pastore, 1952), which inspired a number of additional investigations on the topic (e.g., Cohen, 1955; Kregarman & Worchel, 1961; Rothaus & Worchel, 1960). However, one response to this proposition is that the original 1939 hypothesis includes these instances in its theorizing, as an arbitrary frustration produces a thwarting of an expected reward while non-arbitrary frustrations (e.g., the bus drives past your stop with a sign reading "On way to garage") prevent one from expecting a reward in the first place (Berkowitz, 1993a).

Cognitive Neoassociation Theory

Although some of the basic tenets of the frustration-aggression hypothesis remain well supported, the relationship of frustrations (and other aversive events) on aggression are best understood by considering the degree to which negative affect is aroused by the event (Berkowitz, 1989). In other words, negative affect serves as a mediator of the frustration-aggression effect (and many other effects), which helps bring theoretical clarity to other findings such as the role of arbitrariness in frustration effects (i.e., arbitrary frustrations elicit more negative affect). The cognitive neoassociation model serves as a theoretical account that generalizes more effectively to all aversive experiences (Berkowitz, 1989). This model presents several stages, the first of which is the generation of negative affect due to the aversive event. The associative aspect of the model relies on the notion that semantic memory consists of a network of interrelated concepts, scripts, and behavioral propensities, some of which are linked to negative affect. In other words, negative affect automatically activates "a variety of expressive-motor reactions, feelings, thoughts, and memories that are associated with both flight and fight tendencies" (Berkowitz, 1989, p. 69). Personal histories of learning, genetic propensities, and various situational factors collectively influence the likelihood of either a fight or flight response. Once the initial aversive event is experienced, more complex cognitive operations such as attribution processes (Anderson et al., 1996), self-regulation processes (Anderson & Bushman, 2002), self-efficacy expectations (Bandura, 1977), and outcome expectancies (Bandura, 1986) interact to produce a variety of possible aggressive and/or nonaggressive affective, cognitive, and behavioral outcomes.

Excitation Transfer

Another theory relevant to the study of aversive experience is excitation transfer theory (Zillmann, 1971). The theory relies on an understanding of physiological arousal and of attribution processes, specifically the misattribution of arousal derived from one situation to a stimulus (or set of stimuli) in a subsequent situation. Physiological arousal requires some time to dissipate, very often longer than the individual perceives. When individuals are aroused in one situation (e.g., from climbing stairs), some portion of that arousal persists into the next situation (e.g., meeting a professor). One tool that people use to understand their environment is the monitoring of their own physiological state, which helps them interpret how they are feeling or reacting to current events. Therefore, when a provocation is experienced in the subsequent environment (for example), the residual arousal derived from the initial situation can be misinterpreted or "misattributed" as having resulted from the provocateur's behavior, which ultimately increases the perception of one's own anger and, consequently, the likelihood and severity of retaliation. Such misattribution of arousal has been shown in a variety of situations with a variety of positive and negative behaviors. In one study (Zillmann & Bryant, 1974), researchers tested this theory by randomly assigning participants to either thread discs onto a wire or go for a bike ride. The bike riding condition elicited significantly greater arousal levels compared to the disc threading condition. Participants were then asked to play a Battleship type game with a confederate in which aversive noise blasts were administered as feedback for misses. After the first game, participants were randomly assigned to overhear an insult from the confederate. As predicted, participants who had ridden the bicycle and were insulted behaved more aggressively in the noise blast task.

Modern Social-Cognitive Theories

Modern social-cognitive theories (e.g., social learning theory, social cognitive theory, script theory) all incorporate a number of constructs and processes that account for aversive event effects on aggressive behavior (see Chapter 1 of this volume). The most comprehensive of these models, as applied to aggression, is the General Aggression Model (Anderson & Bushman, 2002). In this model, aversive events are seen as increasing the likelihood of aggressive behavior in much the same way as described by the cognitive neoassociation model (Berkowitz, 1989) and the excitation model (Zillmann, 1971), but it also takes into account other cognitive, affective, and past learning history factors, as well as biological factors. For example, beliefs about one's ability to carry out behavioral plans that come to mind (i.e., efficacy expectation), about the likely outcomes of the plans (outcome expectations), and about the normativeness or appropriateness of the behavioral plan all depend on past history, and all influence the likelihood that a particular behavioral plan (or script) will be carried out. Furthermore, many (most?) of these decisions can take place quickly and without conscious awareness. Details about the General Aggression Model are beyond the scope and page limits of this chapter, of course, but a more detailed discussion is available elsewhere in this volume (see Chapter 12).

Specific Aversive Events

In this section we describe a few of the research findings from more specific areas of research on how commonly experienced aversive events influence aggressive and violent behavior.

Provocation

Provocation is possibly the single most important cause of aggression (Anderson & Bushman, 2002). Provocations are by definition interpersonal, and come in a variety of forms including (but not limited to) the thwarting of one's goals, insults, passive-aggressiveness (if detected), and physical aggression. The well-known effect of provocation on aggression was studied in relation to gender differences in aggression in a meta-analysis (Bettencourt & Miller, 1996), which found a strong effect of provocation on aggression (median Cohen's $d = 0.86$). The meta-analysis also discovered an interesting interaction between provocation and gender effect. At low levels of provocation, males on average behaved more aggressively than females. However, at high levels of provocation this gender difference was greatly reduced. This finding illustrates the power of situational factors (provocation) to overwhelm individual difference factors (gender) given sufficient intensity.

Pain

Animal Studies

Perhaps one of the most commonly experienced aversive events is physical pain. Research on pain and aggression has a long history that focused largely on animal behavior. Although much of this research focused on the aggressive reactions of rats following painful electric stimulation, similar effects are seen across many species, including snakes, chickens, hamsters, gophers, monkeys, cats, and even turtles (Ulrich et al., 1965). A consistent finding in this literature is that pain increases aggression. However, several moderators of this effect have described mitigating and intensifying conditions.

Given that much of this research has used electric shocks, several moderation tests have focused on varying the duration, intensity, frequency, and consistency of the shocks (Ulrich et al., 1965; Tedeschi et al., 1959). In each of these tests, experimenters established optimal "windows" of effectiveness for each variable in which shocks most readily produced an aggressive response. This finding underlies a common theme in research on aversive events: that extremely low levels of aversive stimulation often fail to increase aggression due to the relatively low degree of elicited arousal, whereas at extremely high levels of aversive stimulation, the individual is overwhelmed by the sensory input, drawing attention away from the aggressive target (and toward the source of the aversive stimulus, to the sensation itself, or to potential avenues of escape) or physically weakening the person, ultimately resulting in a decline in the likelihood of aggressive responding.

Other moderators tested include the temporal length of rat pairing sessions, sensory impairment, physical orientation, size of the chamber, and the physical orientation of the rats (Ulrich & Azrin, 1962). Unsurprisingly, these situational manipulations produced considerable variation in the shock-induced aggressive behaviors. For example, chamber size produced a rather dramatic influence on the pain-aggression response; larger cage sizes (24 × 24 in.) produced a mere 2% of fighting responses following the administration of a shock compared to a 90%

response rate in smaller cages (6 × 6 in.; Ulrich & Azrin, 1965), which suggests that crowding is an unpleasant state that increases aggression.

Human Studies

These findings served as a foundation of the study of the pain–aggression link, but there are limitations in generalizing such findings to human aggression. Research on the pain–aggression effect on humans has been a difficult one to advance because of ethical considerations. Thus, much of this research has been restricted to correlational studies of individuals experiencing chronic pain. In one such study (Margari et al., 2014), chronic pain patients were more likely than control participants to indicate that they had engaged in verbal aggression toward others within the past week, but not physical aggression. Of course, causal direction is difficult to establish with such studies; perhaps chronically angry or aggressive individuals are more prone to injury.

Experimental work with humans has been restricted to mildly painful stimuli. For instance, in one study a clever method was developed in order to better understand the motivational consequences of pain elicitation (Berkowitz et al., 1981). Women asked to submerge their hands in painfully cold water delivered more painful noise blasts to a confederate when they believed that this noise would harm the confederate's performance compared to when they believed the noise would motivate the confederate to perform better, suggesting that pain induces a motivation to harm others, even when those others are not the source of the pain. Other experimental studies have investigated the cognitive repercussions of painful stimuli. For example, participants in one study first completed a measure of trait hostility, and then held their non-writing arm in a painful position (the others held their arm in a comfortable position) while rating the similarity of pairs of words (Anderson et al., 1998). Some of the words were clearly aggressive in meaning (e.g., *kill*), whereas others were words were more ambiguous (e.g., *wound*). Pain increased the perceived similarity of aggressive-ambiguous word pairs, and of aggressive-aggressive word pairs, but only for participants who scored high on trait hostility. Furthermore, the pain manipulation significantly increased feelings of anger.

Although limited in size, the relatively small research literature yielded advances in understanding some of the goals associated with the pain–aggression relationship, providing evidence for the activation of a motivation to deter painful stimulation by aggressing, in addition to a pain-induced motivation to harm others (Berkowitz, 1993b; Berkowitz et al., 1981).

Bitter Taste

Recent research suggests that bitter tastes can temporarily cause increases in aggression-related affect and aggressive behavior. One set of three laboratory experiments found that consuming a bitter-tasting drink (relative to a sweet or neutral drink) increased state hostility (anger) and aggressive behavior, regardless of whether the participants were provoked (Sagioglou & Greitemeyer, 2014).

Ambient Temperature

Ambient temperature is somewhat different from most other aversive events in that it isn't so much an "event" as it is a pervasive aversive situation. The relationship between hot temperatures and aggression is one that many of us are familiar with, if not at a scientific level, at a linguistic one. Numerous descriptions in the English language entertain the relationship between heat and aggression, as when referring to one's "hot-headed" coworker or a "heated" debate between colleagues. Research indicates that the layperson believes that heat increases aggression (Anderson & Anderson, 1998), and that this belief is so linguistically embedded that mere exposure to hot temperature words primes aggressive cognitions and triggers perceptual biases (DeWall & Bushman, 2009). Of course, a social belief that heat increases aggression does not make it so. However, there is considerable evidence that hot temperatures can and do increase aggressive and even violent behavior.

The Heat Paradox

There is a paradox between two seemingly disparate effects of heat. Heat is believed to increase aggressive behavior. However, heat makes people feel sluggish (Anderson & Anderson, 1998), reducing motivation to act. The paradox is that heat appears to simultaneously reduce energy levels while increasing aggression, an activity that usually requires considerable energy and effort.

As we will discuss in the next section, the heat-induced increase in aggression is well supported in the scientific literature. However, the reference to reduced alertness and energy is more complicated. One study found that heat stress increases physiological arousal, as measured by heart rate, but it also decreases perceived arousal (Anderson et al., 1995). Furthermore, numerous findings indicate that heat stress impairs performance on a variety of cognitive tasks (for a review, see Anderson & Anderson, 1998). Despite the complexity of this issue, the simple answer is that uncomfortable temperatures generate negative affect, which leads to a cascade of cognitive and emotional processes that tend to increase aggression (Berkowitz, 1993a, 1993b). If the apparent reduction in motivation resulting from heat does indeed reduce aggression, this reduction is overpowered by these other effects of heat discomfort, which we describe next.

Heat and Aggression: Field Studies

Many studies of temperature effects on aggressive behavior use data gathered in real-world contexts, including archival studies of violent and nonviolent crime, as well as other types of aggression. Such archival studies yield very consistent results. For instance, violent crime rates are higher on hot days than on cold days, in hot months relative to cooler months, and in hot years relative to cooler years (Anderson, 1989; Anderson et al., 1997); these effects do not occur for nonviolent crimes. This is consistent with other research showing that heat stress increases negative affect (which helps drive most violent crimes) but has little impact on aggressive thought processes (which may underlie many nonviolent crimes) (Anderson et al., 1996). And although there are plausible alternative explanations of the heat-aggression relation for each individual type of archival study, when tested empirically all of those alternative explanations have failed to account for the heat-aggression effect, leaving the original heat hypothesis as the simplest and most consistently supported explanation (for a review, see Anderson et al., 2000).

For example, one could posit that violent crime rates are higher in U.S. southern cities compared to northern cities because of cultural differences (e.g., a Southern culture of honor or violence; Nisbett & Cohen, 1996), or a higher prevalence of poverty (Guerra et al., 1995), not because of temperature effects. One method of testing such possibilities is to statistically control for the relevant alternative explanation variables, and then see whether the heat-aggression effect remains significant. When this is done, the heat-aggression effect remains significant (Anderson & Anderson, 1996). Furthermore, the Southern culture of honor and various other region-related alternative explanations can't explain seasonal effects (e.g., Anderson, 1987) or why hotter summers yield a relatively larger seasonal effect on U.S. violence rates (Anderson et al., 1998; Anderson & DeLisi, 2011).

Other field studies have examined less extreme forms of aggressive behavior. In one study (Kenrick & MacFarlane, 1986), confederate drivers frustrated other drivers in a Phoenix, Arizona, intersection by failing to drive forward when the light turned green. The aggression measure was the number of times that the target drivers (participants)—located immediately behind the confederate—honked their horns. There was a linear increase in frequency of horn honking as temperature increased. Importantly, this effect was largest among vehicles with an open window—suggesting the effects were strongest among those who were unprotected from the heat by air conditioners.

In another field study (Reifman et al., 1991), researchers collected archival data from the 1986–1988 baseball seasons. They were interested in whether the temperature recorded at the time of the game was related to the number of times in which batters were hit by a pitch during the game. As baseball enthusiasts know, "crowding the plate" can be seen as an aggressive act by a batter, and pitchers sometimes respond by throwing at or very close to such batters to "brush them back." Furthermore, pitchers sometimes throw directly at a batter in retaliation for some prior event in the game (e.g., a teammate getting hit by a pitch in the prior inning). As predicted by the heat hypothesis, even after controlling for a number of game-related factors (e.g., errors, attendance, wild pitches, walks), pitchers struck batters more frequently on hot days than on cooler days.

Heat and Aggression: Laboratory Experiments

In science, the most convincing support for a causal interpretation usually comes from experimental work. Unfortunately, experimental work on the heat-aggression effect has produced mixed results, likely because of methodological problems with early studies (for a review, see Anderson et al., 2000). A meta-analysis on early work in this area found a small but significant positive relationship between heat and aggression in those studies in which other provocations were not present, but a non-significant heat effect in those studies in which other negative events were also present. These studies were thus considered inconclusive.

Heat and Aggression: The Linear versus Curvilinear Debate

Some scholars have claimed to show a curvilinear effect of heat on aggression, with maximal aggression occurring at some moderately warm temperature (e.g., 80°F, 27°C). In other words, the shape of the curve relating heat stress to aggression—from comfortable (e.g., 72°F, 22°C) through moderately warm to hot (90°F, 32°C) was hypothesized to be an inverted "U." This suggestion comes from field studies of riots and other violent crimes (e.g., Baron & Ransberger, 1978; Cohn & Rotton, 1997), and from laboratory studies that found mixed results of heat manipulations, with hot temperatures sometimes leading to greater aggression and sometimes to less aggression (e.g., Baron & Bell, 1976). Interestingly, early laboratory experiments that led some authors to propose a downturn at hot temperatures never demonstrated a curvilinear effect; none of them manipulated temperature throughout the full range necessary to test the inverted "U."

Indeed, only one set of temperature-aggression experiments have manipulated temperatures across the range necessary to test the shape function, that is, from *comfortable* to *too warm* to *hot* (Anderson et al., 2000).[1] In the first experiment, participants did a filler task for about 10 minutes while in a cubicle set at one of the randomly assigned temperatures. Then, while still in the cubicles, they watched four brief videos of dating couples having a conversational interaction. The participants' task was to rate each interaction on 28 adjectives, 10 of which were hostility-related. The most hostile ratings were made by participants in the warm conditions, not the hot participants. This suggests that those in the hot conditions were aware of possible biases induced by being very hot and attempted to adjust their ratings accordingly.

The second experiment used the same experimental manipulation of temperature, but the main dependent variable was a measure of retaliatory aggression, in which the participant could punish a person who had aggressed against him or her in an earlier part of the study session. Of particular importance are the results from participants who had been highly provoked. On the first retaliation opportunity, the highest levels of aggression were delivered by those in the hot condition, the least by those in the comfortable condition, a linear effect. However, after this initial "outburst," hot condition participants reduce their aggressive punishments to a level almost as low as comfortable participants, whereas those in the warm condition continued to aggress at a moderately high level, thereby producing the long sought after inverted "U." These "post-outburst" aggression results matched the hostility perception results of the first experiment, further suggesting that when the aversive condition (i.e., hot ambient temperature) was obvious, there was some attempt to take the aversive situation into account in responding to provocation. Of course, in the real world an initial heat-induced outburst of aggression typically provokes the recipient of that outburst into responding aggressively before any later moderation of aggression can take place, thereby yielding linear effects of heat stress on real-world aggression and violence.

In the few field studies that have reported a downturn in aggression at very hot temperatures, the curvilinear effects have all been shown to be artifactual results of inappropriate data analyses. When appropriate data analyses were applied to the same data, there was no evidence of a downturn in aggression at even the highest temperatures (e.g., Bushman et al., 2005a, b; Carlsmith & Anderson, 1979). That is, the heat-aggression relation appears to be essentially linear. Of course, "the relationship must become curvilinear at some point, because at extremely high temperatures everyone gets sick and dies, precluding aggressive acts" (Anderson & Anderson, 1984, p. 96).

Needless to say, the effect of temperature on aggressive inclination and behavior is not a simple one. At this point in time, several conclusions and at least one speculation are warranted. It is clear that in the real world, hotter temperatures are associated with greater aggressive and violent behavior; there is no valid evidence of an inverted "U" in such studies. Laboratory data suggest that this heat effect is mediated primarily by increased irritability, but that may well include not only a direct effect on aggressive emotion, but also an indirect effect on aggressive perception or cognition, which are known to be increased by feelings of anger. In any case, more research is needed to thoroughly test both mediators and moderators of ambient temperature effects on aggression.

Stress

The experience of stress can be thought of as a much broader category of aversive conditions than those discussed in previous sections, encapsulating a wide variety of negative experiences. In this section we give examples of a number of these stressful experiences.

Several aversive experiences often associated with stress involve time pressures, threats of danger, and interpersonal confrontations. These sometimes occur while driving, especially in new or congested traffic routes. Research reveals that congested driving conditions are associated with aggressive responding (e.g., tailgating, horn honking, swearing at other drivers) and stress (Hennessy & Wiesenthal, 1999). Once stressed drivers arrive at their destination, it is likely that the driving-based stress will lead to increases in aggressive behavior at the destination, as predicted by excitation transfer theory (Zillmann, 1971). In one study (Hennessy, 2008), drivers recorded their experience of stress during a commute to work. The researchers also collected reports of workplace aggression at the end of their shift. The results showed that individuals who had experienced stress during their commute were more likely to aggress at work in the form of increased hostility directed at coworkers as well as increases in obstructive behavior. Similarly, stressors encountered at work such as confusion about roles or interpersonal conflicts, are associated with increases in aggressive behavior (e.g., making fun of others, sabotaging others' work; Chen & Spector, 1992; Taylor & Kluemper, 2012).

Crowding is another source of stress, especially when endured for long periods of time. However, high population density can be a source for positive experiences such as during a sporting event, concert, or a county fair (Bushman & Huesmann, 2010). For this reason, researchers distinguish between high population density and crowding. Density is the number of people in a given area, whereas crowding is the subjective and unpleasant feeling that there are too many people in a given area. For instance, in one study prison inmates' perceived crowding was related to increases in stress, as well as a tendency to exhibit a hostile attribution bias (Lawrence & Andrews, 2004).

Whereas these examples provide evidence of short-term effects of stress on aggression, there also are many enduring sources of stress that individuals must tolerate over extended periods of time. Persistent stress can not only produce increases in aggression in the short-term (i.e., following each instance of stress) but can build long-term propensities toward aggression through a confluence of learning processes that can complicate the seemingly simple relationship between aversive experience and aggression (e.g., by teaching the stressed individual that aggressive responses are successful and appropriate; Anderson & Bushman, 2002). These processes work in tandem with the short-term effects we've already described, producing increases in aggression that are multiplicative and not simply additive (Garmezy, 1987).

In one study (Guerra et al., 1995), for instance, nearly 2,000 children from two separate cities were followed over a two-year period. Researchers collected data directly from these children as well as their teachers and archival records. They asked children to report whether they had experienced any of 10 major negative life events, such as whether a family member had become seriously ill or whether the child had been placed in foster care. Importantly, they also measured children's beliefs about the appropriateness of aggression and their actual aggressiveness as reported by their peers and teachers. They found that across all children, low socioeconomic status was associated with increases in the likelihood of having stressful experiences, and in normative beliefs supporting aggressive behavior. However, the relationships between these variables differed as a function of ethnic group membership.

Another study examined the potential mediating role of emotional dysregulation in the stress-aggression relationship in approximately 1,500 middle school students (Herts et al., 2012). Emotional dysregulation measures assessed children's ability to understand others' emotions, their tendency to ruminate about past events, as well as their ability to regulate their own sadness and anger. Stressful life events and peer victimization served as the stress indicator, and self-reported aggressive acts were also measured. The researchers found a robust positive relationship between stress and aggression, which was mediated by emotional dysregulation. Another study found a similar pattern in which stress increased anger and hostility, which in turn increased aggression (Sprague et al., 2011). Such studies provide valuable insights into the consequences of stressful events and point the way to potential treatment options for children and adults under extreme stress.

Other longitudinal work has focused on stress in romantic relationships. In one study (Langer et al., 2008), changes observed over time in chronic stressors in domains unrelated to the relationship (e.g., work, finances, health, school) were mirrored by changes in physical aggressiveness toward the significant other (e.g., pushing, grabbing, shoving, hitting, or throwing items at one's partner). Further, these stress–aggression relationships were present for both husbands and wives. Similar findings have also been reported in other studies (e.g., Barling & Rosenbaum, 1986; Cano & Vivian, 2003).

Discussion

Depending on one's level of analysis, the effects of aversive experience on aggressive outcomes may appear to be both simple and highly complex. At the broadest level, aversive experiences reliably elicit aggression. More focused investigations, however, reveal that aversive experiences initiate a cascade of psychological consequences that result in aggressive behaviors, which then influence the person's social environment, often resulting in additional aversive experiences.

The effects of aversive experience are therefore not simply unidirectional in which negativity from the world is simply "injected" into individuals who then express it. Understanding human aggression requires a highly dynamic account that is exemplified by modern social-cognitive theories such as General Aggression Model (Anderson & Bushman, 2002). Aversive events serve as a situational risk factor that influences a variety of highly interactive internal states including aggressive affect, cognitions, and arousal. Decision-making processes then result in the execution of aggressive (or nonaggressive) behaviors. The long-term effects of aversive experience are the result of learning processes in which (broadly speaking) individuals' cognitive associations, motor propensities, beliefs, attitudes, and perceptual and attentional processes produce stability in environmental responding over time.

Indeed, there is a great deal yet to be understood about the role of aversive experience in generating aggressive and violent behavior, both in the immediate situation and developmentally over time. The motivational and emotional under-pinnings of aversive events and their consequences have received some attention, but more work is needed in developing a richer understanding of the cognitive and emotional consequences of aversive experience and their implications for behavior (e.g., Anderson et al., 1998). On an even finer grain of analysis, there is much more yet to be understood about the biological consequences of aversive events and how those consequences influence future social and emotional events. There also is a need to tie together the study of aversive events with other risk factors for aggression (i.e., examine interactions), given the ubiquity of aversive experience and its probable relevance in the production of day-to-day aggressive acts. It is our belief that General Aggression Model is a useful framework for such work, and our hope that this chapter serves to inspire this future work.

Note

1 These studies also included cold and cool temperature conditions, which will not be discussed here because of space constraints.

References

Anderson, C. A. (1987). Temperature and aggression: Effects on quarterly, yearly, and city rates of violent and nonviolent crime. *Journal of Personality and Social Psychology, 52*(6), 1161.

Anderson, C. A. (1989). Temperature and aggression: Ubiquitous effects of heat on the occurrence of human violence. *Psychological Bulletin, 106,* 74–96.

Anderson, C. A., & Anderson, D. C. (1984). Ambient temperature and violent crime: Tests of the linear and curvilinear hypotheses. *Journal of Personality and Social Psychology, 46,* 91–97.

Anderson, C. A., & Anderson, K. B. (1996). Violent crime rate studies in philosophical context: A destructive testing approach to heat and southern culture of violence effects. *Journal of Personality and Social Psychology, 70,* 740–756.

Anderson, C. A., & Anderson, K. B. (1998). Temperature and aggression: Paradox, controversy, and a (fairly) clear picture. In R. G. Geen & E. Donnerstein (Eds.), *Human aggression: Theories, research, and implications for social policy* (pp. 247–298). San Diego, CA: Academic Press.

Anderson, C. A., Anderson, K. B., & Deuser, W. E. (1996). Examining an affective aggression framework: Weapon and temperature effects on aggressive thoughts, affect, and attitudes. *Personality and Social Psychology Bulletin, 22,* 366–376.

Anderson, K. B., Anderson, C. A., Dill, K. E., & Deuser, W. E. (1998). The interactive relations between trait hostility, pain, and aggressive thoughts. *Aggressive Behavior, 24,* 161–171.

Anderson, C. A., Anderson, K. B., Dorr, N., DeNeve, K. M., & Flanagan, M. (2000). Temperature and aggression. *Chapter in Advances in Experimental Social Psychology, 32,* 63–133.

Anderson, C. A., & Bushman, B. J. (2002). Human aggression. *Annual Review of Psychology, 53,* 27–51.

Anderson, C. A., Bushman, B. J., & Groom, R. W. (1997). Hot years and serious and deadly assault: Empirical tests of the heat hypothesis. *Journal of Personality and Social Psychology, 73,* 1213–1223.

Anderson, C.A., Bushman, B.J., & Groom, R.W. (1997). Hot years and serious and deadly assault: Empirical tests of the heat hypothesis. *Journal of Personality and Social Psychology, 73*, 1213–1223.

Anderson, C. A., & DeLisi, M. (2011). Implications of global climate change for violence in developed and developing countries. In J. Forgas, A. Kruglanski, & K. Williams (Eds.), *The psychology of social conflict and aggression* (pp. 249–265). New York: Psychology Press.

Anderson, C. A., Deuser, W. E., & DeNeve, K. (1995). Hot temperatures, hostile affect, hostile cognition, and arousal: Test of a general model of affective aggression. *Personality and Social Psychology Bulletin, 21*, 434–448.

Anderson, C.A., Gentile, D.A., & Buckley, K.E. (2007). *Violent video game effects on children and adolescents: Theory, research, and public policy.* New York: Oxford University Press.

Anderson, C. A., Krull, D. S., & Weiner, B. (1996). Explanations: Processes and consequences. Chapter in E. T. Higgins & A. W. Kruglanski (Eds.), *Social psychology: Handbook of basic principles* (pp. 271–296). New York: Guilford Press.

Bandura, A. (1977). Self-efficacy: Toward a unifying theory of behavioral change. *Psychological Review, 84*(2), 191–215.

Bandura, A. (1986). *Social foundations of thought and action: A social cognitive theory.* Rockville, MD: Prentice-Hall.

Barling, J., & Rosenbaum, A. (1986). Work stressors and wife abuse. *Journal of Applied Psychology, 71*, 346–348.

Baron, R. A. & Bell, P. A. (1976). Aggression and heat: The influence of ambient temperature, negative affect, and a cooling drink on physical aggression. *Journal of Personality & Social Psychology, 33*, 245–255.

Baron, R. A. & Ransberger, V. M. (1978). Ambient temperature and the occurrence of collective violence: The "long, hot summer" revisited. *Journal of Personality and Social Psychology, 36*, 351–360.

Bartholow, B. D., Anderson, C. A., Carnagey, N. L., & Benjamin, A. J. (2005). Interactive effects of life experience and situational cues on aggression: The weapons priming effect in hunters and nonhunters. *Journal of Experimental Social Psychology, 41*, 48–60.

Berkowitz, L. (1989). Frustration-aggression hypothesis: Examination and reformulation. *Psychological Bulletin, 106*(1), 59–73.

Berkowitz, L. (1993a). *Aggression: Its causes, consequences, and control.* Doubleday, NY: McGraw-Hill Book Company.

Berkowitz, L. (1993b). Pain and aggression: Some findings and implications. *Motivation and Emotion, 17*(3), 277–293.

Berkowitz, L., Cochran, S. T., & Embree, M. C. (1981). Physical pain and the goal of aversively stimulated aggression. *Journal of Personality and Social Psychology, 40*, 687–700.

Bettencourt, B., & Miller, N. (1996). Gender differences in aggression as a function of provocation: A meta-analysis. *Psychological Bulletin, 119*(3), 422.

Bushman, B. J., & Huesmann, L. R. (2010). Aggression. In S. T. Fiske, D. T. Gilbert, & G. Lindzey (Eds.), *Handbook of social psychology* (5th ed., pp. 833–863). New York: John Wiley & Sons.

Bushman, B. J., Wang, M. C., & Anderson, C. A. (2005a). Is the curve relating temperature to aggression linear or curvilinear? Assaults and temperature in Minneapolis reexamined. *Journal of Personality and Social Psychology, 89*(1), 62–66.

Bushman, B. J., Wang, M. C., & Anderson, C. A. (2005b). Is the curve relating temperature to aggression linear or curvilinear? A response to Bell (2005) and to Cohn and Rotton (2005). *Journal of Personality and Social Psychology, 89*(1), 74–77.

Cano, A., & Vivian, D. (2003). Are life stressors associated with marital violence? *Journal of Family Psychology, 17*, 302–314.

Carlsmith, J. M., & Anderson, C. A. (1979). Ambient temperature and the occurrence of collective violence: A new analysis. *Journal of Personality and Social Psychology, 37*, 337–344.

Chen, P. Y., & Spector, P. E. (1992). Relationships of work stressors with aggression, withdrawal, theft and substance use: An exploratory study. *Journal of Occupational and Organizational Psychology, 65*, 177–184

Cohen, A. R. (1955). Social norms, arbitrariness of frustration, and status of the agent of frustration in the frustration-aggression hypothesis. *The Journal of Abnormal and Social Psychology, 51*(2), 222–226.

Cohn, E. G., & Rotton, J. (1997). Assault as a function of time and temperature: A moderator-variable time-series analysis. *Journal of Personality and Social Psychology, 72*, 1322–1334.

DeWall, N. C., & Bushman, B. J. (2009). Hot under the collar in a lukewarm environment: Words associated with hot temperature increase aggressive thoughts and hostile perceptions. *Journal of Experimental Social Psychology, 45*, 1045–1047.

Dollard, J., Miller, N. E., Doob, L. W., Mowrer, O. H., & Sears, R. R. (1939). *Frustration and aggression*. New Haven, CT: Yale University Press.

Garmezy, N. (1987). Stress, competence, and development: Continuities in the study of schizophrenic adults, children vulnerable to psychopathology, and the search for stress-resistant children. *American Journal of Orthopsychiatry, 57*, 159–174.

Gentile, D. A., & Bushman, B. J. (2012). Reassessing media violence effects using a risk and resilience approach to understanding aggression. *Psychology of Popular Media Culture, 1*(3), 138.

Guerra, N. G., Huesmann, L. R., Tolan, P. H., Van Acker, R., & Eron, L. D. (1995). Stressful events and individual beliefs as correlates of economic disadvantage and aggression among urban children. *Journal of Consulting and Clinical Psychology, 63*(4), 518.

Hennessy, D. A. (2008). The impact of commuter stress on workplace aggression. *Journal of Applied Social Psychology, 38*(9), 2315–2335.

Hennessy, D. A., & Wiesenthal, D. L. (1999). Traffic congestion, driver stress, and driver aggression. *Aggressive Behavior, 25*, 409–423.

Herts, K. L., McLaughlin, K. A., & Hatzenbuehler, M. L. (2012). Emotion dysregulation as a mechanism linking stress exposure to adolescent aggressive behavior. *Journal of Abnormal Child Psychology, 40*, 1111–1122.

Kenrick, D. T., & MacFarlane, S. W. (1986). Ambient temperature and horn honking: A field study of the heat/aggression relationship. *Environment and Behavior, 18*(2), 179–191.

Kregarman, J. J., & Worchel, P. (1961). Arbitrariness of frustration and aggression. *The Journal of Abnormal and Social Psychology, 63*(1), 183–187.

Langer, A., Lawrence, E., & Barry, R. A. (2008). Using a vulnerability-stress-adaptation framework to predict physical aggression trajectories in newlywed marriage. *Journal of Consulting and Clinical Psychology, 76*(5), 756–768.

Lawrence, C., & Andrews, K. (2004). The influence of perceived prison crowding on male inmates' perception of aggressive events. *Aggressive Behavior, 30* (4), 273–283.

Margari, F., Lorusso, M., Matera, E., Pastore, A., Zagaria, G., Bruno, F., . . . & Margari, L. (2014). Aggression, impulsivity, and suicide risk in benign chronic pain patients–a cross-sectional study. *Neuropsychiatric Disease and Treatment, 10*, 1613.

Nisbett, R. E., & Cohen, D. (1996). *Culture of honor: The psychology of violence in the south*. Boulder, CO: Westview Press.

Pastore, N. (1952). The role of arbitrariness in the frustration-aggression hypothesis. *The Journal of Abnormal and Social Psychology, 47*(3), 728.

Reifman, A., Larrick, R., & Fein, S. (1991). Temper and temperature on the diamond: The heat-aggression relationship in major league baseball. *Personality and Social Psychology Bulletin, 17*(5), 580–585.

Rothaus, P., & Worchel, P. (1960). The inhibition of aggression under non-arbitrary frustration. *Journal of Personality, 28*, 108–117.

Sagioglou, C., & Greitemeyer, T. (2014). Bitter taste causes hostility. *Personality and Social Psychology Bulletin, 40*, 1589–1597.

Sprague, J., Verona, E., Kalkhoff, W., & Kilmer, A. (2011). Moderators and mediators of the stress-aggression relationship: Executive function and state anger. *Emotion, 11*(1), 61–73.

Taylor, S. G., & Kluemper, D. H. (2012). Linking perceptions of role stress and incivility to workplace aggression: The moderating role of personality. *Journal of Occupational Health Psychology, 17*(3), 316–329.

Tedeschi, R. E., Tedeschi, D. H., Mucha, A., Cook, L., Mattis, P. A., & Fellows, E. J. (1959). Effects of various centrally acting drugs on fighting behavior of mice. *Journal of Pharmacology and Experimental Therapeutics, 125*(1), 28–34.

Ulrich, R. E., & Azrin, N. H. (1962). Reflective fighting in response to aversive stimulation. *Journal of Experimental Analysis of Behavior, 5*(4), 511.

Ulrich, R. E., Hutchinson, R. R., & Azrin, N. H. (1965). Pain-elicited aggression. *The Psychological Record, 15*, 111–126.

Zillmann, D. (1971). Excitation transfer in communication-mediated aggressive behavior. *Journal of Experimental Social Psychology, 7*(4), 419–434.

Zillmann, D., & Bryant, J. (1974). Effect of residual excitation on the emotional response to provocation and delayed aggressive behavior. *Journal of Personality and Social Psychology, 30*(6), 782–791.

10

OSTRACISM AND AGGRESSION

*Eric D. Wesselmann, Dongning Ren,
and Kipling D. Williams*

Humans desire to connect socially with others, and they experience negative physical and psychological outcomes when this need is thwarted (Baumeister & Leary, 1995). Ostracism (i.e., being excluded and ignored) and other forms of social exclusion are common negative social experiences that thwart this need for social connection (Williams, 2009).[1] Ostracism can occur *physically* (e.g., being exiled or incarcerated; Boehm, 1986; Mahdi, 1986; Zippelius, 1986), *socially* (being ignored and excluded while in the physical face-to-face presence of others; Warburton et al., 2006; Wesselmann et al., 2012; Williams & Sommer, 1997), or in *cyber* interactions (e.g., chat rooms, text messages, video chats, social networking sites, and online games; Goodacre & Zadro, 2010; Smith & Williams, 2004; Tobin et al., 2015; Williams et al., 2000; Williams et al., 2002; Wolf et al., 2014). Even minimal social cues that suggest one is relationally devalued (e.g., averted eye gaze, hurtful laughter, or uncomfortable silences) can elicit feelings of ostracism (Böckler et al., 2014; Klages & Wirth, 2014; Koudenburg et al., 2011; Wirth et al., 2010).

Ostracism's Effects over Time

Ostracism causes a range of negative physical and psychological outcomes. The Temporal Model of Ostracism (Figure 10.1; Williams, 2009) theorizes a three-stage temporal structure to explain the effects of ostracism on individuals. In the *Reflexive* stage, ostracized individuals immediately experience pain, as demonstrated in research using both neurological and self-report measures (Eisenberger et al., 2003; Kross et al., 2011; MacDonald & Leary, 2005; Onoda et al., 2010). Additionally, ostracized individuals experience heightened cortisol levels and cardiovascular problems (Dickerson & Kemeny, 2004; Gunnar et al., 2003; Josephs et al., 2012; Moor et al., 2010); increased negative affect, such as anger, jealousy,

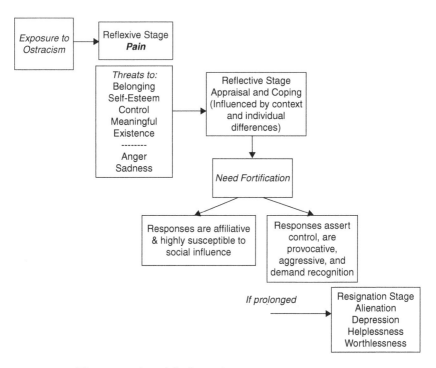

FIGURE 10.1 The temporal model of ostracism

sadness, and shame (Chow et al., 2008; Gerber & Wheeler, 2009; Harmon-Jones et al., 2009; Peterson et al., 2011; Westermann et al., 2015; Williams, 2009); decreased self-regulation (Baumeister et al., 2005; DeWall et al., 2012; Oaten et al., 2008); increased ruminative thought patterns (Zwolinski, 2012); and feelings of dehumanization (Bastian & Haslam, 2010). Ostracism also thwarts core psychological needs: specifically, an individual's need for *belonging, self-esteem, control,* and *meaningful existence* (Williams, 2009). These negative effects occur regardless of who (stranger, acquaintance, or loved one) is the source of the ostracism or their motive behind the treatment (Nezlek et al., 2012; Williams, 2009). These negative effects have few situational or dispositional moderators, demonstrating that ostracism is a ubiquitously adverse experience (Wesselmann et al., 2015).

The *Reflective* stage focuses on the cognitive and behavioral processes that ostracized individuals use to recover thwarted basic needs (Williams, 2009). Experimental data suggest that most ostracized individuals begin recovering within minutes after the event occurs (Wirth & Williams, 2009; cf. Buelow et al., 2015). Ostracized individuals can use several different cognitive strategies to alleviate their pain, such as recalling ostracism from an outsider's (compared to first-person) perspective (Lau et al., 2009), focusing their attention on the present moment (Molet et al., 2013), or self-affirming social-relevant values or relationships (Knowles et al., 2010).

Moreover, ostracized individuals can recover by reminding themselves of a posi-tive social relationship, whether it be with another person, a deity, a pet, or a symbolic/parasocial relationship with a fictitious character (e.g., Aydin et al., 2010; Derrick et al., 2009; Laurin et al., 2014; McConnell et al., 2011; Pfundmair et al., 2015; Twenge et al., 2007).

Paradoxical Behavioral Responses to Ostracism

Most research on the Reflective stage investigates the behavioral strategies that facilitate basic need recovery from ostracism. Many researchers have argued that humans are biologically predisposed to form social connections with others, and that when these connections are threatened they should be motivated immediately to repair these connections or find alternative relationships to fulfill their need to belong (e.g., Lieberman, 2013; Maner et al., 2007; Williams, 2009). Indeed, sev-eral studies demonstrate that ostracized individuals behave more *pro*-socially than included individuals, and these reactions seem to be in the service of reestablish-ing social connections to others (see Wesselmann et al., 2015, for review).

Paradoxically, research demonstrates that ostracized individuals also behave more *anti*-socially than included individuals. Researchers have measured aggres-sion in various ways, ranging from behavioral temptations for physical and social aggression, to actual behaviors such as providing a target negative evaluations, delivering aversive noise blasts, ostensibly forcing someone to consume hot sauce when the person previously indicated hating spicy food, and exhibiting counter-productive work behaviors in the organizational context (Buckley et al., 2004; Hitlan & Noel, 2009; Twenge et al., 2001; Warburton et al., 2006). This aggression is not simply retaliatory. Indeed, ostracism elicits an aggressive response toward the *source* of ostracism (Buckley et al., 2004; Bushman & Baumeister, 1998; Chow et al., 2008; Twenge et al., 2001; Twenge & Campbell, 2003; van Beest et al., 2012), as well as *bystanders* (Gaertner et al., 2008) and *innocent* targets (Twenge et al., 2001; Twenge & Campbell, 2003; Warburton et al., 2006; Wesselmann et al., 2010). Even simply recalling a time when one had been ostracized is enough to evoke aggres-sive responses (Riva et al., 2011).

Theorists argue that these two contradictory patterns can be reconciled: pro- and anti-social responses should be focused on fortifying specific psychological needs, depending upon what is most important (or simply most available) to the ostracized person (DeWall & Richman, 2011; Smart Richman & Leary, 2009; Twenge, 2005; Williams, 2007; Williams & Wesselmann, 2011). Specifically, pro-social behaviors should fortify *inclusionary* needs (belonging and self-esteem) because they are more likely to facilitate social connections, whereas anti-social behaviors should fortify *power/provocation* needs (control and meaningful exist-ence) because these behaviors should at least provoke acknowledgement if someone cannot achieve re-inclusion or anticipates future ostracism (Gerber & Wheeler, 2009; Sommer & Bernieri, 2014; Williams, 2009).

Experimental research supports the argument that ostracized individuals respond preferentially based on specific needs; we will focus on the link between power/provocation needs and aggression (see Wesselmann et al., 2015, for a review of the link between inclusionary needs and pro-social behavior). Previous research demonstrated that only individuals' threatened need for control mediated the link between ostracism and aggression (Schoel et al., 2014). Other research suggests that participants' self-control resources help mitigate aggressive responses to ostracism (Chester et al., 2014; Pfundmair et al., 2015). Further, experimentally fortifying ostracized individuals' sense of control either directly or symbolically reduces their psychological distress and ultimately their aggressive responses (Bozin & Yoder, 2008; Huang et al., 2013; Kuehn et al., 2015; Warburton et al., 2006; Waytz et al., 2015; Zhou et al., 2009). Conversely, additional control threats can exacerbate aggressive responses to ostracism. Individuals who are ostracized unexpectedly experience a threat to their predictive control—they perceive a deficiency in their ability to read social signals. Subsequently, they show more aggressive responses than individuals who can predict future ostracism (Wesselmann et al., 2010).

Thus far, experimental research has focused on threats and fortification to the need for control, but neglected the need for meaningful existence. One unpublished study provided preliminary evidence that when given both pro- and anti-social responses, ostracized participants preferred the responses that had the most meaningful impact regardless of social acceptability—they only showed a preference for anti-social responses when the targets were those who ostracized them (Domachowska et al., 2014). Other research demonstrated that unfair ostracism (compared with fair ostracism) negatively impacted both control and meaningful existence needs more than belonging and self-esteem needs, and also increased anti-social behavioral temptations (Tuscherer et al., 2015). It is important to note that although ostracism research treats each of the four needs as conceptually distinct, typically they are intercorrelated and often combined into one aggregate measure (Williams, 2009). Thus, it is possible that by fortifying control or meaningful existence, there may be some fortification spillover into belonging and self-esteem and vice versa. For example, some research finds that fortifying the inclusionary needs can also reduce ostracized participants' desire to respond aggressively (DeWall et al., 2010; Twenge et al., 2007).

Individual Differences in Aggressive Responses

Even though experimental research demonstrates that individuals respond to ostracism with aggression, not all individuals respond equally. Research suggests that certain individual differences intensify aggressive responses to ostracism. For example, individuals differ in their sensitivity to rejection (i.e., how commonly they expect and readily perceive rejection cues; Downey & Feldman, 1996), and this should influence their reactions to specific instances of ostracism. Researchers typically assess rejection sensitivity by asking participants to imagine a variety of situations (e.g., "You ask someone in one of your classes to coffee") in which they could be accepted or rejected by others, and participants indicate 1) how anxious they would be about the outcome and 2) how likely they would be accepted in each situation. In laboratory research, ostracized individuals who are higher in rejection sensitivity respond more aggressively than individuals lower in rejection sensitivity (Ayduk et al., 2008; Dotan-Eliaz et al., 2009; Pfundmair et al., 2015).

Additionally, individuals differ in the degree to which they believe partners in interpersonal relationships either are inherently compatible or they are not; any relationship struggles are diagnostic that the relationship is doomed (destiny beliefs; Knee et al., 2003). Research demonstrates that individuals who endorse these types of beliefs also respond more aggressively to laboratory manipulations of ostracism compared with individuals lower in these traits (Chen et al., 2012). Ostracized individuals high in these traits likely assume that they can expect ostracism in the future, and thus the power/provocation need cluster should be more salient to them than the inclusionary needs cluster. Therefore, these individuals should favor anti-social responses over pro-social responses.

Furthermore, individuals high in narcissism respond more negatively to ostracism (and other social threats) than individuals low in narcissism (Chester & DeWall, 2015; Thomaes et al., 2011; Twenge & Campbell, 2003). Narcissistic individuals think they are special people who deserve special treatment, and when they do not get the special treatment they think they are entitled to, they respond to others aggressively (e.g., Bushman & Baumeister, 1998). One explanation is that, with inflated self-esteem, narcissistic individuals expect more inclusion (and less ostracism) in social interactions than individuals who are low in narcissism. Given that unexpected ostracism provides a double threat and intensifies aggressive responses, it is not surprising that narcissistic individuals respond the most aggressively to ostracism.

Chronic Ostracism and Extreme Violent Outcomes

Some individuals experience ostracism repeatedly and find any attempts to become reconnected thwarted consistently. These individuals enter the *Resignation* stage, accepting their outcast status and experiencing extreme negative outcomes due to exacerbated need threat (i.e., feelings of alienation, depression, helplessness, and meaninglessness; Williams, 2009). Some chronically ostracized individuals may disengage from social relationships to avoid future ostracism (Leitner et al., 2014; Wesselmann et al., 2014), but others may choose to respond with extreme hostility.

School Shootings

Systematic analyses of mass violence in schools suggest that perpetrators experienced (or at least perceived) chronic ostracism by their peers, teachers, and perhaps others in the larger community (Leary et al., 2003; Oksanen et al., 2014; Sommer et al., 2014; Williams & Wesselmann, 2011). Ostracism increases the degree to which individuals develop hostile cognitions, encouraging them to perceive individual acts as aggressive and likely to occur in the future; these cognitions are a key mediator in the link between ostracism and aggressive responses (DeWall et al., 2009; Reijntjes et al., 2011). It is likely that chronically ostracized individuals would develop hostile attributional biases that would make them dispositionally aggressive (i.e., Anderson & Bushman, 2002) to any negative social interaction whether it directly or indirectly made them feel ostracized. Further, the more an individual comes to view him or herself as an outsider, the more everyone else may seem like an antagonistic *collective* worthy of revenge (Gaertner et al., 2008); aggression against any one "member" (even an innocent person) may serve to satisfy the ostracized person's desire to fortify his or her need for control or meaningful existence. Importantly, ostracism seems to be a necessary component for understanding school shootings, but it is not sufficient by itself to produce mass violence. A systematic profile of school shooters between 1995 and 2001 found that in addition to perceived chronic ostracism, most shooters also exhibited one or more of three risk factors: psychological problems, familiarity with and interest in weapons, and fascination with morbid topics (Leary et al., 2003).

Radicalization and Extreme Groups

Research demonstrates that experimental manipulations of ostracism make individuals focus more on re-inclusion strategies, including showing interest in joining new groups (Maner et al., 2007; Molden et al., 2009). Further, ostracism manipulations make individuals more susceptible to social influence tactics (i.e., compliance, conformity, and obedience; Carter-Sowell et al., 2008; DeWall, 2010; Riva et al., 2014; Williams et al., 2000). Many of these studies involve encouraging ostracized individuals to engage in mundane and harmless behaviors, but some studies find that ostracized individuals may engage in illegal behavior (i.e., drug use), especially if it is in the service of social connection (DeWall & Richman, 2011; Mead et al., 2011).

It is possible that some individuals who experience ostracism chronically may become desperate for re-inclusion by anyone, even extreme groups (e.g., predatory or extremist religious cults; Wesselmann & Williams, 2010) or homegrown terrorist organizations (Knapton, 2014). Theory and research suggest that terrorists perceive their actions as a way to regain a sense of meaning, significance, or control (Jonas et al., 2014; Kruglanski, 2003; Kruglanski et al., 2009; Kruglanski & Orehek, 2011). Laboratory experiments demonstrate that individuals who are ostracized tend to derogate the ostracizers and perceive them as a collective outgroup (Gaertner et al., 2008), and that ostracized groups are more aggressive than ostracized individuals (van Beest et al., 2012). Thus, individuals who perceive they are members of groups that are chronically ostracized by larger society may seek out others who feel similarly disenchanted, and if these groups adopt a view that aggression is the best way to reestablish a sense of control and meaning, terrorist activities may become an attractive option (Knapton, 2014). Further, individuals who perceive their social group in familial terms (i.e., *identity fusion*) may become increasingly devoted to their group after experiencing ostracism (Gómez et al., 2011), which in turn can facilitate one's willingness to kill or be killed for their group (Swann et al., 2010).

Reducing Aggression?

What may be some potential strategies to help reduce aggressive responses to ostracism? At the individual level, studies suggest there may be biomedical treatments that can mitigate the psychological distress individuals experience during ostracism. Ostracism is experienced neurologically as pain; thus, chemicals that can numb pain receptors reduce the negative effects of a single ostracism experience (Deckman et al., 2014; DeWall et al., 2010). Noninvasive stimulation of brain regions associated with pain regulation can also reduce the distress of and aggressive responses to ostracism (Riva et al., 2012; Riva et al., 2015). There may also be cognitive tactics for reducing aggression that do not necessitate biomedical interventions. Encouraging individuals to focus more on long-term rather than short-term future outcomes (Balliet & Ferris, 2013), or to develop self-control/ mindfulness skills (Denson, 2015; Molet et al., 2013), may reduce the likelihood of responding aggressively to ostracism.

Little research directly addresses how to discourage ostracized individuals or groups from engaging in large-scale violence (e.g., school shootings or terrorist activities). Many individuals experience ostracism daily (Nezlek et al., 2012), but most do not engage in violence or terrorist activities. Ostracism could be a triggering mechanism that motivates individuals with psychological problems and a fascination with death and weapons (Leary et al., 2003), either to strike out violently alone, or to seek out groups that feel similarly (especially if those groups have access to weaponry). For these individuals or groups, chronic exposure to ostracism with little hope of re-inclusion may lead them to consider violence or terrorism as the only way to achieve desired control and attention. Groups who are ostracized by other groups or society generally may develop tighter in-group identities and have less tolerance of deviation within the group and a stronger commitment to group goals. This climate, combined with the possibility that group members reinforce calls for provocational action to achieve their goals, might provoke ostracized groups to violence more quickly than it would for individuals.

An ideal solution to prevent violent responses might be to change the geopolitical climate such that no individuals or social groups felt ostracized from larger society, but this type of solution seems highly unlikely given the universality of the use of ostracism across cultures and even species (Williams, 2009). An alternative option to focus on in the short term might be to change some of the beliefs that these individuals and groups hold about aggression, encouraging them to focus on alternative ways of exerting control or meaning that are productive and peaceful (e.g., Lickel et al., 2006). Regarding individuals who seek out extremist groups, an additional strategy would be to reduce the desire for individuals to join these groups initially. Theory and data suggest that when individuals feel ostracized by the larger culture because of their race, ethnicity, or religion (e.g., citizens or immigrants of Arabic descent, Muslims), they begin to feel less connected with the dominant culture and thus may find homegrown terrorist groups to be a welcoming community that affords them ways to assert their social identity (Knapton, 2014; Schaafsma & Williams, 2012). Thus, societies may curb this tendency by reducing the marginalization of certain social groups within their borders and instead emphasizing an inclusive collective identity that values diversity of its members while welcoming members of all social groups within its collective.

Note

1 Researchers often use the terms exclusion, ostracism, and rejection synonymously. However, there are debates about how these and other phenomena (e.g., discrimination, bullying) differ theoretically and empirically (Smart Richman & Leary, 2009; Williams, 2009). We acknowledge these debates but choose to use the term *ostracism* for simplicity because most of the outcomes we discuss occur similarly across phenomena, regardless of whether or not one is being explicitly ignored (Wesselmann et al., 2016).

References

Anderson, C. A., & Bushman, B. J. (2002). Human aggression. *Annual Review of Psychology, 53*, 27–51.

Aydin, N., Fischer, P., & Frey, D. (2010). Turing to God in the face of ostracism: Effects of social exclusion on religiousness. *Personality and Social Psychology Bulletin, 36*, 742–753.

Ayduk, Ö., Gyurak, A., & Luerssen, A. (2008). Individual differences in the rejection–aggression link in the hot sauce paradigm: The case of rejection sensitivity. *Journal of Experimental Social Psychology, 44*, 775–782.

Balliet, D., & Ferris, D. (2013). Ostracism and prosocial behavior: A social dilemma perspective. *Organizational Behavior & Human Decision Processes, 120*, 298–308.

Bastian, B., & Haslam, N. (2010). Excluded from humanity: The dehumanizing effects of social ostracism. *Journal of Experimental Social Psychology, 46*, 107–113.

Baumeister, R. F., DeWall, C. N., Ciarocco, N. J., & Twenge, J. M. (2005). Social exclusion impairs self-regulation. *Journal of Personality and Social Psychology, 88*, 589–604.

Baumeister, R. F., & Leary, M. R. (1995). The need to belong: Desire for inter-personal attachments as a fundamental human motivation. *Psychological Bulletin, 117*, 497–529.

Böckler, A., Hömke, P., & Sebanz, N. (2014). Invisible man: Exclusion from shared attention affects gaze behavior and self-reports. *Social Psychological and Personality Science, 5*, 140–148.

Boehm, C. (1986). Capital punishment in tribal Montenegro: Implications for law, biology, and theory of social control. *Ethology and Sociobiology, 7*, 305–320.

Bozin, M. A., & Yoder, J. D. (2008). Social status, not gender alone, is implicated in different reactions by women and men to social ostracism. *Sex Roles, 58*, 713–720.

Buckley, K. E., Winkel, R. E., & Leary, M. R. (2004). Reactions to acceptance and rejection: Effects of level and sequence of relational evaluation. *Journal of Experimental Social Psychology, 40*, 14–28.

Buelow, M. T., Okdie, B. M., Brunell, A. B., & Trost, Z. (2015). Stuck in a moment and you cannot get out of it: The lingering effects of ostracism on cognition and satisfaction of basic needs. *Personality and Individual Differences, 76*, 39–43.

Bushman, B. J., & Baumeister, R. F. (1998). Threatened egotism, narcissism, self-esteem, and direct and displaced aggression: Does self-love or self-hate lead to violence? *Journal of Personality and Social Psychology, 75*, 219–229.

Carter-Sowell, A. R., Chen, Z., & Williams, K. D. (2008). Ostracism increases social susceptibility. *Social Influence, 3*, 143–153.

Chen, Z., DeWall, C., Poon, K., & Chen, E. (2012). When destiny hurts: Implicit theories of relationships moderate aggressive responses to ostracism. *Journal of Experimental Social Psychology, 48*, 1029–1036.

Chester, D. S., & DeWall, C. N. (2015). Sound the alarm: The effect of narcissism on retaliatory aggression is moderated by dACC reactivity to rejection. *Journal of Personality*. DOI:10.1111/jopy.12164.

Chester, D. S., Eisenberger, N. I., Pond Jr, R. S., Richman, S. B., Bushman, B. J., & De Wall, C. N. (2014). The interactive effect of social pain and executive functioning on aggression: An fMRI experiment. *Social Cognitive and Affective Neuroscience, 9*, 699–704.

Chow, R. M., Tiedens, L. Z., & Govan, C. L. (2008). Excluded emotions: The role of anger in antisocial responses to ostracism. *Journal of Experimental Social Psychology, 44*, 896–903.

Deckman, T., DeWall, C. N., Way, B. Gilman, R., & Richman, S. (2014). Can marijuana reduce social pain? *Social and Personality Psychology Science, 5*, 131–139.

Denson, T. F. (2015). Four promising psychological interventions for reducing reactive aggression. *Current Opinion in Behavioral Sciences, 3*, 136–141.

DeWall, C. N. (2010). Forming a basis for acceptance: Excluded people form attitudes to agree with potential affiliates. *Social Influence, 5*, 245–260.

DeWall, C. N., Gilman, R., Sharif, V., Carboni, I., & Rice, K. G. (2012). Left out, sluggardly, and blue: Low self-control mediates the relationship between ostracism and depression. *Personality and Individual Differences, 53*, 832–837.

DeWall, C. N., MacDonald, G., Webster, G. D., Masten, C., Baumeister, R. F., Powell, C., Combs, D., Schurtz, D. R., Stillman, T. F., Tice, D. M., & Eisenberger, N. I. (2010). Acetaminophen reduces social pain: Behavioral and neural evidence. *Psychological Science*, 21, 931–937.

DeWall, C. N., & Richman, S. B. (2011). Social exclusion and the desire to reconnect. *Social and Personality Psychology Compass, 5*, 919–932.

DeWall, C. N., Twenge, J. M., Bushman, B., Im, C., & Williams, K. D. (2010). A little acceptance goes a long way: Applying Social Impact Theory to the rejection-aggression link. *Social Psychological and Personality Science, 1*, 168–174.

DeWall, C. N., Twenge, J. M., Gitter, S. A., & Baumeister, R. F. (2009). It's the thought that counts: The role of hostile cognition in shaping aggressive responses to social exclusion. *Journal of Personality and Social Psychology, 96*, 45–59.

Derrick, J. L., Gabriel, S., & Hugenberg, K. (2009). Social surrogacy: How favored television programs provide the experience of belonging. *Journal of Experimental Social Psychology, 45*, 352–362.

Dickerson, S. S., & Kemeny, M. E. (2004). Acute stressors and cortisol responses: A theoretical integration and synthesis of laboratory research. *Psychological Bulletin, 130*, 355–391.

Domachowska, I., Schade, H., Mitchell, A., & Williams, K. D. (2014). *Hurt or help, I just want to matter: Reconciling prosocial and aggressive responses to ostracism.* Amsterdam: European Association of Experimental Social Psychology.

Dotan-Eliaz, O., Sommer, K. L., & Rubin, Y. S. (2009). Multilingual groups: Effects of linguistic ostracism on felt rejection and anger, coworker attraction, perceived team potency, and creative performance. *Basic and Applied Social Psychology, 31*, 363–375.

Downey, G., & Feldman, S. I. (1996). Implications of rejection sensitivity for intimate relationships. *Journal of Personality and Social Psychology, 70*, 1327–1343.

Eisenberger, N. I., Lieberman, M. D., & Williams, K. D. (2003). Does rejection hurt? An fMRI study of social exclusion. *Science, 302*, 290–292.

Gaertner, L., Iuzzini, J., & O'Mara, E. M. (2008). When rejection by one fosters aggression against many: Multiple-victim aggression as a consequence of social rejection and perceived groupness. *Journal of Experimental Social Psychology, 44*, 958–970.

Gerber, J., & Wheeler, L. (2009). On being rejected: A meta-analysis of experimental research on rejection. *Perspectives on Psychological Science, 4*, 468–488.

Gómez, Á., Morales, J. F., Hart, S., Vázquez, A., & Swann, W. B. (2011). Rejected and excluded forevermore, but even more devoted irrevocable ostracism intensifies loyalty to the group among identity-fused persons. *Personality and Social Psychology Bulletin, 37*, 1574–1586.

Goodacre, R., & Zadro, L. (2010). O-Cam: A new paradigm for investigating the effects of ostracism. *Behavioral Research Methods, 42*, 768–774.

Gunnar, M. R., Sebanc, A. M., Tout, K., Donzella, B., & van Dulmen, M. M. H. (2003). Peer rejection, temperament, and cortisol activity in preschoolers. *Developmental Psychology, 43*, 346–368.

Harmon-Jones, E., Peterson, C. K., & Haris, C. R. (2009). Jealousy: Novel methods and neural correlates. *Emotion, 9*, 113–117.

Hitlan, R. T., & Noel, J. (2009). The influence of workplace exclusion and personality on counterproductive work behaviours: An interactionist perspective. *European Journal of Work and Organizational Psychology, 18*, 477–502.

Huang, J. Y., Ackerman, J. M., & Bargh, J. A. (2013). Superman to the rescue: Simulating physical invulnerability attenuates exclusion-related interpersonal biases. *Journal of Experimental Social Psychology, 49*, 349–354.

Jonas, E., McGregor, I., Klackl, J., Agroskin, D., Fritsche, I., Holbrook, C., . . . & Quirin, M. (2014). Threat and defense: From anxiety to approach. *Advances in Experimental Social Psychology, 49*, 219–286.

Josephs, R. A., Telch, M. J., Hixon, J. G., Evans, J. J., Lee, H., Knopik, V. S., McGeary, J. E., Hariri, A. R., & Beevers, C. G. (2012). Genetic and hormonal sensitivity to threat: Testing a serotonin transporter genotype × testosterone interaction. *Psychoneuroendocrinology, 37*, 752–761.

Klages, S. V., & Wirth, J. H. (2014). Excluded by laughter: Laughing until it hurts someone else. *The Journal of Social Psychology, 154*, 8–13.

Knapton, H. M. (2014). The recruitment and radicalisation of western citizens: Does ostracism have a role in homegrown terrorism? *Journal of European Psychology Students, 5*, 38–48.

Knee, C. R., Patrick, H., & Lonsbary, C. (2003). Implicit theories of relationships: Orientations toward evaluation and cultivation. *Personality and Social Psychology Review, 7*, 41–55.

Knowles, M. L., Lucas, G. M., Molden, D. C., Gardner, W. L., & Dean, K. K. (2010). There's no substitute for belonging: Self-affirmation following social and nonsocial threats. *Personality and Social Psychology Bulletin, 36*, 173–186.

Koudenburg, N., Postmes, T., & Gordijn, E. H. (2011). Disrupting the flow: How brief silences in group conversations affect social needs. *Journal of Experimental Social Psychology, 47*, 512–515.

Kross, E., Berman, M. G., Mischel, W., Smith, E. E., & Wager, T. D. (2011). Social rejection shares somatosensory representations with physical pain. *Proceedings of the National Academy of Sciences, 108*, 6270–6275.

Kruglanski, A. W. (2003, April). *Terrorism as a tactic of minority influence*. Paper presented at F. Buttera and J. Levine (Chairs). Active Minorities: Hoping and Coping. Grenoble, France.

Kruglanski, A. W., Chen, X., Dechesne, M., Fishman, S., & Edward, O. (2009). Fully committed: Suicide bombers' motivation and the quest for personal significance. *Political Psychology, 30*, 331–357.

Kruglanski, A. W., & Orehek, E. (2011). The role of the quest for personal significance in motivating terrorism. In J. P. Forgas, A. W. Kruglanski, & K. D. Williams (Eds.), *The psychology of social conflict and aggression* (pp. 153–164). New York: Psychology Press.

Kuehn, M. M., Chen, S., & Gordon, A.M. (2015). Having a thicker skin: Social power buffers the negative effects of social rejection. *Social Psychological and Personality Science,* DOI:1948550615580170.

Lau, G., Moulds, M. L., & Richardson, R. (2009). Ostracism: How much it hurts depends on how you remember it. *Emotion, 9*, 430–434

Laurin, K., Schumann, K., & Holmes, J. G. (2014). A relationship with God? Connecting with the divine to assuage fears of interpersonal rejection. *Social Psychological and Personality Science, 5*, 777–785.

Leary, M. R., Kowalski, R. M., Smith, L., & Phillips, S. (2003). Teasing, rejection, and violence: Case studies of the school shootings. *Aggressive Behavior, 29*, 202–214.

Leitner, J. B., Hehman, E., Deegan, M. P., & Jones, J. M. (2014). Adaptive disengagement buffers self-esteem from negative social feedback. *Personality and Social Psychology Bulletin, 40*, 1435–1450,

Lickel, B., Miller, N., Stenstrom, D. M., Denson, T. F., & Schmader, T. (2006). Vicarious retribution: The role of collective blame in intergroup aggression. *Personality and Social Psychology Review, 10*, 372–390.

Lieberman, M. D. (2013). *Social: Why our brains are wired to connect*. New York: Crown Publishers.

MacDonald, G., & Leary, M. R. (2005). Why does social exclusion hurt? The relationship between social and physical pain. *Psychological Bulletin, 131*, 202–223.

Mahdi, N. Q., (1986). Pukhtunwali: Ostracism and honor among the Pathan Hill Tribes. *Ethology and Sociobiology, 7*, 295–304.

Maner, J. K., DeWall, C. N., Baumeister, R. F., & Schaller, M. (2007). Does social exclusion motivate interpersonal reconnection? Resolving the" porcupine problem." *Journal of Personality and Social Psychology, 92*, 42–55.

McConnell, A. R., Brown, C. M., Shoda, M. T., Stayton, L. E., & Martin, C. E. (2011). Friends with benefits: On the positive consequences of pet ownership. *Journal of Personality and Social Psychology, 101*, 1239–1252.

Mead, N. L., Baumeister, R. F., Stillman, T. F., Rawn, C. D., & Vohs, K. D. (2011). Social exclusion causes people to spend and consume strategically in the service of affiliation. *Journal of Consumer Research, 37*, 902–919.

Molden, D.C., Lucas, G. M., Gardner, W. L., Dean, K., & Knowles, M. L. (2009). Motivations for prevention or promotion following social exclusion: Being rejected versus being ignored. *Journal of Personality and Social Psychology, 96*, 415–431.

Molet, M., Macquet, B., Lefebvre, O., & Williams, K. D. (2013). A focused attention intervention for coping with ostracism. *Consciousness and Cognition, 22*, 1262–1270.

Moor, B. G., Crone, E. A., & van der Molen, M. W. (2010). The heartbreak of social rejection: Heart rate deceleration in response to unexpected peer rejection. *Psychological Science, 21*, 1326–1333.

Nezlek, J. B., Wesselmann, E. D., Wheeler, L., & Williams, K. D. (2012). Ostracism in everyday life. *Group Dynamics: Theory, Research, and Practice, 16*, 91–104.

Oaten, M., Williams, K. D., Jones, A., & Zadro, L. (2008). The effects of ostracism on self-regulation in the socially anxious. *Journal of Social and Clinical Psychology, 27*, 471–504.

Oksanen, A., Kaltiala-Heino, R., Kiilakoski, T., & Lindberg, N. (2014). Bullying, romantic rejection, and conflicts with teachers: A Finnish perspective. *International Journal of Developmental Science, 8*, 37–41.

Onoda, K., Okamoto, Y., Nakashima, K., Nittono, H., Yoshimura, S., Yamawaki, S., Yamaguchi, S., & Ura, M. (2010). Does low self-esteem enhance social pain? The relationship between trait self-esteem and anterior cingulate cortex activation induced by ostracism. *Social Cognitive and Affective Neuroscience, 5*, 385–391.

Peterson, C. K., Gravens, L. C., & Harmon-Jones, E. (2011). Asymmetric frontal cortical activity and negative affective responses to ostracism. *Social Cognitive and Affective Neuroscience, 6*, 277–285.

Pfundmair, M., DeWall, C. N., Fries, V., Geiger, B., Krämer, T., Krug, S., Frey, D., & Aydin, N. (2015). Sugar or spice: Using I³ metatheory to understand how and why glucose reduces rejection-related aggression. *Aggressive Behavior.* DOI: 10.1002/ab.21593

Pfundmair, M., Eyssel, F., Graupmann, V., Frey, D., & Aydin, N. (2015). Wanna play? The role of self-construal when using gadgets to cope with ostracism. *Social Influence.* DOI: 10.1080/15534510.2015.1074102

Reijntjes, A., Thomaes, S., Kamphuis, J. H., Bushman, B. J., De Castro, B. O., & Telch, M. J. (2011). Explaining the paradoxical rejection-aggression link: The mediating effects of hostile intent attributions, anger, and decreases in state self-esteem on peer rejection-induced aggression in youth. *Personality and Social Psychology Bulletin, 37*, 955–963.

Riva, P., Lauro, L. J. R., DeWall, C. N., & Bushman, B. J. (2012). Buffer the pain away stimulating the right ventrolateral prefrontal cortex reduces pain following social exclusion. *Psychological Science, 23*, 1473–1475.

Riva, P., Romero Lauro, L. J., DeWall, C. N., Chester, D. S., & Bushman, B. J. (2015). Reducing aggressive responses to social exclusion using transcranial direct current stimulation. *Social Cognitive and Affective Neuroscience, 10*, 352–356.

Riva, P., Williams, K. D., Torstrick, A. M., & Montali, L. (2014). Orders to shoot (a camera): Effect of ostracism on obedience. *The Journal of Social Psychology, 154*, 208–216.

Riva, P., Wirth, J. H., & Williams, K. D. (2011). The consequences of pain: The social and physical pains overlap on psychological responses. *European Journal of Social Psychology, 41*, 681–687.

Schaafsma, J., & Williams, K. D. (2012). Exclusion, intergroup hostility, and religious fundamentalism. *Journal of Experimental Social Psychology, 48*, 829–837.

Schoel, C., Eck, J., & Greifeneder, R. (2014). A matter of vertical position: Consequences of ostracism differ for those above versus below its perpetrators. *Social Psychological and Personality Science, 5*, 149–157.

Smart Richman, L., & Leary, M. R. (2009). Reactions to discrimination, stigmatization, ostracism, and other forms of interpersonal rejection: A multimotive model. *Psychological Review, 116*, 365–383.

Smith, A., & Williams, K. D. (2004). R U There? Effects of ostracism by cell phone messages. *Group Dynamics: Theory, Research, and Practice, 8*, 291–301.

Sommer, F., Leuschner, V., & Scheithauer, H. (2014). Bullying, romantic rejection, and conflicts with teachers: The crucial role of social dynamics in the development of school shootings–A systematic review. *International Journal of Developmental Science, 8*, 3–24.

Sommer, K. L., & Bernieri, F. (2014). Minimizing the pain and probability of rejection evidence for relational distancing and proximity seeking within face-to-face interactions. *Social Psychological and Personality Science*. Published online before print September 9, 2014, doi: 10.1177/1948550614549384.

Swann, W. B., Gómez, Á., Dovidio, J. F., Hart, S., & Jetten, J. (2010). Dying and killing for one's group identity fusion moderates responses to intergroup versions of the trolley problem. *Psychological Science, 21*, 1176–1183.

Thomaes, S., Stegge, H., Olthof, T., Bushman, B. J., & Nezlek, J. B. (2011). Turning shame inside-out: "Humiliated fury" in young adolescents. *Emotion, 11*, 786–793.

Tobin, S. J., Vanman, E. J., Verreynne, M., & Saeri, A. K. (2015). Threats to belonging on Facebook: Lurking and ostracism. *Social Influence, 10*, 31–42.

Tuscherer, T., Sacco, D. F., Wirth, J. H., Claypool, H. M., Hugenberg, K., & Wesselmann, E. D. (2015). Responses to exclusion are moderated by its perceived fairness. *European Journal of Social Psychology*. Manuscript in press.

Twenge, J. M. (2005). When does social rejection lead to aggression? The influences of situations, narcissism, emotion, and replenishing connections. In K. D. Williams, J. P. Forgas, & W. von Hippel (Eds.), *The social outcast: Ostracism, social exclusion, rejection, and bullying* (pp. 201–212). New York: Psychology Press.

Twenge, J. M., Baumeister, R. F., Tice, D. M., & Stucke, T. S. (2001). If you can't join them, beat them: Effects of social exclusion on aggressive behavior. *Journal of Personality and Social Psychology, 81*, 1058–1069.

Twenge, J. M., & Campbell, W. K. (2003). "Isn't it fun to get the respect that we're going to deserve?" Narcissism, social rejection, and aggression. *Personality and Social Psychology Bulletin, 29*, 261–272.

Twenge, J. M., Zhang, L., Catanese, K. R., Dolan-Pascoe, B., Lyche, L. R., & Baumeister, R. F. (2007). Replenishing connectedness: Reminders of social activity reduce aggression after social exclusion. *British Journal of Social Psychology, 46*, 205–224.

van Beest, I., Carter-Sowell, A. R., van Dijk, E., & Williams, K. D. (2012). Groups being ostracized by groups: Is the pain shared, is recovery quicker, and are groups more likely to be aggressive?. *Group Dynamics: Theory, Research, and Practice, 16*, 241–254.

Warburton, W. A., Williams, K. D., & Cairns, D. R. (2006). When ostracism leads to aggression: The moderating effects of control deprivation. *Journal of Experimental Social Psychology, 42*, 213–220.

Waytz, A., Chou, E. Y., Magee, J. C., & Galinsky, A. D. (2015). Not so lonely at the top: The relationship between power and loneliness. *Organizational Behavior and Human Decision Processes, 130*, 69–78.

Wesselmann, E. D., Butler, F. A., Williams, K. D., & Pickett, C. L. (2010). Adding injury to insult: Unexpected rejection leads to more aggressive responses. *Aggressive Behavior, 36*, 232–237.

Wesselmann, E. D., Cardoso, F. D., Slater, S., & Williams, K. D. (2012). To be looked at as though air: Civil attention matters. *Psychological Science, 23*, 166–168.

Wesselmann, E. D., Grzybowski, M. R., Steakley-Freeman, D. M., DeSouza, E. R., Nezlek, J. B., & Williams, K. D. (2016). Social Exclusion in everyday life. In P. Riva & J. Eck (Eds.), *Social exclusion: Psychological approaches to understanding and reducing its impact* (pp. 3–23). New York: Springer.

Wesselmann, E. D., Hales, A. H., Ren, D., & Williams, K. D. (2015). Ostracism threatens personal security: A temporal need threat framework. In P. Carroll, R. Arkin, & A. Wichman (Eds.), *Handbook of personal security* (pp. 191–206). New York: Psychology Press.

Wesselmann, E. D., Ren, D., & Williams, K. D. (2015). Motivations for responses to ostracism. *Frontiers in Psychology, 6*, 40. doi: 10.3389/fpsyg.2015.00040

Wesselmann, E. D., & Williams, K. D. (2010). The potential balm of religion and spirituality for recovering from ostracism. *Journal of Management, Spirituality, and Religion, 7*, 29–45.

Wesselmann, E. D., Williams, K. D., Ren, D., & Hales, A. (2014). Ostracism and solitude. In R. J. Coplan & J. Bowker (Eds.), *A handbook of solitude: Psychological perspectives on social isolation, social withdrawal, and being alone* (pp. 224–241). Malden, MA: Wiley-Blackwell.

Westermann, S., Rief, W., Euteneuer, F., & Kohlmann, S. (2015). Social exclusion and shame in obesity. *Eating Behaviors, 17*, 74–76.

Williams, K. D. (2007). Ostracism. *Annual Review of Psychology, 58*, 425–452.

Williams, K. D. (2009). Ostracism: Effects of being excluded and ignored. In M. Zanna (Ed.), *Advances in experimental social psychology* (pp. 275–314). New York: Academic Press.

Williams, K. D., Cheung, C. K. T., & Choi, W. (2000). Cyberostracism: Effects of being ignored over the Internet. *Journal of Personality and Social Psychology, 79*, 748–762.

Williams, K. D., Govan, C. L., Croker, V., Tynan, D., Cruickshank, M., Lam, A. (2002). Investigations into differences between social and cyberostracism. *Group Dynamics: Theory, Research, and Practice, 6*, 65–77.

Williams, K. D., & Sommer, K. L. (1997). Social ostracism by coworkers: Does rejection lead to social loafing or compensation. *Personality and Social Psychology Bulletin, 23*, 693–706.

Williams, K. D., & Wesselmann, E. D. (2011). The link between ostracism and aggression. In J. P. Forgas, A. W. Kruglanski, & K. D. Williams (Eds.), *The psychology of social conflict and aggression* (pp. 37–51). New York: Psychology Press.

Wirth, J. H., Sacco, D. F., Hugenberg, K., & Williams, K. D. (2010). Eye gaze as relational evaluation: Averted eye gaze leads to feelings of ostracism and relational devaluation. *Personality and Social Psychology Bulletin, 36*, 869–882.

Wirth, J. H., & Williams, K. D. (2009). "They don't like our kind": Consequences of being ostracized while possessing a group membership. *Group Processes and Intergroup Relations, 12*, 111–127.

Wolf, W., Levordashka, A., Ruff, J. R., Kraaijeveld, S., Lueckmann, J. M., & Williams, K. D. (2014). Ostracism Online: A social media ostracism paradigm. *Behavior Research Methods, 47*, 361–373.

Zhou, X., Vohs, K. D., & Baumeister, R. F. (2009). The symbolic power of money reminders of money alter social distress and physical pain. *Psychological Science, 20*, 700–706.

Zippelius, R. (1986). Exclusion and shunning as legal and social sanctions. *Ethology and Sociobiology, 7*, 159–166.

Zwolinski, J. (2012). Psychological and neuroendocrine reactivity to ostracism. *Aggressive Behavior, 38*, 108–125.

11

GUN VIOLENCE

Wendy Cukier, Sarah Allen Eagen,
and Gwendoline Decat

> *While male-dominated societies often justify small arms possession through the alleged*
> *need to protect vulnerable women, women actually face greater danger of violence when*
> *their families and communities are armed.*
>
> Barbara Frey, Special Rapporteur on Human Rights
> and Small Arms (2002)

The terrible irony is that while firearms are strongly linked to traditional notions of masculinity and promoted as a means of self-protection, particularly in the United States, the empirical evidence suggests that quite the contrary is true—where there are more firearms, risks of violence increase (Krug et al., 2002). Legal guns are often misused by their owners, particularly in violence against women and in suicide. Legal guns are also sold illegally or stolen, fuelling illegal markets (Cook et al., 2009). Firearms, then, factor into violence in several ways (Coupland, 1996). First, they increase lethality of violent attempts, whether in the context of interpersonal violence or self-directed violence (suicide attempts) (Kellermann et al., 1992). Lax regulation and enforcement increase the chances that danger-ous people will gain access to firearms (Chapdelaine, 1996). Second, they figure prominently in the culture of violence and notions of masculinity that link male-ness to violence (Goldstein, 2001). Finally, the political economy associated with the weapons industry and gun lobby exercise significant (and distorting) effects on beliefs and political systems (Diaz, 1999). This chapter will review the empirical evidence related to these three issues (Cukier & Sidel, 2005).

Public health and criminology literatures, and to a lesser extent the peace and conflict literatures, focus on the role of firearms in increasing the lethality of violence. Where firearms are concerned, the United States is unique in many

TABLE 11.1 Countries with the Highest Rates of Reported Firearms Deaths (per 100,000)*

Country	Year	Total Reported Firearm Deaths (Minimum)	Total Firearm Death Rate (Minimum)	% That Are Homicides
Colombia	2002	22,827	55.7	93%
Venezuela	2000	5,689	34.3	95%
South Africa	2002	11,709	26.8	97%
El Salvador	2001	1,641	25.8	98%
Brazil	2002	38,088	21.7	97%
Puerto Rico	2001	734	19.1	91%
Jamaica	1997	450	18.6	98%
Guatemala	2000	2,109	18.5	NA
Honduras	1999	1,677	16.2	NA
Uruguay	2000	104	13.9	22%
Ecuador	2000	1,321	13.4	80%
Argentina	2001	4,327	11.5	38%
USA	2001	29,753	10.3	38%

Firearm death rate among 112 countries (Cukier and Sidel, 2005)

respects. It has the highest rate of gun death among high-income nations, ranking thirteenth in reported firearm deaths with 112 other developing and post-conflict nations.

To prevent an illness or injury, public health experts consider preventive action to control the agent and the vehicle to protect the host. In 2009, the World Health Organization (WHO) has identified "reducing access to lethal means" as one of its violence prevention strategies (WHO, 2009). In the case of injury due to gunshot wounds, the agent is the force deployed by firing a gun, the vehicle is the gun or ammunition, and the human host is the victim. Access to firearms and ammunition constitutes the universal link—the one against which we can take action—in the chain of events leading to any injury with a firearm (Chapdelaine, 1996). It may be defined in a number of ways, including the percentage of households where firearms are present (or various surrogate measures) (Miller & Cohen, 1997), or the ease with which individuals can obtain firearms and ammunition in a given place at a given time. A number of researchers have maintained that there is sufficient evidence to conclude that rates of firearms death and injury are linked to access to firearms (Hemenway, 2004). There is a strong correlation between the percentage of households with firearms and firearm death rates (homicide, suicide and unintentional deaths) among industrialized countries (see Figure 11.1).

Although rates of violence per se are not directly affected by the availability of firearms, rates of lethal violence are. High levels of gun use in assault and robbery in the United States, for example, are strongly associated with elevated U.S. death rates from violence, and it has been established that gun ownership and gun violence tend to rise and fall together (Wintemute, 2008). A number of studies

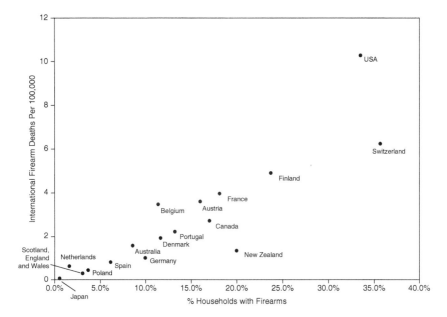

FIGURE 11.1 Rate of firearm ownership (% of households) and deaths (per 100,000) for industrialized countries.

have examined the difference in outcomes between assaults with knives compared to assaults with firearms and have concluded that the objective dangerousness of the instrument used in violent assaults has a direct and measurable impact on the number of victims who will die in the attack, known as the "instrumentality effect" (Phillips & Maume, 2007). Not only has this been shown to be the case where guns are used instead of knives, but increased use of particular types of firearms, such as high-caliber handguns or military assault weapons, have also been linked to increases in death rates (Chapdelaine, 1996).

In an analysis of 14 countries, the correlation between gun ownership and gun suicide was also significant, as was the correlation of rate of gun ownership with overall suicide rates (Kellermann et al., 1992). After accounting for several independent risk factors, another study concluded that keeping one or more firearms was associated with a 4.8-fold higher risk of suicide in the home (Kellermann et al., 1992). The risks are higher, particularly for adolescents, in homes in which the guns were kept loaded and unlocked (Brent et al., 1991). One study suggested a 93% correlation between the rate of households with firearms and the firearm death rate (consisting mainly of suicides) (Miller & Cohen 1997). This is also seen on a regional basis within country. For example, a 1990–1992 study conducted revealed that nearly half of all suicides in rural regions in the province of Quebec, Canada, involved firearms, whereas in urban areas such as Montreal, they accounted for only 14% (Simon et al., 1996).

Many of the research projects examining the accessibility thesis have conducted comparisons of homes in which firearms are present to those in which they are not (Kellermann et al., 1993). A homicide of a family member was 2.7 times more likely to occur in a home with a firearm than in a home without a gun (Kellerman et al., 1993). In another study, based on a standardized survey of victimization in 54 countries, gun ownership was significantly related to both the level of robberies and the level of sexual assaults (Mayhew & Van Dijk, 1997). Additionally, it was concluded that high levels of gun ownership, such as in the United States, the former Yugoslavia, South Africa and several Latin American countries, are strongly related to higher levels of violence generally (Mayhew & Van Dijk, 1997).

Although more research could illuminate the interaction between the range of factors shaping the demand for firearms, at the societal level and at the individual level (such as criminal activity, drug use, and parental factors), there is a growing body of literature that reveals a relationship between access to firearms, firearms death rates and certain types of crime (Hemenway & Miller, 2000). This underpins the notion that reducing access to firearms through regulation will reduce the lethality of assaults and suicide attempts.

Comparisons between Canada and the United States are instructive. The United States has a higher rate of gun ownership per capita, particularly handguns, than any other industrialized country in the world. Approximately 40% of U.S. households have firearms (Graduate Institute of International Studies, 2002). Estimates of the rate of gun ownership and the number of guns, however, vary considerably. In the United States, a country with a population of 290 million, it is estimated that there are more than 200 million firearms owned, one-third of them handguns. One-sixth of the handguns owned are regularly carried by their owners, approximately half in the owners' cars and the other half on the owners' persons (Cook & Ludwig, 1996). Per capita rates of firearm ownership in the United States also exceed those of 14 other nations for which data are available (Graduate Institute of International Studies, 2002). Indeed, the Small Arms Survey estimates that more than 40% of all the guns in the world are in the United States, not only fuelling violence in the United States but internationally, as U.S. guns are smuggled into proximate countries like Canada and Mexico and around the world (Cook, Cukier, & Krause, 2009). In contrast, in Canada, a country with 32 million people, it is estimated that there are approximately 7 million firearms, only about 450,000 of them handguns. Approximately 18% of Canadian households have firearms (Environics Research Group, 2003). Handguns are strictly regulated and few citizens (about 50) have permits to carry them for self-protection.

The rates of death from firearms in Canada and the United States have been studied, and one of the most well-known analyses was a comparison of Seattle, Washington, and Vancouver, British Columbia. This study showed that despite similarities in size and demographics, there are huge differences in the rate of firearm homicide as a result of the differences in the availability of firearms in the two countries (Sloan et al., 1988).

International studies have suggested that availability of firearms is connected to rates of lethal violence where other factors are held constant (Cukier & Sidel, 2005). For example, one study found a direct relationship between the rates of firearm ownership in 25 high-income countries and both the female firearm homicide and overall homicides (Hemenway et al., 2002).

Of particular interest is the comparison of the United States and Canada, two countries that are similar (though not identical) in terms of culture, history and general socioeconomic conditions. For example, in 2013, rates of homicide without guns are comparable, 1.06 per 100,000 for Canada versus 1.55 per 100,000 for the United States. However rates of homicide *with guns* are dramatically different. The U.S. rate of homicides with firearms is 3.55 per 100,000—more than nine times the Canadian rate of 0.38 per 100,000. In 2013, there were a total of 131 murders with guns in all of Canada, a country of more than 30 million people. In the United States there were 11,208. If the difference were broad drivers of violence, we would expect the murder rates without guns to also be significantly higher. The fact that there is such a stark difference between homicide rates with and without firearms in the two countries cannot be explained in any other way than the difference in the access to firearms (see Table 11.2 and Figure 11.2).

Similarly, rates of robberies without firearms are comparable, but rates of robberies with firearms are dramatically different, suggesting that the availability of firearms is a key factor driving rates of lethal violence and robbery. Although some claim that international rates of gun violence are not associated with firearm ownership rates, typically these studies do not differentiate high-income from low-income countries or reference rates of "violence" broadly (Slack, 2009). And indeed, countries like Great Britain and Australia report higher rates of assaults, for

TABLE 11.2 Comparison of Homicide Rates in Canada and the United States in 2013 (gunpolicy.org, 2015)

2013	Canada	US	Comparison US vs. Canada
Total Homicide	512	16,121	
Rate of Homicide	1.44 per 100,000	5.1 per 100,000	3.5x
Total Homicide with Firearms	131	11,208	
Rate of Homicide with Firearms	0.38 per 100,000	3.55 per 100,000	9.3x
Homicides without Guns	381	4,913	
Rates of Homicides without Guns	1.06 per 100,000	1.55 per 100,000	1.5x
Total Handgun Homicides	86	5,782	
Rates of Handgun Homicides	0.25 per 100,000	1.82 per 100,000	7.3x

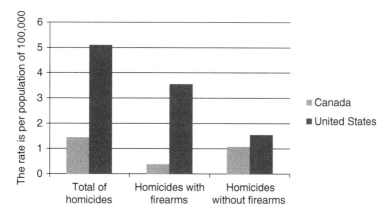

FIGURE 11.2 Comparison of homicide rates in Canada and the United States (2013).

example, than the United States, but their rates of lethal violence are much lower. In 2011, for example, the United States had 11,068 homicides with firearms (3.55 per 100,000), the United Kingdom had 38 (0.06 per 100,000) and Australia had 31 (0.14 per 100,000). In spite of this evidence, there are claims that arming for self-protection reduces violence (Kleck, 1997; Lott, 2000; Mauser, 2006). Some of these claims rest on self-reported responses to the survey item: "Have you or a member of your family used a firearm in the last five years to defend yourself against an animal or a person?" (Kleck, 1997; Mauser, 2006). They then take the response rates and extrapolate to the general population. The methodology used has been soundly critiqued. Dr. David Hemenway, a professor at Harvard University, noted that this method is based on incorrect assertions and misleading statements, comparing it to a 1995 survey by NBC which asked 1,500 Americans, "Have you personally ever been in contact with aliens from another planet or not?" Extrapolating the results (0.6%) to the entire U.S. population would suggest that 1.2 million Americans have been in actual contact with aliens. Other studies have attempted to compare local crime rates relative to "shall carry" regulations, but ignore the fact that states have open borders and there is considerable evidence that guns flow from unregulated to regulated states (Lott, 2000). Within the United States, the studies comparing one community to another or one state to another are often confounded by a variety of factors. However, the evidence comparing industrial countries reinforces the notion that access to firearms is linked to firearm deaths (Cukier & Sidel, 2005).

In considering particular forms of violence—violence against women in particular, as well as suicide—easy availability of firearms is a major risk factor. The presence of a firearm is one of the strongest risk factors for domestic homicide in both the United States (Campbell et al., 2003) and Canada (Cukier & Sidel, 2005). More recently, an analysis of 24 countries with comprehensive data on the types of weapons used in committing femicides revealed a direct correlation between femicide rates and the use of firearms (Geneva Declaration Secretariat, 2011).Generally, countries with higher rates of femicide had a higher percentage of the femicides committed with firearms, reinforcing the lethality of firearms. Among the countries examined, firearms were used in one-third of the femicides, but in countries such as Brazil, Colombia, El Salvador, Guatemala, and Honduras, firearms were used in more than 60% of femicides (Geneva Declaration Secretariat, 2011). However, media focus on random acts of violence, combined with the traditional constructions of "crime" and "the criminal element," have downplayed domestic violence.

Not only are women more at risk from civilian weapons than military weapons in many regions, but the evidence shows clearly that women are just as likely to be victimized by their intimate partners as by "criminals" or "combatants" (Boyd, 2014). This pattern—seen in contexts as diverse as rural Alberta, Canada, and Cambodian refugee camps—highlights the importance of controlling the availability of firearms. Women are primarily at risk from legal guns in the hands of legal gun owners. Consequently, many women's organizations insist that "the distinction between 'the criminal element' and 'law abiding citizens' is meaningless in the context of violence against women" (Alberta Council of Women's Shelters, 1998).

Where guns are widely available they tend to be used in suicides. For example, 93% of suicides attempted with firearms succeed (Cukier & Chapdelaine, 2001). In the United States, guns are used in more than half of all suicides (CDC, 2013), and the risks are much higher that a suicide will occur when a gun is in the home (Kposowa et al., 2016). In areas where gun ownership is prevalent—for example, in rural communities of Australia or Canada—guns figure prominently in suicide (Palmer, 2014). The association between possession of firearms in the home and suicide rates has been the subject of considerable research in contexts such as the United States, Canada, Australia, Switzerland, and elsewhere (Cukier & Sidel, 2005; Kellerman et al., 1992).

A range of approaches have been taken to reduce access to firearms, generally focusing on screening and licensing, safe storage, record keeping and prohibitions on weapons where the risk is considered to outweigh the utility and to a lesser extent, education. Extensive research has investigated the impact of different measures on the availability of firearms, suicide and crime rates. Again, while context plays an important role and the enforcement of laws is as important as the regulations themselves, there is evidence to suggest that some forms of regulation are effective in reducing access to firearms; again, in this regard, the contrast between Canada and the United States is instructive (Cukier & Sidel, 2005).

Firearms and the Culture of Violence

In the most basic sense, increased weapon availability has been shown to fuel a "culture of violence." Armed violence promotes fear, which in turn promotes arming, which again promotes violence. For example, one criminologist suggested that stricter controls on firearms both reflect and shape values, particularly the "culture of violence," in the same way legislation has been observed to have long-term effects on other behaviors (Gartner, 2000). However, the notion that the unrestrained access to firearms fuels a "culture of violence" is by no means new.

Most of the existing work exploring demand for firearms is silent on one of the factors found across nations, both in times of war and in times of peace: the majority of those who use and misuse firearms are men. Traditional male roles as providers, warriors or police officers often entail the use of firearms, but even among civilian populations, demand for both legal and illegal guns is much higher among men than women. This would appear to suggest that in order to develop effective strategies to stem the misuse and proliferation of firearms we must understand the ways in which concepts of masculinity affect demand. Conventional notions of masculinity ascribe the role of protector and defender to men, and for many, gun ownership is a symbol of masculine power and status.

Although violence is not an exclusively male practice, guns are linked to masculine identity. The values, social practices and institutions that together constitute this gun culture include "consumerist militarism," which can be defined as the normalization and even glorification of war, weaponry, military force and violence through TV, films, books, songs, dances, games, sports and toys. In South Africa, for example, demand for guns is a socially constructed concept that is embedded in culture (Cock, 1997). Dealing with the culture of violence is, therefore, an essential part of a strategy to counter violence.

Nowhere is the strong association of guns and masculinity stronger than in U.S. culture. The symbolic significance of guns has been made explicit in many ways (Goldstein, 2001). For example, guns are essential equipment for cowboys and warriors, both of which play a significant role in the mythology of history in the United States. Some criminologists have argued that empirical evidence indicates that cultural factors are stronger predictors of violence than economic factors (Gartner, 2000). Gartner (2000) notes that societies that are frequently at war consistently have higher rates of interpersonal and within-group violence. Homicide rates within participant nations have consistently remained high after wars whether the nation has won or lost (Meddings, 1997). Similarly, societies with violent sports and that permit corporal and capital punishments tend to have higher levels of interpersonal violence (Gartner, 2000). In such societies, male children are typically socialized for aggression, in part to equip them for adult roles as warriors (Gartner, 2000). Empirical research into attitudes towards killing in various contexts also reveals a strong association between attitudes that include the willingness to kill to protect property, to avenge the rape of a child, or to lend support for capital punishment with homicide rates and attitudes to gun ownership (McAlister, 2001; Cohen, 1998; Cukier & Sheptycki, 2012). The relationships among gun laws, rates of gun ownership and societal values are potentially complex and mutually influencing. Society shapes its laws and its laws shape society.

The (re)production of notions of masculinity are critical to understanding the demand for firearms, an often neglected area of research. There is an important need to examine notions of masculinity, the roles that guns play in male culture, and ways to decouple these. To date most discussions of the role of gender are relegated to "gender studies" rather than addressed in the dominant literatures.

In Western industrialized societies, the media is one of the principal conduits of culture. American media in particular tends to portray heroes using violence as a justified means of resolving conflict (American Academy of Pediatrics, 2001). Comparable work suggests a link between gender, media violence and behavior (Page, 2009), although the definitions, analysis and explanatory frameworks differ. Research has tended to focus on exposure to guns and violence. Content analyses, for example, have focused on violent acts, on how the protagonists are depicted, as well as on the association between exposure to violence in the media and a variety of physical and/or mental health problems among children and adolescents. Some of these disorders studied include aggressive behavior and the desensitization to violence and fear. It has been noted that "titillating violence in sexual contexts and comic violence are particularly dangerous, because they associate positive feelings with hurting others" (AAP, 2001). For example, a broad-based study for UNESCO concluded that there were not simple causal relations but broader effects on psychology and behavior as a result of video game violence (von Feilitzen, 2000).

The American Pediatric Association has concluded, "The murder rate of young blacks rose 300% during the three decades after television's introduction in the US. Although exposure to media violence is not the sole factor contributing to aggression, anti-social attitudes, and violence among children and adolescents, it is an important health risk factor" (von Feilitzen, 2000). Similar studies have been conducted across different cultures and countries such as South Africa (Centerwall, 1992).

Another intersection of gun culture, the media and gender can be found in entertainment media. Studies of U.S. television and film have illuminated the relationship between firearms and masculinity in the United States as revealed in Hollywood action films. Scholars have discussed the rise of white, violent men such as Sylvester Stallone, Arnold Schwarzenegger, and Bruce Willis as cinematic heroes for whom guns are iconic. It has been suggested that the appeal of these stereotypes is particularly strong among disempowered white working-class men. Furthermore, it has been noted that the depiction of gun use in films, particularly the use of guns for self-protection, is very much at odds with the reality of gun use by U.S. men. The masculine discourse of self-protection is pervasive even though it flies in the face of reality. Moreover, critics have also discussed the "mythic" constructions of gunplay in U.S. movies (Arjet, 2002).

It is critical in the exploring the media-culture-violence link that one understands that it is only one factor among many. Often it is used to minimize other factors such as social economic disparity, inequity, or access to firearms. Following the Columbine school shootings in the United States, National Rifle Association

(NRA) president Charlton Heston maintained that it was not the availability of guns that was an issue but rather violent video games. This thesis has been advanced by some researchers who explicitly oppose gun control (Centerwall, 1992). Even Michael Moore's documentary, *Bowling for Columbine*, which suggested the U.S. culture of violence was the principal differentiator between the United States and Canada, downplayed the availability of guns as a factor.

The analysis of empirical studies must consequently be carefully nuanced. Some researchers frame their analysis in terms of gender stereotypes and role models in order to examine how violence affects girls and boys in different ways. Others suggest that extensive exposure to violent media is symptomatic of other problems such as a lack of parental care and supervision, while still others examine it in terms of violent media's contribution to a broader "culture of violence." The perspectives that focus on "cultures of violence" rather than on simple cause-and-effect relationships appear to be the most promising (Gerbner & Gross, 1980).

According to one scholar, "Guns are an important signifier of virility and power and hence an important way violent masculinity is constructed and then sold to audience. In fact, the presence of guns in magazine and newspaper ads is crucial to communicating the extent of a movie's violent content . . . images of gun-toting macho males pervade the visual landscape" (Katz, 1995, pp. 349–358).

To date, there is limited evidence that efforts to increase gun ownership among women have been successful. In fact, *Ms.* magazine has critiqued this new "power feminism" and most women's organizations have reinforced the fact that where there are more guns, more women are likely to be killed by their partners (Jones, 1994).

The Political Economy of Firearms

The movie *Making a Killing* documents in considerable detail the way in which gun manufacturers and their allies exert enormous control over the American political systems (Diaz, 1999). The economic might of the gun lobby is used to influence politicians and to promote laws that help expand the market. For example, laws which permit civilians to carry concealed weapons in the United States (Hargrove, 1995), and more recently the U.S. Supreme Court decision striking down a ban on handguns in Washington, DC (*D.C. vs. Heller*, 2008), are seen by the firearms industry as expanding the market for handguns in spite of conclusive evidence of their lack of benefit in terms of self-protection (Anderson, 1996; Thurman, 1995). In spite of its limitations, Michael Moore's film *Bowling for Columbine* also attempted to portray complex relationships between the gun industry and lobby, the culture of fear, and death that is almost uniquely American.

Recent polling in the United States from Pew (2015), for example, showed the vast majority of Americans support stricter control measures, including background checks for gun shows and private sales (85%), preventing individuals with a history of mental illness from getting access to firearms (79%), national databases tracking firearm sales (including secondary sales) (70%), and even a ban on military assault weapons (57%). There are big differences between Republicans and Democrats on some of these issues.

Yet there has been little progress in strengthening firearms laws at the national level and, if anything, the United States is one of the few countries in the world that has relaxed controls on firearms in recent years. Part of the challenge in the United States is the lack of campaign spending limits, which allows special interests to distort political processes. Even in countries like Canada, South Africa, Brazil and Australia, the gun lobby has been effective in blocking stronger laws and, in some cases, relaxing laws that have been introduced (Hearn, 2005). At the international level, firearm manufacturers have thwarted efforts by the United Nations to establish global standards to combat the illegal gun trade (Goldring, 1999).

One scholar argues that the NRA's production of a "faceless and nameless threat, one which terrorizes us in our most intimate spaces . . . is not intended exclusively to demonstrate that Americans must have the right to keep and bear arms. Instead, the NRA manufactures its own politically potent mode of masculinity by way of a strategically constructed threat" (O'Neill, 2004). Manufacturers advertise extensively in NRA publications, *American Rifleman* and *American Hunter*, providing about 8% of the NRA's overall revenues (Spitzer, 1995). Other reciprocal relationships exist; for example, manufacturers distribute NRA membership materials in their packaging and the NRA provides discount gun purchase offers as well as publicity and advertising.

Fear for personal safety at home and on the streets is a significant factor influencing firearm demand in countries that allow carrying guns for personal protection (Udulutch, 1989). As the former NRA president Wayne Lapierre put it, "The market's being driven by fear" (Anderson, 1996). Several states have enacted statutes permitting individuals to carry a concealed firearm. These laws are seen by the firearms industry as expanding the market for handguns in spite of conclusive evidence of their lack of benefit in terms of self-protection (Thurman, 1995). Even in countries like Canada where there is no legislative basis to support arming for self-protection, gun lobby rhetoric mirrors the NRA, particularly efforts to market to women (O'Neill, 2004). As the director of the Violence Policy Center suggests, "Lethality in guns is like nicotine in cigarettes—an addictive hook set deep into the irrational side of its customers" (Diaz, 1999). The gun industry links its advertising and promotional efforts to the fantasies of its customers. Assault weapons sales got a huge boost from the film *Rambo*, and the Austrian-made Glock got a push from California governor Arnold Schwarzenegger. Companies with strong links to military and policing markets exploited this relationship in their marketing efforts. For example, some companies published advertisements aimed at civilians that emphasized the military lineage of their weapons (Cukier et al., 2008).

Other factors also appear to shape demand. For example, dealers claim that the assault weapons ban increased the value of assault weapons in circulation and drove up demand. The terrorist attacks of 9/11 also appear to have caused a spike in American gun sales, although the perceived link between carrying a handgun and preventing terrorist attacks is unclear.

Manufacturers received considerable reinforcement in their efforts from the wide range of firearms magazine publishers and associations that reinforced the "fear factor" and promoted arming. As one gun industry publication noted: "While you may not have an overwhelming number of customers who would carry two firearms, it does open a new market, each backup gun you sell brings with it ancillary sales of ankle holsters, pocket holsters or belly bands, perhaps some Speed Strips for spare ammo and of course ammo itself" (Diaz, 1999). There is evidence that some gun manufacturers, like tobacco companies, are targeting youth in order to sustain markets (Diaz, 1999). There have been parallels between the effects of the gun lobby and the tobacco lobby to shape the research agenda and to block regulatory efforts (Kellermann, 1997). Firearms associations have also been accused of marketing guns to teens and children under the guise of teaching firearm safety. A U.S. study from the Violence Policy Center entitled "Eddie the Eagle: Joe Camel with Feathers" documented the technique of luring young people into the gun culture at a very young age under the pretext of teaching them firearm safety (VPC, 2007). Parallel efforts have been documented in other countries. In Canada, for example, the National Firearms Association (NFA) advises against storing firearms safely (required under Canadian law), in favor, instead, of "gunproofing children," a strategy that involves teaching them how to load, aim and fire guns, even though the Canadian Paediatric Society insists that this actually puts children and youth at risk (Frappier et al., 2005).

Conclusion

The role of firearms in violence has been the subject of much debate. There are few issues that are as controversial and emotionally laden. Sorting through the extensive research at the local, national and international levels is challenging, and untangling the politics that frame the debate and discourses is difficult. On balance, the research seems to support the notion that the availability of firearms is linked to the lethality of violence, although there is considerable disagreement regarding the policies and processes most effective in reducing inappropriate access. Additionally, guns figure prominently in the socialization of boys and in cultures of violence reinforcing notions that firearms have defensive functions, in spite of the extensive evidence that suggests that firearms in the home heighten the risk of suicide and homicides. Finally, there are few lobby groups in the world that exercise the influence of the National Firearms Association in the United States or around the globe. The political economy that underpins the construction of firearms and the very real opposition to firearm control and efforts to further erode regulations in the name of individual liberty or the "right" to bear arms creates enormous distortions.

References

Alberta Council of Women's Shelters. (1998). Affidavit: The Firearms Act (Canada), 128 C.C.C. (3d) 225 at 339 (Alta. C.A.).

American Academy of Paediatrics, Committee on Public Education. (2001). Media violence. *Paediatrics*, *18*(5), 1222–1226.

Anderson, J. (1996). *Inside the NRA: Armed and dangerous: An exposé*. Beverly Hills, CA: Dove Books.

Arjet, R. (2002). *Gunplay: Men, guns and action films in the United States*. Atlanta, GA: Emory University.

Boyd, R. (2014). *The search for lasting peace*. Farnham: Ashgate.

Brent, D. A., Perper, J. A., Allman, C. J., Moritz, G. M., Wartella, M. E., & Zelenak, J. P. (1991). The presence and accessibility of firearms in the homes of adolescent suicides. *Journal of the American Medical Association*, *266*, 2989–2995.

Campbell, J. C., Webster, D., Koziol-McLain, J., Block, C. R., Campbell, D. W., Curry, M. A., Gary, F., Sachs, J., Sharps, P. W., Ulrich, Y., Wilt, S., Manganello, J., Schollenberger, X., Xu, X., & Frye, V. (2003). Risk factors for femicide in abusive relationships: Results from a multi-site case control study. *American Journal of Public Health*, *93*(7), 1089.

Centers for Disease Control and Prevention. (2013). Suicide and self-inflicted injury. From "Deaths: Final data for 2013." Retrieved from www.cdc.gov/nchs/fastats/suicide.htm

Centerwall, B. S. (1992). Television violence: The scale of the problem and where we go from here. *JAMA*, *267*, 3059–3063.

Chapdelaine, A. (1996). Firearms injury prevention and gun control in Canada. *Canadian Medical Association Journal*, *155*, 9.

Chapman, S. (1998). *Over our dead bodies: Port Arthur and Australia's fight for gun control*. Sydney: Pluto Press.

Cock, J. (1997). Fixing our sights: A sociological perspective on gun violence in contemporary South Africa. *Society in Transition*, *28*(1/4), 70–81.

Cohen, D. (1998). Culture, social organization and patterns of violence. *Journal of Personality and Social Psychology*, *75*(2), 408–419

Cook, P. J., Cukier, W., & K. Krauss. (2009). The illicit firearms trade in North America. *Criminology & Criminal Justice*, *9*(3), 265–286.

Cook, P. J., & Ludwig, J. (1996). *Guns in America: Results of a national survey on ownership and use of firearms*. Washington, DC: U.S. Department of Justice, National Institute of Justice.

Coupland, R. (1996). The effect of weapons on health. *Lancet*, *347*, 450–451.

Cukier, W., & Chapdelaine, A. (2001). Global trade in small arms: Public health effects and interventions. A joint publication of International Physicians for the Prevention of Nuclear War (IPPNW) and SAFER-Net.

Cukier, W., Rodrigues, S., & Eagen, S. (2008). The political economy of guns: Globalization and resistance. Critical Management Studies Research Workshop Pre-Academy of Management Annual Meeting, Los Angeles, California.

Cukier, W., & Sheptycki, J. (2012). Globalization of gun culture transnational reflections on pistolization and masculinity, flows and resistance. *International Journal of Law, Crime and Justice*, *40*(1), 3–19.

Cukier, W., & Sidel, V. (2005). *The global gun epidemic*. Westport, CT: Praeger.

Diaz, T. (1999). *Making a Killing*. New York: The New Press.

District of Columbia v. Heller. (2008). 554 U.S. 570, 588.

Environics Research Group. (2003). Majority support for gun control; majority support continuation of national firearms registry. Kingston, ON: Queens University. Retrieved

November 9, 2006, from: www.queensu.ca/cora/polls/2003/February21-Support_for_Gun_Control.pdf

Frappier, J.Y., Leonard, K.A., & Sacks, D. (2005). Youth and firearms in Canada. *Paediatric Child Health, 10*(8), 473–477.

Frey, B. M. (2002). *The question of the trade, carrying and use of small arms and light weapons in the context of human rights and humanitarian norms.* Working Paper Submitted by and in Accordance with Sub-Commission Decisions 2001/120, May 30.

Gartner, R. (2000). Cross cultural aspects of interpersonal violence: A Review of the international empirical evidence, Chapter presented at the International Conference on Crime and Violence: Causes and Policy Responses.

Geneva Declaration Secretariat. (2011). *Global Burden of Armed Violence 2011: Lethal Encounters.* Cambridge: Cambridge University Press.

Gerbner, G., & Gross, L. (1980). Living with television: The violence profile. *Journal of Communication, 30*(3), 10–29.

Goldring, N. (1999). The NRA goes global. *Bulletin of the Automatic Scientists, 55*(1), 61–65.

Goldstein, J. S. (2001). *War and gender: How gender shapes the war system and vice versa.* Oakland: University of California Press.

Graduate Institute of International Studies (GIIS). (2002). *Small arms aurvey 2002: Counting the human cost.* Oxford: Oxford University Press.

Hargrove, T. (1995, November 22). Focus on stopping violence. *The Atlanta Journal-Constitution*, A4.

Hearn, Kelly. (October 21, 2005). As Brazil Votes to Ban Guns, NRA Joins the Fight, *The Nation.*

Hemenway, D. (2004). *Private guns, public health.* Ann Arbor: University of Michigan Press.

Hemenway, D., & Miller, M. (2000). Firearm availability and homicide rates across 26 high-income countries. *Journal of Trauma, 49*, 985–988.

Hemenway, D., Shinoda-Tagawa, T., & M. Miller. (2002). Firearm availability and female homicide victimization rates across 25 populous high-income countries. *Journal of the American Medical Women's Association, 57*, 100–104.

Jones, A. (1994). Is this power feminism?—The push to get women hooked on guns. *Ms. Magazine, 41*, 36–37.

Katz, J. (1995). Advertising and the construction of violent white masculinity. In G. Dines & J. Humez (Eds.), *Gender, race and class in media: A text reader* (pp. 349–358). Thousand Oaks, CA: Sage Publications.

Kellermann, A. J. (1997). Comment: Gunsmoke—changing public attitudes towards smoking and firearms. *American Journal of Public Health, 87*(6), 910–913.

Kellerman, A. L., Rivara, F. P., Rushforth, N. B., Banton, J. G., Reay, D. T., Francisco, J. T., Locci, A. B., Hackman, B. B., & Somes, G. (1993). Gun ownership as a risk factor for homicide in the home. *New England Journal of Medicine, 329*, 1084–1091.

Kellerman, A. L., Rivara, F. P., Somes, G., Reay, D. T., Francisco, J., Banton, J. G., Prodzinski, J., Flinger, C., & Hackman, B. B. (1992). Suicide in the home in relation to gun ownership. *New England Journal of Medicine, 327*, 467–472.

Kleck, G. (1997). *Targeting guns: Firearms and their control.* New York: Aldine de Gruyter.

Kposowa, A., Hamilton, D., & Wang, K. (2016). Impact of firearm availability and gun regulation on state suicide rates, suicide and life-threatening behavior [early view]. Retrieved from http://onlinelibrary.wiley.com/doi/10.1111/sltb.12243/full

Krug, E., Dahlberg, L., Mercy, J.A., Zwi, A.B., & Lozano, R. (2002). *World report on violence and health.* Geneva: WHO.

Lott, J. (2000). *More guns, less crime: Understanding crime and gun control laws.* Chicago: University of Chicago Press.

McAlister, A. (2001). Homicide rates and attitudes towards killing in fifteen nations. Aiming for Prevention Conference, Helsinki Finland, October 28–30.

Mathews, S., Abrahams, N., Martin, L., Vetten, L., Van der Merwe, L., & Jewkes, R. (2004). *Every six hours a woman is killed by her intimate partner': A National Study of Female Homicide in South Africa.* Medical Research Council Policy Brief. Cape Town: Medical Research Council. 1–4.

Mauser, G. (2006). Armed self-defense the Canadian case. *Journal of Criminal Justice,* 24(5), 393–406.

Mayhew, P., Jan, J. M., & van Dijk. (1997). *Criminal victimization in eleven industrialized countries.* WODC report. The Hague: Ministry of Justice of the Netherlands. 162.

Meddings, D.R. (1997). Weapons injuries during and after periods of conflict: Retrospective analysis. *British Medical Journal, 315,* 1417–1420.

Miller, T. R., & Cohen, M. A. (1997). Costs of gunshot and cut/stab wounds in the United States with some Canadian comparisons. *Accident Analysis and Prevention, 29*(3), 329–341.

O'Neill, K. (2004). I need a hero: Gender and the rhetorical dimension of the NRA's use of media. Retrieved July 14, 2008 from: http://beard.dialnsa.edu/~treis/pdf/NRA%20use%20of%20Media.pdf.

Page, E. (2009). *Men, masculinity and guns: Can we break the link?* London: IANSA Women's Network.

Palmer, S. (2014). *Suicide: Strategies and interventions for reduction and prevention.* London: Routledge.

Pew (2015). Continued bipartisan support for expanded background checks on gun sales. Downloaded at www.people-press.org/2015/08/13/continued-bipartisan-support-for-expanded-background-checks-on-gun-sales/

Phillips, S., & Maume, M. O. (2007). Have gun will shoot? Weapon instrumentality, intent, and the violent escalation of conflict. *Homicide Studies, 11*(4), 272–294.

Simon, R., Chouinard, M., & Gravel, C. (1996). Suicide and firearms. In J. McIntosh (Ed.), *Suicide '96* (pp. 35–37). Washington, DC: American Association of Suicidology.

Slack, J. (2009). The most violent country in Europe: Britain is also worse than South Africa and U.S. *The Daily Mail.* July 2.

Sloan, J. H., Kellermann, A. L., Reay, D. T., Ferris, J. A., Koepsell, T., Rivara, F. P., Rice, C., Gray, L. & LoGerfo, J. (1988). Handgun regulations, crime, assaults and homicide: A tale of two cities. *New England Journal of Medicine, 319,* 1256–1262.

Spitzer, R. J. (1995). *The politics of gun control.* New Jersey: Chatham House Publishers.

Thurman, R. (1995, May). Shooting industry suffers sales slump. *Industry in Review,* 62.

Udulutch, M. (1989). The constitutional implications of gun control and several realistic gun control proposals. *American Journal of Criminology, 17*(14), 19, 21.

Violence Policy Centre. (2007). *Joe Camel with feathers: How the NRA with gun and tobacco industry dollars uses its Eddie Eagle program to market guns to kids.* Washington: Violence Policy Centre.

Von Feilitzen, C., & Carlsson, U. (December 2000). Children in the New Media Landscape Games, Pornography, Perceptions, UNESCO/Goteburg University.

Wintemute, G. J. (2008). Guns, fear, the constitution, and the public's health. *New England Journal of Medicine, 358,* 1421–1424.

WHO. (2009). Guns, knives, and pesticides: Reducing access to lethal means. (Series of briefings on violence prevention: The evidence). Retrieved from http://whqlibdoc.who.int/publications/2009/9789241597739_eng.pdf

12

AGGRESSIVE CUES

Weapons and Violent Media

Brad J. Bushman

> "I have a love interest in every one of my films—a gun."
>
> Arnold Schwarzenegger

There are plenty of guns in the world, especially in United States. The United States is the most heavily armed society in the world, with about 90 guns for every 100 citizens (MacInnis, 2007). Although the United States is only about 5% of the world's population, U.S. citizens possess over 30% of the world's guns. But you don't need to live in the United States to be exposed to guns. There are images of guns everywhere, especially in the mass media. Guns are not just in Arnold Schwarzenegger's films, either. For example, a recent study found that the amount of gun violence in the top-selling Hollywood films rated "PG-13" (for ages 13+) has more than tripled since the rating was introduced in 1985 (Bushman et al., 2013).

This chapter examines the effects of aggressive cues on aggression and violence. It examines the effects of weapons that are merely present and are not being used by anyone, called the *weapons effect*. It also examines the effects of violent content in the mass media, called *media violence effects*. This chapter contains five major sections. First, I define the terms *aggression* and *violence*. Second, I present the General Aggression Model as a theoretical framework for understanding aggressive cue effects. Third, I briefly discuss the methods researchers use to study aggressive cue effects. Fourth, I discuss research findings on the weapons effect. Fifth, I will discuss research findings on media violence effects.

Defining Aggression and Violence

It is useful to begin with definitions of aggression and violence, especially since laypeople and researchers sometimes use these terms differently. Laypeople may describe a salesperson who tries really hard to sell them something as "aggressive." The salesperson does not, however, want to harm anyone. Most researchers define *aggression* as any behavior intended to harm another person who does not want to be harmed (Baron & Richardson, 1994). This definition includes four important features. First, aggression is an outward behavior that can be seen, such as one person cursing, slapping, hitting, stabbing, or shooting another person. Aggression is not an emotion that occurs inside a person, such as an angry feeling. Aggression is not a thought that occurs inside a person's head, such as mentally rehearsing a murder. Second, aggression involves at least two people. Thus, suicide would be excluded. Third, aggression is intentional. Aggression is not accidental, such as when a drunk driver accidentally runs over a child. In addition, not all intentional behaviors that hurt others are aggressive behaviors. For example, a dentist intentionally gives a patient a painful shot of Novocain, but the goal is to help rather than hurt the patient. Fourth, the victim wants to avoid the pain. Thus, sadomasochistic sex play would be excluded, because the masochist actively seeks to be harmed. Note that behaviors that are intended to harm others but fail to cause the intended harm are still acts of aggression. For example, if a person intentionally shoots a gun at you but misses, it is still counts as an act of aggression.

Most researchers define *violence* as any behavior intended to cause extreme physical harm, such as injury or death, to another person who does not want to be harmed (Bushman & Huesmann, 2010). Thus, violence is an extreme form of aggression. All violent acts are aggressive, but not all aggressive acts are violent—only acts intended to cause extreme physical harm are classified as violent. The U.S. Federal Bureau of Investigation (FBI) classifies four crimes as violent: murder, aggravated assault, forcible rape, and robbery. Researchers would also classify other physically aggressive acts as violent, such as slapping someone hard across the face. But a husband who constantly screams at his wife would not be committing an act of violence by this definition.

This definition of violence can also be applied to media violence, which is any behavior intended to cause extreme physical harm to another character who does not want to be harmed. This definition of media violence is very similar to definitions used to analyze violent content in various forms of media. For example, several previous content analyses of films have defined *violence* as "Physical acts where the aggressor makes or attempts to make some physical contact with the intention of causing injury or death" (e.g., Bushman et al., 2013; Sargent et al., 2002). Likewise, the National Television Violence Study (1996, 1997, 1998) defined *violence* as "any overt depiction of a credible threat of physical force or the actual use of such force intended to physically harm an animate being or group of beings." The media characters could take various forms (e.g., actual people, animals, realistic characters, fictitious characters, cartoon characters).

Researchers have used different theories to explain aggression and violence. This chapter uses the General Aggression Model (e.g., Anderson & Bushman, 2002a), described next.

General Aggression Model

The General Aggression Model (e.g., Anderson & Bushman, 2002a) provides a useful framework for understanding aggression (see Figure 12.1) and violence (DeWall et al., 2011). In the model, two types of input variables can influence aggression: personal and situational. Personal variables include all the characteristics that the person brings to the situation (e.g., gender, age, genetic predispositions, hormones such as testosterone, personality traits, attitudes, values, beliefs). Situational variables include all the external factors that can influence aggression (e.g., exposure to aggressive cues such as weapons and violent media exposure, provocation, frustration, alcohol, hot temperatures, crowding, the presence of others).

According to the General Aggression Model, personal and situational variables jointly influence one's internal state, which includes aggressive thoughts, angry feelings, and physiological arousal (e.g., skin conductance, heart rate, blood pressure). Thus, there are three possible routes to aggression—through aggressive thoughts, angry feelings, and physiological arousal. However, these routes are not mutually exclusive or even independent, as indicated by the dashed lines with double-headed arrows shown in Figure 12.1. For example, someone who has aggressive ideas might also feel angry and have elevated blood pressure. Someone who has aggressive thoughts, who feels angry inside, and who is highly aroused and stressed out should be more likely to lash out at others aggressively than someone who has no aggressive thoughts, who does not feel angry, and who is calm.

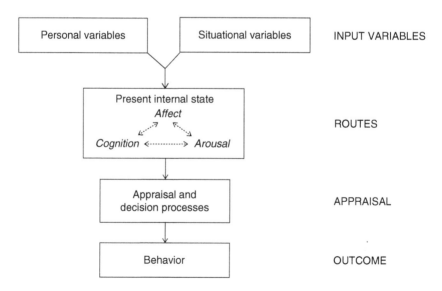

FIGURE 12.1 The General Aggression Model.

Adapted from Anderson and Bushman (2002a) and Krahé (2013).

According to the General Aggression Model, internal states can influence appraisal and decision processes. First, there is an immediate initial appraisal of whether the situation is dangerous, threatening, or warrants aggression. This initial appraisal might lead directly to an automatic or impulsive behavior, or it might lead to a reappraisal. If the initial appraisal is judged to be unsatisfactory and if the person has sufficient time and cognitive resources, reappraisal occurs (Barlett & Anderson, 2011). During reappraisal, the person considers alternative explanations of the situation and alternative behavioral options. When the appraisal is judged to be satisfactory, or when time or resources become insufficient, the appraisal process terminates and the person engages in the behavior, which completes one cycle.

Research has shown that three hostile biases can influence appraisal and decision processes: (1) hostile attribution bias, (2) hostile perception bias, and (3) hostile expectation bias (Dill et al., 1997). The *hostile attribution bias* is the tendency to perceive ambiguous actions by others as aggressive. For example, if a person bumps into you, a hostile attribution would be that the person did it on purpose to harm you. The *hostile perception bias* is the tendency to perceive ambiguous social interactions as being aggressive. For example, if you see two people having a conversation, a hostile perception would be that they are arguing or getting ready to fight. The *hostile expectation bias* is the tendency to assume that people will react to potential conflicts with aggression. For example, if you bump into another person, a hostile expectation would be that the person will assume that you did it on purpose and will attack you in return. These hostile biases can influence people to behave more aggressively themselves.

Each cycle can be viewed as a learning trial in which the person utilizes, develops, and reinforces knowledge structures associated with the episode. *Knowledge structures* are organized packets of information that are stored in memory. These knowledge structures form when a set of related concepts is frequently brought to mind or activated. How people construe and respond to their world depends in part on the knowledge structures they use. From a social-cognitive perspective, personality is the sum of a person's knowledge structures and emotional proclivities (e.g., Mischel & Shoda, 1995).

Methods Used to Study the Effects of Aggressive Cues

Researchers have used three types of methods to study aggressive cue effects: (1) experiments, (2) cross-sectional correlational studies, and (3) longitudinal studies. Each method has its own unique strengths and weaknesses.

Experiments

An experiment has two essential features: control and random assignment. The first feature is control over the procedures. The researcher manipulates the independent variable and holds all other variables constant. Participants are treated identically except for the level of the independent variable they are exposed to. By exercising control, the researcher attempts to ensure that any differences observed on the dependent variables were caused by the independent variable. The second feature is random assignment. Participants are randomly assigned to the levels of the independent variable. By randomly assigning participants to groups, the researcher attempts to ensure that there are no initial differences between groups. For example, if participants are randomly assigned to play a violent versus a non-violent video game, the two groups should be equally aggressive before gameplay. One cannot say that all the aggressive people played the violent game, because it is equally likely that aggressive people played the nonviolent game. Random assignment is the great equalizer, especially with large samples. The primary strength of experiments is that they allow researchers to make causal inferences. The primary weakness of experiments is that the settings and measures tend to be artificial, and they tend to rely on undergraduate student participants.

Cross-Sectional Correlational Studies

In a cross-sectional correlational study, the researcher measures the variables of interest, as well as possible confounding variables. The measurements are taken at only one point in time and are then analyzed to see if they are correlated, after controlling for the confounding variables. The primary strength of cross-sectional correlational studies is that they can be used when experiments cannot be used, and they allow researchers to examine more extreme forms of behavior (e.g., violent criminal behavior). Their primary weakness is that they cannot be used to make causal inference, as suggested by the familiar phrase: "correlation does not imply causation."

Longitudinal Studies

Longitudinal studies are like cross-sectional correlational studies except that researchers take multiple measurements on the same group of individuals over an extended period of time, even decades. Longitudinal studies allow researchers to look at long-term effects of violent media. They also allow researchers to test whether exposure to violent media predicts later aggression, whether aggressive individuals seek out violent media, or both. Their primary weakness is that they take a lot of resources to conduct (e.g., time, money).

Meta-Analysis

As the number of studies on a topic grows, it becomes increasingly important to review, summarize, and integrate study findings. One useful tool for doing this is a *meta-analysis*, which "refers to the analysis of analyses . . . the statistical analysis of a large collection of analysis results from individual studies for the purpose of integrating findings" (Glass, 1976, p. 3). In a meta-analysis, the reviewer uses statistical procedures to integrate the findings from a collection of studies, and describes the results using numerical effect-size estimates. Studies with larger samples are given more weight when computing the average effect-size estimate. The two most common effect-size estimates in the social sciences are the *correlation coefficient*, which gives the strength and direction of the linear relationship between two quantitative variables, and the *standardized mean difference*, which gives the difference between two means in standard deviation units. Conventional values for "small," "medium," and "large" effects are .1, .3, and .5 for the correlation, and 0.20, 0.50, and 0.80 for the standardized mean difference, respectively (Cohen, 1988).

Triangulation

Each research method has its own strengths and weaknesses. When different research methods yield the same pattern of results, one can have more confidence in the results. When the results from different methodologies converge, it is called *triangulation*. The term triangulation comes from surveying techniques that determine a single point with the convergence of measurements taken from two different points (Rothbauer, 2008). For example, Figure 12.2 shows the results of a

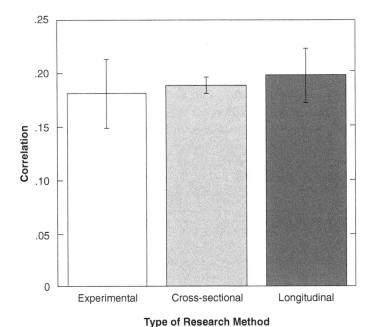

FIGURE 12.2   Average correlations and confidence intervals for different types of studies examining the link between violent video gameplay and aggressive behavior. Based on data from Anderson et al. (2010). Capped vertical bars denote 95% confidence interval limits.

meta-analysis on the effects of violent video games on aggression (Anderson et al., 2010). As can be seen in Figure 12.2, very similar results were obtained for experimental, cross-sectional, and longitudinal studies. This triangulation of results across methods increases our confidence that there is a link between exposure to violent games and aggression.

Next we turn to research findings on the weapons effect. These findings are based on experiments conducted in the laboratory and in the field.

Weapons Effect

> "Guns not only permit violence, they can stimulate it as well. The finger pulls the trigger, but the trigger may also be pulling the finger."
>
> Leonard Berkowitz

Obviously, using a gun can increase aggression and violence, but can just seeing a gun increase aggression? In 1967, Leonard Berkowitz and Anthony LePage conducted an experiment to find out. Male college students were tested in pairs, but one of them was actually an accomplice of the experimenter that was pretending to be a participant (called a "confederate"). The two students evaluated each other's performance on a task (e.g., listing ideas a used car salesperson might use to sell more cars). The "evaluations" were the number of stressful electrical shocks given to the other person. First, the confederate evaluated the participant's performance by using either one shock (low anger condition) or seven shocks (high anger condition). Next, the participant "evaluated" the confederate's performance. The number of electrical shocks the participant chose for the confederate was used to measure aggression. The participant was seated at a table that had a shotgun and a revolver on it, or badminton racquets and shuttlecocks. The items on the table were described as part of another study that another experimenter had supposedly forgotten to put away. There was also a control condition with no items on the table. The experimenter told participants to ignore the items on the table, but apparently they could not. Angered participants who saw the guns were more aggressive than the other participants. Berkowitz and LePage called this effect the *weapons effect*.

The weapons effect has been replicated many times, both inside and outside the lab. In this section I summarize the results of a recent meta-analytic review of weapons effect experiments (Benjamin & Bushman, 2016). The General Aggression Model (e.g., Anderson & Bushman, 2002a), described previously, was used as a theoretical foundation for this meta-analysis. The meta-analysis tested whether gender, age, and provocation moderate the effects of weapons on aggressive thoughts, angry feelings, hostile appraisals, and aggressive behavior. Thus, within the General Aggression Model framework, participant gender and age are personal variables, and exposure to weapons and provocation are situational variables. Two of the three routes to aggression were examined—aggressive thoughts and angry feelings. Unfortunately, no research has tested the effects of weapons on physiological arousal. This meta-analysis also considered the effects of weapons on hostile appraisals and on aggressive behavior.

In weapons effect studies, aggressive cognition is typically measured using the amount of time it takes (measured in milliseconds) to respond to aggressive and nonaggressive words, either by pressing a computer button or by speaking the word aloud. Participants in some studies complete word fragments as quickly as possible. For example, the word fragment K I _ _ can be completed to form the aggressive word KILL, or it can be completed to form a nonaggressive word such as KITE or KIND or KISS. In other studies, participants read a paragraph about an individual named "Donald" who engages in a series of ambiguously hostile behaviors (e.g., refusing to pay rent until his apartment is repainted), and then evaluate "Donald" using positive traits (e.g., DEPENDABLE, KIND), and negative traits (e.g., HOSTILE, UNFRIENDLY). The negative traits are used to measure aggressive cognition.

Aggressive affect is most often measured using mood scales. For example, participants rate how they feel "right now" using a list of adjectives, including some that measure aggressive affect (e.g., ANGRY, FURIOUS, IRRITABLE).

Hostile appraisals are measured in several different ways. For example, one study measured speed of fist clenching, as a form of automatic appraisal (da Gloria et al., 1989). Other studies measured how disagreeable, hostile, and angry participants thought a target person was, as a form of controlled reappraisal (e.g., Holbrook et al., 2014).

In laboratory experiments involving adults, aggression has most typically been measured using electric shocks (e.g., number, intensity, duration) given to a confederate pretending to be another participant. Other studies have measured the intensity of unpleasant noise blasts given to a confederate through headphones, and allocation of hot sauce to a confederate who hates spicy food. Verbal measures of aggression have included negative evaluations of experimenters and confederates. In field experiments involving adults, aggression has been measured either by the number of horn honks given to a confederate who is stalled at a traffic light, or the number of wet sponges thrown at a confederate (Simons et al., 1976). In field experiments involving children, aggression has been measured using behaviors observed in interactions with other children, such as pushing, shoving, kicking, tripping, and hitting.

In addition to the moderator variables provocation and participant age and gender, several methodological moderator variables were examined in this meta-analysis, including whether participants saw actual weapons or photos of weapons, whether the weapons were real or toys, type of weapons shown (i.e., guns, knives, or a mixture of various weapons), whether the study was conducted in a laboratory or field setting, and whether the study findings were published in a peer-reviewed journal.

The meta-analysis included 151 effects from 75 independent experiments involving 6,524 participants (Benjamin & Bushman, 2016). The results are depicted in Figure 12.3. Overall, exposure to weapons increased aggressive thoughts, hostile appraisals, and aggressive behavior. The average weapons effect for angry feelings was in the predicted direction, but was not significant. The weapons effect occurred both inside and outside the laboratory, regardless of whether individuals were provoked, regardless of whether individuals saw actual weapons or photos of weapons, and regardless of the type of weapons they saw. The weapons effect even occurred for toy weapons in studies involving children. There was little evidence of publication bias.

The results from this meta-analysis are generally consistent with the General Aggression Model. However, only 7 studies examined the effect of weapons on angry feelings, and no studies examined the effect of weapons on physiological arousal. The results from this meta-analysis indicate that the mere presence of weapons can increase hostile appraisals. Seeing weapons can cause people to believe that others are threatening, angry, and disagreeable. Most important, seeing weapons can make people more aggressive.

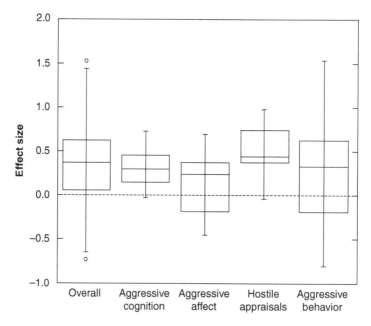

FIGURE 12.3   Weapons effect on aggressive thoughts, angry feelings, hostile appraisals, and aggressive behavior separately. Standardized mean difference was Hedge's g, which controls for small sample bias. Capped vertical bars denote 95% confidence intervals.

The findings from this meta-analysis have important practical implications, especially in societies where weapons such as guns are highly visible. Understanding the weapons effect can help parents with children. Research has shown that children are naturally curious about guns, have difficulty distinguishing a real gun from a toy gun, are prone to handle guns, and can shoot themselves or others with guns (American Academy of Pediatrics, 2013). In the United States, about 35% of homes with children have at least one gun, but in only 39% of these homes are guns locked up, unloaded, and separate from ammunition, as recommended by the American Academy of Pediatrics (Schuster et al., 2000). Some of these guns are in plain sight, such as in glass cabinets, on racks, or on shelves. To reduce the weapons effect, parents can keep guns out of sight of family members. As the English writer John Heywood said, "Out of sight out of mind." Parents can also give their children toys other than guns to play with.

Next we turn to research findings on the media violence effects. In the mass media, guns and other weapons are not merely present. Instead, weapons are often actively used to harm and kill other media characters.

Media Violence Effects

A fact of life in the twenty-first century is that most people are immersed in media, like fish in water. Electronic devices such as smartphones, tablets, television sets, computers, and video game consoles provide users with virtually unlimited access to media. Much of the media that people are exposed to contain violence, whether on television (e.g., Hetsroni, 2007; Lyons, 2013; National Television Violence Study, 1996, 1997, 1998), in movies (e.g., Bushman et al., 2013; Yokota & Thompson, 2000), in video games (e.g., Dill et al., 2005), or even in advertisements (e.g., Jones et al., 2010).

Several meta-analytic reviews have integrated the results from hundreds of studies on media violence effects (e.g., Anderson et al., 2010; Anderson & Bushman, 2002b; Bushman & Huesmann, 2006; Greitemeyer & Mügge, 2014; Paik & Comstock, 1994). The results from these meta-analyses indicate that violent media increase aggressive thoughts, angry feelings, and physiological arousal—the three routes to aggression outlined in the General Aggression Model. For example, consider the top three bars of Figure 12.4, from a meta-analysis of violent video game effects (Anderson et al., 2010).

Violent media can influence feelings other than anger. Numerous studies have shown that violent media can decrease feelings of empathy for others (e.g., see bottom bar of Figure 12.4). After seeing so much violence in the mass media, people can become desensitized to violence in the real world. When people become "comfortably numb" to the pain and suffering of others (Bushman & Anderson, 2009), they are less helpful to those in need (e.g., see fifth bar of Figure 12.4).

According to Cultivation Theory (Gerbner, 1998), heavy exposure to violent media can also increase feelings of fear. Research has shown that heavy television

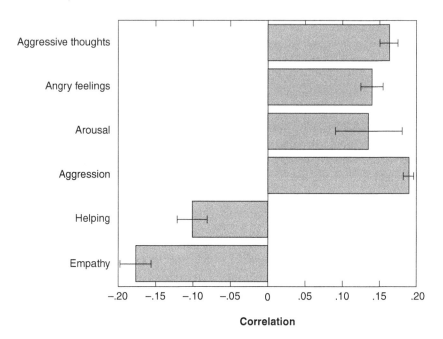

FIGURE 12.4 Results from a meta-analytic review of 381 violent video game effects from studies involving 130,295 participants (Anderson et al., 2010). Capped vertical bars denote 95% confidence interval limits.

viewers are more fearful about becoming victims of violence, are more distrustful of others, and are more likely to perceive the world as a dangerous, mean, and hostile place—called the *mean world syndrome* (e.g., Gerbner & Gross, 1976). One meta-analysis found an average correlation of .10 across 32 studies on the link between television exposure and fear of violence (Morgan & Shanahan, 1997). Thus, exposure to violent media can increase feelings of anger and fear, and decrease feelings of empathy.

The General Aggression Model also predicts that exposure to media violence can increase hostile appraisals,, which are more proximal to aggressive behavior. Consistent with this prediction, a recent meta-analysis found an average correlation of .20 (95% CI = .14, .26) across 37 studies involving 10,410 participants (Bushman, in press).

Numerous studies have shown a link between violent media and aggression (e.g., see the fourth bar in Figure 12.4), and experimental studies show the link is causal (e.g., see first bar in Figure 12.2). But does exposure to violent media cause violent behavior? That is a difficult question to answer conclusively. As noted earlier, experiments are the preferred method for making causal conclusions. However, it is unethical for researchers to allow participants to engage in violent criminal behavior in laboratory experiments. Very few analog experiments have included measures of violent behavior. In one experiment (Konijn et al., 2007), adolescent boys were given the opportunity to blast an ostensible opponent with loud noise through headphones after being randomly assigned to play a violent or nonviolent video game. The noise levels ranged from 0 to 10, and the boys were told that noise levels 8, 9, and 10 could cause "permanent hearing damage" to their ostensible partner. This meets the definition of "violence" given earlier, because the boys believed they could cause extreme physical damage to another boy.[1] The results showed that boys who played a violent game and strongly identified with the violent game character selected noise levels loud enough to cause permanent hearing damage to their ostensible partner. For example, during the debriefing one boy who played a violent game said, "I blasted him with level 10 noise because he deserved it, I know he can get hearing damage, but I don't care!"

Although there are very few experiments on the link between exposure to media violence and violent behavior, there are a number of cross-sectional and longitudinal studies on this topic. One meta-analysis found an average correlation of .10 across 58 studies between exposure to media violence and "criminal violence against a person (e.g., homicide, suicide, stabbing, etc.)" (Paik & Comstock, 1994). The same meta-analysis found an average correlation of .23 across 271 studies between exposure to TV violence and "physical violence against a person (non-illegal behavior)" (Paik & Comstock, 1994). In sum, research from meta-analytic reviews shows that exposure to media violence is a risk factor for both aggressive and violent behavior.

Violent media can have harmful effects on males and females of all ages, regardless of whether they live in Western or Eastern countries (e.g., Anderson et al., 2010). However, some people may be more vulnerable to violent media effects than others, just like some people are more vulnerable to cigarettes than others. For example, some vulnerable groups are individuals who are already characteristically aggressive (e.g., Bushman, 1995), individuals who tend to justify immoral behaviors (Gabbiadini et al., 2014), and individuals who are high in neuroticism and low in agreeableness and conscientiousness (Markey & Markey, 2010).

Conclusion

Many people seem to be like Arnold Schwarzenegger—they love violent media and guns. This love affair may be harmful, however, because research has clearly shown that exposure to aggressive cues such as weapons and violence in the media can make people more aggressive, more numb to the pain and suffering of others, and more afraid of becoming violence victims.

Note

1 Although the noise levels were loud, nobody got hearing damage. Level 10 noise was 105 decibels, about the same volume as a fire alarm.

References

American Academy of Pediatrics (2013, 18 June). *Is there a gun where your child plays? Asking can save lives*. Retrieved from www.aap.org/en-us/about-the-aap/aap-press-room/pages/Is-there-a-Gun-Where-Your-Child-Plays-Asking-Can-Save-Lives.aspx

Anderson, C. A., & Bushman, B. J. (2002a). Human aggression. *Annual Review of Psychology, 53*, 27–51. DOI:10.1146/annurev.psych.53.100901.135231

Anderson, C. A., & Bushman, B. J. (2002b). Media violence and societal violence. *Science, 295*(5564), 2377–2378. DOI:10.1126/science.1070765

Anderson, C. A., Shibuya, A., Ihori, N., Swing, E. L., Bushman, B. J., Sakamoto, A., Rothstein, H. R., & Saleem, M. (2010). Violent video game effects on aggression, empathy, and prosocial behavior in Eastern and Western countries: A meta-analytic review. *Psychological Bulletin, 136*(2), 151–173. DOI:10.1037/a0018251

Barlett, C. P., & Anderson, C. A. (2011). Reappraising the situation and its impact on aggressive behavior. *Personality and Social Psychology Bulletin, 37*(12), 1564–1573. DOI:10.1177/0146167211423671

Baron, R. A., & Richardson, D. R. (1994). *Human aggression* (2nd ed.). New York: Plenum.

Benjamin, A. J., Jr., & Bushman, B. J. (2016). *Effects of the mere presence of weapons on aggressive thoughts, angry feelings, hostile appraisals, and aggressive behavior: A meta-analytic review of the weapons effect literature*. Manuscript under review.

Berkowitz, L., & LePage, A. (1967). Weapons as aggression-eliciting stimuli. *Journal of Personality and Social Psychology, 7*, 202–207. DOI:10.1037/h0025008

Bushman, B. J. (1995). Moderating role of trait aggressiveness in the effects of violent media on aggression. *Journal of Personality and Social Psychology, 69*(5), 950–960. DOI:10.1037/0022-3514.69.5.950

Bushman, B. J. (in press). Violent media and hostile appraisals: A meta-analytic review. *Aggressive Behavior*.

Bushman, B. J., & Anderson, C. A. (2009). Comfortably numb: Desensitizing effects of violent media on helping others. *Psychological Science, 21*(3), 273–277. DOI:10.1111/j.1467-9280.2009.02287.x

Bushman, B. J., & Huesmann, L. R. (2006). Short-term and long-term effects of violent media on aggression in children and adults. *Archives of Pediatrics & Adolescent Medicine, 160*(4), 348–352. DOI:10.1001/archpedi.160.4.348

Bushman, B. J., & Huesmann, L. R. (2010). Aggression. In S. T. Fiske, D. T. Gilbert, & G. Lindzey (Eds.), *Handbook of social psychology* (5th ed., Ch. 23, pp. 833–863). New York: John Wiley & Sons.

Bushman, B. J., Jamieson, P. E., Weitz, I., & Romer, D. (2013). Gun violence trends in movies. *Pediatrics, 132*(6), 1014–1018. DOI:10.1542/peds.2013-1600

Cohen, J. (1988). *Statistical power analysis for the behavioral sciences* (2nd ed.). Hillsdale, NJ: Lawrence Erlbaum.

da Gloria, J., Duda, D., Pahlavan, F., & Bonnet, P. (1989). "Weapons effect" revisited: Motor effects of the reception of aversive stimulation and exposure to pictures of firearms. *Aggressive Behavior, 15*, 265–271. DOI:10.1002/ab.2480150401

DeWall, C. N., Anderson, C. A., & Bushman, B. J. (2011). The General Aggression Model: Theoretical extensions to violence. *Psychology of Violence, 1*(3), 245–258. DOI:10.1037/a0023842

Dill, K. E., Anderson, C. A., Anderson, K. B., & Deuser, W. E. (1997). Effects of aggressive personality on social expectations and social perceptions. *Journal of Research in Personality, 31*, 272–292.

Dill, K. E., Gentile, D. A., Richter, W. A., & Dill, J. C. (2005). Violence, sex, race and age in popular video games: A content analysis. In E. Cole & J. Henderson Daniel (Eds.), *Featuring females: Feminist analyses of the media* (pp. 115–130). Washington, DC: American Psychological Association.

Gabbiadini, A., Riva, P., Andrighetto, L., Volpato, C., & Bushman, B. J. (2014). Moral disengagement moderates the effect of violent video games on self-control, cheating and aggression. *Social Psychological and Personality Science, 5*(4), 451–458. DOI: 10.1177/1948550613509286

Gerbner, G. (1998). Cultivation analysis: An overview. *Mass Communication & Society, 1*(3–4), 175–194. DOI:10.1080/15205436.1998.9677855

Gerbner, G., & Gross, L. (1976). Living with television: The violence profile. *Journal of Communication, 26*(2), 172–199. DOI:10.1111/j.1460–2466.1976.tb01397.x

Gerbner, G., & Gross, L. (1980). Living with television: The violence profile. *Journal of Communication, 30*(3), 10–29.

Glass, G.V. (1976). Primary, secondary, and meta-analysis of research. *Educational Researcher, 5*(10), 3–8. DOI:10.3102/0013189X005010003

Greitemeyer, T., & Mügge, D. O. (2014). Video games do affect social outcomes: A meta-analytic review of the effects of violent and prosocial video game play. *Personality and Social Psychology Bulletin, 40*(5), 578–589. DOI:10.1177/0146167213520459

Hetsroni, A. (2007). Four decades of violent content on prime-time network programming: A longitudinal meta-analytic review. *Journal of Communication, 57*(4), 759–784.

Holbrook, C., Galperin, A., Fessler, D. M. T., Johnson, K. L., Bryant, G. A., & Haselton, M. G. (2014). If looks could kill: Anger attributions are intensified by affordances for doing harm. *Emotion, 14*, 455–461. DOI:10.1037/a0035826

Jones, T., Cunningham, P. H., & Gallagher, K. (2010). Violence in advertising: A multi-layered content analysis. *Journal of Advertising, 39*(4), 11–36. DOI:10.2753/JOA0091–3367390402

Konijn, E. A., Nije Bijvank, M., & Bushman, B. J. (2007). I wish I were a warrior: The role of wishful identification in effects of violent video games on aggression in adolescent boys. *Developmental Psychology, 43*(4), 1038–1044. DOI: 10.1037/0012–1649.43.4.1038

Krahé, B. (2013). *The social psychology of aggression* (2nd ed.). New York: Psychology Press.

Lyons, M. (2013, April 17). Maxing out on murder: Good luck finding decent TV drama without rape or killing. *Vulture.* Retrieved from www.vulture.com/2013/04/maxing-out-on-murder-shows.html

MacInnis, L. (2007, August 28). U.S. most armed country with 90 guns per 100 people. *Reuters News.* Retrieved from www.reuters.com/article/2007/08/28/us-world-firearms-idUSL2834893820070828

Markey, P. M., & Markey, C. N. (2010). Vulnerability to violent video games: A review and integration of personality research. *Review of General Psychology, 14*(2), 82–91. DOI:10.1037/a0019000

Mischel, W., & Shoda, Y. (1995). A cognitive-affective system theory of personality: Reconceptualizing situations, dispositions, dynamics, and invariance in personality structure. *Psychological Review, 102*(2), 246–268. DOI:10.1037/0033–295X.102.2.246

Morgan, M., & Shanahan, J. (1997). Two decades of cultivation research: An appraisal and a meta-analysis. Communication Yearbook, 20, 1–45.

National Television Violence Study (1996). *National television violence study* (Vol. 1). Thousand Oaks, CA: Sage.

National Television Violence Study (1997). *National television violence study* (Vol. 2). Studio City, CA: Mediascope.

National Television Violence Study (1998). *National television violence study* (Vol. 3). Santa Barbara, CA: The Center for Communication and Social Policy, University of California, Santa Barbara.

Paik, H., & Comstock, G. (1994). The effects of television violence on antisocial behavior: A meta-analysis. *Communication Research, 12,* 516–546. DOI:10.1177/009365094021004004

Rothbauer, P. (2008). Triangulation. In L. M. Given (Ed.), *The SAGE encyclopedia of qualitative research methods* (pp. 892–894). Thousand Oaks, CA: Sage Publications.

Sargent, J. D., Heatherton, T. F., Ahrens, M. B., Dalton, M. A., Tickle, J. J., & Beach, M. L. (2002). Adolescent exposure to extremely violent movies. *Journal of Adolescent Health,* 31(6), 449–454.

Schuster, M. A., Franke, T. M., Bastian, A. M., Sor, S., & Halfon, N. (2000). Firearm storage patterns in U.S. homes with children. *American Journal of Public Health, 90,* 588–594. DOI:10.2105/AJPH.90.4.588

Simons, L. S., Fenn, M. R., Layton, J. F., & Turner, C. W. (1976). Verhalten en eimen aggressions-spiel auf dem vergnugnungsplatz (Aggressive behavior in a game at the amusement park). In J. Koch (Ed.), *Altruismus und aggression: Das fieldexperiment in der sozialpsychology 1 (Altruism and aggression: The field experiment in social psychology 1)* (pp. 141–148). Weinheim and Basel, Weinheim, Germany: Beltz Verlag.

Turner, C. W., Layton, J. F., & Simons, L. S. (1975). Naturalistic studies of aggressive behavior: Aggressive stimuli, victim visibility, and horn honking. *Journal of Personality and Social Psychology, 31,* 1098–1107. DOI:10.1037/h0076960

Yokota, F., & Thompson K. M. (2000). Violence in G-rated animated films. *Journal of the American Medical Association, 283*(20), 2716–2720. DOI:10.1001/jama.283.20.2716

13

EFFECTS OF ALCOHOL AND OTHER DRUGS ON HUMAN AGGRESSION

Dominic J. Parrott and Christopher I. Eckhardt

Author Note

Preparation of this chapter was supported in part by grant R01-AA-020578 from the National Institute on Alcohol Abuse and Alcoholism awarded to both authors.

The notion of a linkage between alcohol and other drugs to acts of aggression is hardly a recent phenomenon, and is even evident in historical records of ancient Greece in the fourth and fifth centuries BC (Nencini, 1997). In the mid-nineteenth century, adherents to the temperance movement in the United States advanced the argument that if alcohol makes people do and feel things differently than they would normally, then alcohol could clearly be viewed as a cause of criminal behavior (Crichtlow, 1986). This notion of alcohol and other drugs destroying self-control and promoting deviance quickly infiltrated society's attitudes about the typical causes of aggression and violent crime and, despite the many and varied shifts in attitudes toward alcohol and substance use over time, continues to persist. Frequent news reports of murders, robberies, and other violent crimes that appear to involve substance use provide ongoing reinforcement of the notion that alcohol and substance use and violent crime are associated.

Empirical support for this association is extensive, especially as it relates to alcohol and aggression. Formative research on the causes of homicides over a four-year period indicated that the offender or victim had been drinking in over 60% of homicide incidents, with both offender and victim drinking in over 40% of homicides (Wolfgang, 1958). Since this seminal publication, subsequent cross-sectional research has supported the notion that around 50% of aggressive incidents seem to involve drinking by offenders and victims (Murdoch et al., 1990; Pernanen, 1991; Pittman & Handy, 1964), with one report indicating alcohol involvement in 100% of homicide incidents stemming specifically from arguments (Lindqvist, 1986). In a large population-based survey of married or cohabitating couples in the United States, rates of partner-directed aggression were approximately three times higher among chronic heavy drinkers than among couples who refrain from drinking alcohol (Kantor & Straus, 1987). The large amount of cross-sectional data supporting the alcohol-aggression link in turn spurred a flurry of laboratory studies examining the effects of acute alcohol intoxication on aggression, with findings demonstrating that alcohol intoxication reliably increased aggressive responding (e.g., Shuntich & Taylor, 1972; Zeichner & Pihl, 1979). Thus, by the late 1980s and early 1990s, there appeared to be clear evidence from multiple sources of data that alcohol use is an important risk factor for aggressive behavior.

Subsequent quantitative and qualitative literature reviews assessed whether the overall pattern of data support the expected alcohol-aggression link (Bushman, 1997; Bushman & Cooper, 1990; Ito et al., 1996; Lipsey et al., 1997; Parker & Auerhahn, 1998). Although these reviews consistently reported significant positive associations between alcohol use and aggression, there was a growing recognition that this relation was neither as strong, nor as clear, as previously assumed. Reported effect sizes have typically been in the medium range (e.g., $r = .54$ in Ito et al., 1996; $r = .61$ in Bushman & Cooper, 1990), calling into question the assumption of a simple linear relationship between alcohol and aggression. Instead, reviews suggested that a variety of moderating variables account for the heterogeneous results (e.g., Chermack & Giancola, 1997; Pihl & Sutton, 2009). For instance, larger alcohol-aggression effect sizes were reported for intoxicated individuals with higher levels of anxiety, greater inhibition conflict, and more anger/hostility/frustration as well as for intoxicated individuals who consumed a higher alcohol dose or distilled beverages, did not have a nonaggressive response alternative, and perceived a possibility to be retaliated against. Smaller effects were noted with increased provocation levels and self-focused attention, during distraction conditions, and when experimenters were blind to alcohol condition (e.g., Bushman & Cooper, 1990; Ito et al., 1996).

The recognition that alcohol was neither a necessary nor sufficient cause of aggressive behavior also supported the need to further distinguish between pharmacological and psychological factors, as well as their interaction, in understanding substance-induced aggression. While the assumption has been that the specific pharmacodynamics of alcohol's effects on various central nervous system components are proximal causes of aggression, it is also plausible that alcohol and other substances affect interpersonal behaviors through their effects on cognitive and affective systems that alter how the individual interprets social situations (Goldman et al., 1999). This view, termed the expectancy model, gained popularity following a seminal publication that argued that "people learn about drunkenness what their society 'knows' about drunkenness; and, accepting and acting upon the understandings thus imparted to them, they become the living confirmation of their society's teachings" (MacAndrew & Edgerton, 1969, p. 88). Much has been devoted to understanding whether culturally shared expectancies and beliefs about the consequences of alcohol use have specific influences on social interactions involving alcohol consumption. However, in studies using expectancy controls (i.e., "placebo" participants who believe they are receiving alcohol but in fact receive very little or no alcohol), there is little evidence to support the notion that alcohol-related aggression is better explained by expectancies rather than alcohol itself. Rather, most research indicates that pharmacologic factors are necessary to understand alcohol-related aggression (Quigley & Leonard, 2006).

Given the reviewed literature, the present chapter will emphasize pharmacological-based theories of substance-related violence. It is also worth noting that the overwhelming majority of research on substance-related violence has involved alcohol. Moreover, the majority of substance-related deleterious social effects are related to alcohol rather than other drugs. As such, unless otherwise noted, our review will be specific to the alcohol-aggression link.

Theories of Alcohol-Related Aggression

Social scientists have advanced numerous theories to explain the pharmacological effect of alcohol on aggressive behavior (Giancola, 2000; Graham, 1980). The *disinhibition model* is one of the first explanatory models and emphasizes alcohol's general disinhibiting effect on behavior. This model posits that alcohol directly impairs brain centers responsible for inhibiting socially inappropriate behavior, including aggression. However, the extant literature clearly indicates that alcohol facilitates aggression to a greater extent for certain "at risk" individuals and in certain "at risk" situations (Pihl & Sutton, 2009). Thus, the disinhibition model is unable to explain in whom, and under what conditions, a disinhibited state will lead to aggression.

As an alternative to the disinhibition model, numerous indirect causal models have been advanced. The most accepted of these are founded upon the view that the alcohol-aggression relation is mediated by alcohol-induced changes in physiological arousal and/or impairment of cognitive functioning or some neurological system. These theories are reviewed in detail below.

Physiological Arousal

Increased arousal is positively associated with aggressive behavior (Anderson & Bushman, 2002; Rule & Nesdale, 1976). Moreover, alcohol increases arousal on the ascending limb and decreases arousal on the descending limb of the breath alcohol concentration curve. Accordingly, the stimulant effects (e.g., vigor) and sedative effects (e.g., fatigue) of alcohol intoxication are most prominent on the ascending and descending limb, respectively (Addicott et al., 2007; Martin et al., 1993). In view of these effects, it is not surprising that aggression most often occurs during the ascending limb of intoxication (Giancola & Zeichner, 1997), and that heightened arousal is more strongly associated with aggression among intoxicated persons (Giancola et al., 1998).

Anxiolysis-Disinhibition

Alcohol is posited to facilitate aggression by reducing anxiety (Ito et al., 1996; Pihl et al., 1993). Typically, neural "warning signals" that arise from threatening cues in the environment elicit anxiety and subsequently inhibit aggression. The pharmacological effects of alcohol disrupt these "warning signals" via impairment of the functioning of the prefrontal cortex and its subcortical connections. As a result, the anxiety response is muted and aggressive behavior is more likely. These basic tenets of the anxiolysis-disinhibition hypothesis have been established in earlier studies (e.g., Conger, 1956; Taylor & Chermack, 1993; Washburne, 1956; Wilson, 1988) and supported indirectly by later studies. Most notably, a meta-analysis of 49 studies demonstrated that the effect size of acute alcohol intoxication on aggression increased as the strength of anxiety-producing cues increased (Ito et al., 1996). The authors concluded that intoxicated individuals experienced anxiolysis and, as a result, were "relatively free from anxiety-related inhibition, leading to increased aggression in intoxicated relative to sober persons" (p. 72).

Given these findings, the aggression-promoting effects of alcohol seem readily, and succinctly, explained by anxiolysis. However, the link between alcohol and the anxiety response is complex. For instance, support for the notion that alcohol intoxication invariably decreases anxiety is equivocal (Cappell & Herman, 1972; Greeley & Oei, 1999; Sayette, 1993), leading to the advancement of other models that may explain these contradictory findings. A notable example is the appraisal-disruption model (Sayette, 1993), which purports that effects of alcohol on anxiety depend upon the temporal relationship between alcohol consumption and exposure to anxiety-producing cues. When alcohol consumption precedes exposure to anxiogenic cues, alcohol disrupts initial appraisal of these cues and, consequently, attenuates the spread of activation to threat-related information stored in memory. In turn, this impairment results in anxiolysis. However, when exposure to anxiety-producing cues precedes alcohol consumption, encoding of threat-related information is not impaired and may even be enhanced. In these instances, alcohol is posited to increase anxiety.

Using this model to understand the alcohol-aggression relation, alcohol should increase aggression via anxiolysis when threatening and/or anxiety-producing cues *follow* alcohol consumption; however, when such cues precede alcohol consumption, alcohol should increase anxiety. A recent study supports this latter hypothesis and showed that alcohol-facilitated increases in anxiety also facilitated aggressive behavior (Parrott et al., 2012). Collectively, this literature underscores the complexity of the alcohol-aggression relation and its numerous putative mechanisms.

Self-Awareness

Self-awareness theory posits that when attention is focused on the self, automatic comparisons between self and social standards of appropriate behavior are initiated (Silvia & Duval, 2001). Alcohol intoxication reduces self-awareness by disrupting the encoding of self-relevant information that could be used to modulate behavior in accordance with nonaggressive social norms (Hull, 1981; Hull et al., 1983). Indeed, alcohol has a weaker effect on aggression when participants' attention is focused on self-relevant information (Ito et al., 1996). For example, experimental inducement of participants' self-awareness via the addition of mirrors or emphasis of one's behavior in relation to nonaggressive norms reduces alcohol-related aggression toward oneself (Berman et al., 2009), and others (Bailey et al., 1983; Jeavons & Taylor, 1985), in social drinking samples and heavy-drinking men (Gallagher & Parrott, in press).

Executive Functioning

Executive functioning is a broad construct that is important to behavioral self-regulation. It comprises numerous neurocognitive domains that are critical to the planning and execution of adaptive behavioral responses, including attentional control, response inhibition, working memory, cognitive flexibility, and self-monitoring (Anderson et al., 2008). One scholar posited that executive functioning may both mediate and moderate the effect of alcohol on aggression (Giancola, 2000). Thus, alcohol may (1) disrupt executive functioning, which then dysregulates goal-directed behavior and subsequently increases the likelihood of aggression (a mediator model), and/or (2) increase aggression to a greater extent in persons with low, relative to high, premorbid executive functioning (a moderator model).

Extant literature supports both hypotheses. Numerous studies indicate that alcohol consumption impairs executive functioning (e.g., Curtin & Fairchild, 2003; Hoaken et al., 1998; Peterson et al., 1990), and that impairment in executive functioning is associated with aggressive behavior (Fishbein, 2000). In addition, studies indicate that alcohol facilitates aggression to a greater extent among persons who possess lower levels of sober-state executive functioning (Giancola, 2004; Giancola et al., 2006; Hoaken et al., 1998).

Alcohol Myopia

The alcohol-aggression relation is most frequently interpreted from the etiologic standpoint of Alcohol Myopia Theory (Steele & Josephs, 1990; Steele & Southwick, 1985). This theory purports that the pharmacological properties of alcohol narrow attentional focus, restrict the internal and external cues that individuals perceive, and reduce individuals' capacity to process meaning from information they do perceive. One related model, the Attention-Allocation Model, posits that alcohol impairs attentional capacity, which then restricts the inebriate's ability to perceive and process instigatory and inhibitory cues. As a result, intoxicated individuals allocate their attention such that they perceive and process only the most salient cues of a situation (e.g., a verbal insult) and exclude less salient inhibitory cues (e.g., legal consequences of aggression).

Alcohol Myopia Theory has garnered ample empirical support. Laboratory data suggest that alcohol use increases or decreases aggression depending upon whether attention is manipulated toward cues that promote (e.g., provocation) or inhibit (e.g., nonaggressive norms) aggression, respectively. For instance, distraction from provocative cues reduces physical aggression among intoxicated men (Gallagher & Parrott, 2011; Giancola & Corman, 2007). Meta-analytic reviews evidence smaller effect sizes of alcohol on aggression when participants are distracted (Bushman & Cooper, 1990). Cross-sectional studies suggest that heavy drinking is associated with aggression primarily among hostile individuals who endorse dispositional tendencies toward aggression-related cognitive biases (Leonard & Blane, 1992) or who are susceptible to alcohol-related shifts in attention toward provocative cues (e.g., low mindfulness: Gallagher et al., 2010). Accordingly, prior research has demonstrated that individuals at risk for aggression show attentional biases toward aggression-relevant contextual stimuli (Eckhardt & Cohen, 1997; Smith & Waterman, 2004). Thus, it follows from Alcohol Myopia Theory that alcohol use may potentiate aggression by narrowing attention onto salient, provocative cues, especially in high-risk individuals. While prior research has examined the moderating effects of information processing biases (e.g., executive functioning deficits; Giancola, 2004), the mediational attention allocation hypothesis assumed to underlie the alcohol-aggression association has received scant empirical attention (Gallagher & Parrott, 2011).

The Attention-Allocation Model has largely been used to explain why alcohol increases aggressive behavior (Giancola et al., 2010). However, this model also makes the counterintuitive prediction that alcohol intoxication can actually decrease aggression, even below that of sober individuals. Specifically, in a situation where non-provocative cues are most salient, the narrowed attentional capacity of the inebriate will be focused on those cues, leaving little space in working memory to focus on less salient provocative cues. In contrast, sober persons faced with the same situation possess enough working memory to allot attention to provocative and non-provocative cues, thus increasing their risk of aggression above that of intoxicated persons. Data support this counterintuitive prediction (Bailey et al., 1983; Gallagher & Parrott, 2011, in press; Giancola et al., 2011; Giancola & Corman, 2007), which carries compelling implications for interventions designed to prevent or reduce alcohol-related aggression (Giancola et al., 2009). These implications are discussed in more detail later in this chapter.

Instigation × Impellance × Inhibitor (I³) Theory

The theories reviewed above provide useful frameworks for understanding how a particular class of variables may be involved with substance-related aggression. However, each is understandably limited in scope. By organizing these theories and supportive evidence within a single conceptual framework, the fundamental principles and processes that underlie substance-related aggression may be better understood.

One such "meta-theory," called I³ Theory ("I-Cubed"), is a multifactorial process-level model that predicts myriad behaviors, including aggression (Finkel, 2007, 2014; Finkel & Eckhardt, 2013). Like other meta-theoretical approaches, such as the General Aggression Model (Anderson & Bushman, 2002), I³ Theory does not restrict the prediction of aggression to one decisive risk factor (or set of factors) or to one particular theoretical level of analysis (e.g., intrapersonal vs. interpersonal). Rather, I³ Theory suggests that scholars can predict whether a given social interaction will result in aggression if they can discern the strength of instigation, degree of impellance, and presence of inhibitory factors. Despite the limitations of the monotheoretical approaches reviewed above, each can contribute to an I³ analysis of aggression as long as a process or set of processes through which their hypothesized risk factors promote aggressive responding (Finkel, 2014). Once these factors are organized into the I³ framework, their effects on aggressive responding as well as their interactions with other relevant risk factors can be examined. The three process domains of I³ Theory are defined below.

Instigating Factors

Instigating factors normatively produce an urge to behave aggressively (e.g., provocation, relationship conflict). These factors provide the initial momentum toward an aggressive action that represents the availability of an aggressive response. Of course, availability of an aggressive response does not mandate its implementation. People are exposed to instigating influences every day, but few actually produce subsequent aggression. Thus, other processes are necessary to determine whether someone will perpetrate aggression at a specific point in time.

Impelling Factors

Impelling factors are dispositional and/or situational factors that psychologically prepare an individual to experience a strong urge to aggress when encountering instigation in a particular context. For example, a person with high trait anger is prone to aggression (Birkley & Eckhardt, 2015), but contextual or situational instigators must first provide the initial urge toward aggression. High trait anger represents an impeller, which amplifies the instigating cue beyond that which would occur if the cue was presented alone. Just like a pool of gasoline will not ignite without an incendiary device, instigating and impelling factors interact to create an individual's "urge-readiness," or the likelihood that the person will experience a strong inclination to act aggressively in that particular context.

Inhibiting/Disinhibiting Factors

Inhibitory factors increase the likelihood that a person will be able to resist an urge to behave aggressively in the presence of a given instigatory cue. Inhibiting factors set the threshold beyond which aggressive urges would result in aggressive behavior. The integrity of these inhibitory capabilities may be compromised by various *disinhibiting* influences, which decrease the effectiveness of inhibitory efforts and, therefore, decrease the likelihood that a person will be able to resist an aggressive urge. A variety of disinhibiting cognitive processes appear to support the "moral disengagement" that accompanies destructive human behavior, including interpersonal aggression, such as constructing a moral justification for aggression, euphemistic labeling and advantageous comparisons designed to minimize the impact of aggression, displacement and diffusion of responsibility, blaming and dehumanizing the aggressive target, and distorting the consequences of aggression (Bandura, 1999). In the specific context of interpersonal aggression, researchers have also examined several types of disinhibiting influences associated with an increased risk for aggression, including cognitive resource depletion, relationship commitment, physical pain, and—of relevance to this chapter—alcohol intoxication (Berkowitz, 1993; Finkel et al., 2009; Giancola et al., 2010). The difference between inhibiting and disinhibiting influences constitutes a person's "urge-impedance," or the overall ability of an individual to inhibit an aggressive inclination.

A key advantage of using I^3 Theory to understand substance-related aggression rests in its interactional framework. The model suggests that we may be able to predict, with greater accuracy, whether a given social interchange will result in aggressive or nonaggressive responding if we can discern the strength and patterning of instigation, impellance, and inhibition factors. Prior research has supported the use of the Instigation × Impellance × Inhibition interaction to predict non-intoxicated interpersonal aggression (Finkel et al., 2012; Sinclair et al., 2011; Slotter et al., 2012). Notably, one laboratory-based study found that high trait anger (high impellance) was associated with higher aggression in response to provocation (strong instigation), but only among men who were intoxicated (high disinhibition) and reported low levels of anger control (low inhibition; Parrott & Zeichner, 2002). This finding represents a prime application of the I^3 interactional framework and how knowledge of the interplay among these three processes may be both *necessary and sufficient* for predicting alcohol-facilitated aggression.

Proposed Mechanisms of Alcohol-Facilitated Aggression

A singular advantage to a unifying model such as I³ Theory is its theoretical inclusiveness, which allows researchers to incorporate the most empirically supported theories available as a means of establishing empirically based, multifactorial conceptualizations of aggression risk. Specific theories can then be brought to bear to examine how hypotheses related to risk can be translated into process-oriented mediation models. For example, while research has clearly established that alcohol-facilitated aggression is more likely when the perpetrator (a) is provoked (i.e., the role of *Instigation*) and (b) possesses particular aggressogenic traits (i.e., the role of *Impellers*), evidence is converging that the pathway from alcohol intoxication to aggressive behavior primarily involves factors specifically related to *Inhibition* (e.g., Pihl et al., 2003). Thus, alcohol does not appear to unilaterally impel acts of aggression via direct pharmacologic manipulation; rather, alcohol intoxication produces key neuropsychological changes that alter executive functioning and impede self-regulatory capacities (Giancola et al., 2010).

As reviewed earlier, Alcohol Myopia Theory has garnered substantial empirical support as a model for understanding *how* alcohol affects inhibitory processes related to human behavior, including aggression (Giancola et al., 2010). While it is clear that Alcohol Myopia Theory is a well-supported model that fleshes out the inhibitory process dimension of the I³ meta-theory, the intervening processes by which attentional biases increase (or decrease) the probability of an aggressive response to a provocative situation remain largely unstudied. To address this important gap in the literature, researchers sought to explain the mechanisms that are likely to mediate the association between attention allocation and interpersonal aggression (Giancola et al., 2010). These proposed mechanisms of Alcohol Myopia Theory are discussed below.

Increased Negative Affect and Anger

Building on cognitive-neoassociationistic theory (Berkowitz, 1990, 1993), alcohol-induced attention toward provocation is posited to produce a state of general negative affect that may subsequently generate a refined affective state of anger. Angry affect may then promote aggression by activating aggression-impelling scripts in the associative network that invoke concepts of revenge and retaliation, further focusing the individual on the actions of the instigator, and producing a state of excited arousal that impels an approach behavior such as aggression.

Support for this approach comes from studies of the interaction between alcohol intoxication and trait, as well as state, anger as risk factors for aggression (Eckhardt, 2007; Parrott & Zeichner, 2002; Parrott et al., 2003). Collectively, this line of research finds that alcohol facilitates anger and aggression, especially among individuals who are high in trait anger. Building upon these results, it is likely that biased attention toward conflict-laden, prepotent contextual stimuli may automatically activate affective changes that increase the likelihood of an aggressive response (Anderson & Bushman, 2002).

Hostile Cognitive Rumination

A variety of models that outline aggression etiology (e.g., Anderson & Bushman, 2002; Berkowitz, 2008; Huesmann, 1988) predict that attentional biases favoring conflict and aggression lead to excessive rumination about the provocation, the transgressor, and the behavioral responses required to resolve the provocative situation. This prediction has been supported in conditions involving an insulting provocation delivered by a laboratory confederate (Bushman et al., 2005), after imagining anger-inducing autobiographical memories (Rusting & Nolen-Hoeksema, 1998), and in prior research with partner violent males (Eckhardt et al., 1998; 2002).

Together, these findings suggest that one important impellance pathway through which alcohol-induced attentional biases may increase aggression risk is by concentrating subsequent cognitive processes on the hostile transgression. Support for this view comes from studies of the interaction between alcohol and trait variables associated with rumination or suppression on aggressive behavior (Borders & Giancola, 2011; Gallagher et al., 2014). These experimental studies suggest that under conditions of interpersonal provocation, alcohol intoxication produces a myopic focus on hostile thoughts. Thus, it is likely that these cognitive distortions serve as critical information cues that prolong angry affect and guide the transgressed toward an aggressive resolution of the conflict.

Self-awareness

As previously reviewed (e.g., Hull, 1981; Hull et al., 1983), alcohol-induced reductions in self-awareness are posited to facilitate aggressive behavior. Thus, manipulations or interventions that redirect the inebriate's attention onto cues that promote self-awareness should effectively reduce intoxicated aggression. Consistent with this view, meta-analytic findings indicate smaller effect sizes of alcohol on aggression when social drinking participants' attention was focused on self-relevant information (Ito et al., 1996). More recent experimental studies have extended these findings to self-directed aggression (e.g., Berman et al., 2009) and heavy drinkers (Gallagher & Parrott, in press). Collectively, this literature indicates that, by increasing self-awareness, the inebriate is distracted from provocation *and* able to process cues of inhibition. As a result, intoxicated aggression is less likely.

Summary

I[3] Theory provides a heuristic framework that integrates numerous approaches that have been successful in understanding (1) the cognitive, affective, and behavioral risk factors for alcohol-facilitated interpersonal aggression, and (2) theoretically relevant mechanisms of aggression. Collectively, accounting for multiple determinants and mechanisms of alcohol- and substance-related aggression within a parsimonious framework provides the foundation for the construction of effective treatments to prevent alcohol- and substance-related aggression.

Alcohol and Aggression: Notable Areas of Study

Alcohol use has also been associated with specific categories of interpersonal aggression. Prior reviews of the association between alcohol use and sexual aggression have been exclusively qualitative in nature, and suggest that alcohol use is indeed a proximal risk factor for sexual aggression (Abbey et al., 2014; Testa, 2002). With regard to alcohol use and intimate partner violence, three meta-analytic reviews have reported similar results, with overall effect sizes in the moderate range ($d = 0.47$ to 0.57) across 50 studies investigating physical intimate partner violence and perpetrator alcohol use (Ferrer et al., 2004; Foran & O'Leary, 2008; Stith et al., 2004).

However, these reviews have examined a variety of sources of alcohol use data, and therefore have not specifically addressed the extent to which the *acute effects* of alcohol intoxication have direct effects on aggressive responding. A recent meta-analytic review sought to bridge this gap and reported associations between acute alcohol use and male-to-female aggression (Crane et al., in press). Across 22 studies involving over 2,500 participants, the overall effect was significant and small to moderate in size ($d = 0.36$) and suggested that males who drank alcohol showed more laboratory aggression toward females than males who received no alcohol. The effects of acute alcohol intoxication had similar effects on general aggression ($d = 0.32$), sexual aggression ($d = 0.32$), and intimate partner violence ($d = 0.45$), and were consistent across a variety of potential moderators.

Relative to sexual aggression and intimate partner violence, research on the link between acute alcohol intoxication and bias-motivated aggression toward stigmatized groups is limited (Hull & Van Treuren, 1986; Parrott & Miller, 2009). Because the adverse effects of such violence extend beyond the physical victim to larger social groups (Herek & McLemore, 2013; Meyer, 2003), the public health significance is substantial. Studies of intergroup bias indicate that alcohol increases the expression of prejudice, stereotyping, and discrimination (Bartholow et al., 2006; Reeves & Nagoshi, 1993; Stepanova et al., 2012). Consistent with these data, several studies suggest that alcohol facilitates aggression toward stigmatized groups. One cross-sectional, survey-based investigation found that approximately 33% of hate crime perpetrators were intoxicated at the time of their offense (Dunbar, 2003). Another study assessed men's daily reports of alcohol use and perpetration of aggression toward a gay man or lesbian. Results indicated that the odds of aggression toward a gay man or lesbian increased significantly on a day when heterosexual men consumed alcohol (Parrott et al., 2010). Finally, a recent experimental study that used a laboratory aggression task found that alcohol facilitated heterosexual men's bias-motivated aggression toward a gay male, but not toward a lesbian (Parrott & Lisco, 2015).

Together these results converge with prior conclusions suggesting that alcohol consumption should be considered a contributing cause of interpersonal aggression (Leonard, 2005), although additional research is needed to more carefully examine potential moderators of these effects and to examine other categories of aggressive behavior (e.g., female-to-male aggression).

Effects of Other Drugs on Human Aggression

It is clear that substance use is associated with aggressive behavior. However, the nature of that relationship is exceedingly complex and likely explained by direct pharmacological effects as well as indirect effects associated with the use and procurement of illicit substances. Drugs are typically classified according to their effects on behavior: central nervous system (CNS) depressants (e.g., benzodiazepines, barbiturates), CNS stimulants (e.g., cocaine, methamphetamine), marijuana, opiates, and psychedelics-hallucinogens. We organize our review according to these classifications. As in the preceding review of the relation between alcohol and aggression, we focus only on the direct, pharmacological effects of drugs on aggression.

The relation between CNS depressants (excluding alcohol) and aggression is rather well-established and shows that ingestion of these drugs increases aggressive behavior (Bushman, 1993). For instance, experimental studies show that benzodiazepines increase aggression (e.g., Berman & Taylor, 1995), primarily at lower doses and among individuals with aggression-promoting personality traits (Ben-Porath & Taylor, 2002).

In contrast, multiple reviews (e.g., Hoaken & Stewart, 2003; Taylor & Hulsizer, 1998) highlight inconsistent support for the view that the pharmacological properties of CNS stimulants increase aggression. At present, the most conservative conclusion is that these drugs do not increase aggression and, instead, any observed relation is due to third variable explanations (e.g., trait aggression, antisocial behavior). The research literature on the relation between marijuana and aggression is somewhat more consistent, though it renders a similar conclusion. Most experimental studies have examined the specific pharmacological effect of tetrahydrocannabinol (THC) on aggression and found that aggression is more likely suppressed, rather than facilitated, at moderate to high doses (e.g., Myerscough & Taylor, 1985; Taylor et al., 1976). Like CNS stimulants, it is posited that any observed relation between marijuana and aggression is better explained by individual differences or, with regard to intimate partner violence, couple-level factors (Testa & Brown, 2015; Testa et al., 2011).

Evidence to support a facilitative effect of acute opiate use on aggressive behavior is very limited. Quite the opposite, it is widely accepted that opiate use suppresses aggressive behavior. Notably, studies suggest that opiate withdrawal, which is characterized by heightened agitation, irritability, and negative affect, may facilitate aggression in response to provocation (Roth, 1994). Such data support the view that it is the psychological and physiological reactions to opiate withdrawal, rather than its pharmacological properties, that facilitate aggression. Similarly, there is little evidence to support acute use of psychedelics as a facilitator of aggressive behavior. Reviews of the literature highlight correlational data that suggest a relation between phencyclidine (PCP) and aggression (e.g., Boles & Miotto, 2003; Taylor & Hulsizer, 1998); however, these data are difficult to interpret due to methodological limitations.

Prevention and Intervention

The preceding review clearly demonstrates that the pharmacological effects of alcohol and other drugs are a contributing cause of human aggression. In stark contrast to this literature, evidence-based programs to prevent or reduce alcohol- and substance-related aggression are quite limited. Existing approaches to prevention and intervention generally target the individual and attempt to decrease aggression by preventing or reducing alcohol or substance use. However, pertinent literature suggests the utility of alternative individual-level as well as societal-level approaches.

Reducing Consumption or Abstinence

Given the well-established link between alcohol and certain drugs and aggression— especially among at-risk individuals—it seems reasonable to presume that removing this risk factor (alcohol or drug use) would result in a concomitant reduction in aggressive behavior. Evidence to date from the alcohol literature supports this notion: reducing problematic drinking during treatment (e.g., a spouse-involved alcoholism treatment) also leads to reductions in aggression among intimate partners (O'Farrell & Murphy, 1995; O'Farrell et al., 2003; Stuart et al., 2003), with reductions in intimate partner violence (IPV) stable over a two-year follow-up period (O'Farrell et al., 1999). Still other research has examined combined treatments for substance use problems and IPV, which have potentially important benefits concerning cost savings in time and personnel and a greater likelihood of treatment compliance (Murphy & Ting, 2010). Results of the small number of studies evaluating such combined treatments are encouraging, with offenders in the combined treatment condition more likely to initiate and remain in treatment (Goldkamp et al., 1996) and report more days abstinent (Easton et al., 2007). While some findings suggest that a combined treatment results in as much intimate partner violence reduction as traditional intimate partner violence–focused treatments over the course of the intervention (Kraanen et al., 2013), the aggression-reducing impact of the combined substance use/intimate partner violence interventions have yet to be established at meaningful follow-up periods (i.e., more than six months post-intervention). Thus, there remains an unmet need for individual-level interventions that employ an integrated focus on aggression and substance use (McMurran, 2012). Overall, results of this emerging research area suggest that effective treatment for substance use disorders is related to reductions in intimate partner violence, and that such treatments should be meaningfully incorporated into a coordinated community response to interpersonal violence (Murphy & Ting, 2010).

Attention-Allocation Model-Inspired Interventions

Even if treatment for an alcohol or substance use disorder was deemed a first-line intervention for aggression, the reality is that many patients do not achieve sustained abstinence, and the long-term effects of these interventions are unknown. As such, there has been a call in the literature for research to examine interventions for alcohol-related aggression that are applied *during* episodes of acute intoxication (Gallagher & Parrott, 2011; Giancola et al., 2009; Giancola et al., 2011; Giancola et al., 2010). Proposed approaches to intervention, and the evidence base upon which they are based, are grounded in the Attention-Allocation Model (Steele & Josephs, 1990), which asserts that intoxicated individuals allocate their attention such that they perceive and process only the most salient cues of a situation. As described earlier, the Attention-Allocation Model allows for the counterintuitive hypothesis that intoxicated persons will behave less aggressively than sober individuals if their attention is redirected away from cues of instigation by more salient cues of inhibition.

Interventions grounded in this model call for the use of highly salient and easy-to-process cues that are non-provocative, nonaggressive, and/or inhibitory. As a result, the inebriate's attention should be redirected away from hostile provocative cues onto more salient nonaggressive and/or inhibitory cues. With a focus on such cues, cognitive (e.g., low self-awareness, angry cognitions) and emotional states (e.g., anger, low empathy) associated with aggressive behavior should be attenuated.

At the societal level, public interventions designed to manipulate the attentional focus of inebriates have been proposed, such as flashing signs in bars that proscribe violence (Gallagher et al., 2010; Giancola et al., 2009, 2010). Indeed, the bar setting has been identified as an under-studied but highly feasible point of intervention for alcohol-related aggression (Graham & Homel, 2008; Leonard et al., 2003). For example, research has implicated several environmental characteristics common to bars that increase the risk of alcohol-related aggression, including crowding, poor traffic flow, dancing, pool playing, excessive noise, and even the sound of music (Graham, 2009; Leonard et al., 2003)! However, the feasibility of modifying these characteristics has been questioned. Thus, the idea of manipulating attention via implementation of cues that deter violence or enhance self-awareness carries potential but has yet to be rigorously tested.

Outside of public settings, the most common location for alcohol-related violence is in the home and involves romantic partners (Leonard et al., 2002). To tailor Attention-Allocation Model-based interventions to the individual, individualized plans could be developed that would employ physical cues of nonviolence as well as partners or other family members as agents of attentional redirection. For instance, nondescript "anti-violence" chips—akin to the sobriety chips used in Alcoholics Anonymous—could be carried to remind the person of his or her commitment to nonviolence. As opposed to this "top-down" approach of saturating an inebriate's environment with inhibitory cues, an alternative "bottom-up" approach can be used to influence the type of cues toward which an inebriate would be likely to attend. Specifically, attentional bias modification tasks make subtle changes to automatized attention allocation processes to influence what information is likely to be perceived. These tasks have been used successfully to direct attention away from anxiety-provoking threat cues and reduce anxiety-related symptoms (Dennis & O'Toole, 2014). Though untested, this approach holds promise as a method to reduce attention toward aggressive cues and ultimately decrease alcohol-related aggression in response to provocation.

Third-Party (Bystander) Intervention

Interventions designed to reduce or prevent intoxicated or non-intoxicated aggression have historically targeted potential perpetrators or victims. However, the field has witnessed a paradigm shift that focuses on the potential impact of *bystanders* in preventing violence (e.g., Banyard et al., 2007; Berkowitz, 2002). Indeed, bystanders are present across numerous interpersonal violence situations (Hamby et al., in press) and thus represent a potentially important target for prevention efforts. In essence, the bystander approach to violence prevention aims to prepare individuals to intervene when they witness situations that involve or could potentially lead to interpersonal aggression. Bystander prevention strategies represent a heterogeneous collection of techniques including social marketing campaigns, structured psychoeducational programs, and bystander skill-building interventions that seek to empower men and women to intervene in high-risk situations to prevent aggression.

The bystander approach is founded on an extensive social psychological literature (Fischer et al., 2011). The classic bystander finding suggests that when more people are present, any one person is less likely to intervene (Latané & Darley, 1970). However, for situations that require multiple interveners, people are more likely to engage in prosocial bystander behavior when they first see one or more others engage in that behavior (Carlo & Randall, 2001; Levine & Hogg 2009), *including instances of interpersonal violence* (Christy & Voigt, 1994). Not surprisingly, bystander programs—which seek to facilitate bystanders' engagement in prosocial intervention behavior—have been identified as a promising strategy to prevent sexual violence (Katz & Moore, 2013) and IPV (McMahon & Dick, 2011).

Unfortunately, this extensive evidence base does not account for the role of alcohol use, nor has it been evaluated across other interpersonal violence situations where alcohol is involved. For instance, campus sexual violence often occurs at or after attending bars or parties where attendees drink alcohol (Armstrong et al., 2006; Flack et al., 2007; Planty, 2002), and approximately 80% of men endorse perpetrating unwanted physical contact against a woman in a bar (Thompson & Cracco, 2008). Alcohol-related aggression in bars and other public venues is also highly likely to occur in the presence of bystanders, yet only one study has examined the likelihood of bystander intervention in a drinking context. Results indicated that 79% of bystanders did not intervene when sexual violence occurred in a bar (Graham et al., 2014). However, this study did not assess why bystanders failed to intervene, or even if they, the perpetrator, or the victim had consumed alcohol.

In summary, much work lies ahead to better evaluate the effectiveness of bystander intervention programming in the prevention of alcohol- and substance-related violence. However, this area represents one potentially fruitful approach to violence prevention that, at minimum, nicely complements existing approaches.

Conclusion

The study of alcohol and other drugs' effects on human aggression has a long history. The present chapter demonstrates that there is little debate on several fundamental points: (1) the pharmacological effects of alcohol and certain other drugs cause aggressive behavior; (2) this relationship is exceedingly complex, as evidenced by myriad moderating variables and various putative mechanisms by which aggression is facilitated in at-risk individuals and/or situations; and (3) effective interventions that break this robust and complicated association are limited. Thus, the next generation of research in this area must bring greater clarity to this complex association such that intervention-based research and practice can more effectively address this critical public health problem.

References

Abbey, A., Wegner, R., Woerner, J., Pegram, S. E., & Pierce, J. (2014). Review of survey and experimental research that examine the relationship between alcohol consumption and men's sexual aggression perpetration. *Trauma, Violence, & Abuse, 15*, 265–282.

Addicott, M. A., Marsh-Richard, D. M., Mathias, C. W., & Dougherty, D. M. (2007). The biphasic effects of alcohol: Comparisons of subjective and objective measures of stimulation, sedation, and physical activity. *Alcoholism: Clinical and Experimental Research, 31*, 1883–1890. doi: 10.1111/j.1530–0277.2007.00518.x

Anderson, C. A., & Bushman, B. J. (2002). Human aggression. *Annual Review of Psychology, 53*, 27–51. doi: 10.1146/annurev.psych.53.100901.135231

Anderson, V., Jacobs, R., & Anderson, P. J. (2008). *Executive functions and the frontal lobes: A lifespan perspective.* Philadelphia, PA: Taylor & Francis.

Armstrong, E. A., Hamilton, L., & Sweeney, B. (2006). Sexual assault on campus: A multi-level, integrative approach to party rape. *Social Problems, 53*, 483–499. doi: http://dx.doi.org/10.1525/sp.2006.53.4.483

Bailey, D. S., Leonard, K. E., Cranston, J. W., & Taylor, S. P. (1983). Effects of alcohol and self-awareness on human physical aggression. *Personality and Social Psychology Bulletin, 9*, 289–295. doi: 10.1177/0146167283092014

Bandura, A. (1999). Moral disengagement in the perpetration of inhumanities. *Personality & Social Psychology Review, 3*, 193–209. doi: 10.1207/s15327957pspr0303_3

Banyard, V. L., Moynihan, M. M., & Plante, E. G. (2007). Sexual violence prevention through bystander education: An experimental evaluation. *Journal of Community Psychology, 35*, 463–481. doi: 10.1002/jcop.20159

Bartholow, B. D., Dickter, C. L., & Sestir, M. A. (2006). Stereotype activation and control of race bias: Cognitive control of inhibition and its impairment by alcohol. *Journal of Personality and Social Psychology, 90*, 272–287. doi:10.1037/0022–3514.90.2.272

Ben-Porath, D. D., & Taylor, S. P. (2002). The effects of diazepam (valium) and aggressive disposition on human aggression: An experimental investigation. *Addictive Behaviors, 27*, 167–177. doi:10.1016/S0306–4603(00)00175–1

Berkowitz, A. (2002). Fostering men's responsibility for preventing sexual assault. In P. A. Schewe (Ed.), *Preventing violence in relationships: Interventions across the life span.* (pp. 163–196). Washington, DC, US: American Psychological Association.

Berkowitz, L. (1990). On the formation and regulation of anger and aggression: A cognitive-neoassociationistic analysis. *American Psychologist, 45*, 494–503. doi: 10.1037/0003–066X.45.4.494

Berkowitz, L. (1993). Towards a general theory of anger and emotional aggression: Implications of the cognitive-neoassociationistic perspective for the analysis of anger and other emotions. In R. S. Wyer, Jr. & T. K. Srull (Eds.), *Perspectives on anger and emotion* (pp. 1–46). Hillsdale, NJ; England: Lawrence Erlbaum Associates.

Berkowitz, L. (2008). On the consideration of automatic as well as controlled psychological processes in aggression. *Aggressive Behavior, 34*, 117–129. doi: 10.1002/ab.20244

Berman, M., Bradley, T., Fanning, J., & McCloskey, M. (2009). Self-focused attention reduces self-injurious behavior in alcohol-intoxicated men. *Substance Use and Misuse, 44*, 1280–1297. doi: 10.1080/10826080902961328

Berman, M. E., & Taylor, S. (1995). The effects of triazolam on aggression in men. *Experimental and Clinical Psychopharmacology, 3*, 411–416. http://dx.doi.org/10.1037/1064–1297.3.4.411

Birkley, E., & Eckhardt, C. I. (2015). Anger, hostility, internalizing negative emotions, and intimate partner violence perpetration: A meta-analytic review. *Clinical Psychology Review, 37*, 40–56. DOI: 10.1016/j.cpr.2015.01.002

Boles, S. M., & Miotto, K. (2003). Substance abuse and violence: A review of the literature. *Aggression and Violent Behavior, 8*, 155–174. doi:10.1016/S1359–1789(01)00057-X

Borders, A., & Giancola, P. R. (2011). Trait and state hostile rumination facilitate alcohol-related aggression. *Journal of Studies on Alcohol and Drugs, 72*, 545–554.

Bushman, B. J. (1993). Human aggression while under the influence of alcohol and other drugs: An integrative research review. *Current Directions in Psychological Science, 2*(5), 148–152. doi: 10.1111/1467-8721.ep10768961

Bushman, B. J. (1997). Effects of alcohol on human aggression: Validity of proposed explanations. *Recent Developments in Alcoholism, 13*, 227–244.

Bushman, B. J., Bonacci, A. M., Pedersen, W. C., Vasquez, E. A., & Miller, N. (2005). Chewing on it can chew you up: Effects of rumination on triggered displaced aggression. *Journal of Personality and Social Psychology, 88*, 969–983. doi: 10.1037/0022–3514.88.6.969

Bushman, B. J., & Cooper, H. M. (1990). Effects of alcohol on human aggression: An integrative research review. *Psychological Bulletin, 107*, 341–354. http://dx.doi.org/10.1037/0033–2909.107.3.341

Cappell, H., & Herman, C. P. (1972). Alcohol and tension reduction: A review. *Quarterly Journal of Studies on Alcohol, 33*, 33–64.

Carlo, G., & Randall, B. (2001). Are all prosocial behaviors equal?: A socioecological developmental conception of prosocial behavior. In F. Columbus (Ed.), *Advances in psychology research, Volume II* (pp. 151–170). Huntington, NY: Nova Science Publishers.

Chermack, S. T., & Giancola, P. R. (1997). The relation between alcohol and aggression: An integrated biopsychosocial conceptualization. *Clinical Psychology Review, 17*, 621–649. doi:10.1016/S0272–7358(97)00038-X

Conger, J. (1956). Reinforcement theory and dynamics of alcoholism. *Quarterly Journal of Studies on Alcohol, 17*, 296–305.

Christy, C. A., & Voigt, H. (1994). Bystander responses to public episodes of child abuse. *Journal of Applied Social Psychology, 24*, 824–847. doi: 10.1111/j.1559–1816.1994.tb00614.x

Crane, C. A., Godleski, S. A., Przybyla, S. M., Schlauch, R. C., & Testa, M. (in press). The proximal effects of acute alcohol consumption on male-to-female aggression: A meta-analytic review of the experimental literature. *Trauma, Violence, and Abuse.*

Crichtlow, B. (1986). The powers of John Barleycorn: Beliefs about the effects of alcohol on social behavior. *American Psychologist, 41*, 751–764. doi: http://dx.doi.org/10.1037/0003–066X.41.7.751

Curtin, J. J., & Fairchild, B. A. (2003). Alcohol and cognitive control: Implications for regulation of behavior during response conflict. *Journal of Abnormal Psychology, 112*, 424–436. doi: http://dx.doi.org/10.1037/0021–843X.112.3.424

Dennis, T. A., & O'Toole, L. J. (2014). Mental health on the go: Effects of a gamified attention-bias modification mobile application in trait-anxious adults. *Clinical Psychological Science, 2*, 576–590. doi: 10.1177/2167702614522228

Dunbar, E. (2003). Symbolic, relational, and ideological signifiers of bias-motivated offenders: Toward a strategy of assessment. *American Journal of Orthopsychiatry, 73*, 203–211. doi: http://dx.doi.org/10.1037/0002–9432.73.2.203

Easton, C. J., Mandel, D. L., Hunkele, K. A., Nich, C., Rounsaville, B. J., & Carroll, K. M. (2007). A cognitive behavioral therapy for alcohol-dependent domestic violence offenders: An integrated substance abuse-domestic violence treatment approach (SADV). *The American Journal on Addictions, 16*, 24–31. doi:10.1080/10550490601077809

Eckhardt, C. I. (2007). Effects of alcohol intoxication on anger experience and expression among partner assaultive men. *Journal of Consulting and Clinical Psychology, 75*, 61–71. doi: 10.1037/0022–006X.75.1.61

Eckhardt, C., Barbour, K. A., & Davison, G. C. (1998). Articulated thoughts of maritally violent and nonviolent men during anger arousal. *Journal of Consulting and Clinical Psychology, 66*, 259–269. doi: http://dx.doi.org/10.1037/0022–006X.66.2.259

Eckhardt, C. I., & Cohen, D. J. (1997). Attention to anger-relevant and irrelevant stimuli following naturalistic insult. *Personality and Individual Differences, 23*, 619–629. doi:10.1016/S0191–8869(97)00074–3

Eckhardt, C., Jamison, T. R., & Watts, K. (2002). Anger experience and expression among male dating violence perpetrators during anger arousal. *Journal of Interpersonal Violence, 17*, 1102–1114. doi: 10.1177/08862600223666

Ferrer, V., Bosch, E., Garcia, E., Manassero, M. A., & Gili, M. (2004). Meta-analytic study of differential characteristics between batterers and non-batterers: The case of psychopathology and consumption of alcohol and drugs. *Psykhe, 13*, 141–156.

Finkel, E. J. (2007). Impelling and inhibiting forces in the perpetration of intimate partner violence. *Review of General Psychology, 11*, 193–207. doi: 10.1037/1089–2680.11.2.193

Finkel, E.J. (2014). The I-cubed model: Metatheory, theory, and evidence. In J.M. Olson & M.P. Zanna (Eds.), *Advances in experimental social psychology* (pp. 1–104). San Diego: Academic Press.

Finkel, E. J., DeWall, C. N., Slotter, E. B., McNulty, J. K., Pond, R. S., Jr., & Atkins, D.C. (2012). Using I³ theory to clarify when dispositional aggressiveness predicts intimate partner violence perpetration. *Journal of Personality and Social Psychology, 102*, 533–549. doi: 10.1037/a0025651

Finkel, E. J., DeWall, C. N., Slotter, E. B., Oaten, M., & Foshee, V. A. (2009). Self-regulatory failure and intimate partner violence perpetration. *Journal of Personality and Social Psychology, 97*, 483–499. doi: 10.1037/a0015433

Finkel, E. J., & Eckhardt, C. I. (2013). *Intimate partner violence*. In J. A. Simpson & L. Campbell (Eds.), *Handbook of close relationships* (pp. 452–474). New York: Oxford.

Fischer, P., Krueger, J. I., Greitemeyer, T., Vogrincic, C., Kastenmüller, A., Frey, D., Heene, M., Wicher, M., & Kainbacher, M. (2011). The bystander-effect: A meta-analytic review on bystander intervention in dangerous and non-dangerous emergencies. *Psychological Bulletin, 137*, 517–537. doi: http://dx.doi.org/10.1037/a0023304

Fishbein, D. (2000). Neuropsychological function, drug abuse, and violence: A conceptual framework. *Criminal Justice and Behavior, 27*, 139–159. doi: 10.1177/0093854800027002001

Flack, W. F., Daubman, K. A, Caron, M. L., Asadorian, J. A., D'Aureli, N. R., Gigliotti, S. N., Hall, A. T., Kiser, S., & Stine, E. R. (2007). Risk factors and consequences of unwanted sex among university students: Hooking up, alcohol, and stress response. *Journal of Interpersonal Violence, 22*, 139–57. doi: 10.1177/0886260506295354

Foran, H. M., & O'Leary, K. D. (2008). Alcohol and intimate partner violence: A meta-analytic review. *Clinical Psychology Review, 28*, 1222–1234. doi: 10.1016/j.cpr.2008.05.001

Gallagher, K. E., Hudepohl, A. D., & Parrott, D. J. (2010). The power of being present: The role of mindfulness on the relation between men's alcohol use and sexual aggression toward intimate partners. *Aggressive Behavior, 36*, 405–413. doi: 10.1002/ab.20351

Gallagher, K. E., Lisco, C. G., Parrott, D. J., & Giancola, P. R. (2014). Effects of thought suppression on provoked men's alcohol-related physical aggression in the laboratory. *Psychology of Violence, 4*, 78–89. http://dx.doi.org/10.1037/a0032304

Gallagher, K. E., & Parrott, D. J. (2011). Does distraction reduce the alcohol-aggression relation?: A cognitive and behavioral test of the attention-allocation model. *Journal of Consulting and Clinical Psychology, 79*, 319–329. doi:10.1037/a0023065

Gallagher, K. E., & Parrott, D. J. (In press). A self-awareness intervention for heavy drinking men's alcohol-related aggression toward women. *Journal of Consulting and Clinical Psychology*. doi:http://dx.doi.org/10.1037/ccp0000118

Giancola, P. (2000). Executive functioning: A conceptual framework for alcohol-related aggression. *Experimental and Clinical Psychopharmacology, 8*, 576–597. doi: http://dx.doi.org/10.1037/1064–1297.8.4.576

Giancola, P.R. (2004). Executive functioning and alcohol-related aggression. *Journal of Abnormal Psychology, 113*, 541–555. doi: http://dx.doi.org/10.1037/0021–843X.113.4.541

Giancola, P. R., & Corman, M. D. (2007). Alcohol and aggression: A test of the attention-allocation model. *Psychological Science, 18*, 649–655. doi: 10.1111/j.1467–9280.2007.01953.x

Giancola, P. R., Duke, A. A. & Ritz, K. Z. (2011). Alcohol, violence, and the alcohol myopia model: Preliminary findings and implications for prevention. *Addictive Behaviors, 36*, 1019–1022. doi:10.1016/j.addbeh.2011.05.006

Giancola, P. R., Josephs, R. A., DeWall, C. N., & Gunn, R. L. (2009). Applying the attention-allocation model to the explanation of alcohol-related aggression: Implications for prevention. *Substance Use and Misuse, 44,* 1263–1279. doi: 10.1080/108260809 02960049

Giancola, P. R., Josephs, R. A., Parrott, D. J., & Duke, A. A. (2010). Alcohol myopia revisited: Clarifying aggression and other acts of disinhibition through a distorted lens. *Perspectives on Psychological Science, 5,* 265–278. doi: 10.1177/1745691610369467

Giancola, P. R., Parrott, D. J., & Roth, R. M. (2006). The influence of difficult temperament on alcohol-related aggression: Better accounted for by executive functioning? *Addictive Behaviors, 31,* 2169–2187. doi:10.1016/j.addbeh.2006.02.019

Giancola, P. R., Reagin, C. M., Van Weenen, R. V., & Zeichner, A. (1998). Alcohol-induced stimulation and sedation: Relation to physical aggression. *The Journal of General Psychology, 125,* 297–304. doi: 10.1080/00221309809595339

Giancola, P., & Zeichner, A. (1997). The biphasic effects of alcohol on human aggression. *Journal of Abnormal Psychology, 106,* 598–607. doi: http://dx.doi.org/10.1037/0021-843X. 106.4.598

Goldkamp, J. S., Weiland, D., Collins, M., & White, M. (1996). *The role of drug and alcohol abuse in domestic violence and its treatment: Dade County's domestic violence court experiment (final report).* Philadelphia, PA: Crime and Justice Research Institute.

Goldman, M. S., Del Boca, F. K., & Darkes, J. (1999). Alcohol expectancy theory: The application of cognitive neuroscience. In K. E. Leonard & H. T. Blane (Eds.), *Psychological theories of drinking and alcoholism* (pp. 203–246). New York: Guilford.

Graham, K. (1980). Theories of intoxicated aggression. *Canadian Journal of Behavioural Science, 12,* 141–158. doi: http://dx.doi.org/10.1037/h0081045

Graham, K. (2009). They fight because we let them! Applying a situational crime prevention model to barroom violence. *Drug and Alcohol Review, 28,* 103–109. doi: 10.1111/j.1465-3362.2008.00038.x

Graham, K., Bernards, S., Wayne Osgood, D., Abbey, A., Parks, M., Flynn, A., Dumas, T., & Wells, S. (2014). "Blurred lines?" Sexual aggression and barroom culture. *Alcoholism: Clinical and Experimental Research, 38,* 1416–1424. doi: 10.1111/acer.12356

Graham, K., & Homel, R. (2008). *Raising the bar: Preventing aggression in and around bars, pubs, and clubs.* Portland, Oregon: Willan Publishing.

Greeley, J., & Oei, T. (1999). Alcohol and tension reduction. In K. E. Leonard & H. T. Blane (Eds.), *Psychological theories of drinking and alcoholism* (2nd ed., pp. 14–53). New York: Guilford Press.

Hamby, S., Weber, M. C., Grych, J., & Banyard, V. (in press). What difference do bystanders make?: The association of bystander involvement with victim outcomes in a community sample. *Psychology of Violence.* doi:10.1037/a0039073

Herek, G. M., & McLemore, K. A. (2013). Sexual prejudice. *Annual Review of Psychology, 64,* 309–333. doi:10.1146/annurev-psych-113011-143826

Hoaken, P., Assaad, J., & Pihl, R. O. (1998). Cognitive functioning and the inhibition of alcohol-induced aggression. *Journal of Studies on Alcohol, 59,* 599–607. doi: http://dx.doi.org/10.15288/jsa.1998.59.599

Hoaken, P. N., & Stewart, S. H. (2003). Drugs of abuse and the elicitation of human aggressive behavior. *Addictive behaviors, 28,* 1533–1554. doi:10.1016/j.addbeh.2003.08.033

Huesmann, L. R. (1988). An information processing model for the development of aggression. *Aggressive Behavior, 14,* 13–24. doi: 10.1002/1098–2337(1988)14:1<13::AID-AB2480140104>3.0.CO;2-J

Hull, J. (1981). A self-awareness model of the causes and effects of alcohol consumption. *Journal of Abnormal Psychology, 90*, 586–600. doi: http://dx.doi.org/10.1037/0021–843X.90.6.586

Hull, J., Levenson, R., Young, & Sher, K. (1983). Self-awareness-reducing effects of alcohol consumption. *Journal of Personality and Social Psychology, 44*, 461–473. doi: http://dx.doi.org/10.1037/0022–3514.44.3.461

Hull, J. G., & Van Treuren, R. R. (1986). Experimental social psychology and the causes and effects of alcohol consumption. In H. D. Cappell (Ed.), *Research advances in alcohol and drug problems* (pp. 211–244). New York: Plenum Press.

Ito, T., Miller, N., & Pollock, V. (1996). Alcohol and aggression: A meta-analysis of the moderating effects of inhibitory cues, triggering events, and self-focused attention. *Psychological Bulletin, 120*, 60–82. doi: http://dx.doi.org/10.1037/0033–2909.120.1.60

Jeavons, C., & Taylor, S. (1985). The control of alcohol-related aggression: Redirecting the inebriate's attention to socially appropriate conduct. *Aggressive Behavior, 11*, 93–101. doi:10.1002/1098–2337(1985)11:2<93::AID-AB2480110202>3.0.CO;2-Y

Katz, J., & Moore, J. (2013). Bystander education training for campus sexual assault prevention: An initial meta-analysis. *Violence and Victims, 28*, 1054–1067. doi:10.1891/0886–6708.VV-D-12–00113

Kantor, G. K., & Straus, M. A. (1987). The "drunken bum" theory of wife beating. *Social Problems, 34*, 213–230. doi: http://dx.doi.org/10.2307/800763

Kraanen, F. L., Vedel, E., Scholing, A., & Emmelkamp, P. M. (2013). The comparative effectiveness of integrated treatment for substance abuse and partner violence (I-StoP) and substance abuse treatment alone: A randomized controlled trial. *BMC Psychiatry, 13*, 189. doi:10.1186/1471–244X-13–189

Latané, B., & Darley, J. M. (1970). *The unresponsive bystander: Why doesn't he help?* New York: Meredith Corporation.

Leonard, K. E. (2005). Alcohol and intimate partner violence: When can we say that heavy drinking is a contributing cause of violence? *Addiction, 100*, 422–425. doi: 10.1111/j.1360–0443.2005.00994.x

Leonard, K. E., & Blane, H. T. (1992). Alcohol and marital aggression in a national sample of young men. *Journal of Interpersonal Violence, 7*, 19–30. doi: 10.1177/088626092007001002

Leonard, K. E., Quigley, B. M., & Collins, R. L. (2002). Physical aggression in the lives of young adults: Prevalence, location, and severity among college and community samples. *Journal of Interpersonal Violence, 17*, 533–550.

Leonard, K. E., Quigley, B. M., & Collins, R. L. (2003). Drinking, personality, and bar environmental characteristics as predictors of involvement in barroom aggression. *Addictive Behaviors, 28*, 1681–1700. doi: 10.1177/0886260502017005004

Levine, J. M., & Hogg, M. A. (2009). *Encyclopedia of group processes and intergroup relations.* Thousand Oaks, CA: Sage.

Lindqvist, P. (1986). Criminal homicide in northern Sweden 1970–1981: Alcohol intoxication, alcohol abuse and mental disease. *International Journal of Law and Psychiatry, 8*, 19–37. doi:10.1016/0160–2527(86)90081–6

Lipsey, M. W., Wilson, D. B., Cohen, M. A., & Derzon, J. H. (1997). Is there a causal relationship between alcohol use and violence? A synthesis of evidence. In M. Galanter (Ed.), *Recent developments in alcoholism: Alcohol and violence* (Vol. 13, pp. 245–282). New York: Plenum Press.

MacAndrew, C., & Edgerton, R. B. (1969). *Drunken comportment: A social explanation.* Chicago: Aldine.

McMahon, S., & Dick, A. (2011). "Being in a room with like-minded men": An exploratory study of men's participation in a bystander intervention program to prevent intimate partner violence. *The Journal of Men's Studies, 19,* 3–18. doi:10.3149/jms.1901.3

McMurran, M. (2012). Individual-level interventions for alcohol-related violence: A Rapid Evidence Assessment (REA). *Criminal Behaviour and Mental Health, 22,* 14–28. doi: 10.1002/cbm.821

Martin, C. S., Earleywine, M., Musty, R. E., Perrine, M. W., & Swift, R. M. (1993). Development and validation of the biphasic alcohol effects scale. *Alcoholism: Clinical and Experimental Research, 17,* 140–146. doi: 10.1111/j.1530–0277.1993.tb00739.x

Meyer, I. (2003). Prejudice, social stress, and mental health in lesbian, gay, and bisexual populations: Conceptual issues and research evidence. *Psychological Bulletin, 129,* 674–697. doi: 10.1037/0033–2909.129.5.674.

Murdoch, D., Pihl, R., & Ross, D. (1990). Alcohol and crimes of violence: Present issues. *Substance Use & Misuse, 25,* 1065–1081. doi: 10.3109/10826089009058873

Murphy, C. M., & Ting, L. (2010). The effects of treatment for substance use problems on intimate partner violence: A review of empirical data. *Aggression and Violent Behavior, 15,* 325–333. doi:10.1016/j.avb.2010.01.006

Myerscough, R., & Taylor, S. P. (1985). The effects of marijuana on human physical aggression. *Journal of Personality and Social Psychology, 49,* 1541–1546. doi: http://dx.doi.org/10.1037/0022–3514.49.6.1541

Nencini, P. (1997). The rules of drug taking: Wine and poppy derivatives in the ancient world. III. Wine as an instrument of aggressive behavior in the ancient world. *Substance Use & Misuse, 32,* 361–367. doi:10.3109/10826089709055857

O'Farrell, T. J., Fals-Stewart, W., Murphy, M., & Murphy, C. M. (2003). Partner violence before and after individually based alcoholism treatment for male alcoholic patients. *Journal of Consulting and Clinical Psychology, 71,* 92–102. doi: http://dx.doi.org/10.1037/0022–006X.71.1.92

O'Farrell, T., & Murphy, C. M. (1995). Marital violence before and after alcoholism treatment. *Journal of Consulting and Clinical Psychology, 63,* 256–262. doi: http://dx.doi.org/10.1037/0022–006X.63.2.256

O'Farrell, T. J., Van Hutton, V., & Murphy, C. M. (1999). Domestic violence before and after alcoholism treatment: A two-year longitudinal study. *Journal of Studies on Alcohol, 60,* 317–321. doi: http://dx.doi.org/10.15288/jsa.1999.60.317

Parker, R. N., & Auerhahn, K. (1998). Alcohol, drugs, and violence. *Annual Review of Sociology, 24,* 291–311.

Parrott, D. J., Gallagher, K. E., Vincent, W., & Bakeman, R. (2010). The link between alcohol use and aggression toward sexual minorities: An event-based analysis. *Psychology of Addictive Behaviors, 24,* 516–521. http://dx.doi.org/10.1037/a0019040

Parrott, D. J., Gallagher, K. E., & Zeichner, A. (2012). Liquid courage or liquid fear: Alcohol intoxication and anxiety facilitate physical aggression. *Substance Use and Misuse, 47,* 774–786. doi: 10.3109/10826084.2012.667182

Parrott, D. J., & Lisco, C. G. (2015). Effects of alcohol and sexual prejudice on aggression toward sexual minorities. *Psychology of Violence, 5,* 256–265. doi: http://dx.doi.org/10.1037/a0037479

Parrott, D. J., & Miller, C. A. (2009). Alcohol consumption-related antigay aggression: Theoretical considerations for individual- and societal-level interventions. *Substance Use and Misuse, 44,* 1377–1398. doi:10.1080/10826080902961526

Parrott, D. J., & Zeichner, A. (2002). Effects of alcohol and trait anger on physical aggression in men. *Journal of Studies on Alcohol, 63*, 196–204. doi: http://dx.doi.org/10.15288/jsa.2002.63.196

Parrott, D. J., Zeichner, A., & Stephens, D. (2003). Effects of alcohol, personality, and provocation on the expression of anger in men: A facial coding analysis. *Alcoholism: Clinical and Experimental Research, 27*, 937–945. doi: 10.1111/j.1530–0277.2003.tb04418.x

Pernanen, K. (1991). *Alcohol in human violence.* New York: Guilford Press.

Peterson, J., Rothfleisch, J., Zelazo, P., & Pihl, R. (1990). Acute alcohol intoxication and cognitive functioning. *Journal of Studies on Alcohol, 51*, 114–122. doi: http://dx.doi.org/10.15288/jsa.1990.51.114

Pihl, R. O., Assaad, J. M., & Hoaken, P. N. S. (2003). The alcohol-aggression relationship and differential sensitivity to alcohol. *Aggressive Behavior, 29*, 302–315. doi: 10.1002/ab.10072

Pihl, R., Peterson, J., & Lau, M. (1993). A biosocial model of the alcohol-aggression relationship. *Journal of Studies on Alcohol (Suppl. 11)*, 128–139.

Pihl, R. O., & Sutton, R. (2009). Drugs and aggression readily mix; so what now? *Substance Use & Misuse, 44*, 1188–1203. doi: 10.1080/10826080902959884

Pittman, D. J., & Handy, W. (1964). Patterns in criminal aggravated assault. *Journal of Criminal Law, Criminology and Police Science, 55*, 462–470.

Planty, M. (2002). *Third-party involvement in violent crime, 1993–1999.* National Institute of Justice, Bureau of Justice Statistics Special Report. Rockville, MD. Justice Statistics Clearinghouse/NCJRS. NCJ 189100.

Quigley, B. M., & Leonard, K. E. (2006). Alcohol expectancies and intoxicated aggression. *Aggression and Violent Behavior, 11*, 484–496. doi:10.1016/j.avb.2006.01.008

Reeves, S. B., & Nagoshi, C. T. (1993). Effects of alcohol administration on the disinhibition of racial prejudice. *Alcoholism: Clinical and Experimental Research, 17*, 1066–1071. doi:10.1111/j.1530–0277.1993.tb05665.x

Roth, J. A. (1994). *Psychoactive substances and violence.* Washington, DC: National Institute of Justice, Office of Justice Programs.

Rule, B. G., & Nesdale, A. R. (1976). Emotional arousal and aggressive behavior. *Psychological Bulletin, 83*, 851–863. doi: http://dx.doi.org/10.1037/0033–2909.83.5.851

Rusting, C. L., & Nolen-Hoeksema, S. (1998). Regulating responses to anger: Effects of rumination and distraction on angry mood. *Journal of Personality and Social Psychology, 74*, 790–803. doi: http://dx.doi.org/10.1037/0022–3514.74.3.790

Sayette, M. A. (1993). An appraisal-disruption model of alcohol's effects on stress responses in social drinkers. *Psychological Bulletin, 114*, 459–476. doi: http://dx.doi.org/10.1037/0033–2909.114.3.459

Shuntich, R. J., & Taylor, S. P. (1972). The effects of alcohol on human physical aggression. *Journal of Experimental Research in Personality, 6*, 34–38.

Silvia, P. J., & Duval, T. S. (2001). Objective self-awareness theory: Recent progress and enduring problems. *Personality and Social Psychology Review, 5*, 230–241. doi: 10.1207/S15327957PSPR0503_4

Sinclair, H. C., Ladny, R. T., & Lyndon, A. E. (2011). Adding insult to injury: Effects of interpersonal rejection types, rejection sensitivity, and self-regulation on obsessive relational intrusion. *Aggressive Behavior, 37*, 503–520. doi: 10.1002/ab.20412

Slotter, E. B., Finkel, E. J., DeWall, C. N., Pond Jr., R. S., Lambert, N. M., Bodenhausen, G.V., & Fincham, F. D. (2012). Putting the brakes on aggression toward a romantic partner: The inhibitory influence of relationship commitment. *Journal of Personality and Social Psychology, 102,* 291–305. doi: http://dx.doi.org/10.1037/a0024915

Smith, P., & Waterman, M. (2004). Role of experience in processing bias for aggressive words in forensic and non-forensic populations. *Aggressive Behavior, 30,* 105–122. doi: 10.1002/ab.20001

Steele, C. M., & Josephs, R. (1990). Alcohol Myopia: Its prized and dangerous effects. *American Psychologist, 45,* 921–933. doi: http://dx.doi.org/10.1037/0003–066X.45.8.921

Steele, C. M., & Southwick, L. (1985). Alcohol and social behavior: I. The psychology of drunken excess. *Journal of Personality and Social Psychology, 48,* 18–34. doi: http://dx.doi.org/10.1037/0022–3514.48.1.18

Stepanova, E. V., Bartholow, B. D., Saults, J., & Friedman, R. S. (2012). Alcohol-related cues promote automatic racial bias. *Journal of Experimental Social Psychology, 48,* 905–911. doi:10.1016/j.jesp.2012.02.006

Stith, S. M., Smith, D. B., Penn, C. E., Ward, D. B., & Tritt, D. (2004). Intimate partner physical abuse perpetration and victimization risk factors: A meta-analytic review. *Aggression and Violent Behavior, 10,* 65–98. doi: 10.1016/j.avb.2003.09.001

Stuart, G. L., Moore, T. M., Kahler, C. W., & Ramsey, S. E. (2003). Substance abuse and relationship violence among men court-referred to batterers' intervention programs. *Substance Abuse, 24,* 107–122. doi: 10.1080/08897070309511539

Taylor, S., & Chermack, S. (1993). Alcohol, drugs and human physical aggression. *Journal of Studies on Alcohol, (Suppl. 11),* 78–88.

Taylor, S. P., & Hulsizer, M. R. (1998). Psychoactive drugs and human aggression. In R. G. Geen & E. Donnerstein (Eds.), *Human aggression: Theories, research, and implications for social policy* (pp. 139–165). San Diego, CA: Academic Press.

Taylor, S. P., Vardaris, R. M., Rawtich, A. B., Gammon, C. B., Cranston, J. W., & Lubetkin, A. I. (1976). The effects of alcohol and delta-9-tetrahydrocannabinol on human physical aggression. *Aggressive Behavior, 2,* 153–161. doi: 10.1002/1098–2337(1976)2:2 <153::AID-AB2480020206>3.0.CO;2–9

Testa, M. (2002). The impact of men's alcohol consumption on perpetration of sexual aggression. *Clinical Psychology Review, 22,* 1239–1263. doi:10.1016/S0272–7358(02)00204–0

Testa, M., & Brown, W. C. (2015). Does marijuana use contribute to intimate partner aggression? A brief review and directions for future research. *Current Opinion in Psychology, 5,* 6–12. doi:10.1016/j.copsyc.2015.03.002

Testa, M., Hoffman, J. H., & Leonard, K. E. (2011). Female intimate partner violence perpetration: Stability and predictors of mutual and nonmutual aggression across the first year of college. *Aggressive Behavior, 37,* 362–373. doi: 10.1002/ab.20391

Thompson, E. H., & Cracco, E. J. (2008). Sexual aggression in bars: What college men can normalize. *The Journal of Men's Studies, 16,* 82–96. doi: 10.3149/jms.1601.82

Washburne, C. (1956). Alcohol, self and the group. *Quarterly Journal of Studies on Alcohol, 17,* 108–123.

Wilson, G. T. (1988). Alcohol and anxiety. *Behaviour Research and Therapy, 26,* 369–381. doi:10.1016/0005–7967(88)90070–8

Wolfgang, M. E. (1958). *Patterns in criminal homicide.* Philadelphia, PA: University of Pennsylvania Press.

Zeichner, A., & Pihl, R. O. (1979). Effects of alcohol and behavior contingencies on human aggression. *Journal of Abnormal Psychology, 88,* 153–160. doi: http://dx.doi.org/10.1037/0021–843X.88.2.153

PART IV

Targets of Aggression and Violence

14

CYBER BULLYING

A Critical Overview

Dan Olweus

A strong societal interest in the phenomenon of what has later been called bullying first started in Sweden in the late 1960s and early 1970s under the designation "mobbing." At that time, there existed basically no empirical research data to shed light on the many issues and concerns involved in the general Swedish debate about the phenomenon. Against this background, I initiated, in the early 1970s, what is usually considered to be the first systematic research project on bullying by peers. This project was first published as a book in Swedish in 1973 (Olweus, 1973). In 1978, a somewhat expanded version of this book appeared in the United States under the title *Aggression in the Schools: Bullies and Whipping Boys* (Olweus, 1978). In the context of the translation, I decided to replace the term "mobbing" with the term "bullying" (Olweus, 2013). And most of the international attention to these problems over the past 25 years or so concerns some variant of the term bullying and not mobbing (which term, however, has been retained in the Scandinavian countries).

In this chapter, my main focus will be on cyber bullying, that is, bullying with electronic forms of contact or communication such as mobile/cell phones and the Internet. Cyber bullying is a relatively new phenomenon that has received a lot of concerned attention from both researchers and the media for about 10 years. Although a good deal of research has been conducted on cyber bullying, this emerging field has somewhat unclear boundaries and has to address some challenges and unsolved problems. A key problem has been and is: Can cyber bullying be conceptualized just as a subcategory or form of traditional bullying, or should it be best regarded as a distinct phenomenon with special characteristics that make it (partly) different from traditional bullying? (e.g., Menesini, 2012; Olweus, 2012a, b). In the process of presenting a good deal of empirical research facts and some myths about cyber bullying, this problem will run through the chapter, and my answer to the problem will appear at the end of the chapter as a tentative conclusion. So, let us start with definitional issues.

Definition of Bullying and Cyber Bullying

At the time of initiation of my first research project on bullying, it was not possible, or even desirable, to set forth a very stringent definition of bullying. However, the need for a relatively clear and circumscribed definition became urgent in connection with a government-initiated campaign against bullying in Norway in 1983. In that context, the following definition was developed: "A student is being bullied or victimized when he or she is exposed, repeatedly and over time, to negative actions on the part of one or more other students" (Olweus, 1993, p. 9). It is a negative action when someone intentionally inflicts, or attempts to inflict, injury or discomfort upon another, which is the definition of aggressive behavior. Negative actions can be carried out by words, by physical contact, or in other ways such as making faces or mean gestures, backbiting, and intentional exclusion from a group. These forms of bullying are usually named (direct) verbal, (direct) physical, and indirect or relational bullying.

Even if a single instance of more serious harassment can be regarded as bullying under certain circumstances, the definition given above emphasizes negative actions that are carried out with *some repetitiveness*. In order to use the term bullying, there should also be an *imbalance in power or strength*, an asymmetric power relationship between perpetrator(s) and target: The student who is exposed to the negative actions has a hard time defending himself or herself. In line with this reasoning, we do not call it bullying when there is a conflict or aggressive interchange between two persons of approximately the same physical or mental strength.

In this definition, the phenomenon of bullying is thus characterized by the three criteria: (a) It is aggressive behavior or intentional "harm doing" (b) which is usually carried out with some repetitiveness (c) in an interpersonal relationship characterized by an imbalance of power, favoring the perpetrator(s). One might add that the bullying behavior usually occurs without apparent provocation and can be considered a form of proactive aggression in which the targeted individual is actively sought out. This definition also makes it clear that bullying can be considered a form of peer abuse.

Use of these three criteria has been well accepted among both researchers and practitioners for a number of years (e.g., Smith & Brain, 2000; Smith et al., 2013). However, with the advent of *cyber bullying*, that is, bullying via electronic forms of contact or communication—such as emails, mobile phone calls, text messages, chat room, instant messaging, website—concerns have been raised about whether and possibly how both the repetitiveness and the power imbalance criteria in the general definition can be applied to bullying with electronic means. The issue of whether and how the key criteria of traditional bullying can be applied to cyber bullying is discussed in considerable detail in a recent essay (Smith et al., 2013). After thoughtful consideration of a number of different aspects, the authors reach the tentative conclusion that the key criteria defining traditional bullying are largely applicable to cyber bullying as well. They suggest, for example, that the imbalance of power can be assessed "in terms of differences in technological know-how between perpetrator and victim, relative anonymity, social status, number of friends, or marginalized group position" (p. 36). And the criterion of repetition may have to be understood in a somewhat different way, with a focus on how many individuals can be reached with a negative message rather than on the perpetrator's cyber behavior, which is often a single act. Although the issue of the defining criteria of cyber bullying is still debated among researchers in the field and will probably need some further refinements, the position taken here is fairly close to my own and represents in my view a step in the right direction (for more information, see, e.g., Bauman et al., 2013; Olweus, 2012a, b; Smith et al., 2013).

Some Factors Affecting Prevalence

Science and news reports suggest that cyber bullying is a very frequent phenomenon among today's children and youth, and that the frequency (percent) or prevalence of the phenomenon has increased dramatically in recent years. Most prevalence estimates are derived from self-report questionnaires administered to the youths themselves (who presumably are the ones who can best respond to a question about whether they have been bullied). Generally, prevalence rates show extremely large variation, from 1%–2% up to 40%–50% or even more. Accordingly, it is very difficult for schools, parents, and others to know why this is so, and what a reasonably correct estimate might be. A number of studies with very high prevalence rates has made many schools believe that cyber bullying, and not traditional bullying, is the key problem they have to address. Before looking at some empirical analyses of prevalence, it may be useful to briefly consider three factors that influence the reported prevalence estimates and may contribute to the prevailing confusion: (1) the reference period, (2) the choice of cutoff point (response alternative), and (3) the context of measurement.

To get a meaningful prevalence estimate one must decide upon a specific time period—usually called the *reference period*—to which the question and response alternatives refer (Olweus, 1979, 1993). Examples include "How often have you been bullied/cyber bullied) in the past year" or "in the past couple of months," which constitute period prevalence rates. Prevalence rates will typically increase with the length of the reference period. Sometimes unusually high prevalence values turn out on closer inspection to be "lifetime prevalence estimates," that is, they measure responses to questions of the type: Have you ever been bullied? With regard to cyber bullying, the "lifetime" reference period is about 10 years. The same time periods must of course be used to make meaningful comparisons.

Sometimes diverging estimates are simply a consequence of markedly different reference periods (see, e.g., Olweus, 2012b).

Another factor of importance is *cutoff point* (response alternative) used in deciding when a respondent is considered being bullied. In the Olweus Bullying Questionnaire (OBQ, Olweus, 1996), for example, the various response alternatives to the global question about being bullied at school (in the past couple of months) are: "I haven't been bullied at school in the past couple of months," "it has only happened once or twice," "2 or 3 times a month," "about once a week," and "several times a week." After a detailed discussion of conceptual and strategic arguments and several empirical analyses, it was decided that individuals who respond "2 or 3 times a month" or more often can be classified (for research purposes) as "being bullied" (Solberg & Olweus, 2003). The cutoff point at "2 or 3 times a week" has been used in a number of large-scale research studies on bullying as a lower boundary, but in some other large-scale studies the "once or twice" response has been used instead, usually with considerably higher prevalence rates. In evaluating the contribution of a particular research study with regard to prevalence estimation, it is thus quite important to consider the frequency response alternatives used in the particular study, and not lump together results based on divergent cutoff points in the same category.

One obvious reason why some researchers have reported high or very high prevalence figures of cyber bullying is that cyber bullying has been studied "in isolation," that is, outside the general context of (traditional) bullying. To put cyber bullying in proper perspective, it is in my view necessary to study it in *the context of (traditional) bullying* more generally. One cannot talk about a phenomenon as bullying unless a reasonably precise definition has been provided to the respondents or the formulation of the questions or other measures used make it quite clear that the contents conform to what is usually implied in bullying. As explained above, bullying implies a special form of usually repeated aggressive behavior in the context of a power-imbalanced relationship, and the term should not be used as a blanket term for any form of negative or aggressive act (cf. Hunter et al., 2007; Olweus, 2010, 2013; Solberg et al., 2007). It is important to make a distinction between bullying and general aggression.

Empirical Estimates of Prevalence

In order to get empirical estimates of the prevalence of cyber bullying when studied in the context of traditional bullying, we administered the OBQ to a total of 440,000 U.S. students in grades 3–12 from 2007 to 2010 (Olweus, 2012a). The formulation of the cyber bullying item reads: "I was bullied with mean and hurtful messages, calls, or pictures, or in other ways on my mobile phone or over the internet (computer). (Please remember that it is not bullying when it is done in friendly and playful way.)"

To put the estimates of cyber bullying in relation to estimates of traditional bullying, we chose one item on direct verbal bullying for comparison. This item reads as follows: "I was called mean names, was made fun of, or teased in a hurtful way." Direct negative verbal comments are a characteristic of almost all traditional forms of bullying and can in a sense be seen as prototypical of such behavior. The questionnaire also contains parallel items about bullying other students, verbally or electronically.

All items on bullying were preceded with a rather detailed definition of bullying, underlining intentionality, some repetitiveness, and a power imbalance between target and perpetrator (see, e.g., Olweus, 2012a). Although use of single items may seem to be non-optimal from a psychometric point of view, for some areas of investigation including bullying, global single items can capture a lot of valid information and actually predict concurrent criteria as well as or even better than a whole scale of eight to nine bullying items (e.g., Olweus, 2013, p. 762).

The results obtained when cyber bullying is studied in the context of other forms of bullying is shown in Figures 14.1 and 14.2. Figure 14.1 illustrates the results for being exposed to direct verbal bullying and to cyber bullying, respectively, for the four consecutive years between 2007 and 2010. The average across-time prevalence for being verbally bullied is 17.3%, and the corresponding figure for being cyber bullied is 4.5%. The average for bullying others verbally is 9.6%, whereas the corresponding figure for cyber bullying others is 2.8% (Figure 14.2).

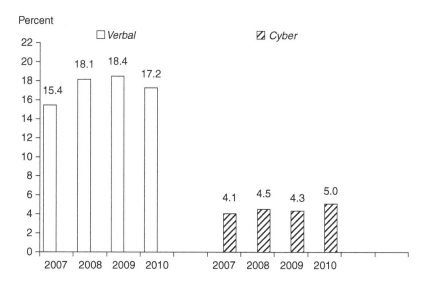

FIGURE 14.1 Time series data for 2007–2010 for verbal bullying (being verbally bullied) and cyber bullying (being bullied electronically). Data from all over the USA. Total n = 447,000.

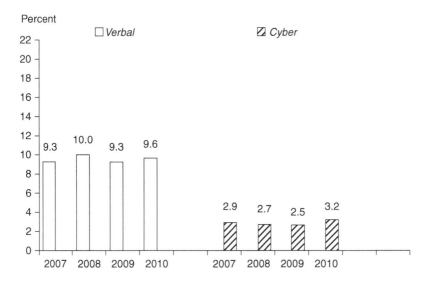

FIGURE 14.2 Time series data for 2007–2010 for verbal bullying (verbally bullying other students) and cyber bullying (bullying other students electronically). Data from all over the USA. Total n = 440,000.

Very much the same pattern of results—but with lower prevalence levels—were obtained for a large Norwegian sample where a collection of 41 schools were followed over a five-year period from 2006 to 2010 (see Olweus, 2012a). A number of other studies with a similar approach, many of which were based on quite large samples, have reported comparable prevalence figures (see Olweus, 2012b).

As can be seen in the two figures and in the Norwegian data (Olweus, 2012a), basically no systematic change in prevalence has occurred over the time periods studied, from 2006 to 2010. Norwegian follow-up data for 2013 and 2014 also indicated no increase; if anything, there was a decrease.

As documented by the reported prevalence percentages based on two very solid samples with different designs, cyber bullying is actually a quite low-prevalence phenomenon, representing only some 25% to 35% of the level of traditional bullying by direct verbal means. It is obvious that the "psychological threshold" for endorsing the global items on cyber bullying is much higher than for direct verbal bullying. The two global questions about cyber bullying are actually among the various bullying items/forms with the lowest prevalence rates. And even if one takes into account the possibility that certain forms of cyber bullying such as being exposed to a single episode of a personally embarrassing picture might not be adequately classified as being bullied ("2 or 3 times a month" or more), there is no doubt that there are *many more children and youth involved in traditional (verbal) bullying than in cyber bullying.* As a check on the robustness of the findings described, the reported empirical prevalence and time series analyses were also performed with the response alternative of "once or twice" (and not "2 or 3 times a month") as a lower-bound criterion for being classified as being bullied/bullying others. The pattern of results for these analyses remained very much the same.

Degree of Overlap of Traditional Bullying with Cyber Bullying

Another claim made by the media and some researchers is that the new form of cyber bullying has created many new victims and perpetrators of bullying. One way to empirically check on this claim is to investigate how large a percentage of respondents who have been cyber bullied are also bullied in traditional ways. In our own analyses, we cross-classified the dichotomized electronic being bullied variable (not cyber bullied vs. cyber bullied two or three times a month or more) with a dichotomized traditional being bullied variable representing all eight forms of being bullied in the OBQ (direct verbal, physical, and indirect) (see Olweus, 2012a for details). This cross-classification thus informs us about the degree of overlap between any form of being bullied traditionally and being cyber bullied.

The empirical results documented a very high degree of overlap. Of students who had been exposed to cyber bullying in the U.S. sample, 88% had been bullied in at least one traditional way. Also, for cyber bullying others, the overlap was 88%. The results for the Oslo schools were similar, with degree of overlap being 93% and 91%, respectively. In these analyses, only about 10% of the students involved in cyber bullying had only been cyber bullied or had only cyber bullied others.

In other studies, the degree of overlap varies a good deal from about 50% (e.g., Ybarra & Mitchell, 2004) to over 67% (e.g., Hinduja & Patchin, 2012) to 75% (Smith et al., 2008, Table 2, p. 380) to 90% (Salmivalli & Pöyhönen, 2012, p. 64; our own data). These somewhat varying results are likely to be related to choice of variables, measurement context (bullying or general aggression/harassment), reliability of measurement, and so forth. Nonetheless, a general conclusion can be drawn that the new electronic media seem to have actually created relatively few new victims or bullies.

Are There Negative Effects of Cyber Bullying, and How Do We Find Out?

Both media and researchers have reported that there are many serious negative effects of cyber bullying, typically of the same kind as effects of traditional bullying: depression; low self-esteem; anxiety; suicidal ideation, attempts, and completions; and psychosomatic problems like headaches and sleep disturbances, to name a few. Although cyber bullied children certainly report such problems or symptoms, it is difficult to know to what extent these problems actually are a consequence of cyber bullying. This is because the great majority of cyber bullied children and youth are also bullied in traditional ways, as documented above. How do we try to find out what the "true" effects of cyber bullying are, independent of possible effects of traditional bullying?

Here we will look at this problem in several different ways.

One way is to ask a sample of students whether they think being exposed to cyber bullying in various media channels would have more, the same, or less impact on victims than traditional bullying, rating their perceptions on an impact scale (Smith et al., 2008). Results in this study varied a good deal, with being exposed to a (presumably embarrassing) picture/video clip being perceived as having the most negative impact. Several other examples/media channels seemed to have considerably less impact.

A more direct way is to compare the percentages of bullied students who reported that they were not bothered or felt nothing when they were bullied in traditional and/or electronic ways. In a large-scale study with participants from England, Spain, and Italy (Ortega et al., 2012), 36% of cyber victims and 25% of traditional victims reported not being bothered. An Australian study gave very similar figures, 30% and 14% respectively (Campbell et al., 2012). In addition, almost 60% of students who were both traditional and cyber victims said that the negative impact of traditional bullying was worse than cyber bullying, whereas 12% said the opposite, and 28% found them equally bad. There are obviously more cyber than traditional victims who report not being much or at all affected by the bullying.

A third way of exploring the current issue is to categorize participants from large studies into four mutually exclusive groups: (1) pure traditional victims, (2) pure cyber victims, (3) combined traditional and cyber victims, and (4) non-involved participants. These groups can then be compared on one or more relevant outcome variables such as depression, low self-esteem, or anxiety. In this context, particular interest is attached to the pure cyber victim group. In the study of U.S. students with low self-esteem as the outcome variable (Olweus, 2012a, p. 533), the small group of pure cyber victims, that is, students who had been bullied with electronic but not traditional means (representing approximately 1.5% of the total sample of 2,800 students), had significantly worse results than the noninvolved students. Their level of low self-esteem was about the same as that of the group of traditional victims but clearly lower than for the group of combined victims.

In a Finnish study with a similar design but also including longitudinal outcome data, the small group of pure cyber victims (n = 94 or 0.5% of the large total sample of more than 17,000 students) had the lowest levels of depression at one-year follow-up and did not differ in that respect from the noninvolved group (Salmivalli et al., 2013). And the (lack of) social/peer acceptance variable was basically unrelated to cyber victimization. The authors concluded that "the extremely small group of electronically-only victims is selected on a different basis than those targeted traditionally . . . among the relatively well-adjusted and socially accepted students" (pp. 450–451) in this study.

In this context, it is also interesting to note that the small pure cyber-victim group (n = 81 or 1.4% of the total sample) in a study by Brighi et al. (2012) on several dimensions of self-esteem related to areas such as peers and sports did not differ from the noninvolved group (Table 3.7, p. 46).

A fourth way is to use a regression framework to find out to what extent a natural outcome variable such as depression or low self-esteem can be predicted from being cyber bullied over and above being bullied in traditional ways. If being cyber bullied is found to have a significant effect, this is often interpreted as evidence that cyber bullying is a distinct phenomenon with special characteristics that make it different from traditional forms of bullying.

In one U.S. study with data from Kowalski et al. (2008) and reported in Olweus (2012a), the addition of being cyber bullied did not increase prediction of low self-esteem after being traditionally bullied had been accounted for (results based on the combined group).

However, with depression or internalizing symptoms as the outcome variable, at least four recent studies have reported significant additive effects of being cyber bullied over and above the effects of being traditionally bullied (Bonanno & Hymel, 2013; Machmutow et al., 2012; Menesini et al., 2012; Perren, 2010). With the possible exception of the last study, the amount of additional predicted variance was quite small, between 0.8% and 1.5%.

Should such results be seen as an indication that being cyber bullied is a distinct phenomenon? If one takes as a point of departure the theoretical position that being cyber bullied is just a form of being bullied, on a par with other forms of being bullied, it becomes natural to check if being cyber bullied is more predictive of a relevant outcome variable than other forms of being bullied. An empirical check of this possibility was undertaken, using the outcome variable of low self-esteem from the U.S. study already mentioned (Olweus, 2012a). The global variable of being bullied (using the whole sample) predicted 8.3% of the variance in low self-esteem. Adding the being cyber bullied variable increased the predicted variance to 11.0%, representing a 2.7% increase. This was comparable to adding an item on indirect bullying, "being left out," which increased the predicted variance amount to 11.7%, representing a 3.4% increase. When a similar analysis was conducted using the scale of seven items of different forms of being bullied (with exclusion of the "being left out" variable), the amount of added variance for the being left out variable was somewhat smaller but still larger than the added variance predicted by the being cyber bullied variable. Very likely, most items representing different forms of being bullied contain some portion of specific variance that may correlate with a suitable outcome variable over and above the prediction by a global variable of being bullied or a sum scale of the bullied items. Obviously, finding that being cyber bullied predicts a significant increase of variance in a suitable outcome variable cannot without further analyses be taken as an indication that cyber bullying should best be regarded as a distinct phenomenon—possibly except if the increase is markedly higher for being cyber bullied than for other forms of being bullied.

Reflecting on the results of the possible negative effects of cyber bullying, one is struck by two facts: (1) Many reports have not measured or taken into account effects of concurrent traditional bullying, which makes it impossible to evaluate the extent to which cyber bullying may have a negative effect (over and above traditional bullying). (2) There seems to be considerable variability with regard to possible negative effects. When as many as a third of cyber victims report that they aren't bothered or feel nothing, it is obvious that some behaviors that they classify as cyber bullying are relatively non-serious. At the same time, it is equally clear that some forms of cyber bullying, such as having false rumors spread on the Internet or being exposed to a website with a personally embarrassing picture or video, can be very hurtful and distressing. Accordingly, there is a need for more fine-grained measurement of cyber bullying variables in order to achieve a more coherent picture on this important point.

More generally, if a researcher is just interested in applying a prediction perspective, it is reasonable to expect that the addition of a cyber bullying variable in many cases will increase the amount of variance explained (as will other forms of traditional bullying often do, if treated as separate predictors).

How Can Cyber Bullying Be Reduced or Prevented?

Because it is often reported that cyber bullying is a very frequent phenomenon with severe consequences for targeted youth, it has been argued that intervention efforts and resources nowadays should primarily focus on the problem of cyber bullying. Others have contended that ordinary anti-bullying programs that were primarily developed to counter and reduce traditional bullying, such as the Olweus Bullying Prevention Program (Olweus & Limber, 2010) or the KiVa program (Salmivalli et al., 2013), must also incorporate distinctive program components to deal with the special features of cyber bullying. What is the empirical evidence for such positions?

A few studies have evaluated the value and effects of a relatively technological approach using psychoeducational interventions designed to increase Internet safety and decrease risky online behavior among middle-school students (Mishna et al., 2011). The authors of this small-scale meta-analysis concluded that there were clear indications of increased Internet knowledge, but none of the three interventions seemed to change the students' own risky or inappropriate online behavior.

A more direct approach to the problem was taken in two studies with programs that focused on changing cyber bullying behavior, the ConRed program (Ortega-Ruiz et al., 2012) and the Cyber Friendly Schools Program (Cross et al., 2015). The first of these studies, covering a short-term (three-month) intervention in three schools (n = 893), reported significant but small reductions in levels of both cyber victimization and cyber bullying. In the longitudinal, randomized Cyber Friendly Schools study, using two-part growth modeling analysis of the outcome variables, the difference between intervention and control groups was only significant in the binary part of the model and only for the period from Time 1 to Time 2, and not for Time 2 to Time 3. In less technical language, this means that "the intervention and control groups differed regarding the odds of involvement in cyber bullying behavior, but not on the extent of involvement in the behavior when it occurred" (Cross et al., 2015, p. 9). This result was found for both cyber victimization and cyber bullying (for the first time period), representing a positive result on 4 out of 16 tests. The total sample comprised approximately 3,300 students in the 13–15 year age range.

As there is a high degree of overlap between traditional bullying and cyber bullying and the former is much more frequent, it is a meaningful goal to explore if cyber bullying also can be reduced with a general, school-based anti-bullying program with key focus on traditional bullying. There are (at least) two randomized control studies with such an approach, one being based on the Austrian ViSC Social Competence program (Gradinger et al., 2015) and the other on the Finnish KiVa program (Williford et al., 2013). Both these studies, using large samples (n = 2,042 and n = 18,412, respectively) and sophisticated methods of data analysis, documented clear relative reductions for the program students for both cyber victimization and cyber bullying from pre- to posttest over a one-year period. However, in the KiVa study, the effect on cyber bullying (perpetration) was qualified by age, implying positive effects for younger students but no significant effects for older students.

In summary, the studies on intervention with a main focus on cyber bullying/victimization have given mixed results and few guidelines as to how these problems can be reduced or prevented with such an approach. In some contrast, the two general anti-bullying programs seemed to be able to achieve positive results on cyber victimization and cyber bullying (conditional on age in the KiVa project), also in the absence of program components with a special focus on the electronic forms of bullying.

Summing Up

By and large, it seems that the usual criteria of traditional bullying can also be applied to cyber bullying but will probably need some further refinement. At the same time, it is important to realize on this point that some traditional forms of bullying such as having rumors spread are fairly similar to cyber bullying behaviors with regard to spreading mechanisms. Furthermore, as summarized in Olweus (2012a), it has been found that cyber and traditional items belong to the same latent factor or dimension in exploratory and confirmatory factor analyses as well as in more advanced item response theory (IRT) analyses. Preliminary analyses have also shown that cyber bullying items seem to function very much as items on traditional bullying (Olweus, 2012a, p. 530), with a largely monotone-increasing relation between the usual frequency categories (including the occasional "once or twice" option) and a natural outcome variable (level of low self-esteem).

If measured in an appropriate (bullying) context, cyber victimization/bullying is a low base rate phenomenon with many fewer students involved compared to traditional forms of bullying. But this is also true of other forms of/items on traditional bullying, such as "being threatened or forced to do things I didn't want to do." Contrary to many media and also researcher reports, the prevalence of cyber victimization/bullying has not increased over the past 8–10 years, as is also the case with traditional forms of victimization/bullying. Although a low base rate phenomenon, it is obvious that some special forms of cyber bullying such as having degrading and embarrassing pictures or videos posted can be very hurtful. Such events seem to be quite rare, however.

Some studies have documented that addition of cyber variables to traditional variables can increase prediction, but as was demonstrated with some traditional indirect items, similar or even somewhat stronger predictions can be obtained if such items are added to a global item or a scale of several items on traditional bullying. Accordingly, increased prediction cannot in itself and without further analyses be taken as an indication that cyber victimization/bullying qualifies as a phenomenon that is fundamentally different from traditional bullying.

In addition, with regard to intervention, the studies conducted so far seem to indicate that ordinary anti-bullying programs such as ViSC or KiVa, without a special focus on cyber bullying, can achieve more positive and consistent results than programs that are particularly geared toward the reduction and prevention of cyber bullying.

All of these facts are consistent with a view that conceptualizes cyber victimization/bullying as a form of bullying and not as a phenomenon that is fundamentally or qualitatively different from traditional bullying. Such a conclusion would of course be welcome from a theoretical perspective of parsimony or simplicity, implying that these on the surface fairly different behaviors can be subsumed under the same conceptual umbrella. This would probably mean that several of the noted differences between cyber victimization and traditional victimization are of relatively little importance from the perspective of the recipient.

On the other hand, little is gained by trying to force phenomena with markedly different characteristics under the same conceptual umbrella. Although cyber bullying and traditional bullying behaviors are largely similar, on at least two counts cyber bullying variables seem to behave differently than traditional bullying variables. First, the correlation between cyber victimization and cyber bullying is typically larger than the correlation between corresponding variables for various traditional forms (such as being left out/excluding the target or being physically bullied/bullying the target physically; Kowalski et al., 2014). Second, in spite of the fact that cyber victimization/bullying is a low base rate phenomenon—which usually implies that the item/variable reflects a high level of seriousness or severity—the percentage of cyber victims who feel nothing or aren't bothered is clearly lower than for traditional forms of bullying. This paradox might possibly indicate that there occurs in the digital world a certain amount of relatively benign teasing or joking that is not considered very threatening or hurtful by the recipient and is often reciprocated in kind. And one reason why the base rate of cyber bullying others is very low might well reflect the fact that sending a nasty cyber message after all requires some planning and determination and in addition may leave some digital traces that can lead to identification and disclosure of the perpetrator. With the empirical evidence available at this point in time, it is not possible to decide if these characteristics of cyber bullying are just an indication of measurement or other problems or if they represent genuinely different characteristics or mechanisms.

A Tentative Conclusion

In conclusion, most of the empirical facts and deliberations about cyber bullying reported above are consistent with the view of cyber bullying as a form of bullying, on a par with other forms such as verbal, physical, and indirect/relational. However, because some of the reported facts are based a limited amount of research, such a conclusion should be regarded as tentative. The emerging field of cyber bullying is in a relatively early phase, and there is a clear need for more conceptual, methodological, and empirical research on many of the issues discussed in this chapter.

To build a useful and coherent body of knowledge, it essential that future research efforts measure the phenomenon of cyber victimization/bullying in a "bullying context." This is important so that researchers can separate out from their bullying data less serious forms of cyber aggression or harassment where the perpetrator(s) and the targeted child or youth don't belong to the same classrooms, schools, or other social units, and the targeted individual may have no idea of who the perpetrator is. We have to remember that most students who are cyber bullied are also bullied in traditional ways, and such students should therefore be able to provide some good or at least tentative pointers as to which student or students might be involved in the perpetration. A key goal of our research and intervention work is identification of the existence and prevalence of individuals in a particular unit who have been exposed to power abuse by peers. This collection of individuals has one essential characteristic in common: They are being systematically bullied by peers. And the many negative long-term outcomes that have gradually been identified in long-term research concern these individuals (e.g., Olweus & Breivik, 2014; Ttofi et al., 2011) and not individuals who have been exposed to one or more episodes of traditional or cyber aggression or harassment.

I want to emphasize that my intention in writing this chapter has not been to downplay or trivialize cyber bullying. However, in order for research and intervention work on cyber bullying to proceed in a systematic and fruitful way, I think it is necessary to place it in proper context and to communicate a somewhat more realistic picture of its prevalence and nature. In addition, from a practical and prevention/intervention perspective, attention to cyber bullying cases can often represent a useful new approach to change and also lead to a disclosure of what actually goes on in terms of traditional bullying in the school context.

References

Bauman, M., Underwood, M. K., & Card, N. A. (2013) Definitions: Another perspective and a proposal for beginning with cyberaggression. In S. Bauman, J. Walker, & D. Cross (Eds.), *Principles of cyberbullying research: Definition, measures, and methods* (pp. 41–46). Philadelphia, PA: Routledge.

Bonanno, R. A., & Hymel, S. (2013). Cyber bullying and internalizing difficulties: Above and beyond the impact of traditional forms of bullying. *Journal of Youth and Adolescence, 42*, 685–697.

Brighi, A., Melotti, G., Guarini, A., Genta, M. L., Ortega, R., Mora-Merchán, J., Smith, P. K., & Thompson, F. (2012). Self-esteem and loneliness in relation to cyberbullying in three European countries. In Q. Li, D. Cross, & P. K. Smith (Eds.), *Cyberbullying in the global playground: Research from international perspectives* (pp. 32–56). Chichester, UK: Wiley-Blackwell.

Campbell, M., Spears, B., Slee, P., Butler, D., & Kift, S. (2012). Victims' perceptions of traditional and cyberbullying, and the psychological correlates of their victimization. *Emotional and Behavioural Difficulties, 17*, 389–401.

Cross, D., Shaw, T., Hadwen, K., Cardoso, P., Slee, P., Roberts, C., Thomas, L., & Barnes, A. (2015). Longitudinal impact of the Cyber Friendly Schools Program on Adolescents' Cyberbullying Behavior. *Aggressive Behavior, 42*, 166–180.

Gradinger, P., Yanagida, T., Strohmeier, D., & Spiel, C. (2015). Prevention of cyberbullying and cyber victimization: Evaluation of the ViSC Social Competence Program. *Journal of School Violence, 14*, 87–110.

Hinduja, S., & Patchin, J. W. (2012). Cyberbullying: Neither an epidemic nor a rarity. *European Journal of Developmental Psychology, 9*, 539–543.

Hunter, S. C., Boyle, J. M. E., & Warden, D. (2007). Perceptions and correlates of peer-victimization and bullying. *British Journal of Educational Psychology, 77*, 797–810.

Kowalski, R. M., Giumetti, G. W., Schroeder, A. N., & Latanner, M. R. (2014). Bullying in the digital age: A critical review and meta-analysis of cyberbullying research among youth. *Psychological Bulletin, 140*, 1073–1137.

Kowalski, R. M., Limber, S. P., & Agatston, P. W. (2008). *Cyber bullying: Bullying in the digital age*. Malden, MA: Blackwell Publishing.

Machmutow, K., Perren, S., Sticca, F., & Alsaker, F. D. (2012). Peer victimization and depressive symptoms: Can specific coping strategies buffer the negative impact of cyber victimization? *Emotional and Behavioural Difficulties, 17*, 389–401.

Menesini, E. (2012). Cyberbullying: The right value of the phenomenon. Comment on the paper: Cyberbullying: An overrated phenomenon? *European Journal of Developmental Psychology, 9*, 544–552.

Menesini, E., Calussi, P., & Nocentini, A. (2012). Cyberbullying and traditional bullying: Unique, additive and synergistic effects on psychological health symptoms. In Q. Li, D.

Cross, & P. K. Smith (Eds.), *Cyberbullying in the global playground: Research from* international *perspectives* (pp. 245–262). Chichester, UK: Wiley-Blackwell.

Mishna, F., Cook, C., Saini, M., Wu, M.-J., & MacFaddon, R. (2011). Interventions to prevent and reduce cyber abuse of youth: A systematic review. *Research on Social Work Practice, 21,* 5–14.

Olweus, D. (1973). *Hackkycklingar och översittare: Forskning om skolmobning.* Stockholm: Almqvist and Wiksell.

Olweus, D. (1978). *Aggression in the schools. Bullies and whipping boys.* Washington, DC: Hemisphere Press (Wiley).

Olweus, D. (1979). Stability of aggressive reaction patterns in males: A review. *Psychological Bulletin, 86,* 852–875.

Olweus, D. (1989). Prevalence and incidence in the study of anti-social behavior: Definitions and measurement. In M. Klein (Ed.), *Cross-national research in self-reported crime and delinquency* (pp. 187–201). Dordrecht, The Netherlands: Kluwer.

Olweus, D. (1993). *Bullying at school: What we know and what we can do.* Oxford: Blackwell Publishers.

Olweus, D. (1996). *The revised Olweus Bully/Victim Questionnaire.* Mimeo. Bergen, Norway: Research Center for Health Promotion (HEMIL), University of Bergen.

Olweus, D. (2010). Understanding and researching bullying: Some critical issues. In S. S. Jimerson, S. M. Swearer, & D. L. Espelage (Eds.), *Handbook of bullying in schools: An international perspective* (pp. 9–33). New York: Routledge.

Olweus, D. (2012a). Invited discussion paper. Cyber bullying: An overrated phenomenon. *European Journal of Developmental Psychology, 9,* 520–538.

Olweus, D. (2012b). Commentary. Comments on cyberbullying article: A rejoinder. *European Journal of Developmental Psychology, 9,* 559–568.

Olweus, D. (2013). School bullying: Development and some important challenges. *Annual Review of Clinical Psychology, 14,* 1–30.

Olweus, D., & Breivik, K. (2014). Plight of victims of school bullying: The opposite of well-being. In B.-A. Asher, F. Casas, I. Frones, & J. E. Korbin (Eds.), *Handbook of child well-being* (pp. 2593–2616). Heidelberg, Germany: Springer.

Olweus, D., & Limber, S. P. (2010). The Olweus bullying prevention program: Implementation and evaluation over two decades. In S. R. Jimerson, S. M. Swearer, & D. L. Espelage (Eds.), *Handbook of bullying in schools: An international perspective* (pp. 377–401). New York: Routledge.

Ortega-Ruiz, R., del Rey, R., & Casas, J. A. (2012). Knowing, building and living together on Internet and social networks: The ConRed Cyberbullying Prevention Program. *International Journal of Conflict and Violence, 6,* 303–313.

Ortega, R., Elipe, P., Mora-Merchán, J.A., Genta, M.L., Brighi, A., Guarini, A., Smith, P.K., Thompson, F., & Tippett, N. (2012). The emotional impact of bullying and cyberbullying on victims: A European cross-national study. *Aggressive Behavior, 38,* 342–356.

Perren, S., Dooley, J., Shaw, T., & Cross, D. (2010). Bullying in schools and cyberspace: Associations with depressive symptoms in Swiss and Australian adolescents. *Child and Adolescent Psychiatry and Mental Health, 4,* 28–39.

Salmivalli, C., & Pöyhönen, V. (2012). Cyberbullying in Finland. In Q. Li, D. Cross, & P. K. Smith (Eds.), *Cyberbullying in the global playground: Research from international perspectives* (pp. 57–72). Chichester, UK: Wiley-Blackwell.

Salmivalli, C., Sainio, M., & Hodges, E. V. E. (2013). Electronic victimization: Correlates, antecedents, and consequences among elementary and middle school students. *Journal of Clinical Child and Adolescent Psychology, 42,* 442–453.

Smith, P. K., & Brain, P. (2000). Bullying in schools: Lessons from two decades of research. *Aggressive Behavior, 26*(1), 1–9.

Smith, P. K., del Barrio, C., & Tokunaga, R. (2013). Definitions of bullying and cyberbullying: How useful are the terms? In S. Bauman, J. Walker, & D. Cross (Eds.), *Principles of cyberbullying research: Definition, measures, and methods* (pp. 26–40). Philadelphia, PA: Routledge.

Smith, P. K., Mahdavi, J., Carvalho, M., Fisher, S., Russell, S., & Tippett, N. (2008). Cyberbullying: Its nature and impact in secondary school pupils. *Journal of Child Psychology and Psychiatry, 49*, 376–385.

Solberg, M. E., & Olweus, D. (2003). Prevalence estimation of school bullying with the Olweus Bully/Victim Questionnaire. *Aggressive Behavior, 29*, 239–268.

Solberg, M. E., Olweus, D., & Endresen, I. M. (2007). Bullies and victims at school: Are they the same pupils? *British Journal of Educational Psychology, 77*, 441–464.

Tokunaga, R. S. (2010). Following you home from school: A critical review and synthesis of research on cyberbullying victimization. *Computers in Human Behavior, 26*, 277–287.

Ttofi, M. M., Farrington, D. P., Lösel, F., & Loeber, R. (2011). Do the victims of school bullies tend to become depressed later in life? A systematic review and meta-analysis of longitudinal studies. *Journal of Aggression, Conflict and Peace Research, 3*, 63–73.

Williford, A., Elledge, L. C., Boulton, A. J., DePaolis, K. J., Little, T. D., & Salmivalli, C. (2013). Effects of the KiVa Antibullying Program on cyberbullying and cybervictimization frequency among Finnish youth. *Journal of Clinical Child and Adolescent Psychology, 42*, 820–833.

Ybarra, M. L., & Mitchell, J. K. (2004). Online aggressor/targets, aggressors, and targets: A comparison of associated youth characteristics. *Journal of Child Psychology and Psychiatry, 45*, 1308–1316.

15

VIOLENCE AGAINST WOMEN

Barbara Krahé

Violence against women causes suffering and misery to victims and their families and also places a heavy burden on societies worldwide. It mostly happens within intimate relationships or between people known to each other. We begin by introducing the construct of violence against women as a social construction. Next, data are presented from the international research literature on the prevalence of two major forms of violence against women, physical and sexual victimization by an intimate partner and sexual victimization by men outside intimate relationships. This is followed by a brief review of the debate on the role of gender differences in perpetrating intimate partner violence, critiquing the claim that women are as likely or even more likely than men to show physical aggression against an intimate partner. The predominant explanations of why men engage in aggressive behavior toward women focus on different levels, from the macro level of society to the individual level of the perpetrator. Approaches at preventing violence against women are discussed in the final section.

Introduction: Violence against Women as a Social Construction

Violence against women is recognized as a serious social problem and a criminal offence in many, but by no means all, countries in the world (Turquet et al., 2011). Historically, condemning men's violence against women is a recent development. For a long time, women were considered the property of men, be they fathers, husbands, employers, or other men holding power over them. Accordingly, harm inflicted on women by men was considered the legitimate exercise of the right to domination and control. This view is still prevalent in some parts of the world, notably in societies characterized by a strong hierarchical structure and inequality of power beyond the domain of gender relations (Devries et al., 2013). Thus, any discussion of the research on violence against women needs to be located within the historical and cross-cultural coordinates of how the roles of men and women are defined in a given society, designating the construct of violence against women as a "social construction."

Understanding violence against women as a social construction means to acknowledge that what is considered violence against women at any given point in time reflects the prevailing social norms about appropriate interactions between men and women. For studying violence against women, especially in cross-cultural research designed to establish and compare the prevalence of violence against women in different countries and cultural groups, the fact that the very definition of the concept is socially constructed creates problems, as we will see in the next section.

Violence against women is a form of gender-based aggression because it is connected to the membership of perpetrator and victims in distinct gender groups. It comprises any behavior intended by a male actor to cause harm to a female target. Current research on violence against women can be subdivided into two strands. The first is the extensive field of research on intimate partner violence (see Chapter 16 of this volume), focusing on violence inflicted on women by their male partners. In this field of research, the majority of studies have investigated the infliction of physical harm, but there are also studies looking at another form of aggression against women, namely psychological maltreatment by intimate partners. This form of aggression is also more difficult to define and measure, which is why it will not be discussed in detail in the present chapter (see, however, Carney & Barner, 2012, for a review of this body of research). The second strand of research is directed at the problem of sexual aggression. This strand overlaps with the first in that many acts of sexual aggression are committed by perpetrators in a relationship with the victim, as denoted by the concepts of marital rape and date rape. However, sexual assaults are also committed by acquaintances outside an intimate relationship or by total strangers. In the present chapter, we will review evidence about both intimate partner violence and non-intimate sexual aggression to provide an overview of the extent to which women experience these two forms of gender-based aggression, what explains violence against women, how victims are affected in their sexual, physical, and mental health, and what can be done to prevent violence against women.

Definition and Prevalence of Violence against Women

A recent comprehensive examination of the prevalence of intimate partner violence and non-intimate sexual assault was published by the World Health Organization (WHO, 2013). The report considers violence against women as encompassing

> many forms of violence, including violence by an intimate partner (intimate partner violence) and rape/sexual assault and other forms of sexual

violence perpetrated by someone other than a partner (non-partner sexual violence) as well as female genital manipulation, honour killings, and the trafficking of women.

(WHO, 2013, p. 4)

In the present chapter, we will focus physical and sexual violence by an intimate partner as well as non-partner sexual assault. Based on the definitions adopted by the World Health Organization report, *physical violence* is defined as being slapped or having something thrown at the person that could hurt her, being pushed or shoved, being hit with a fist or something else that could hurt, being kicked, dragged, or beaten up, being choked or burnt on purpose, and/or being threatened with, or actually, having a gun, knife, or other weapon used on the person. *Sexual violence* is defined as being physically forced to have sexual intercourse when the person did not want to, having sexual intercourse because the person was afraid of what her partner might do, and/or being forced to do something sexual that she found humiliating or degrading (WHO, 2013, p. 6).

Setting a lower age boundary of 15 years and including only women who had ever been in a relationship, the report compiled evidence from 151 original population-based studies from 81 countries to establish the lifetime prevalence rate of women's experience of physical and sexual victimization by an intimate partner. Countries were classified into regions according to the standard classification adopted by the WHO, as shown in Table 15.1. Across all included countries, the mean rate of women experiencing physical assault, sexual assault, or both from an intimate partner was 30%, but there was considerable variation by region, as shown in Table 15.1. In a second analysis, the report compiled evidence

TABLE 15.1 Lifetime Prevalence in % of Violence against Women Worldwide (WHO, 2013)

	Physical and/or sexual intimate partner violence among ever-partnered women	Non-partner sexual violence
Low- and middle-income regions		
Africa	36.6	11.9
Americas	29.8	10.7
Eastern Mediterranean	37.0	—[a]
Europe	25.4	5.2
South-East Asia	37.7	4.9
Western Pacific	24.6	6.8
High-income regions	23.2	12.6
Overall rate	**30.0**	**7.2**

Adapted from WHO, 2013. See p. 17 and p. 19 for the figures in this table and p. 18 for countries included in each category. [a]No data were found for countries in this region.

of the prevalence rates of non-partner sexual assault among women regardless of whether they had ever been in a relationship, showing that on average 7.2% of women reported non-partner sexual assault. The figures, also shown in Table 15.1, again reveal substantial variability between regions.

As the report is based on original studies using different definitions and measures of violence against women, part of the variability we see in the prevalence rates is due to differences in scope and methodology of the research that informed the report. Furthermore, as noted above, what is considered violence against women is socially constructed and varies between cultures, so even at the conceptual level, studies are likely to address different phenomena. This difficulty of comparing prevalence rates from different studies is a problem that not only affects cross-cultural analyses but also hampers the interpretation of prevalence rates within single countries (Krahé et al., 2014).

In addition to national surveys that formed the basis of the WHO report, official crime statistics provide data about the scale of intimate partner violence and non-partner sexual assault, but these figures only include cases reported to the police. As both forms of violence against women are vastly underreported (Palermo et al., 2014; Temkin & Krahé, 2008), there is a general consensus that crime statistics do not reflect the true extent to which women experience intimate partner violence or sexual assault by acquaintances and strangers.

A highly controversial issue in interpreting the scale of violence against women is how prevalence rates for women's victimization in intimate relationships compare to those for men. Victimization surveys identify women as more vulnerable to intimate partner violence compared to men. For example, the victimization rate by non-sexual partner abuse of 23.8% for women in the 2012–13 Crime Survey for England and Wales contrasts with a rate of 11.1% for men (Office for National Statistics, 2014). Women are also more likely than men to suffer injuries as a result of their partner's aggressive actions (Rennison & Welchans, 2000), up to the point that they are more likely to be killed by an intimate partner (Campbell et al., 2007).

By contrast, research studies using the Conflict Tactics Scales (Straus, 1979; Straus et al., 1996) to assess experiences of physical and sexual assault in intimate relationship often reveal that men report higher rates of victimization by their female partners than women report by their male partners (see Archer, 2000, for a meta-analysis). On this measure, participants are presented with a list of minor and severe acts of physical aggression and asked to indicate if and how many times they have experienced the behavior in question from an intimate partner in a specified time period (e.g., the past year). In addition, a scale measuring injuries suffered by a partner is included. Table 15.2 illustrates this measure by presenting example items of the physical assault, sexual assault, and injury scales of the revised Conflict Tactics Scales (CTS2; Straus et al., 1996).

In a meta-analysis including 82 studies, women were found to be slightly more likely than men to show physical aggression toward a partner (an effect size of $d = -0.05$; Archer, 2000). However, women were more likely to be injured as a

TABLE 15.2 Example Items from the Revised Conflict Tactics Scales (Straus et al., 1996)

Scale	Example item
Physical assault	
Minor	My partner threw something at me that could hurt.
Severe	My partner slammed me against a wall.
Sexual assault	
Minor	My partner insisted on sex when I did not want to but did not use physical force.
Severe	My partner used threats to make me have sex.
Injury	
Minor	I had a sprain, bruise, or small cut because of a fight with my partner.
Severe	I needed to see a doctor because of a fight with my partner, but he didn't.

Response scale: 1 (once in the past year) to 6 (more than 20 times in the past year); N = this has never happened; B = not in the past year but it happened before.

result of their intimate partner's aggressive behavior than were men (an effect size of $d = 0.15$). This finding may explain why men feature more prominently as perpetrators of interpersonal violence in crime statistics: if men's aggressive behaviors are more likely to lead to injuries, they are more likely to be reported to the police and be counted in official records. Critics have argued that the overrepresentation of women as perpetrators of intimate partner violence in studies using the CTS is distorted because this instrument records acts of violence without taking their context into account (Dobash & Dobash, 2004). In particular, it does not consider whether the behavior shown is an unprovoked attack or a defensive response to a previous attack, so that an act of self-defense by a woman is counted in the same way as the initial assault by her male partner.

It is now widely acknowledged by researchers that intimate partner violence is not a unitary phenomenon but comprises different forms, contexts, and underlying dynamics. Scholars have distinguished three types of intimate partner violence, differing in the involvement of men and women as perpetrators and victims (Kelly & Johnson, 2008). The first type is called *coercive controlling violence*, involving emotionally abusive intimidation and physical violence. It is a stable relationship feature and more often shown by men than by women. The second type is called *violent resistance* in response to a coercive controlling partner, more often shown by women than by men (see also a recent review by Hamberger & Larsen, 2015). The third and most common type is called *situational couple violence*, arising *ad hoc* out of everyday conflict situations rather than being a stable pattern in a relationship. This form of intimate violence appears to be shown equally by men and women. Almost all the studies claiming gender symmetry in intimate partner violence use general community samples in which gender symmetry appears as a result of lumping together the different forms of intimate partner violence (Johnson & Ferraro, 2000). Researchers now widely agree that progress in the understanding of the dynamics of intimate partner violence will have to go beyond purely act-based descriptions and pay greater attention to the specific forms and contexts in which assaults on intimate partners take place (Frieze, 2000).

For sexual assault, the figures comparing women's and men's victimization rates provide a clear and uncontroversial picture: women are far more likely to be victimized by a male perpetrator than men are to be victimized by a female perpetrator. For example, in the latest Crime Survey for England and Wales, 19.1% of women but only 2.7% of men reported at least one incident of victimization since the age of 16 (Office for National Statistics, 2014). In the United States, data from the 2010 National Intimate Partner and Sexual Violence Survey showed that 18.3% of women reported a lifetime history of rape victimization compared to 1.4% of men (Black et al., 2011).

From the evidence discussed in this section, it is clear that physical and sexual violence inflicted by an intimate partner is a reality for many women. The likelihood of being sexually assaulted by a man outside an intimate relationship is far lower than being sexually assaulted by a romantic or dating partner, contradicting the stereotype of the "real rape" as an attack by a stranger (see Temkin & Krahé, 2008, on the "real rape" stereotype). Beyond demonstrating that violent victimization affects women worldwide, it is important to understand why it is that so many relationships that should be built on trust, respect, and loving interactions also involve behaviors that intentionally harm the romantic partner and what explains the experience of coercive sex by women from men with whom they are not in an intimate relationship.

Explanations of Violence against Women

In this section, we will review explanations of why men show physical and sexual violence against women, which can be assigned to three levels: (a) the macro level of the society, or social group, in which violence against women occurs, (b) the dyadic level of relationship functioning and interaction patterns between the partners, and (c) the individual level of the perpetrator. In addition, we will look at specific situational circumstances that may precipitate violence against women.

Macro-Level Explanations

Theories at the macro level consider causes of violence against women that lie in the social structure and value systems of a society or a particular social group. The extent to which violence is culturally accepted in a society is thought to affect the prevalence of violence against intimate partners. Specifically, the acceptance of violence has been linked to the patriarchal structure of societies that create a favorable context for men's violence against female partners (Marin & Russo,

1999). Patriarchal societies are characterized by a clear-cut power differential between men and women, with men dominating women in most areas of public and private life. Male dominance is linked to a positive evaluation of male assertiveness and aggressiveness. In these societies, social institutions are dominated by men, making it hard for women to be acknowledged as victims of male violence, to secure help, and to enforce the legal prosecution of perpetrators. Although linking violence against women to power differentials in society would seem plausible, there is limited empirical evidence from psychology to support this notion (Eckhardt, 2011). An exception is the work examining differences in the acceptability of physical partner abuse in cultures differing in the endorsement of a "culture of honor" (Vandello & Cohen, 2008). In honor cultures, it is important for men to uphold an image of toughness, which includes making sure their partner behaves in accordance with prevailing standards of female decency. If men see women as violating the honor code, physical violence is accepted in these cultures as a legitimate way of restoring their threatened male identity. The extent to which men have dominance over women was also shown to be relevant to gender differences in intimate partner violence in a study including victimization rates in 16 countries (Archer, 2006). The less power women had in the respective country, the higher their victimization rates were compared to those of men.

Macro-level explanations identify certain social norms and values that allow intimate partner violence to happen and go unsanctioned. However, they cannot address the issue of why intimate partner violence occurs in some relationships, but not others, and is performed by some individuals, and not others under the same societal conditions.

Dyad-Level Explanations

At the dyad level, explanations look at the relationship as the unit of analysis and try to identify structural features of relationship functioning that increase the likelihood of aggression. Low marital satisfaction was identified as a risk factor of physical partner violence in both men and women in a meta-analysis (Stith et al., 2008). Moreover, abuse is more likely to occur in relationships based on patriarchal attitudes and role divisions in which the man dominates the relationship and has power over his female partner, physically, materially, and in terms of decision-making. This is particularly true for cultures linking male dominance to the concept of honor, in which a man's social status and reputation are defined through the extent to which he has control over his female partner (Vandello & Cohen, 2003).

Individual-Level Explanations

Finally, research has examined causes for intimate partner violence at the level of the individual perpetrator, considering a range of socio-demographic and personal characteristics of men acting violently against their female partners.

A meta-analysis of risk factors for physical partner abuse showed that younger, less educated, and less affluent men were more likely to abuse their partners than were older, more educated, and more affluent men (Stith et al., 2004). However, personality variables were more closely associated with the risk of partner abuse in men than these socio-demographic characteristics. Individuals suffering from personality disorders or mental illness have a higher risk of abusing their partner (Eckhardt, 2011), particularly because they have problems controlling angry feelings and aggressive impulses (Birkley & Eckhardt, 2015). Endorsement of the traditional male gender role and attitudes condoning violence, dispositional proneness to anger, and attachment difficulties, particularly jealousy, were found to increase the likelihood that men become abusive toward an intimate partner (Stith et al., 2004).

Situational Precipitation of Violence against Women

The most prominent situational characteristic implicated in violence against an intimate partner is alcohol use. Although alcohol intoxication is not necessarily a cause of intimate partner violence, it is likely to lower the threshold for aggressive behavior in conflict situations with a partner. Meta-analytic evidence showed small to moderate associations between drinking and perpetration of intimate partner violence among both men and women (Foran & O'Leary, 2008). Parallel findings for a range of drugs other than alcohol were obtained in another meta-analysis (Moore et al., 2008), which found that the association with intimate partner violence was strongest for cocaine. Moreover, acts of physical aggression tend to be more severe and more likely to lead to serious harm when the perpetrator, the victim, or both are drunk, as shown in data from 13 countries across the world (Graham et al., 2011). Adding to these findings on the role of alcohol in perpetrating violence against a partner, a recent meta-analysis showed that alcohol consumption was also linked to the odds of victimization among women (Devries et al., 2014).

Alcohol is also involved on a large scale in sexual aggression toward women. It is estimated that about half of all sexual assaults are committed by men who are under the influence of alcohol, and half of all victims of sexual aggression were drinking at the time of the assault (Abbey et al., 2004). Situational drinking and general habits of heavy drinking have been identified as a risk factor for sexual aggression victimization and perpetration in several longitudinal and cross-cultural studies (e.g., Abbey & McAuslan, 2004; Krahé et al., 2015; Swartout & White, 2010).

The explanations discussed in this section addressed different variables associated with an increased likelihood of showing violent behavior toward an intimate partner and engaging in sexual aggression toward women. None of them can aspire, nor, indeed, claims, to predict exactly which relationships will become violent. Not every man growing up in a patriarchal society turns into an abuser, nor does everyone experiencing marital conflict or drinking in sexual interactions.

Macro-level factors, such as cultural norms, are relatively stable and continuously present. They provide the background against which individuals engage in aggressive behavior. Dyadic and individual factors, such as high level of marital conflict and individual attitudes about violence, have a more immediate impact on the unfolding of aggressive interactions. It is the combination and interaction of these different risk factors that eventually precipitate physical and sexual aggression toward women.

Consequences of Violence against Women

Intimate partner violence leads to a variety of physical consequences, such as serious injuries, higher incidence of stress-related physical illnesses, and economic effects, such as poverty as a result of leaving an abusive relationship or due to employment instability (Coker et al., 2011). In addition, the psychological impact of victimization on the victim's mental health and well-being is substantial. Many victims of physical partner violence are traumatized by the experience, especially because severe forms of partner abuse tend to persist over time. A meta-analysis revealed that the mean rate of post-traumatic stress disorder (PTSD) among female victims of physical partner abuse was 63%, the mean rate of depression was 47%, and the mean rate of suicidality was 17% (Golding, 1999). A more recent meta-analytic review found a two- to threefold higher risk of developing major depressive disorder in women exposed to intimate partner violence in comparison to non-victimized women (Beydoun et al., 2012). Beyond these national data, the WHO (2013) report summarizes evidence on the adverse health effects of exposure to intimate partner violence and non-partner sexual assault across studies from a wide range of countries, as presented in Table 15.3.

TABLE 15.3 Selected Health Outcomes among Women Victimized by an Intimate Partner (based on WHO, 2013, pp. 29–30)

	N Studies	Odds Ratio*
Intimate partner violence		
Sexual health		
AIDS/HIV	17	1.52
Sexually transmitted disease	21	1.81
Mental health		
Unipolar depressive disorder	16	1.97
Alcohol use disorders	36	1.82
Injuries	11	2.92
Non-partner sexual violence		
Unipolar depressive disorder	5	2.59
Alcohol use disorders	5	2.33

* Denotes the increase in likelihood of suffering the respective adverse health outcome in victimized compared to non-victimized women.

The figures show that women who experienced physical violence from an intimate partner were almost twice as likely as women without a victimization history to suffer from mental health problems, such as depression and alcohol-related problems, and were 1.5 times more likely to be infected with HIV.

The consequences of a sexual assault on the victim are no less severe (see Martin et al., 2011, for a review). As shown in Table 15.3, the WHO survey revealed that women who suffered sexual violence from a non-partner were 2.5 times more likely to suffer from depression and alcohol-related problems compared to non-victimized women. Furthermore, research has shown that many victims develop the symptomatology of PTSD in the weeks and months following the assault, and sexual assault has been identified as one of the strongest risk factors for PTSD in women (Klump, 2008). In fact, the finding that women show higher rates of PTSD in the general population compared to men has been attributed to the higher prevalence of sexual victimization among women (Tolin & Foa, 2008). Women who experienced sexual assault also had a higher risk of suicide (Ullman, 2004), and women who experienced repeated victimization had higher rates of PTSD than first-time victims (Najdowski & Ullman, 2011).

Victims of sexual aggression not only have to come to terms with the emotional trauma of the assault itself, they also have to cope with the reactions of others who learn about their fate. These reactions, by legal and medical professionals as well as friends and family members, are often perceived as unsupportive, sometimes even as a "second assault." There is a widespread tendency to blame the victim of a sexual assault, unparalleled in judgments of victims of other criminal offences (Bieneck & Krahé, 2011). A large body of evidence has shown that certain victim characteristics, such as low social status, higher number of sexual partners, and pre-rape behavior that is at odds with female role requirements, are linked to higher attributions of responsibility to the victim (Temkin & Krahé, 2008). The tendency to hold victims responsible for being sexually assaulted is seen as a major factor in the low conviction rate for rape that has plagued the legal systems of many countries (Krahé, 2016).

Intimate partner violence and sexual aggression are not only deeply disturbing to individual victims and their families, they also carry high costs for societies as a whole. A report by the World Health Organization details the economic burden of different forms of partner abuse (Waters et al., 2004). For example, one study estimated the costs of rape in the United States in terms of medical treatment as well as impairment of mental health, productivity, and quality of life at $47,000 per case (Miller et al., 1993). In a survey of over 3,000 women in the United States, the annual health care costs were found to be 19% higher among victims of intimate partner violence than among non-victimized women (Rivara et al., 2007).

Preventing Violence against Women

We saw in the last section that partner abuse may lead to long-term psychological distress and impairment. To ameliorate these adverse effects, a critical first step is to stop the violence. Being entrapped in abusive relationships because of psychological mechanisms, such as denial, self-blame, and adaptation to violence, is a common fate of victims of partner violence. Even of those who try to leave a violent relationship and seek refuge in shelters for battered women, about a third eventually return to their abusive partners, with some studies suggesting even higher figures (Barnett et al., 2011). Thus, empowering women to gain independence from abusive partners, psychologically, economically, and in terms of managing their everyday lives, must be a key objective of intervention work with victims of partner abuse.

To prevent violence against women from happening in the first place, developing effective interventions is a primary concern of practitioners and policy makers, and there is a wide range of approaches toward achieving this goal (as reviewed by Ellsberg et al., 2015). In this section, we will review approaches located at two levels: the macro level of society and the individual level of perpetrators and victims.

Societal-Level Measures

One way in which intimate partner violence can be tackled at the societal level is by means of the legal system. Legal regulations have been introduced to enhance the protection of victims and improve the detection of intimate partner violence. For example, many countries now have the instrument of imposing *restraining orders* on individuals who have used or threatened to use violence against intimate partners. This instrument stops abusers from getting close to the persons they threaten to attack and enforces legal sanctions in case the order is violated. Other legal regulations are designed to increase the odds of criminal prosecution of intimate partner violence offenders in the form of *warrantless arrests* or *mandatory arrest* policies in cases of intimate partner violence. These criminal justice responses to violence appear to have some success in protecting women (Goodman & Epstein, 2011). Evaluations of success are mostly based on official records of increases in the number of arrests and criminal prosecutions in intimate partner violence incidents. At the same time, there have also been critical voices. For example, it has been argued that restraining orders may serve to escalate rather than de-escalate intimate partner conflicts because they lead to anger and frustration in the aggressor, and that mandatory arrest policies have increased the number of victims who were arrested alongside the aggressor (e.g., Hovmand et al., 2009).

Another approach for dealing with intimate partner violence at the societal level consists in improving *protective services* offering support to the victims. Measures include the provision of sheltered accommodation for women and children who suffered intimate partner violence, regular visits by social workers to families identified as "at risk" to preempt the development of abusive situations, provisions for placing elders abused by their partners into high-quality care, and providing treatment programs for the perpetrators of abuse (Barnett et al., 2011).

Evaluating the effectiveness of macro-level responses to intimate partner violence is difficult, not least because the criteria of success are hard to define. For example, whether the introduction of restraining orders causes rates of intimate partner homicide to decline is almost impossible to establish given the many factors that affect the incidence of such assaults. It has been argued that mandatory reporting laws undermine the autonomy of victims and put them at risk of further violence from the abusive partner (see Bledsoe et al., 2004, for a balanced evaluation).

A societal approach to the prevention of sexual violence against women is to address the low conviction rates in the criminal prosecution of rape by implementing changes in the treatment of rape victims by the police and the medical system. Although these measures are directed, in the first instance, at survivors of sexual assault, they are also intended to have a wider effect on increasing reporting rates by removing the expectation of secondary victimization by police and medical staff as a barrier to reporting. In the United States, programs have been implemented to ensure that sexual assault victims are cared for by specialized teams, such as sexual assault nurse examiners (the SANE program; Campbell & Patterson, 2011). In Britain, specialized Sexual Assault Referral Centres (SARCs) were introduced to better meet the needs of victims and improve the chances of criminal prosecution, and further recommendations for change were made in an independent report to the government (Stern, 2010).

Individual-Level Measures

Several approaches have been developed to address intimate partner violence and sexual aggression at the level of the individual aggressor. One measure is the psycho-educational approach designed to increase men's understanding of the detrimental effects of violence and to challenge role expectations and entitlements regarding male dominance. The second approach draws on cognitive behavioral therapy to help abusers to "unlearn" violent behavior through improving communication skills and anger management. Two meta-analyses investigated the effectiveness of interventions, mainly based on these two approaches, targeting men who had shown violence toward an intimate partner. The first meta-analysis included 44 effect sizes from 22 treatment studies that compared treated abusers with a non-treatment control group (Babcock et al., 2004). Treatment efficacy was measured by the rate of recidivism in terms of the proportion of participants who committed further acts of physical violence in the post-treatment period, established by police records and partner reports. The small effect size led the authors to conclude that the effect of the interventions on reducing recidivism was minimal. The second meta-analysis considered 10 rigorously conducted studies in which participants had been mandated by a court to participate in an intervention program (Feder & Wilson, 2005). Whether or not abusers engaged in further intimate partner violence, established through official records or through victim reports, was the outcome variable. For recidivism rates established by official records, a significant effect size of $d = 0.26$ was found, indicating that participants in the treatment groups had a lower rate of continuing violence than untreated controls. Studies using victim reports as a source of information on whether the participants engaged in further violence against their partner failed to show significant treatment effects. Assuming that victim reports provide a more accurate reflection of repeat abuse, as only a small proportion of abusive incidents are reported to official agencies, this analysis also suggests that the interventions remained largely ineffective in stopping abusive men from engaging in further violence against their female partners.

Individual-level approaches addressing sexual aggression primarily focus on men as potential perpetrators, and many studies have addressed the effectiveness of rape prevention programs (see reviews by Paul & Gray, 2011; Vladutiu et al., 2011). These studies provided evidence for short-term reductions in the acceptance of rape myth downplaying the seriousness of rape and assigning blame to the victim (e.g., Langhinrichsen-Rohling et al., 2011), but the effects tended to disappear within a few weeks post-intervention. Based on evidence that men tend to overestimate the extent to which their peers accept and use sexual aggression, the "social norms approach" considers a correction of these misperceptions as a central element of rape prevention (Fabiano et al., 2003). The aim of this approach is to counter the rape-supportive normative environment by engaging men as social justice allies, both in terms of challenging misperceptions and in promoting active intervention to stop other men from engaging in sexual aggression. An evaluation of a theory-based rape prevention program that included a social norms component and sought to increase men's willingness to intervene as bystanders on behalf of sexual assault victims was conducted by Gidycz et al. (2011). Although the program was successful in reducing the perception of sexual aggression as acceptable and decreasing the rate of sexual aggression, little effect was found in terms of reducing rape myth acceptance and promoting bystander intervention when witnessing a sexual assault.

Complementing rape prevention efforts targeting men, risk reduction programs for women aim at increasing women's awareness and understanding of the risk factors leading to sexual aggression, and enabling them to engage in more effective resistance when faced with a situation where a sexual assault may be imminent (Fisher et al., 2008). The success of these programs appears limited, particularly with women who have experienced a previous sexual assault (Hanson & Gidycz, 1993). However, studies testing programs with a focus on promoting self-protective behavior and overcoming barriers to resistance provided a more positive picture. A systematic evaluation of a risk reduction program found a significant increase in self-protective dating behaviors, more assertive communication in sexual interactions, greater self-efficacy in rejecting unwanted sexual advances, and greater use of resistance tactics in program participants from pretest to the follow-ups after four and seven months compared to a control group (Gidycz et al., 2015). Victimization rates did not differ between the intervention and the control group, but victimized women in the intervention group were less likely to engage in self-blame and more likely to blame the perpetrator.

The research reviewed in this section has shown that effective strategies for preventing violence against women are still few and far between. Although the need to implement legal measures and create secure havens for protecting women against male violence has been recognized and a number of policy steps have been taken, there is not yet conclusive evidence that they achieve the intended goals. Measures at the individual level, potentially easier to evaluate, have shown limited success so far.

Conclusion

The research reviewed in this chapter has provided ample evidence that violence against women is a worldwide problem. In recognition of this pervasive threat to women's health and well-being, the United Nations designated November 25 as the International Day for the Elimination of Violence against Women in 1999. In 2008, the UN Secretary General launched his UNITE campaign to end violence against women, which is inspired by the vision of "a world free from violence against all women and girls" (www.un.org/en/women/endviolence/). Systematic research, as reviewed in this chapter, may serve an important function not only in documenting the scale of violence against women and its consequences to raise awareness about the problem. It also contributes to the understanding of the causes of violence against women that is crucial for the development of theory-based, effective measures of prevention and intervention.

References

Abbey, A., & McAuslan, P. (2004). A longitudinal examination of male college students' perpetration of sexual assault. *Journal of Consulting and Clinical Psychology, 72*, 747–756.

Abbey, A., Zawacki, T., Buck, P. O., Clinton, A. M., & McAuslan, P. (2004). Sexual assault and alcohol consumption: What do we know about their relationship and what types of research are still needed? *Aggression and Violent Behavior, 9*, 271–303.

Archer, J. (2000). Sex differences in aggression between heterosexual partners: A meta-analytic review. *Psychological Bulletin, 126*, 651–680.

Archer, J. (2006). Cross-cultural differences in physical aggression between partners: A social-role analysis. *Personality and Social Psychology Review, 10*, 133–153.

Babcock, J. C., Green, C. E., & Robie, C. (2004). Does batterers' treatment work? A meta-analytic review of domestic violence treatment. *Clinical Psychology Review, 23*, 1023–1053.

Barnett, O. W., Miller-Perrin, C. L., & Perrin, R. D. (2011). *Family violence across the lifespan* (3rd ed.). Thousand Oaks, CA: Sage.

Beydoun, H. A., Beydoun, M. A., Kaufman, J. S., Lo, B., & Zonderman, A. B. (2012). Intimate partner violence against adult women and its association with major depressive disorder, depressive symptoms and postpartum depression: A systematic review and meta-analysis. *Social Science & Medicine, 75*, 959–975.

Bieneck, S., & Krahé, B. (2011). Blaming the victim and exonerating the perpetrator in cases of rape and robbery: Is there a double standard? *Journal of Interpersonal Violence, 26*, 1785–1797.

Birkley, E. L., & Eckhardt, C. (2015). Anger, hostility, internalizing negative emotions, and intimate partner violence perpetration: A meta-analytic review. *Clinical Psychology Review, 37*, 40–56.

Black, M. C., Basile, K. C., Breiding, M. J., Smith, S. G., Walters, M. L., Merrick, M. T., Chen, J., & Stevens, M. R. (2011). *The national intimate partner and sexual violence survey (NISVS): 2010 summary report*. Atlanta, GA: National Center for Injury Prevention and Control, Centers for Disease Control and Prevention. Retrieved from: www.cdc.gov/violenceprevention/pdf/nisvs_report2010-a.pdf

Bledsoe, L. K., Yankeelov, P. A., Barbee, A. P., & Antle, B. F. (2004). Understanding the impact of intimate partner violence mandatory reporting law. *Violence Against Women, 10*, 534–560.

Campbell, J. C., Glass, N., Sharps, P. W., Laughon, K., & Bloom. T. (2007). Intimate partner homicide. Review and implications of research and policy. *Trauma, Violence, & Abuse, 8*, 246–269.

Campbell, R., & Patterson, D. (2011). Services of victims of sexual violence. In M. P. Koss, J. W. White, & A. E. Kazdin (Eds.), *Violence against women and children* (Vol. 2: Navigating solutions, pp. 95–114). Washington, DC: American Psychological Association.

Carney, M. M., & Barner, J. R. (2012). Prevalence of partner abuse: Rates of emotional abuse. *Partner Abuse, 3*, 286–335.

Coker, A. L., Williams, C. M., Follingstad, D. R., & Jordan, C. E. (2011). Psychological, reproductive and maternal health, behavioral, and economic impact of intimate partner violence. In J. W. White, M. P. Koss, & A. E. Kazdin (Eds.), *Violence against women and children* (Vol. 1: Mapping the terrain, pp. 265–284). Washington, DC: American Psychological Association.

Devries, K. M., Mak, J. Y. T., García-Moreno, C., Petzold, M., Child, J. C., Falder, G., Lim, S., Bacchus, L. J., Engell, R. E., Rosenfeld, L., Pallitto, C., Vos, T., Abrahams, N., & Watts, C. H. (2013). The global prevalence of intimate partner violence against women. *Science, 340*(6140), 1527–1528.

Devries, K. M., Child, J. C., Bacchus, L. J., Mak, J., Falder, J., Graham, K., Watts, C., & Heise, L. (2014). Intimate partner violence victimization and alcohol consumption in women: A systematic review and meta-analysis. *Addiction, 109*, 379–391.

Dobash, R. P., & Dobash, R. E. (2004). Women's violence in intimate relationships: Working on a puzzle. *British Journal of Criminology, 44*, 324–349.

Eckhardt, C. (2011). Intimate partner violence: Cognitive, affective, and relational factors. In J. P. Forgas, A. W. Kruglanski, & K. D. Williams (Eds.), *The psychology of social conflict and aggression* (pp. 167–184). New York: Psychology Press.

Ellsberg, M., Arango, D. J., Morton, M., Gennari, F., Kiplesund, S., Contreras, M., & Watts, C. (2015). Prevention of violence against women and girls: What does the evidence say? *The Lancet, 385*, 1555–1565.

Fabiano, P. M., Perkins, H. W., Berkowitz, A., Linkenbach, J., & Stark, C. (2003). Engaging men as social justice allies in ending violence against women: Evidence for a social norms approach. *Journal of American College Health, 52*, 105–112.

Feder, L., & Wilson, D. B. (2005). A meta-analytic review of court-mandated batterer intervention programs: Can courts affect abusers' behavior? *Journal of Experimental Criminology, 1*, 239–262.

Fisher, B. S., Daigle, L. E., & Cullen, F. T. (2008). Rape against women: What can research offer to guide the development of prevention programs and risk reduction interventions? *Journal of Contemporary Criminal Justice, 24,* 163–177.

Foran, H., & O'Leary, K. D. (2008). Alcohol and intimate partner violence: A meta-analytic review. *Clinical Psychology Review, 28,* 1222–1234.

Frieze, I. H. (2000). Violence in close relationships-Development of a research area: Comment on Archer (2000). *Psychological Bulletin, 126,* 681–684.

Gidycz, C. A., Orchowski, L. M., & Berkowitz, A.D. (2011). Preventing sexual aggression among college men: An evaluation of a social norms and bystander intervention program. *Violence Against Women, 17,* 720–742.

Gidycz, C. A., Orchowski, L. M., Probst, D., Edwards, K., Murphy, M., & Tansill, E. (2015). Concurrent administration of sexual assault prevention and risk reduction programming: Outcomes for women. *Violence Against Women, 21,* 780–800.

Golding, J. M. (1999). Intimate partner violence as a risk factor for mental disorders: A meta-analysis. *Journal of Family Violence, 14,* 99–132.

Goodman, L.A., & Epstein, D. (2011). The justice system response to domestic violence. In M.P. Koss, J.W. White, & A.E. Kazdin (Eds.), *Violence against women and children* (Vol. 2: Navigating solutions, pp. 215–235). Washington, DC: American Psychological Association.

Graham, K., Bernards, S., Wilsnack, S. C., & Gmel, G. (2011). Alcohol may not cause partner violence but it seems to make it worse: A cross national comparison of the relationship between alcohol and the severity of partner violence. *Journal of Interpersonal Violence, 26,* 1503–1523.

Hamberger, L. K., & Larsen, S. E. (2015). Men's and women's experience of intimate partner violence: Review of ten years of comparative studies in clinical samples; Part I. *Journal of Family Violence, 30,* 699–717.

Hanson, K. A., & Gidycz, C. A. (1993). Evaluation of a sexual assault prevention program. *Journal of Consulting and Clinical Psychology, 61,* 1046–1052.

Hovmand, P. S., Ford, D. N., Flom, I., & Kyriakakis, S. (2009). Victims arrested for domestic violence: Unintended consequences of arrest policies. *System Dynamics Review, 25,* 161–181.

Johnson, M. P., & Ferraro, K. J. (2000). Research on domestic violence in the 1990s: Making distinctions. *Journal of Marriage and the Family, 62,* 948–963.

Kelly, J. B., & Johnson, M. P. (2008). Differentiation among types of intimate partner violence: Research update and implications for interventions. *Family Court Review, 46,* 476–499.

Klump, M. S. (2008). Posttraumatic stress disorder and sexual assault in women. *Journal of College Student Psychotherapy, 21,* 67–83.

Krahé, B. (2016). Societal responses to sexual violence against women: Rape myths and the "real rape" stereotype. In H. Kury, S. Redo, & E. Shea (Eds.), *Women and children as victims and offenders* (pp. 671–700). New York: Springer.

Krahé, B., Berger, A., Vanwesenbeeck, I., Bianchi, G., Chliaoutakis, J., Fernández-Fuertes, A. A. . . . Zygadło, A. (2015). Prevalence and correlates of young people's sexual aggression perpetration and victimisation in 10 European countries. A multilevel analysis. *Culture, Health & Sexuality, 17,* 682–69.

Krahé, B., Tomaszewska, P., Kuyper, L., & Vanwesenbeeck, I. (2014). Prevalence of sexual aggression among young people in Europe: A review of the evidence from 27 EU countries. *Aggression and Violent Behavior, 19,* 545–558.

Langhinrichsen-Rohling, J., Foubert, J. D., Brasfield, H. M., Hill, B., & Shelley-Tremblay, S. (2011). The men's program: Does it impact college men's self-reported bystander efficacy and willingness to intervene? *Violence Against Women, 17*, 743–759.

Marin, A. J., & Russo, N. F. (1999). Feminist perspectives of male violence against women: Critiquing O'Neil and Harway's model. In M. Harway, & J. M. O'Neil, (Eds.), *What causes men's violence against women?* (pp. 18–35). Thousand Oaks, CA: Sage.

Martin, S. L., Macy, R. J., & Young, S. K. (2011). Health and economic consequences of sexual violence. In J. W. White, M. P. Koss, & A. E. Kazdin (Eds.), *Violence against women and children* (Vol. 1: Mapping the terrain, pp. 173–195). Washington, DC: American Psychological Association.

Miller, T. R., Cohen, M. A., & Rossman, S. B. (1993). Victim costs of violent crime and resulting injuries. *Health Affairs, 12*, 186–197.

Moore, T. M., Stuart, G. L., Meehan, J. C., Rhatinga, D. L., Hellmuth. J. C., & Ken, S. M. (2008). Drug abuse and aggression between intimate partners: A meta-analytic review. *Clinical Psychology Review, 28*, 247–274.

Najdowski, C. J., & Ullman, S. E. (2011). The effects of revictimization on coping and depression in female sexual assault victims. *Journal of Traumatic Stress, 24*, 218–221.

Office for National Statistics (2014). *Chapter 4-Violent crime and sexual offences-Intimate personal violence and partner abuse.* Retrieved from: www.ons.gov.uk/ons/dcp171776_394500.pdf

Palermo, T., Bleck, J., & Peterman, A. (2014). The tip of the iceberg. Reporting and gender-based violence in developing countries. *American Journal of Epidemiology, 179*, 602–612.

Paul, L. A., & Gray, M. J. (2011). Sexual assault programming on college campuses: Using social psychological belief and behavior change principles to improve outcomes. *Trauma, Violence, & Abuse, 12*, 99–109.

Rennison, C. M., & Welchans, S. (2000). *Intimate partner violence.* Bureau of Justice Statistics Special Report, May, 2000. Retrieved from: http://bjs.ojp.usdoj.gov/content/pub/pdf/ipv.pdf

Rivara, F. P., Anderson, M. L., Fishman, P., Boniomi, A. E., Reid, R. J., Carrell, D., & Thompson, R. S. (2007). Healthcare utilization and costs for women with a history of intimate partner violence. *American Journal of Preventive Medicine, 32*, 89–96.

Stern, V. (2010). *The Stern Review. A report by Baroness Vivien Stern CBE of an independent review into how rape complaints are handled by public authorities in England and Wales.* Retrieved from: http://webarchive.nationalarchives.gov.uk/20100418065537/http://equalities.gov.uk/PDF/Stern_Review_acc_FINAL.pdf

Stith, S. M., Green, N. M., Smith, D. B., & Ward, D. B. (2008). Marital satisfaction and marital discord as risk markers for intimate partner violence: A meta-analytic review. *Journal of Family Violence, 23*, 149–160.

Stith, S. M., Smith, D. B., Penn, C. E., Ward, D. B., & Tritt, D. (2004). Intimate partner abuse perpetration and victimization risk factors: A meta-analytic review. *Aggression and Violent Behavior, 10*, 65–98.

Straus, M. A. (1979). Measuring intrafamily conflict and violence: The Conflict Tactics Scales. *Journal of Marriage and the Family, 41*, 75–88.

Straus, M. A., Hamby, S. L. Boney-McCoy, S., & Sugarman, D. B. (1996). The revised Conflict Tactics Scales (CTS2). *Journal of Family Issues, 17*, 283–316.

Swartout, K. M., & White, J. W. (2010). The relationship between drug use and sexual aggression in men across time. *Journal of Interpersonal Violence, 25*, 1716–1735.

Temkin, J., & Krahé, B. (2008). *Sexual assault and the justice gap: A question of attitude.* Oxford: Hart Publishing.

Tolin, D. F., & Foa, E. B. (2008). Sex differences in trauma and posttraumatic stress disorder: A quantitative review of 25 years of research. *Psychological Trauma: Theory, Research, Practice, and Policy, S,* 37–85.

Turquet, L., Seck, P., Azcona, G., Menon, R., Boyce, C., Pierron, N., & Harbour, E. (2011). *Progress of the world's women 2011–2012: In pursuit of justice.* Retrieved from: http://menengage.org/wp-content/uploads/2014/06/Progress_of_the_Worlds_Women_2011.pdf

Ullman, S. E. (2004). Sexual assault victimization and suicidal behavior in women: A review of the literature. *Aggression and Violent Behavior, 9,* 331–351.

Vandello, J. A., & Cohen, D. (2003). Male honor and female fidelity: Implicit cultural scripts that perpetuate domestic violence. *Journal of Personality and Social Psychology, 84,* 997–1010.

Vandello, J. A., & Cohen, D. (2008). Culture, gender, and men's intimate partner violence. *Social and Personality Psychology Compass, 2,* 652–667.

Vladutiu, C. J., Martin, S. L., & Macy, R. (2011). College- or university-based sexual assault prevention programs: A review of program outcomes, characteristics, and recommendations. *Trauma, Violence, & Abuse, 12,* 67–86.

Waters, H., Hyder, A., Rajkotia, Y., Basu, S., Rehwinkel, J.A., & Butchart, A. (2004). *The economic dimensions of interpersonal violence.* Retrieved October 29, 2010, from: http://whqlibdoc.who.int/publications/2004/9241591609.pdf

WHO (2013). *Global and regional estimates of violence against women: Prevalence and health effects of intimate partner violence and non-partner sexual violence.* Retrieved from: www.who.int/iris/bitstream/10665/85239/1/9789241564625_eng.pdf

16

LOVE AND HURT

Why We Aggress Against Loved Ones

C. Nathan DeWall, Kellie R. Lynch,
and Claire M. Renzetti

People need people, but some of our relationships mean more to us than others do. Most people prefer spending their free time with family than with strangers. Few politicians or corporate executive officers (CEOs) leave office in order to spend more time with people they've never met. It's in our nature to favor our family. And the more dire the situation, the stronger our pro-family preference.

Imagine the following scenario. A building is on fire. Three people are trapped inside and plead with you to rescue them. Only one lucky soul will survive. But there is a catch. One person is a direct relative; another person is a distant relative; and the third person is not a relative at all. Whose life do you save? Most people choose their direct relative (Burnstein et al., 1994).

But some of the most horrific and puzzling behavior on record involves aggression toward family members. Consider the case of Lissette Ochoa, who is a member of the Colombian elite social class. In a jealous rage, her husband, Rafael, beat her so severely that she spent a month in the hospital recovering. He was convicted of attempted murder, but only spent three months in jail. Lissette forgave Rafael and agreed to reconcile.

Why do people hurt the ones they love the most? Social psychologists have generally given this question short shrift. Rather than examining aggression within different types of relationships, social psychologists have focused on the underlying causes of aggression between strangers. Those causal factors may or may not apply to aggression toward family members.

Social psychologists do have something to say about aggression within families. This chapter showcases what that might be. Because the evidence is so scarce, we broaden our coverage to social psychological approaches to the study of aggression within close relationships. The first section describes how often intimate partner violence occurs, what forms it can take, and how various demographic factors impact these rates. Next, we discuss three dominant theories of intimate partner violence. The following sections review social, cultural, and biological factors that can increase or decrease intimate partner violence, respectively. We conclude by suggesting potential strategies to reduce such aggression.

How Often Does Aggression within Families Occur?

It is difficult to research things that rarely happen. We live in the most peaceful time in human history (Pinker, 2011). To solve conflict, people rarely resort to violence. Most people will never behave aggressively. They may not even threaten someone physically. People generally treat close relationship partners nicer than they treat strangers and acquaintances. Given the low base rate of aggression, coupled with our generally nicer behavior toward close relationship partners, we have to wonder how often intimate partner violence occurs. Is intimate partner violence a black swan—something that exists, but is so rare and contrary to our expectations of relationships that we deem it unworthy of study?

Intimate partner violence (IPV) is no black swan. IPV occurs at alarmingly high rates. It impacts millions of individuals across the United States (Black et al., 2011) and all over the world (Devries et al, 2013; World Health Organization, 2013). IPV refers to any pattern of behavior intended to gain control or power over a current or former partner. The Centers for Disease Control classifies IPV into the following four types: physical violence, sexual violence, stalking, and psychological aggression (Breiding et al., 2015). Within the United States, national surveys estimate that 22.1% to 35.6% of women, and 7.4% to 28.5% of men have experienced physical violence, sexual violence, and/or stalking at some point in their lives (Black et al., 2011; Tjaden & Thoennes, 2000).

Adolescent and college-aged women (i.e., between the ages of 16 and 24) typically experience higher rates of IPV compared to other age categories (Black et al., 2011; Rennison, 2001), drawing attention to the investigation of dating violence in college samples. A review of dating violence at 31 colleges in 16 countries revealed physical dating violence perpetration rates between 17% and 45%, with similar rates for men and women (Straus, 2004). However, college-aged women are more likely to experience sexual assault than college men (Fisher et al., 2000; Hines & Saudino, 2003; Krebs et al., 2007). Most rates of *completed* sexual assault for college women within the previous school year range from 1.8% to 11% (Fisher et al., 2000; Krebs et al., 2007; Mohler-Kuo et al., 2004) and 3.7% for college men (Krebs et al., 2007). However, research on campus sexual assault typically has not focused specifically on intimate or dating partners, but rather suggests that the vast majority (about 90%) of sexual assaults are perpetrated by someone the victim knows, typically involve drugs or alcohol, and occur most often among first- and second-year students (Fisher et al., 2000; Krebs et al., 2007; Mohler-Kuo et al., 2004; Smith et al., 2003). Comparing rates of IPV across samples can be problematic due to differences in survey methodology and definitions of an "intimate partner" and "violence." As an example, classifying an incident as IPV can be difficult in a college sample given that factors such as "hook-up culture" (Stinson, 2010) can complicate if an individual is defined as an intimate partner versus an acquaintance (Logan et al., 2015).

Similarities between men and women for IPV perpetration, also known as gender symmetry, have been the topic of much discussion among IPV scholars. While there are a substantial number of published studies suggesting that men and women perpetrate IPV at similar rates (for a review, see Archer, 2002), considerable research suggests that there are important gender differences within IPV. For example, women are more likely than men to experience injury and perpetrate IPV in self-defense (Archer, 2000; Black et al., 2011; DeKeseredy & Schwartz, 1998; Hamberger, 2005; Hamberger & Guse, 2002; Kimmel, 2002; Menard et al., 2009; Tjaden & Thoennes, 2000). Further, a cost analysis of IPV injuries found that the average cost of experiencing at least one physical IPV incident was nearly 2.5 times as high for women ($948) than for men ($387; 1995 U.S. dollars; Arias & Corso, 2005).

Gender disparities in estimates of IPV are magnified when taking the context of the incident into account. For example, about 1 in 4 women (25.7%) compared to only 1 in 20 men (5.2%) in the United States have experienced physical violence, rape, or stalking that caused them to be fearful at some point in their lives at the hands of an intimate partner (Black et al., 2011). Gender differences in IPV are particularly large when examining rates of fatal IPV. Of the known U.S. intimate partner homicides in 2010, 39.3% of women versus only 2.8% of men were killed by an intimate partner (Bureau of Justice Statistics, 2013). Similar gender disparities in intimate partner homicide have been found worldwide (35% of women versus 5% of men, World Health Organization, 2013).

Theories of IPV

The history of social psychology is full of theories that attempt to explain why people behave aggressively (see Chapter 1 of this volume). Some prominent examples include frustration-aggression theory (Dollard et al., 1939), cognitive neoassociation theory (Berkowitz, 1989), social learning theory (Bandura, 1977; Mischel & Shoda, 1995), script theory (Huesmann, 1988), excitation transfer theory (Zillmann, 1988), and social interaction theory (Tedeschi & Felson, 1994). Over the course of nearly a century, these theories enjoyed success at predicting how, when, and why aggression occurred. But these theories suffered two limitations. The first is that these theories focused exclusively on one group of people who were on the receiving end of aggression, namely strangers. Each theory also explained only a small piece of the puzzle of what predicted aggression.

Below, we describe dominant theoretical approaches that address these two limitations. First, we discuss the feminist theoretical model that developed outside of social psychology to explain intimate partner violence. Next, we review two influential social psychological theories of aggression—the General Aggression Model (DeWall et al., 2011) and I³ Theory (Finkel, 2014)—that provide broad and coherent frameworks to understand the many causes of aggression between both strangers and close relationship partners.

The Feminist Theoretical Model and Intimate Partner Violence

Outside of social psychology, social scientists have made tremendous headway in formulating explanatory models of intimate partner violence. Explanatory models of IPV may be divided into two types: those that focus on individual-level causal factors and those that focus on structural-level factors. Within each of these categories, there are multiple theories. Feminist theory is a dominant structural-level model for explaining IPV. In fact, current public and research attention to IPV is credited to the resurgence of the feminist movement in the 1970s, which raised awareness of IPV as a *public problem*, rather than a private family issue, which called for public policy solutions, rather than individual treatment (Schechter, 1982).

Feminist theory begins with the assumption that all human behavior, including violent and aggressive behavior, is gendered. That is, human behavior is socially constructed within a cultural context that includes a set of gender norms and roles—rules, expectations, and beliefs about how men and women are *supposed* to act and interact in given situations. In most societies, the social structure that produces and reproduces these gender norms is a *patriarchal* one. A patriarchy is a system of social organization in which men dominate women and what is considered masculine is more highly valued than what is considered feminine. Feminist theory maintains, then, that IPV is a product of male oppression of females in a patriarchal social system, which affords men greater power and privilege. Male privilege and female subordination are preserved through various forms of gender discrimination, and ultimately, through the use of coercive control and violence. Thus, this model sees men as primarily the perpetrators of IPV and women as primarily the victims (Dobash & Dobash, 1979; Hunnicutt, 2009; Renzetti, 2013).

Research on IPV has produced findings in support of feminist theory. For example, studies that examine men's and women's motivations for using violence against an intimate partner show important gender differences. Men are more likely to use violence against an intimate partner when they feel themselves losing control of the relationship or when they interpret their partner's words or behavior as a challenge to their authority. In contrast, women are more likely to use violence, especially severe physical violence, against an intimate partner when they believe they are in imminent danger of being attacked, or to fight back when they are being attacked (Barnett et al., 1997; Dobash & Dobash, 2015; Dobash et al., 1998; Rajan & McCloskey, 2007).

At the same time, however, feminist theory has been criticized on several grounds. Feminists of color, feminists in non-Western societies, lesbian feminists, and others have been critical of the feminist model's emphasis on the primacy of gender. As they point out, gender inequality intersects with other inequalities, including those based on social class, race and ethnicity, sexual orientation, age, and disability status, to influence the behavioral outcomes of different groups of women and men (Crenshaw, 1994; McPhail et al., 2007; Renzetti, 2013). Other critics argue that feminist theory downplays or excuses women's aggression in intimate relationships and mistakenly characterizes it as purely self-defensive (Mills, 2003; Straus, 2007). And still others maintain that feminist theory's emphasis on the structural causes of IPV has resulted in an overreliance on legal and criminal justice responses to the problem, which disproportionately affect the economically disadvantaged and people of color (Richie, 2012). This tendency to focus on institutional responses also overlooks the need to develop responses better suited to individuals' situations, since a one-size-fits-all approach is ineffective (McPhail et al., 2007).

In response to these criticisms, feminist theorists have developed more nuanced theories. For instance, nested ecological framework incorporates individual factors (the ontogenic level), relationship factors (the microsystem), and informal and formal social networks (the exosystem) along with the broader cultural and social context of patriarchy (the macrosystem) (Heise, 1998; see also Brownridge, 2009; Fulu & Miedema, in press; Graham-Bermann & Gross, 2008). Similarly, integrative feminist model "uses a both/end approach" by incorporating multiple models of violence causation, including "the explanatory role of physiological and neurological factors, evolutionary psychology, substance abuse, childhood experiences of violence, intergenerational transmission of violence, shame and humiliation, attachment disorders, lack of anger control, psychopathology and difficult personality traits, general communication and coping skills deficits, personal inadequacy, and violence as a tool for constructing masculinity," while retaining the feminist sociocultural framework "as the glue holding together these puzzle pieces, multiple theories, and interventions" (McPhail et al., 2007, pp. 833–834). While certainly provocative and potentially promising, this feminist theoretical approach must still be subjected to empirical testing.

General Aggression Model

The General Aggression Model (GAM; Figure 16.1) is a dynamic, social-cognitive, and developmental model that blends perspectives from domain-specific theories of aggression (Anderson & Bushman, 2002). It includes situational, personological, and biological variables. These variables serve as inputs to internal states of affect, cognition, and arousal, which in turn feed into appraisal and decision processes. Depending on how people appraise the situation, they will decide to lash out impulsively or engage in thoughtful, peaceful behaviors.

Initial research that tested the GAM focused on aggression between strangers. In recent years, aggression researchers have begun to extend the GAM to

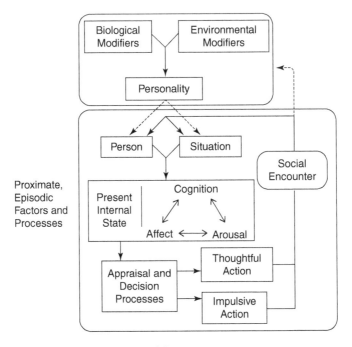

FIGURE 16.1 General Aggression Model.

intimate partner violence (DeWall et al., 2011). This work has focused primarily on how factors that the GAM uses to understand aggression between strangers also increase aggression within romantic relationships. With these extensions in place, social psychologists have become aware that they have a coherent framework to understand aggression within the context of ongoing relationships.

I³ Model

Unlike the GAM, the I³ Model (pronounced I-cubed) began with a clear focus on understanding intimate partner violence (Finkel, 2007; Finkel et al., 2009; Finkel et al., 2012). Later iterations of the I³ Model sought to encompass many other behaviors (Finkel, 2014). But the I³ Model's main assumption remains unchanged: Behavior is determined by a combination of impellance, instigation, and inhibition (hence, the three *I*s in the I³ Model). Impellance refers to the effect of any situational or stable factor that increases the likelihood or intensity of intimate partner violence. Instigation is any factor that triggers an aggressive urge. Inhibiting factors help people override the effects of impellance and instigation on aggression, thereby reducing the likelihood or intensity of intimate partner violence.

The I³ Model can be used to identify individual factors that can increase or decrease intimate partner violence. But its more novel contribution lies in its use of statistical moderation to test how the combination of impelling, instigating, and inhibiting factors interact to predict intimate partner violence. The I^3 Model predicts that the combination of high impellance, high instigation, and low inhibition will create a so-called "perfect storm," in which the likelihood or intensity of intimate partner violence will be highest.

These three theoretical approaches showcase how those inside and outside the field of social psychology have sought to understand the problem of intimate partner violence. Each approach has unique strengths and weaknesses. What follows are empirical applications of these theories to the study of intimate partner violence. Given this volume's emphasis on the social psychology of aggression, we focus on situational, cultural, and biological factors that involve a social component.

Social and Cultural Factors

Social Rejection

People have a fundamental need to belong (Baumeister & Leary, 1995). This need for positive and lasting relationships is among the strongest human motivations and influences our daily thoughts, feelings, and actions. When people feel rejected, it hurts. Neuroimaging evidence suggests that when people relive romantic rejection, blood flows to brain regions that also register physical pain (Kross et al., 2011). Just as physical pain causes aggression, romantic rejection increases intimate partner violence. In one study, some participants imagined experiencing an intense romantic rejection (i.e., "There is nothing I find appealing about you"; Sinclair et al., 2011). Compared with non-rejected people, those who imagined romantic rejection reported more aggressive inclinations toward the rejector. These findings jibe with those from other social psychological studies that point to social rejection as a reliable predictor of aggression (Leary et al., 2006).

Jealousy

Shakespeare called jealousy a "green-eyed monster that makes fun of the victims it devours" (*Othello*, Act 3, Scene 3). Whereas social rejection involves actual loss of a relationship, jealousy occurs when people fear that something or someone threatens the stability of their relationship. Jealousy is consistently related to higher levels of intimate partner violence perpetration, regardless of whether such perpetration involves male-to-female or female-to-male violence (Caldwell et al., 2009; Chiffriller & Hennessy, 2010; Hellmuth et al., 2013).

Culture

There are cross-cultural influences to IPV. A meta-analysis of IPV prevalence in 81 countries revealed that lifetime prevalence rates ranged from 16.3% in East

Asia and 19.3% in Western Europe to 41.7% in South Asia and 65.6% in Central Sub-Saharan Africa (Devries et al., 2013). Such differences in lifetime prevalence rates can be attributed to economic inequality, gender inequalities, social norms that justify IPV, decreased access to fair family law practices (e.g., divorce), and the failure to criminalize IPV (Devries et al., 2013). There are also cultural differences in IPV within the United States. Women of color, particularly African American women, are more likely to experience IPV in their lifetime than White women (Black et al., 2011; Greenfeld et al., 1998; Lipsky et al., 2009; Logan et al., 2006; Tjaden & Thoennes, 2000). However, racial differences in IPV within the United States have often been explained by socioeconomic status and poverty, as racial differences within IPV tend to disappear when controlling for variables such as household income, education, and relationship status (Cho, 2012; Lambert & Firestone, 2000; Rennison & Planty, 2003; Straus & Gelles, 1990).

Cultural norms related to traditional gender roles also impact the occurrence of IPV. For example, there is strong evidence that women who live in rural communities within the United States experience more severe and chronic IPV than women who live in urban communities do (Logan et al., 2003; Logan et al., 2009; Peek-Asa et al., 2011; Shannon et al., 2006). Rural communities typically have cultural norms that reinforce patriarchy (e.g., a wife is her husband's property) and the sentiment that IPV is a private, domestic matter, which can create social isolation and impact help-seeking behaviors or community responses to IPV in rural communities (Lanier & Maume, 2009; Logan et al., 2003; Shannon et al., 2006; Websdale, 1998).

The culture of honor within the American South provides a compelling example of within-cultural differences in attitudes toward intimate partner violence. According to the culture of honor, people are encouraged to defend their reputation if it has been threatened (Vandello & Cohen, 2003). In one striking study, women from the American North and the American South witnessed another woman being slammed against a wall by her boyfriend. In reality, the victim and perpetrator were accomplices of the experimenter. Compared with women from the American North, those from the American South were more accepting of the intimate partner violence they witnessed. These findings suggest that forces between and within cultures can influence intimate partner violence.

Biological and Mental Factors

Glucose

What makes the human brain so special? Size does matter, but it isn't the whole story. Instead, what sets our brain apart from the brains of other animals is our ability to sustain enough energy to feed our 86 billion neurons (Herculano-Houzel, 2012). Glucose is the energy that fuels the brain. It also takes energy to form and maintain relationships. When we lack metabolic energy, our relationships suffer.

The most direct evidence for this point comes from a study of married couples (Bushman et al., 2014). Each day, participants pricked their fingers and used a glucose meter to measure their blood glucose levels. Participants also completed a measure of intimate partner violence inclinations, which took the form of stabbing a voodoo doll that represented their spouse. On days when participants had low glucose levels, they expressed more aggressive inclinations toward their spouse. Participants with lower blood glucose levels were also more likely to physically aggress against their spouse, by ostensibly giving him or her louder blasts of unpleasant noise through headphones. These findings show that low blood sugar may be tied to fights with one's spouse.

Oxytocin

Oxytocin helps people build social bonds. A wave of research has shown that oxytocin makes people more sensitive to social information (Groppe et al., 2013). But oxytocin has a complicated history regarding aggression. To our knowledge, only one experiment has examined how oxytocin affects intimate partner violence (DeWall et al., 2014). In that study, participants were exposed to oxytocin or placebo through nasal spray. Next, they reported their aggressive inclinations toward a romantic partner. Oxytocin increased intimate partner violence inclinations, but this was only true for highly aggressive people. The bottom line: For people who regularly dominate their close relationship partners, boosting their bonding motivation increases their tendency to lash out.

Alcohol

Alcohol is a robust predictor of aggression and violence. Indeed, alcohol-related aggression imposes an estimated $205 billion in annual costs in the United States alone, which is double the economic costs associated with all other drugs combined (Miller et al., 2006). Drinking is primarily a social activity. Over 90% of the time people drink alcohol, they report doing so with other people (Creswell et al., 2014). In one analysis of 50 studies, alcohol increased both male-to-female and female-to-male intimate partner violence (Foran & O'Leary, 2008). The relationship between alcohol intoxication and intimate partner violence is strongest when people experience partner provocation (Watkins et al., 2015).

Genetic Relatedness, or the "Cinderella Effect"

Buried within the fairy tale of Cinderella is the lesson that people act more aggressively toward their stepchildren than they do toward their biological children. Evolutionary psychologists have dubbed this tendency the "Cinderella Effect" (Daly & Wilson, 1999). Indeed, they argue that "a child is one hundred times more likely to be abused or killed by a stepparent than by a genetic parent" (front cover). The main argument is that people have weaker inhibitions against harming those who do not share their genes compared with those who do. Thus, aggression within families depends in large part on the degree of genetic related-ness between family members.

Mental Fatigue

When we feel an aggressive urge, it takes energy to override our impulse to behave aggressively toward our loved ones. Several pieces of evidence point to mental fatigue as a risk factor for intimate partner violence. First, most domestic violence happens between 6:00 p.m. and 6:00 a.m. (Safe Horizon, 2015). Very few people wake up, eat breakfast, and attack their loved ones. More often, peo-ple perpetrate intimate partner violence when they're mentally fatigued. Labora-tory evidence confirms that mental fatigue plays a causal role in shaping intimate partner violence, especially when people are provoked (Finkel et al., 2009, 2012; Watkins et al., 2015).

Interventions

This chapter shows that there is no single cause of intimate partner violence. To prevent intimate partner violence, we suggest that researchers and clinicians focus on more than one risk factor. For example, making sure that people have adequate metabolic energy may reduce intimate partner violence, but this effect will be strengthened if people are also reminded that their partner accepts them, that intimate partner violence is not a desirable method to protect one's reputa-tion, and that limiting their alcohol consumption will make it easier to enjoy their partner's company.

Two other methods show signs of promise as ways to reduce intimate part-ner violence. The first is a short, theory-driven strategy to improve relationship quality, including relationship commitment (Finkel et al., 2013). Commitment to one's partner inhibits intimate partner violence (Slotter et al., 2012). In this inter-vention, some people were asked to reinterpret the meaning of a recent partner conflict by trying to take an objective, third-party perspective. Others were given no additional instructions. Those who took a third-party perspective, compared with those who did not, reported higher levels of relationship quality a year later. Given previous links between relationship quality and intimate partner violence, we predict that such an intervention would also reduce intimate partner violence perpetration. Adopting a third-party perspective does reduce aggression against strangers (Mischkowski et al., 2012), which strengthens our confidence that such an intervention could reduce aggression against family members.

A second intervention sought to build self-control strength (Finkel et al., 2009). Because mental fatigue makes people more susceptible to intimate partner violence, regularly practicing self-control should make people less vulnerable to situations that normally deplete their self-control energy. In this study, some participants practiced self-control for two weeks by either controlling their attention or using their nondominant hand for everyday tasks. A control group did not engage in any self-control-enhancing activities. At the end of two weeks, participants who had practiced self-control were less mentally fatigued when they were exposed to a difficult self-control task. As a result, they also expressed the lowest levels of intimate partner violence inclinations.

Concluding Remarks

Aggression research is an enterprise of continual mystery. Just when we identify and understand one cause of aggression, another one pops up in need of being understood. The situation becomes even more complex when we try to discern why people intentionally harm their loved ones. This chapter made a case for why intimate partner violence deserves the attention of social psychologists, described dominant theoretical models inside and outside of social psychology that have identified factors that increase and decrease intimate partner violence, and reviewed evidence that followed from these models. We hope the chapter spurs social psychologists to study why intimate partner violence occurs—and how it can be prevented.

References

Anderson, C. A., & Bushman, B. J. (2002). Human aggression. *Annual Review of Psychology*, *53*, 27–51.

Archer, J. (2000). Sex differences in aggression between heterosexual partners: A meta-analytic review. *Psychological Bulletin*, *126*(5), 651–680. doi:10.1037/0033–2909.126.5.651

Archer, J. (2002). Sex differences in physically aggressive acts between heterosexual partners: A meta-analytic review. *Aggression and Violent Behavior*, 7, 313–351.

Arias, I., & Corso, P. (2005). Average cost per person victimized by an intimate partner of the opposite gender: A comparison of men and women. *Violence and Victims*, *20*(4), 379–391. doi:10.1891/vivi.2005.20.4.379

Bandura, A. (1977). *Social learning theory*. New York: Prentice Hall.

Barnett, O. W., Lee, C. Y., & Thelan, R. (1997). Gender differences in attributions of self-defense and control interpartner aggression. *Violence Against Women*, *3*(5), 462–481.

Baumeister, R. F., & Leary, M. R. (1995). The need to belong: Desire for interpersonal attachments as a fundamental human motivation. *Psychological Bulletin, 117*, 497–529.

Berkowitz, L. (1989). Frustration-aggression hypothesis: Examination and reformulation. *Psychological Bulletin, 106*, 59–73.

Black, M. C., Basile, K. C., Breiding, M. J., Smith, S. G., Walters, M. L., Merrick, M. T., Chen, J., & Stevens, M. R. (2011). *The national intimate partner and sexual violence survey (NISVS): 2010 summary report*. Atlanta, GA: National Center for Injury Prevention and Control, Centers for Disease Control and Prevention. Retrieved from: www.cdc.gov/violenceprevention/pdf/nisvs_report2010-a.pdf

Breiding, M. J., Basile, K. C., Smith, S. G., Black, M. C., & Mahendra, R. R. (2015). *Intimate partner violence surveillance: Uniform definitions and recommended data elements, version 2.0.*

Atlanta, GA: National Center for Injury Prevention and Control, Centers for Disease Control and Prevention. Retrieved from: www.cdc.gov/violenceprevention/pdf/intimatepartnerviolence.pdf

Brownridge, D.A. (2009). *Violence against women: Vulnerable populations*. New York: Routledge.

Bureau of Justice Statistics. (2013). *Intimate partner violence: Attributes of victimization, 1993–2011*. (NIJ 243300). Retrieved from: www.bjs.gov/content/pub/pdf/ipvav9311.pdf

Burnstein, E., Crandall, C., & Kitayama, S. (1994). Some neo-Darwinian decision rules for altruism: Weighing cues for inclusive fitness as a function of the biological importance of the decision. *Journal of Personality and Social Psychology, 67*, 773–789.

Bushman, B. J., DeWall, C. N., Pond, R. S., Jr., & Hanus, M. D. (2014). Low glucose relates to greater aggression in married couples. *Proceedings of the National Academy of Sciences, 111*, 6254–6257.

Caldwell, J. E., Swan, S. S., Allen, C. T., Sullivan, T. P., & Snow, D. L. (2009). Why I hit him: Women's reasons for intimate partner violence. *Journal of Aggression, Maltreatment, and Trauma, 18*, 672–697.

Chiffriller, S. H., & Hennessy, J. J. (2010). An empirically generated typology of men who batter. *Victims and Offenders, 5*, 1–24.

Cho, H. (2012). Racial differences in the prevalence of intimate partner violence against women and associated factors. *Journal of Interpersonal Violence, 27*, 344–363. doi:10.1177/0886260511416469

Crenshaw, K. (1994). Mapping the margins: Intersectionality, identity politics, and violence against women of color. In M. A. Fineman & R. Mykitiuk (Eds.), *The public nature of private violence* (pp. 93–118). New York: Routledge.

Creswell, K. G., Chung, T., Clark, D. B., & Martin, C. S. (2014). Solitary alcohol use in teens is associated with drinking in response to negative affect and predicts alcohol problems in young adulthood. *Clinical Psychological Science, 2*, 602–610.

Daly, M., & Wilson, M. (1999). *The truth about Cinderella: A Darwinian view of parental love*. New Haven, CT: Yale University Press.

DeKeseredy, W. S., Schwartz, M. D. (1998). *Measuring the extent of woman abuse in intimate heterosexual relationships: A critique of the Conflict Tactics Scales*. National Online Resource Center on Violence Against Women. Retrieved from: www.vawnet.org/Assoc_Files_VAWnet/AR_ctscrit.pdf

Devries, K. M., Mak, J. T., García-Moreno, C., Petzold, M., Child, J. C., Falder, G., & . . . Watts, C. H. (2013). The global prevalence of intimate partner violence against women. *Science, 340*(6140), 1527–1528. doi:10.1126/science.124093

DeWall, C. N., Anderson, C. A., & Bushman, B. J. (2011). The general aggression model: Theoretical extensions to violence. *Psychology of Violence, 1*, 245–258.

DeWall, C. N., Gillath, O., Pressman, S. D., Black, L. L., Bartz, J. A., Moskovitz, J., & Stetler, D. A. (2014). When the love hormone leads to violence: Oxytocin increases intimate partner violence inclinations among high trait aggressive people. *Social Psychological and Personality Science, 5*, 691–697.

Dobash, R. E., & Dobash, R. P. (1979). *Violence against wives*. New York: Free Press.

Dobash, R. E., & Dobash, R. P. (2015). *When men murder women*. New York: Oxford University Press.

Dobash, R. P., Dobash, R. E., Cavanagh, K., & Lewis, R. (1998). Separate and intersecting realities: A comparison of men's and women's accounts of violence against women. *Violence Against Women, 4*(4), 382–414.

Dollard, J., Doob, L., Miller, N., Mowrer, O., & Sears, R. (1939). *Frustration and aggression*. New Haven, CT: Yale University Press.

Finkel, E. J. (2007). Impelling and inhibiting forces in the perpetration of intimate partner violence. *Review of General Psychology, 11*, 193–207.

Finkel, E. J. (2014). The I³ model: Metatheory, theory, and evidence. In J. M. Olson, & M. P. Zanna (Eds.), *Advances in experimental social psychology* (Vol. 49, pp. 1–104). San Diego: Academic Press.

Finkel, E. J., DeWall, C. N., Slotter, E. B., McNulty, J. K., Pond, R. S., Jr., & Atkins, D.C. (2012). Using I³ Theory to clarify when dispositional aggressiveness predicts intimate partner violence perpetration. *Journal of Personality and Social Psychology, 102*, 533–549.

Finkel, E. J., DeWall, C. N., Slotter, E. B., Oaten, M., & Foshee, V. A. (2009). Self-regulatory failure and intimate partner violence perpetration. *Journal of Personality and Social Psychology, 97*, 483–499.

Finkel, E. J., Slotter, E. B., Luchies, L. B., Walton, G. M., & Gross, J. J. (2013). A brief intervention to promote conflict reappraisal preserves marital quality over time. *Psychological Science, 24*, 1595–1601.

Fisher, B. S., Cullen, F. T., & Turner, M. G. (2000). *The sexual victimization of college women.* National Institute of Justice, Bureau of Justice Statistics. Retrieved from: www.ncjrs. gov/pdffiles1/nij/182369.pdf

Foran, H. M., & O'Leary, K. D. (2008). Alcohol and intimate partner violence: A meta-analytic review. *Clinical Psychology Review, 28*, 1222–1234.

Fulu, E., & Miedema, S. (in press). Violence against women: Globalizing the integrated ecological model. *Violence Against Women.*

Graham-Bermann, S., & Gross, M. (2008). Ecological models of violence. In C. M. Renzetti & J. L. Edleson (Eds.), *Encyclopedia of interpersonal violence* (pp. 212–215). Thousand Oaks, CA: SAGE.

Greenfeld, L. A., Rand, M. R., Craven, D., Klaus, P. A., Perkins, C. A., Ringel, C., & . . . Fox, J. A. (1998). *Violence by intimates: Analysis of data on crimes by current or former spouses, boyfriends, and girlfriends.* Bureau of Justice Statistics, U.S. Department of Justice. Retrieved from: http://bjs.gov/content/pub/pdf/vi.pdf

Groppe, S. E., Gossen, A., Rademacher, L., Hahn, A., Westphal, L., Gründer, G., & Spreckelmeyer, K. N. (2013). Oxytocin influences processing of socially relevant cues in the ventral tegmental area of the human brain. *Biological Psychiatry, 74*, 172–179.

Hamberger, L. K. (2005). Men's and women's use of intimate partner violence in clinical samples: Toward a gender-sensitive analysis. *Violence and Victims, 20*(2), 131–151. doi:10.1891/vivi.2005.20.2.131

Hamberger, L. K., & Guse, C. E. (2002). Men's and women's use of intimate partner violence in clinical samples. *Violence Against Women, 8*(11), 1301–1331. doi:10.1177/107780102762478028

Heise, L. L. (1998). Violence against women: An integrated, ecological framework. *Violence Against Women, 4*(3), 262–290.

Hellmuth, J. C., Gordon, K. C., Stuart, G. L., Moore, T. M. (2013). Risk factors for intimate partner violence during pregnancy and postpartum. *Archives of Women's Mental Health, 16*, 19–27.

Herculano-Houzel, S. (2012). The remarkable, yet not extraordinary, human brain as a scaled-up primate brain and its associated cost. *Proceedings of the National Academy of Sciences, 109*, 10661–10668.

Hines, D. A., & Saudino, K. J. (2003). Gender differences in psychological, physical, and sexual aggression among college students using the Revised Conflict Tactics Scales. *Violence and Victims, 18*(2), 197–217. doi:10.1891/vivi.2003.18.2.197

Huesmann, L. R. (1988). An information processing model for the development of aggression. *Aggressive Behavior, 14*, 13–24.

Hunnicutt, G. (2009). Varieties of patriarchy and violence against women: Resurrecting "patriarchy" as a theoretical tool. *Violence Against Women, 15*, 553–573.

Kimmel, M. S. (2002). 'Gender symmetry' in domestic violence: A substantive and methodological research review. *Violence Against Women, 8*(11), 1332–1363. doi:10.1177/107780102762478037

Krebs, C. P., Lindquist, C. H., Warner, T. D., Fisher, B. S., & Martin, S. L. (2007). *The campus sexual assault (CSA) study.* NIJ 221153. National Institute of Justice. Retrieved from: www.ncjrs.gov/pdffiles1/nij/grants/221153.pdf

Kross, E., Berman, M., Mischel, W., Smith, E. E., & Wager, T. (2011). Social rejection shares somatosensory representations with physical pain. *Proceedings of the National Academy of Sciences, 108*(15), 6270–6275.

Lambert, L. C., & Firestone, J. M. (2000). Economic context and multiple abuse techniques. *Violence Against Women, 6*(1), 49–67. doi:10.1177/10778010022181705

Lanier, C., & Maume, M. O. (2009). Intimate partner violence and social isolation across the rural/urban divide. *Violence Against Women, 15*(11), 1311–1330. doi:10.1177/1077801209346711

Leary, M. R., Twenge, J. M., & Quinlivan. E. (2006). Interpersonal rejection as a determinant of anger and aggression. *Personality and Social Psychology Review, 10*, 111–132.

Lipsky, S., Caetano, R., & Roy-Byrne, P. (2009). Racial and ethnic disparities in police-reported intimate partner violence and risk of hospitalization among women. *Women's Health Issues: Official Publication of the Jacobs Institute of Women's Health, 19*(2), 109–118. doi:10.1016/j.whi.2008.09.005

Logan, T. K., Walker, R., & Cole, J. (2015). Silenced suffering: The need for a better understanding of partner sexual violence. *Trauma, Violence, & Abuse, 16*(2), 111–135. doi:10.1177/1524838013517560

Logan, T. K., Walker, R., Cole, J., Ratliff, S., & Leukefeld, C. (2003). Qualitative differences among rural and urban intimate violence victimization experiences and consequences: A pilot study. *Journal of Family Violence, 18*(2), 83–92.

Logan, T., Walker, R., Hoyt, W., & Faragher, T. (2009). *The Kentucky civil protective order study: A rural and urban multiple perspective study of protective order violation consequences, responses, & costs.* NCJ 228350. US Department of Justice, National Institute of Justice. Retrieved from: www.ncjrs.gov/pdffiles1/nij/grants/228350.pdf

Logan, T., Walker, R., Jordan, C., & Leukefeld, C. (2006). *Women and victimization: Contributing factors, interventions, and implications.* Washington, DC: American Psychological Association Press.

McPhail, B. A., Busch, N. B., Kulkarni, S., & Rice, G. (2007). An integrative feminist model: The evolving feminist perspective on intimate partner violence. *Violence Against Women, 13*(8), 817–841.

Menard, K. S., Anderson, A. L., & Godboldt, S. M. (2009). Gender differences in intimate partner recidivism: A 5-year follow-up. *Criminal Justice and Behavior, 36*(1), 61–76. doi:10.1177/0093854808325905.

Miller, T. R., Levy, D. T., Cohen, M. A., & Cox, K. L. C. (2006). Costs of alcohol and drug-involved crime. *Prevention Science, 7*, 333–342.

Mills, L. G. (2003). *Insult to injury: Rethinking our responses to intimate abuse.* Princeton, NJ: Princeton University Press.

Mischel, W., & Shoda, Y. (1995). A cognitive-affective system theory of personality: Reconceptualizing situations, dispositions, dynamics, and invariance in personality structure. *Psychological Review, 102*, 246–268.

Mischkowski, D., Kross, E., & Bushman, B. J. (2012). Flies on the wall are less aggressive: Self-distanced reflection reduces angry feelings, aggressive thoughts, and aggressive behaviors. *Journal of Experimental Social Psychology, 48*(5), 1187–1191. DOI: 10.1016/j. jesp.2012.03.012

Mohler-Kuo, M., Dowdall, G. W., Koss, M. P., & Wechsler, H. (2004). Correlates of rape while intoxicated in a national sample of college women. *Journal of Studies on Alcohol, 65*(1), 37–45.

Peek-Asa, C., Wallis, A., Harland, K., Beyer, K., Dickey, P., & Saftlas, A. (2011). Rural disparity in domestic violence prevalence and access to resources. *Journal of Women's Health, 20*(11), 1743–1749. doi:10.1089/jwh.2011.2891

Pinker, S. (2011). *The better angels of our nature.* New York: Viking.

Rajan, M., & McCloskey, K. A. (2007). Victims of intimate partner violence: Arrest rates across recent studies. *Journal of Aggression, Maltreatment, & Trauma, 15*(3–4), 27–52.

Rennison, C. M. (2001). *Intimate partner violence and age of victim, 1993–99.* U.S. Department of Justice, Bureau of Justice Statistics. Retrieved from: www.hawaii.edu/hivandaids/ Intimate_Partner_Violence_and_Age_of_Victim_1993_99.pdf

Rennison, C., & Planty, M. (2003). Nonlethal intimate partner violence: Examining race, gender, and income patterns. *Violence and Victims, 18*(4), 433–443. doi:10.1891/ vivi.2003.18.4.433

Renzetti, C. M. (2013). *Feminist criminology.* New York: Routledge.

Richie, B. (2012). *Arrested justice: Black women, violence, and America's prison nation.* New York: New York University Press.

Safe Horizon (2015). Retrieved on September 3, 2015 from www.safehorizon.org/page/ domestic-violence-statistics—facts-52.html

Schechter, S. (1982). *Women and male violence: The visions and struggles of the battered women's movement.* Boston: South End Press.

Shannon, L., Logan, T. K., Cole, J., & Medley, K. (2006). Help-Seeking and coping strategies for intimate partner violence in rural and urban women. *Violence And Victims, 21*(2), 167–181. doi:10.1891/vivi.21.2.167

Sinclair, H. C., Ladny, R. T., & Lyndon, A. E. (2011). Adding insult to injury: Effects of interpersonal rejection types, rejection sensitivity, and self-regulation on obsessive relational intrusion. *Aggressive Behavior, 37*, 503–520.

Slotter, E. B., Finkel, E. J., DeWall, C. N., Pond, R. S., Lambert, N. M., Bodenhausen, G.V., & Fincham, F. D. (2012). Putting the brakes on aggression toward a romantic partner: The inhibitory influence of relationship commitment. *Journal of Personality and Social Psychology, 102*, 291–305.

Smith, P. H., White, J. W., & Holland, L. J. (2003). A longitudinal perspective on dating violence among adolescent and college-age women. *American Journal of Public Health, 93*(7), 1104–1109. doi:10.2105/AJPH.93.7.1104

Stinson, R. D. (2010). Hooking up in young adulthood: A review of factors influencing the sexual behavior of college students. *Journal Of College Student Psychotherapy, 24*(2), 98–115. doi:10.1080/87568220903558596

Straus, M. A. (2004). Prevalence of violence against dating partners by male and female university students worldwide. *Violence Against Women, 10*(7), 790–811. doi:10.1177/1077801204265552

Straus, M. A. (2007). Processes explaining the concealment and distortion of evidence on gender symmetry in partner violence. *European Journal on Criminal Policy and Research, 13*(3–4), 227–232.

Straus, M. A., & Gelles, R. J. (1990). *Physical violence in American families: Risk factors and adaptations to violence in 8,145 families.* New Brunswick, NJ: Transaction.

Tedeschi, J. T., & Felson, R. B. (1994). *Violence, aggression, and coercive actions.* Washington, DC: American Psychological Association.

Tjaden, P., & Thoennes, N. (2000). *Full report of the prevalence, incidence, and consequences of violence against women.* Retrieved from: www.ncjrs.gov/pdffiles1/nij/183781.pdf

Vandello, J. A., & Cohen, D. (2003). Male honor and female fidelity: Implicit cultural scripts that perpetuate domestic violence. *Journal of Personality and Social Psychology, 84,* 997–1010.

Watkins, L. E., DiLillo, D., Hoffman, L., & Templin, J. (2015). Do self-control depletion and negative emotion contribute to intimate partner aggression? A lab-based study. *Psychology of Violence, 5,* 35–45.

Watkins, L. E., DiLillo, D., & Maldonado, R. C. (2015). The interactive effects of emotion regulation and alcohol intoxication on lab-based intimate partner aggression. *Psychology of Addictive Behaviors, 29,* 653–663.

Websdale, N. (1998). *Rural woman battering and the justice system: An ethnography.* Thousand Oaks, CA: Sage Publications.

World Health Organization. (2013). *Global and regional estimates of violence against women: Prevalence and health effects of intimate partner violence and non-partner violence.* Retrieved from: http://apps.who.int/iris/bitstream/10665/85239/1/9789241564625_eng.pdf

Zillmann, D. (1988). Cognitive-excitation interdependencies in aggressive behavior. *Aggressive Behavior, 14,* 51–64.

17

AGGRESSION BETWEEN SOCIAL GROUPS

James Densley and Jillian Peterson

Most theories of aggression are rooted in the biological substructure or psychological superstructure of the individual. Early theories were instinctual (Freud, 1930; Lorenz, 1966), inspired in part by the philosopher Thomas Hobbes' (1651) notion that people were violent by nature, predisposed to "war of all against all." Later theories were cognitive, including the popular *frustration-aggression hypothesis* that aggressive behavior results when purposeful activity is interrupted (Dollard et al., 1939), and the *cognitive neoassociation theory* that aggression is primed by aversive stimuli (Berkowitz, 1990). *Social learning* (Bandura, 1977) and *script* (Huesmann, 1998) theories emphasize the acquisition of aggression through direct experience or observation. *Social interaction theory* ties coercive action to the rational pursuit of individual goals (Tedeschi & Felson 1994). *Excitation transfer theory* links aggression to misattributed physiological arousal (Zillmann, 1983).

Even in integrated theories that account for both personal and situational factors (see Anderson & Bushman, 2002), the bulk of the explanatory power is placed on the individual. In other words, the classic developmental and personality theories of aggression do not necessarily constitute theories of *group* aggression, yet groups commit and receive more aggression than individuals (Meier & Hinsz, 2004). Groups large and small are synonymous with aggression in society (Baron & Kerr, 2004; Brewer, 2003), but one readily identifiable group in particular is said to "warrant special attention" (Papachristos, 2013, p. 49). That group is the street gang. Indeed, despite historic declines in crime over the last two decades (see Roeder et al., 2015), gangs and gang-related aggression persist as salient concerns both for research and public policy (Decker et al., 2013).

All gangs are groups, but not all groups are gangs. Over 30,000 homicides in the United States have been attributed to street gangs since the 1990s (Howell & Griffiths, 2015). Gang members have homicide victimization rates at least 100 times greater than the general population (Decker & Pyrooz, 2010). They also engage in aggressive behavior at significantly higher rates than non-gang members and account for the majority of self-reported delinquency in adolescent samples (Thornberry et al., 2003). Gang violence is public and "contagious" in the sense that it is characterized by cyclical and retaliatory exchanges (Decker, 1996; Loftin, 1984; Papachristos et al., 2013). Gang violence has even been described as a "gift" or "gesture that, if accepted, demands to be reciprocated" (Papachristos, 2009, p. 80).

For the above reasons, conventional wisdom holds that gangs are "qualitatively different" (Klein & Maxson, 2006, pp. 11–12) or "somehow more 'groupy' than other delinquent or peer associations" (Papachristos, 2013, p. 49). Popular facilitation and enhancement hypotheses suggest, for example, "The gang is far more than just a collection of individual persons" (Klein, 1995, p. 43), and the collective and normative features of gang membership may have a causal influence on aggression (Thornberry et al., 1993, 2003). Specific mechanisms underlying "group processes" within gangs, however, remain largely unexplored (Decker et al., 2013; Hughes, 2013; Hughes & Short, 2014; Klein, 1995; McGloin & Decker, 2010; Short, 1965; Short & Strodtbeck, 1965).

Group processes (e.g., collective rules, identities, relationships, liabilities) are very much the purview of psychology (Goldstein, 2002), but because sociology and criminology are the traditional disciplinary homes of gang research, psychology has had little impact on the field (see Hennigan & Spanovic, 2011; Wood & Alleyne, 2010). Much like how classic psychological explanations of aggression focus on the individual level (Meier & Hinsz, 2004), extant psychological theories of gang membership focus on the individual level, such as the risk factors that distinguish gang from non-gang youth (Alleyne & Wood, 2010, 2012). The present chapter seeks to remedy this by offering a psychological perspective on gangs as social groups, and aggression as a group process. The aim is to compare gangs with other social groups engaged in aggressive behavior and highlight the potential for social psychology to contribute to our understanding of gang- and group-based aggression.

In-Group Cohesion and Out-Group Conflict

In simple terms, social groups consist of individuals who share a feeling of unity or are bound together in relatively stable patterns of interaction (Hogg, 1992). Membership in social groups, both formally and informally defined, serves a strong individual need for affiliation and acceptance (Tajfel, 1981). Perceiving oneself and others in group terms is a naturally occurring process known as *social categorization* (Allport, 1954; Tajfel & Turner, 1979). The more that individuals identify with the groups to which they belong ("in-groups"), the more they experience competition and conflict with other groups ("out-groups"). And the more two groups experience competition for limited resources, the more intergroup

conflict develops. The famous 1954 "Robbers Cave" field studies in which adolescent campers were divided into temporary groups and placed in competition
with each other perhaps demonstrates this notion best (Sherif, 1966; Sherif et al.,
1961). This "realistic group conflict," rational in the sense that two groups have
incompatible goals and experience a relative sense of deprivation (Jackson, 1993),
explains in part why in times of high unemployment, white people demonstrate
increased hostility toward immigrants and racial/ethnic minorities they believe
have taken or will take their jobs (Craig, 2002; Grimshaw, 1969).

Some groups, like prison gangs, fight to obtain more of a contested resource
(Skarbek, 2014). Other groups, like soccer hooligans, fight just to fight—for them,
fighting is a source of utility (Leeson et al., 2012). Either way, conflict strongly
facilitates cohesiveness, the "quintessential group process" (Klein, 1995, p. 43).
Cohesiveness refers to interpersonal attraction within the group, but also intrapersonal attraction to the group as a whole (Festinger et al., 1950; Hogg, 1992).
Cohesiveness explains in part why gangs are relatively "durable" groups (Klein &
Maxson, 2006, p. 4), even though gang members rarely remain in them for more
than a few years (Krohn & Thornberry, 2008; Pyrooz & Sweeten, 2015). As previously noted, conflict promotes cohesiveness (Klein & Crawford, 1967; Thrasher,
1927). Violence internal to the gang during group functions and initiations, for
example, "serves to intensify the bonds among members" (Decker & Van Winkle,
1996, p. 270). Cohesiveness also promotes conflict. Low cohesiveness is associated
with violence *within* gangs, for instance, whereas high cohesiveness is associated
with violence *between* gangs (Hughes, 2013).

In many ways, "adversarial relations" define gangs (Suttles, 1972, p. 98). Gangs
adopt common names (e.g., Bloods and Crips) and other identity markers (e.g.,
the colors red and blue) both to create superior-inferior boundaries of membership and to enhance their status in comparison to other groups (Felson, 2006). In-
group members use euphemistic language that labels harmful conduct as harmless
or respectable and "techniques of neutralization" (Sykes & Matza, 1957) that
dehumanize or denigrate out-group members and rationalize aggression toward
them (Alleyne et al., 2014). Studies show, for example, offenders will refer to
crime as "business" (Wright & Decker, 1997, p. 68) or to murder as "righteous,"
particularly when it is used to eliminate competitors or protect property rights
(Katz, 1988, p. 12). Resulting in-group and out-group favoritism creates a fas-
cinating double standard—gang members view the traits of their own gang as
virtuous but perceive those same traits in rival groups as vices (Densley, 2013).
Insiders will describe aggressive gangs as assertive, for example, whereas outsiders
will describe them as callous.

Such behaviors extend beyond gangs (see Bar-Tal, 2011). Catholics and Prot-
estants in Northern Ireland, for example, demonstrate similar levels of cognitive dissonance (Cairns et al., 2006). The "clash of civilizations" framework in
fact suggests essentialist religious and ethnic identities result in far more intense
"us versus them" relations (Huntington, 1996). The construction of "polarized

collective identities" accentuates the discursive practice of "othering" necessary to perpetuate cycles of revenge and retaliation and justify violent responses to perceived injustices (Talbot, 2008).

To some extent, however, in-group and out-group preferences are learned through interaction with intimate others (Akers, 2009; Sutherland & Cressey, 1974). The "bunch of guys" theory of leaderless jihad argues terror networks are built through ties of kinship and friendship that often precede the radicalization process (Sageman, 2008). Religious terrorists are heavily schooled in definitions conducive to violent extremism through Islamic schools and madrasahs (Stern, 2003). Suicide terrorists in particular are *trained* to overcome their survival instinct and the fear of death (Kruglanski et al., 2008). For them, like gang members, aggression is conditioned because it has led to desired outcomes for the group when displayed in certain situations in the past.

Obedience to Authority

If aggression is partly learned behavior, is there a master for every apprentice or teacher for every student? Individuals in groups certainly play different roles. Inevitably, there are group leaders and there are people who follow them. The group leaders exert their social influence over other group members, directly or indirectly, guiding group behavior. While strong leaders can guide groups toward prosocial and positive behavior, they can also push group members toward violence and aggression. From strong boys on the playground leading groups of children into bullying, to crime bosses giving direct orders of violence, obedience to authority is an important psychological phenomenon at play in group aggression.

The degree to which people will blindly obey authority to engage in aggressive acts was demonstrated most acutely by Stanley Milgram's famous shock experiments in the early 1960s (Milgram, 1963, 1974). Hoping to demonstrate that the horror that occurred in Nazi Germany could never be repeated in the United States, Milgram recruited average men through a local newspaper ad to participate in his study. Participants sat in a room with a confederate, both drawing slips of paper to discover who would play the "teacher" and who would play the "learner" (both slips actually said "teacher"). Each participant then sat in front of a large apparatus believed to be an electric shock generator (though it was fake) and read a list of word pairs to the "learner." When the learner incorrectly answered one of the questions, participants were told to administer an electric shock— starting at 15 volts and increasing in increments of 15 volts until the lethal maximum of 450 volts. An authority figure in a white lab coat stood near participants, demanding that they continue. Two-thirds of average citizens did—demonstrating a willingness to administer a lethal shock to a stranger under these circumstances (Milgram, 1963, 1974).

This level of blind obedience to authority to engage in violence or aggression is not limited to a laboratory experiment. From 1975 to 1979, for example,

Pol Pot and the Khmer Rouge used similar means of indoctrination and strong institutional control to create an army of child soldiers (Pina e Cunha et al., 2010). The soldiers were indoctrinated to believe in a mysterious ruling entity and taught to show class hatred toward any and all "capitalists" who refused to join the revolution. Children indiscriminately followed orders to engage in arbitrary and extreme violence and torture. They were encouraged to hate their parents and, in many cases, execute them. More than one million people were killed and buried by the Khmer Rouge regime during the "killing fields" era (Martin, 2008).

When mass genocide occurs, blind obedience to violent leaders is a critical component. In fact, "followership" within a country tends to occur if there are certain cultural characteristics present—a history of being devalued, a history of being victimized, and a general authority orientation (Staub, 2014). With these elements present, individuals actively look for leaders to follow (Staub, 2014). Although it may begin as obedience, the people involved soon do more than just obey—they actively participate. As individuals involved in mass violence lose their own agency, they may even feel more powerful, eventually disengaging from their own moral belief system (Bandura, 1999). This process of obedience to authority, turning into blind loyalty, followed by moral disengagement, is the leading explanation for the transformation of the German people under Adolf Hitler and the Nazi Party in the 1930s and the Hutus during the 1994 Rwandan Genocide (Staub, 2014).

Of course, obedience to authority in social groups can occur on a smaller scale than genocide. Obedience to authority can also occur in the context of multiple perpetrator rape. In one study (Porter & Alison, 2004), researchers analyzed records of 210 groups comprising 2 to 13 people who committed gang rapes in England and the United States, examining group behaviors that occurred during the course of the rape (i.e., hostility, dominance, cooperation). Overall, the study demonstrated that members of the group tended to be consistent in their behavior during a rape. The researchers posited that the consistency in violent behavior was due to one group leader exerting control over the other members of the group, resulting in obedience. The central member of the group modeled the type of behavior they expected, eliciting similar responses from the complicit group members.

Leadership is a contested issue in gang research, with many studies depicting gangs as loose-knit organizations with no formal structure (Decker et al., 2008; Weisel, 2002). There is agreement, however, that some gang members, "shot callers," for instance (Howell & Griffiths, 2015), exert greater influence than others because they are more "central" to the gang network or more "embedded" in its fabric (Pyrooz et al., 2013). Such individuals are most susceptible to group processes, but also able to leverage their authority to "compel individuals to engage in what appear to be nonrational behaviors" (Decker et al., 2013, p. 383), especially violence (Densley, 2013). Subordinate gang members internalize their views, which become the lens through which they view life.

Conformity

Conformity is the social process of changing one's behavior because of direct or indirect group pressure, either real or imagined. In one of the early, famous psychological studies of conformity (Asch, 1951), participants sat around a table with six other "participants" (who were confederates). Participants were given a card with a line on it, and asked to identify how long it was by comparing it to three other lines. Initially, all confederates and participants gave the correct answer. But on the third question, all of the confederates gave a clearly wrong answer. One third of the actual participants conformed to the group, providing the obviously wrong answer to the question when asked.

We conform to our social groups for a number of reasons. We look to people around us for information about what to do and how to behave. We want to look good around our friends, families, and peers, and have our behavior approved of. We don't want to do something wrong, and we hate looking stupid or silly. We also conform to people we look up to because we want to be like them. Every day we conform to the people around us through our style of dress, our tastes, our political beliefs—sometimes consciously and usually unconsciously. People can also conform to aggressive or violent behavior within groups.

This phenomenon was studied most famously at Stanford University in the early 1970s. Twenty-four normal male college students were recruited to participate in a two-week study, which involved living in a fake "prison" in the basement of the Stanford psychology building (Haney et al., 1978). The men were randomly assigned to be "guards" (dressed in sunglasses and uniforms) and "prisoners" (deloused and dressed in prison garb). Almost immediately, the guards began abusing their new power, humiliating and degrading the fake prisoners. The situation unraveled quickly, with prisoners developing depression and displaying psychotic behavior, and the study had to be ended after only six days.

The Stanford prison experiment is a quintessential example of everyday people conforming to a group engaging in aggressive behavior; behavior that they would not have performed on their own. The context of the situation and the normative group aggression overrode individuals' own attitudes and morality. This level of group conformity has also been studied outside the lab. For example, in the case of Abu Ghraib prison in Iraq, where in 2003 U.S. Army Reserve officers working the night shift physically and sexually abused and tortured prisoners of war on camera. These military personnel were normal people, overwhelmed by the situation they were placed in, conforming to the aggressive and violent behavior of their colleagues (Zimbardo, 2007). In the end, 11 soldiers were charged with maltreatment, assault, and battery.

Conformity to group aggression has even been studied on the playground. A study of bullying behavior of over 1,200 elementary students found that the class context and group norms had a stronger influence on bullying behavior than individual attitudes (Salmivalli & Voeten, 2004). Group norms had a stronger influence on aggressive behavior among older students than younger ones. Children and adolescents look to their peers to know how to behave. So if aggression or violence occurs within a classroom, it tends to build as more children conform to the group behavior.

As conformity takes place within a group, individual values and viewpoints can be drowned out. *Groupthink* (Janis, 1972) describes members of a close group who emphasize agreement with each other, rather than critically thinking about a decision. As a result, *group polarization* can occur, when a group's point of view gets shifted to an extreme decision or behavior.

Some of the symptoms of groupthink include believing one's own group is invulnerable, stereotyping any out-groups, believing in the group's morality, and putting direct pressure on any dissenters from the group (Janis, 1972). The extent to which members glorify their group contributes to moral disengagement (Bandura, 1999), leading to aggression with little regard for the victims or consequences. Groupthink has been used to explain the echo chamber of prejudice in hate groups (Craig, 2002), the radicalization process in terror groups (Tsintsadze-Maass & Maass, 2014), fraternal hazing and sexual assault on college campuses (Hong, 2000), and even the decision to invade Iraq after the September 11, 2001, terror attacks (Kramer & Michalowski, 2005). In the gang context, groupthink also contributes to "pluralistic ignorance," that is, when group members privately reject a group norm, but incorrectly assume their gang colleagues accept it (Matza, 1964), such as supposedly not caring about going to prison or being violently victimized (Kennedy, 2011), and a "diffusion of responsibility," whereby immersion in the crowd reduces the perceived risk of sanctions and thus increases levels of aggression (Warr, 2002).

Anonymity

Diffusion of responsibility is also more likely to occur under conditions of anonymity. Anonymity has consistently been linked with increases in aggression and violent behavior, in part due to the "deindividuation" process of reduced inhibition and personal responsibility (Zimbardo, 2007). One early study of anonymity found warriors who changed their appearance before going into battle were more likely to torture and mutilate their enemies than warriors who retained their own appearance (Watson, 1973). An examination of violent attacks in Northern Ireland similarly found a significant relationship between wearing a mask to disguise one's identity and increased aggression (Silke, 2001).

Groups inherently make individuals feel more anonymous than they would on their own. Costumes and uniforms, such as those worn by gang members, Ku Klux Klan (KKK) members, soldiers, police officers, prison guards, prisoners, and professional athletes, enhance this feeling (Rehm et al., 1987). Analyses of football, hockey, soccer, and combat sports indicate team aggression can increase simply by virtue of wearing black or red uniforms—colors associated with death and violence, popular among gangs (Attrill et al., 2008; Frank & Gilovich, 1988; Hill & Barton, 2005). Costly initiation rites and indoctrination rituals designed to break down individual identity and increase group loyalty—common among religious cults, secret societies, college sororities and fraternities—further contribute to aggression (Sosis & Bressler, 2003). There is a reason soldiers shave their heads when they enter boot camp—the group becomes an extension of the individual and the individual becomes an extension of the group.

As important as actually being anonymous is the *feeling* of anonymity. In a series of studies of darkness and moral behavior, researchers found that college students were significantly more likely to cheat on a task if they were in a dimly lit room (Zhong et al., 2010). College students also behaved more selfishly in a game when they were wearing sunglasses versus when they were not. Although the students were not actually any more anonymous in the dimly lit room or wearing sunglasses, they *felt* more anonymous. And when we feel anonymous, we are more willing to engage in immoral behaviors that we otherwise wouldn't consider.

The role of anonymity in aggression can also be seen on social media. Threat and insult is the currency of conversation on comment pages, Facebook, Twitter, and YouTube. And the degree of anonymity may be responsible for the aggressiveness of the comments (Thelwall & Sud, 2011). New anonymous apps such as Yik Yak let people post unattributable comments to anyone in their vicinity. Yik Yak has led to anonymous group conversations where the intimidation and threats are so severe that colleges are asking students to stop using the platform (Mahler, 2015). Cyber-aggression is thought to be even more damaging than traditional face-to-face bullying, partially due to the degree of anonymity involved (Sticca & Perren, 2013). Information on real or perceived threats also diffuses quickly on smartphones and social media (Densley, 2013). For gang members especially, *threats* give rise to preemptive aggression (Decker & Van Winkle, 1996). With the integration of technology into everyday life, some gang behaviors that traditionally occurred in person and in public to build collective identity have moved online and out of sight (Pyrooz et al., 2015).

Bringing the Individual Back In

Undoubtedly, the groups we are a part of have a significant impact on our behavior, including aggression. In-group cohesion and out-group conflict, obedience, conformity, groupthink, and anonymity reduce our individual attitudes and inhibition toward aggression and let group norms prevail. However, group behavior can move in either direction—prosocial or antisocial—which is heavily influenced by individual members and, most importantly, the group leaders. "Bad apples" can push group behavior in a negative direction, instigating aggression. A recent analysis of court transcripts of 80 perpetrators of genocide (Hollows & Fritzon, 2012), for instance, found it is critically important to examine the individual psychological motivations of leaders of mass violence, rather than solely focusing on the group processes that perpetuate genocide.

The individual traits of strong leaders within a group do matter. A diagnosis of conduct disorder as a child, for example, predicts which antisocial teenagers are likely to continue aggressive behavior throughout adulthood, regardless of their peer group (Frick et al., 2003; Moffit, 2006). Callous and unemotional traits are also associated with aggression and violence, particularly instrumental aggression over the life span (for a review, see Glenn & Raine, 2009). The "Central 8" individual risk factors for criminal behavior include a history of antisocial behavior, antisocial personality, antisocial cognition (rationalizing and perpetuating criminal activity; Tangney et al., 2007), antisocial peers, troubled family relationships, problems with school or work, recreation problems, and substance abuse (Andrews et al., 2006). It is also well established that a history of trauma or abuse predisposes individuals to aggressive behavior (Lansford et al., 2002).

Groups that contain members with known risk factors for criminal activity are more likely to engage in violence or aggression; especially if these individuals are dynamic leaders, encouraging obedience and conformity from their comrades. But selection into social groups remains an ongoing communicative exchange between the risky individual and the group (see Densley, 2012, 2015). Individuals do not stumble into gangs probabilistically according to risk factors; rather, selection is a two-way street—people choose gangs, but gangs also choose people (Densley, 2012, 2015; Sanchez-Jankowski, 1991). Some individuals will likely engage in aggression in any context. Other individuals will behave aggressively only in specific contexts with certain social processes at play. For these individuals, social groups can be protective or a trigger for aggression. The direction of the push will depend on the individual attributes of the members.

Discussion and Conclusion

This chapter has discussed some of the important psychological processes that account for aggression in social groups. The primary group focus was street gangs, but as can be observed, many other groups share these processes, from hate groups to sports teams, and terror groups to child soldiers. This chapter thus confirms the value of comparisons in gang research (Klein, 2006) and contributes to renewed efforts to insert psychology into gang scholarship (Wood & Alleyne, 2010). Whether gangs are truly "qualitatively different" from other groups remains an open question (Klein & Maxson, 2006), but collaborative efforts to uncover precisely what amount of the relationship between group membership and aggression can be attributed to the "kinds of persons" who select into groups and the "kinds of groups" these individuals select into can only bring us closer to the answer (Thornberry et al., 1993). Criminologists, psychologists, and sociologists have long formed into their own groups, replicating the conflict of the groups they study. This chapter aims to encourage greater interdisciplinary thinking on group processes that contribute to aggressive behavior.

Group processes are not only central to understanding the etiology of aggression, but also to finding workable solutions to it. Breaking the cycle of intergroup aggression is no easy task. In some instances, it eventually reaches a threshold, prompting de-escalation because it draws unwanted attention from police or detracts from other group business (Densley, 2013). In other instances, interventions by third parties (e.g., law enforcement, gang and community leaders) occur, reducing aggressive behavior. Evidence from this chapter suggests intergroup contact under appropriate conditions could reduce aggression by breaking down boundaries and beliefs that develop in the absence of association (see Kennedy, 2011).

At the same time, however, conflict between social groups typically occurs in certain contexts, namely when groups are competing for limited resources (e.g., money, jobs, territory, power). Blind obedience within groups also often occurs among people who have been previously victimized and devalued (Staub, 2014). In order to reduce group aggression, therefore, the larger context in which it occurs also needs to be changed. Increased resources, access to education, employment, and training, and greater self-efficacy and self-worth may all ultimately reduce group aggression by changing the broader landscape in which social groups exist. We must work to reconcile (1) the individual-level correlates and risks associated with aggression, (2) the group processes involved in aggression, and (3) the macro-level context of aggression (Short, 1985, 1998). This chapter focused on the bad *barrels*, that is, the groups and situational forces that facilitate aggression; but the bad *apples*, or individuals predisposed to aggression, and bad *barrel makers*, broader systems that facilitate group aggression, including the people with the power to shape them, still deserve our attention (Zimbardo, 2007, p. 10).

References

Akers, R. (2009). *Social learning and social structure: A general theory of crime*. New Brunswick, NJ: Transaction.

Alleyne, E., Fernandes, I., & Pritchard, E. (2014). Denying humanness to victims: How gang members justify violent behavior. *Group Processes Intergroup Relations, 17*, 750–762.

Alleyne, E., & Wood, J. (2010). Gang involvement: Psychological and behavioral characteristics of gang members, peripheral youth and non-gang youth, *Aggressive Behavior, 36*, 423–436.

Alleyne, E., & Wood, J. (2012). Gang membership: The psychological evidence. In F. Esbensen & C. Maxson (Eds.), *Youth gangs in international perspective* (pp. 151–168). New York: Springer.

Allport, G. (1954). *The nature of prejudice*. Cambridge, MA: Perseus Books.

Anderson, C., & Bushman, B. (2002). Human aggression. *Annual Review of Psychology, 53*, 27–51.

Andrews, D., Bonta, J., & Wormith, S. (2006). The recent past and near future of risk and/ or need assessment. *Crime and Delinquency, 52*, 7–27.

Asch, S. E. (1951). Effects of group pressure upon the modification and distortion of judgement. In H. Guetzkow (Ed.), *Groups, leadership, and men* (pp. 177–190). Pittsburgh, PA: Carnegie Press.

Attrill, M., Gresty, K., Hill, R., & Barton, R. (2008). Red shirt colour is associated with long-term success in English football. *Journal of Sports Sciences, 26*, 577–582.

Bandura, A. (1977). *Social learning theory.* New York: Prentice Hall.

Bandura, A. (1999). Moral disengagement in the preparation of inhumanities. *Personality and Social Psychology Review, 3*, 193–209.

Baron, R., & Kerr, N. (2004). *Group process, group decision, group action* (2nd ed.). Berkshire, UK: Open University Press.

Bar-Tal, D. (2011). Conflicts and social psychology. In D. Bar-Tal (Ed.), *Intergroup conflicts and their resolution: Social psychological perspective* (pp. 217–240). New York: Psychology Press.

Berkowitz, L. (1990). On the formation and regulation of anger and aggression: A cognitive-neoassociationistic analysis. *American Psychologist, 45*, 494–503.

Brewer, M. (2003). *Intergroup relations* (2nd ed.). Berkshire, UK: Open University Press.

Cairns, E., Kenworthy, J., Campbell, A., & Hewstone, M. (2006). The role of in-group identification, religious group membership and intergroup conflict in moderating in-group and out-group affect. *British Journal of Social Psychology, 45*, 701–716.

Craig, K. (2002). Examining hate-motivated aggression: A review of the social psychological literature on hate crimes as a distinct form of aggression. *Aggression and Violent Behavior, 7*, 85–101.

Decker, S. H. (1996). Collective and normative features of gang violence. *Justice Quarterly, 13*, 243–264.

Decker, S. H., Katz, C., & Webb, V. (2008). Understanding the black box of gang organization: Implications for involvement in violent crime, drug sales, and violent victimization. *Crime and Delinquency, 54*, 153–172.

Decker, S. H., Melde, C., & Pyrooz, D. (2013). What do we know about gangs and gang members and where do we go from here? *Justice Quarterly, 30*, 369–402.

Decker, S. H., & Pyrooz, D. (2010). Gang violence worldwide: Context, culture, and country. In Graduate Institute of International and Development Studies, Geneva (Eds.), *Small Arms Survey 2010* (pp. 128–155). Cambridge, UK: Cambridge University Press.

Decker, S. H., & Van Winkle, B. (1996). *Life in the gang: Family, friends, and violence.* Cambridge, UK: Cambridge University Press.

Densley, J. (2012). Street gang recruitment: Signaling, screening, and selection. *Social Problems, 59*, 301–321.

Densley, J. (2013). *How gangs work: An ethnography of youth violence.* New York: Palgrave Macmillan.

Densley, J. (2015). Joining the gang: A process of supply and demand. In S. Decker & D. Pyrooz (Eds.), *The handbook of gangs* (pp. 235–256). New York: Wiley.

Dollard, J., Doob, L., Miller, N., Mowrer, O., & Sears, R. (1939). *Frustration and aggression.* New Haven, CT: Yale University Press.

Felson, M. (2006). The street gang strategy. In M. Felson (Ed.), *Crime and nature* (pp. 305–325). Thousand Oaks, CA: Sage Publications.

Festinger, L., Schachter, S., & Back, K. (1950). The spatial ecology of group formation. In L. Festinger, S. Schachter, & K. W. Back (Eds.), *Social pressure in informal groups* (pp. 141–161). Stanford, CA: Stanford University Press.

Frank, M., & Gilovich, T. (1988). The dark side of self- and social perception: Black uniforms and aggression in professional sports. *Journal of Personality and Social Psychology, 54*, 74–85.

Freud, S. (1930). *Civilization and its discontents*. London: Penguin.

Frick, P. J., Cornell, A. H., & Barry, C. T. (2003). Callous-unemotional traits and conduct problems in the prediction of conduct problem severity, aggression, and self-report of delinquency. *Journal of Abnormal Child Psychology, 31*, 457–470.

Glenn, A. L., & Raine, A. (2009). Psychopathy and instrumental aggression: Evolutionary, neurobiological, and legal perspectives. *International Journal of Law and Psychiatry, 32*, 253–258.

Goldstein, A. (2002). *The psychology of group aggression*. New York: John Wiley.

Grimshaw, A. (1969). *Racial violence in the United States*. Chicago: Aldine.

Haney, C., Banks, C., & Zimbardo, P. (1978). Interpersonal dynamics in a simulated prison. *International Journal of Criminology and Penology, 1*, 9–97.

Hennigan, K., & Spanovic, M. (2011). Gang dynamics through the lens of social identity theory. In F. Esbensen & C. Maxson (Eds.), *Youth gangs in international perspective* (pp. 127–149). New York: Springer.

Hill, R., & Barton, R. (2005). Red enhances human performance in contests. *Nature, 435*, 293.

Hobbes, T. (1651). *Leviathan*. Cambridge, UK: Cambridge University Press.

Hogg, M. (1992). *The social psychology of group cohesiveness*. New York: New York University Press.

Hollows, K., & Fritzon, K. (2012). 'Ordinary men' or 'evil monsters'?: An action systems model of genocidal actions and characteristics of perpetrators. *Law and Human Behavior, 36*, 458–467.

Hong, L. (2000). Toward a transformed approach to prevention: Breaking the link between masculinity and violence. *Journal of American College Health, 48*, 269–279.

Howell, J., & Griffiths, E. (2015). *Gangs in America's communities* (2nd ed.). Thousand Oaks, CA: Sage.

Huesmann, L. (1998). The role of social information processing and cognitive schema in the acquisition and maintenance of habitual aggressive behavior. In R. Geen & E. Donnerstein (Eds.), *Human aggression: Theories, research, and implications for social policy* (pp. 73–109). San Diego: Academic Press.

Hughes, L. (2013). Group cohesiveness, gang member prestige, and delinquency and violence in Chicago, 1959–1962. *Criminology, 51*, 795–832.

Hughes, L., & Short Jr., J. (2014). Partying, cruising, and hanging in the streets: Gangs, routine activities, and delinquency and violence in Chicago, 1959–1962. *Journal of Quantitative Criminology, 30*, 415–451.

Huntington, S. (1996). *The clash of civilizations and the remaking of world order*. New York: Simon and Schuster.

Jackson, J. (1993). Realistic group conflict theory: A review and evaluation of the theoretical and empirical literature. *Psychological Record, 43*, 395–415.

Janis, I. L. (1972). *Victims of groupthink: A psychological study of foreign-policy decisions and fiascoes*. Boston: Houghton Mifflin.

Katz, J. (1988). *Seduction of crime: Moral and sensual attractions in doing evil*. New York: Basic Books.

Kennedy, D. (2011). *Don't shoot: One man, a street fellowship, and the end of violence in inner-city America*. New York: Bloomsbury.

Klein, M. (1995). *The American street gang: Its nature, prevalence, and control*. New York: Oxford University Press.

Klein, M. (2006). The value of comparisons in street gang research. In J. Short Jr., & L. A. Hughes (Eds.), *Studying youth gangs* (pp. 129–143). Oxford, UK: Altamira Press.

Klein, M., & Crawford, L. (1967). Groups, gangs, and cohesiveness. *Journal of Research in Crime and Delinquency, 4,* 63–75.

Klein, M., & Maxson, C. (2006). *Street gang patterns and policies.* New York: Oxford University Press.

Kramer, R. C., & Michalowski, R. J. (2005). War, aggression, and state crime. *British Journal of Criminology, 45,* 446–469.

Krohn, M., & Thornberry, T. (2008). Longitudinal perspectives on adolescent street gangs. In A. Liberman (Ed.), *The long view of crime: A synthesis of longitudinal research* (pp. 128–60). New York: Springer.

Kruglanski, A., Chen, X., & Golec, A. (2008). Individual motivations, the group process and organizational strategies in suicide terrorism. *Journal of Policing, Intelligence and Counter Terrorism, 3,* 70–84.

Lansford, J. E., Dodge, K. A., Pettit, G. S., Bates, J. E., Crozier, J., & Kaplow, J. (2002). Long-term effects of early child physical maltreatment on psychological, behavioral, and academic problems in adolescence: A 12-year prospective study. *Archives of Pediatrics and Adolescent Medicine, 156,* 824–830.

Leeson, P., Smith, D., & Snow, N. (2012). Hooligans. *Revue d'économie politique, 122,* 213–231.

Loftin, C. (1984). Assaultive violence as contagious process. *Bulletin of the New York Academy of Medicine, 62,* 550–555.

Lorenz, K. (1966). *On aggression.* New York: Harcourt, Brace & World.

McGloin, J., & Decker, S. (2010). Theories of gang behavior and public policy. In H. Barlow & S. Decker (Eds.), *Criminology and public policy: Putting theory to work* (pp. 150–166). Philadelphia: Temple University Press.

Mahler, J. (2015, March 8). Who spewed that abuse? Anonymous Yik Yak app isn't telling. *New York Times.* Retrieved from www.nytimes.com/2015/03/09/technology/popular-yik-yak-app-confers-anonymity-and-delivers-abuse.html?_r=0

Martin, D. (2008, March 31). Dith Pran, "Killing Fields" photographer, dies at 65. *The New York Times.* Retrieved from www.nytimes.com/2008/03/31/nyregion/31dith.html?_r=0

Matza, D. (1964). *Delinquency and drift.* New York: Wiley.

Meier, B., & Hinsz, V. (2004). A comparison of human aggression committed by groups and individuals: An interindividual-intergroup discontinuity. *Journal of Experimental Social Psychology, 40,* 551–559.

Milgram, S. (1963). Behavioral study of obedience. *Journal of Abnormal and Social Psychology, 67,* 371–378.

Milgram, S. (1974). *Obedience to authority: An experimental view.* New York: Harber & Row.

Moffitt, T. E. (2006). Life-course-persistent versus adolescent-limited antisocial behavior. In D. Cicchetti & D. J. Cohen (Eds.), *Developmental psychopathology* (2nd ed., pp. 570–598). Hoboken, NJ: John Wiley & Sons.

Papachristos, A. (2009). Murder by structure: Dominance relations and the social structure of gang homicide. *American Journal of Sociology, 115,* 74–128.

Papachristos, A. (2013). The importance of cohesion for gang research, policy, and practice. *Criminology & Public Policy, 12,* 49–58.

Papachristos, A., Hureau, D., & Braga, A. (2013). The corner and the crew: The influence of geography and social networks on gang violence. *American Sociological Review, 78,* 417–47.

Pina e Cunha, M., Rego, A., & Clegg, S. (2010). Obedience and evil: From Milgram and Kampuchea to normal organizations. *Journal of Business Ethics, 97,* 291–309.

Porter, L. E., & Alison, L. J. (2004). Behavioral coherence in violent group activity: An interpersonal model of sexually violent gang behavior. *Aggressive Behavior, 30,* 449–468.

Pyrooz, D., Decker, S., & Moule Jr., R. (2015). Criminal and routine activities in online settings: Gangs, offenders, and the Internet. *Justice Quarterly, 32,* 471–499.

Pyrooz, D., & Sweeten, G. (2015). Gang membership between ages 5 and 17 years in the United States. *Journal of Adolescent Health, 56,* 414–19.

Pyrooz, D., Sweeten, G., & Piquero, A. (2013) Continuity and change in gang membership and gang embeddedness. *Journal of Research in Crime and Delinquency, 50,* 272–299.

Rehm, J., Steinleitner, M., & Lilli, W. (1987). Wearing uniforms and aggression: A field experiment. *European Journal of Social Psychology, 17,* 357–360.

Roeder, O., Eisen, L-B., & Bowling, J. (2015). *What caused the crime decline?* New York: Brennan Center for Justice. Retrieved from www.brennancenter.org/publication/what-caused-crime-decline

Sageman, M. (2008). *The leaderless jihad.* Philadelphia, PA: University of Pennsylvania Press.

Salmivalli, C., & Voeten, M. (2004). Connections between attitudes, group norms, and behavior in bullying situations. *International Journal of Behavior Development, 28,* 246–258.

Sanchez-Jankowski, M. (1991). *Islands in the street: Gangs and American urban society.* Berkeley: University of California Press.

Sherif, M. (1966). *Group conflict and cooperation.* London: Routledge.

Sherif, M., Harvey, O. J., White, B. J., Hood, W. R., & Sherif, C. W. (1961). *Intergroup conflict and cooperation: The Robbers Cave experiment (Vol. 10).* Norman, OK: University Book Exchange.

Short, J. F. Jr. (1965). Social structure and group processes in explanations of gang delinquency. In M. Sherif & C. W. Sherif (Eds.), *Problems of youth: Transition to adulthood in a changing world* (pp. 155–189). Chicago, IL: Aldine.

Short, J. F., Jr. (1985). The level of explanation problem. In R. Meier (Ed.), *Theoretical methods in criminology* (pp. 51–74). Beverly Hills, CA: Sage.

Short, J. F., Jr. (1998). The level of explanation problem revisited: The American Society of Criminology 1997 Presidential Address. *Criminology, 36,* 3–36.

Short, J. F. Jr., & Strodtbeck, F. (1965). *Group process and gang delinquency.* Chicago: University of Chicago Press.

Silke, A. (2001). Deindividuation, anonymity, and violence: Findings from Northern Ireland. *The Journal of Social Psychology, 143,* 293–499.

Skarbek, D. (2014). *The social order of the underworld: How prison gangs govern the American penal system.* Oxford: Oxford University Press.

Sosis, R., & Bressler, E. (2003). Cooperation and commune longevity: A test of the costly signaling theory of religion. *Cross-Cultural Research, 37,* 211–239.

Staub, E. (2014). Obeying, joining, following, resisting, and other processes in the Milgram studies, and in the Holocaust and other genocides: Situations, personality, and bystanders. *Journal of Social Issues, 70,* 501–514.

Stern, J. (2003). *Terror in the name of God: Why religious militants kill.* New York: Harper Collins.

Sticca, F., & Perren, S. (2013). Is cyberbullying worse than traditional bullying? Examining the differential roles of medium, publicity, and anonymity for the perceived severity of bullying. *Journal of Youth Adolescence, 42,* 739–750.

Sutherland, E., & Cressey, D. (1974). *Criminology* (9th ed.). New York: J. B. Lippincott.

Suttles, G. (1972). *The social construction of communities.* Chicago, IL: University of Chicago Press.

Sykes, G., & Matza, D. (1957). Techniques of neutralization: A theory of delinquency. *American Sociological Review, 22,* 664–670.

Tajfel, H. (1981). *Human groups and social categories.* Cambridge, UK: Cambridge University Press.

Tajfel, H., & Turner, J. (1979). An integrative theory of social conflict. In W. Austin & S. Worchel (Eds.), *The social psychology of intergroup relations* (pp. 33–48). Monterey, CA: Brooks/Cole.

Talbot, S. (2008). 'Us' and 'them': Terrorism, conflict and other discursive formations. *Sociological Research Online, 13.* Retrieved from www.socresonline.org.uk/13/1/17.html

Tangney, J. P., Meshek, D., & Stuewig, J. (2007). Working at the social-clinical-community–criminology interface: The George Mason University inmate study. *Journal of Social and Clinical Psychology, 26,* 1–21.

Tedeschi, J., & Felson, R. (1994). *Violence, aggression, and coercive actions.* Washington, DC: American Psychological Association.

Thelwall, M., & Sud, P. (2011). Commenting on YouTube videos: From Guatemalan rock to el big bang. *Journal of the American Society for Information Science and Technology, 63,* 616–629.

Thornberry, T., Krohn, M., Lizotte, A., & Chard-Wierschem, D. (1993). The role of juvenile gangs in facilitating delinquent behavior. *Journal of Research in Crime and Delinquency, 30,* 55–87.

Thornberry, T., Krohn, M., Lizotte, A., Smith, C., & Tobin, T. (2003). *Gangs and delinquency in developmental perspective.* Cambridge, UK: Cambridge University Press.

Thrasher, F. (1927). *The gang: A study of 1,313 gangs in Chicago.* Chicago, IL: University of Chicago Press.

Tsintsadze-Maass, E., & Maass, R. W. (2014). Groupthink and terrorist radicalization. *Terrorism and Political Violence, 26*(5), online first.

Warr, M. (2002). *Companions in crime: The social aspects of criminal conduct.* Cambridge: Cambridge University Press.

Watson, R. I. (1973). Investigation into deindividuation using a cross-cultural survey technique. *Journal of Personality and Social Psychology, 25,* 342–345.

Weisel, D. (2002). The evolution of street gangs: An examination of form and variation. In W. Reed & S. Decker (Eds.), *Responding to gangs: Evaluation and research* (pp. 25–65). Washington, DC: U.S. Department of Justice, National Institute of Justice.

Wood, J., & Alleyne, E. (2010). Street gang theory and research: Where are we now and where do we go from here? *Aggression and Violent Behavior, 15,* 100–111.

Wright, R., & Decker, S. (1997). *Armed robbers in action: Stickups and street culture.* Boston: Northeastern University Press.

Zhong, C. B., Bohns, V. K., & Gino, F. (2010). Good lamps are the best police: Darkness increases dishonesty and self-interested behavior. *Psychological Science, 21*(3), 311–314.

Zillmann, D. (1983). Arousal and aggression. In R. Geen & E. Donnerstein (Eds.), *Aggression: Theoretical and empirical reviews* (Vol. 1, pp. 75–102). New York: Academic Press.

Zimbardo, P. (2007). *The Lucifer effect: Understanding how good people turn evil.* New York: Random House.

18
THE PSYCHOLOGY OF TERRORISM

David Webber and Arie W. Kruglanski

The coordinated attacks attributed to the Islamic State of Iraq and Syria (ISIS; also called Islamic State of Iraq and the Levant, ISIL) across Paris that left 130 civilians dead, the massacre of 2,000 in Baga, Nigeria, by the Boko Haram, or the Boston Marathon bombing in 2013 that killed 3 and injured 264 are but a few examples of the terrorist attacks that, in recent years, have become commonplace across the world. Such occurrences, unfortunately, show no signs of relenting, and they present a particularly vexing challenge to global security (Zarif, 2015). The effort toward combating terrorists and terrorist organizations requires clear military and policing involvement, aimed at protecting innocent civilians and defeating the extremists on the ground. Equally clear is the fact that psychologists also have a seat at this table. Insights gleaned from current empirical studies focused on terrorism, as well as decades of research into psychological processes underlying terrorist activity, are important weapons in the fight against violent extremism.

For instance, one team of researchers examined terrorist organizations through the lens of industrial-organizational psychology (Ligon et al., 2015). From that perspective, attacks, propaganda efforts, and media attention of violent extremist groups can be seen as branding strategies aimed at creating a unique personality for the organization and allowing violent groups to differentiate themselves from each other. Other efforts have aimed specifically at elucidating the components of terrorist propaganda used for message dissemination and fighter recruitment (e.g., Cohen et al., 2015), of which the considerable research into social influence processes and persuasion (e.g., Kruglanski & Thompson, 1999; Petty & Cacioppo, 1986) could provide valuable insights.

For instance, research into the effectiveness of fear appeals may shed light on barbaric and brutal propaganda attempts that include videos of the beheadings of enemy combatants and other atrocities perpetrated recently by violent extremists (e.g., de Hoog et al., 2005; Witte, 1992). This literature could also be leveraged to improve government-created counter narratives aiming to win the hearts and minds of potential extremists (see Katz, 2014, for discussion of a rather unsuccessful counter narrative campaign launched by the U.S. State Department).

In other research streams, social psychologists have actively worked toward understanding peoples' *reactions* to terrorism. Representative of this approach is research conducted in the wake of the 9/11 attacks. This work examined support for retributive military action, and found, for example, that reactions depended on individuals' perceived risk of future terrorist attack (Huddy et al., 2005), as well as individuals' perception of retributive actions as moral and their tendency to dehumanize their targets (McAlister et al., 2006). Research conducted under the auspices of terror management theory (Greenberg et al., 1986) suggests further that these types of reactions arise as a natural defense to the cogent mortality reminders brought home by the terrorist attacks (Landau et al., 2004; Pyszczynski et al., 2003).

Whereas reactions to terrorist attacks are of interest, a more perplexing question is the psychology of violent extremists, and their motivations. Understanding those, hopefully, will allow us to fashion an effective counterterrorism strategy to combat radicalization into violence. The present chapter aims to address these matters.

Defining Violent Extremism

In this chapter we use the terms *violent extremism*, *terrorism*, and *political violence* interchangeably. The underlying essence of these concepts is the endorsement of or engagement in violent action as a means of achieving ideological or political goals. Thus, the actions of a terrorist can be differentiated from those of a mass shooter, for instance, in that the former are politically motivated whereas the latter are not. Broadly speaking, however, violent extremism can be defined as a special case of extremism. Webster's dictionary defines extremism as "exceeding the ordinary, usual or expected" (Webster's Collegiate Dictionary, 1986, p. 441). Thus, a belief or behavior may be considered extreme if it is *deviant* from expected or normative behavior within a population (see Kruglanski et al., 2015, for a discussion of extremism as deviance). Violent extremism is deviant in the sense that most individuals or organizations do not resort to violence as a means of attaining political goals, just like cliff diving is a deviant means toward personal entertainment or anorexia is a deviant means toward weight loss.

Extreme means, however, are not only deviant, but involve choosing a means toward goal attainment that compromises other important goals (Kruglanski, Chernikova, et al., 2014). Thus, not only are choices to become a terrorist or an anorexic non-normative, but both compromise the biological need for survival and the goal of personal health—one chooses to strive toward, for instance, a separate Islamic State (or Caliphate), but to do so, one forgoes basic concerns for one's own safety and security. The question for psychologists, then, is why would an individual choose behavior that is both non-normative, particularly given the strength of pressures to conform or comply with social norms (e.g., Asch, 1955; Sherif, 1936), and contrary, or *counterfinal*, to other concerns?

Internal Attributions

Mental Illness

The most immediate answer concerning motives for extremism involves an internal attribution whereby extremism reflects a unique personality profile or mental illness. Indeed, there is a long history within social psychology demonstrating that dispositional attributions tend to be favored as explanations for behavior (e.g., Gawronski, 2004; Jones & Harris, 1967; Ross, 1977), particularly when the behavior is unique and unusual (e.g., Jones & Nisbett, 1971). It is not surprising then that early psychological accounts of terrorism were of this ilk (e.g., Cooper, 1977; Pearce, 1977; Taylor, 1988). According to these accounts, terrorists were described as suffering from some sort of mental illness or personality disorder such as sociopathy or psychopathy; they were depicted, therefore, as individuals who engage in antisocial behaviors without an understanding of right and wrong and incapable of remorse for their actions.

Relegation of terrorism to a matter of psychopathology is comforting. It reassures us that terrorist acts are perpetrated by a few "crazies," rather than reflecting a potentially widespread social phenomenon. Unfortunately, the evidence for such claims is lacking, and consensus among experts is that instances of mental illness among terrorists are rare (e.g., Silke, 1998; Victoroff, 2005). Data and interviews collected on a host of different terrorist organizations, including those from Northern Ireland, Germany, Colombia, Palestine, Spain, and jihadist terrorists around the globe, find that terrorists are generally quite normal and free of mental illness (Crenshaw, 1981; Ferguson et al., 2008; Heskin, 1984; Merari, 1998; Post et al., 2003; Rasch, 1979; Sageman, 2004).

It is not that mentally ill individuals cannot become terrorists. Life history interviews conducted with 34 members of the U.S. Far Right (a.k.a. white supremacists) revealed that 34% experienced some sort of mental illness (Bubolz & Simi, 2015). Similar percentages have been found among lone actors (e.g., Corner & Gill, 2015; Gill et al., 2014; Gruenewald et al., 2013; Hewitt, 2003). As an example, in a database of 119 lone actors from the United States and United Kingdom, among "true" lone actors—those that truly acted alone, without command and control links to terrorist organizations—roughly 36% had evidence of a mental illness (Gill et al., 2014). When a matched control group of group actors (i.e., "traditional" terrorists) was added to this dataset, it was found that lone actors were 13 times more likely to have a mental illness than group actors (Corner & Gill, 2015). In a similar comparison between lone and group actors within the U.S. Far Right, lone actors evinced a 40% rate of mental illness, relative to 8% among group actors

(Gruenewald et al., 2013). The most straightforward explanation as to why mental illness is more prevalent among lone actors concerns the selection process that individuals must go through to gain membership in a terrorist organization (e.g., Bueno de Mesquita, 2005; Horgan, 2014; Spaaij, 2010). Simply put, when recruiting individuals to carry out an attack, the group typically looks to hire those who are most competent, and whom the organization can trust to effectively carry out an attack. Individuals with mental illness are thus risky recruits and are likely not to pass recruitment criteria. Thus, although they are likely committed to the cause, they are forced to act independently if they are to act at all.

At first blush, mental illness prevalence among lone actors is quite striking. Indeed, the rate is nearly double that of mental illness in the general adult population in the United States (18.5%; Substance Abuse and Mental Health Services Administration, 2014). Still, it must be noted that mental illness is only present in a minority of lone attackers. The actions of roughly 60% of lone attackers (and 90% of group-affiliated attackers) cannot be attributed to mental illness.

Personality

A second form of internal attribution is to personality. Again, researchers in the area agree that no single personality trait or unique personality profile characterizes terrorists as a whole (see Horgan, 2014, for a discussion). Some evidence exists, however, concerning the prevalence of certain traits among specific subsets of terrorists (e.g., Merari et al., 2009). In one study, researchers conducted a psychological assessment of a rare sample of Palestinian prisoners who were (1) would-be suicide attackers arrested before they could successfully complete their mission, (2) terrorists arrested for non-suicide missions, and (3) organizers or launchers of suicide missions (Merari et al., 2009). Results revealed that whereas 69% of the would-be suicide attackers were categorized as having a *dependent-avoidant* personality style, 80%–90% of the remaining groups evinced emotionally unstable personality styles. The researchers argued that this cluster of traits in suicide attackers identifies people who are susceptible to social influence, particularly to that of authority figures. Although such findings point to a unique nexus of traits that may define suicide attackers, all three groups of terrorists were actually defined by different traits. All in all, then, whereas some personality traits (e.g., dependence, persuadability) may render individuals vulnerable to radicalization, no personality traits appear to define root causes or sufficient and necessary conditions for radicalization (e.g., Jamieson, 1989; Kruglanski & Fishman, 2006; Morf, 1970; Rasch, 1979), so attribution to personality seems to constitute an unsatisfying explanation for terrorism.

The Radicalization Process

Other approaches are geared toward understanding the pathways or processes by which normal individuals radicalize, or turn to extremism (Horgan, 2008;

McCauley & Moskalenko, 2008). These approaches recognize that radicalization constitutes a complex phenomenon that occurs at the intersection of various factors. In the sections that follow, we outline three such important factors, which in conjunction may increase the probability of radicalization.

Needs

The first component is the psychological need, or individual motivation underlying radicalization. Though we defined violent extremism as violence enacted for political goals (e.g., removing occupying military forces from one's native land; Pape, 2005), such goals refer to the extremist organization, and not the motivation of the individual that prompts her or him to self-identify with those goals. One perspective identifies the individual motivation as the quest for significance—the fundamental desire to be someone and matter in the eyes of others (Kruglanski et al., 2009, 2013; Kruglanski, Gelfand, et al., 2014). Accordingly, other motivations that had been identified within the terrorism literature, such as revenge, honor, and loyalty (e.g., Bloom, 2004; Gambetta, 2005; Stern, 2004), are perceived as specific instantiations of the broader motive to feel significant (Kruglanski et al., 2009, 2013; Kruglanski, Gelfand, et al., 2014). We also defined extremism as a means that is selected when one motivation becomes dominant and more important than other concerns or goals. As is the case with all motivational forces (Kruglanski, Chernikova, et al., 2014), the motivation to earn significance is not dominant at all times. The radicalization process, therefore, often begins with some kind of triggering event that activates the significance motive.

Significance Loss

The first variety of triggering event occurs when one faces humiliating or shameful circumstances that induce a loss of significance. These feelings of insignificance can arise from attacks levied at one's personal and individual characteristics, or a group to which the individual belongs. In this vein, others have noted that the path toward radicalization often begins with the experience of emotional vulnerability, disenfranchisement, personal victimization, humiliation, relative deprivation, or strain (e.g., Agnew, 2010; Horgan, 2008; McCauley & Moskalenko, 2008; Post et al., 2002; Smith et al., 2012). Through this lens can be viewed case studies of Palestinians volunteering for suicide attacks after experiencing infertility or an HIV diagnosis (Pedahzur, 2005), or Chechen widows turning to extremism after their significant others were killed by Russian forces (Speckhard & Paz, 2012). All these circumstances cause one to feel insignificant, and motivate behavior aimed at remedying the situation. Fighting for one's group as an extremist, and the recognition, honor, and heroism that one could attain in the process, thus becomes a viable means toward significance restoration.

Such claims have also borne out empirically. Within a sample of Muslims living in the diaspora, perceiving oneself as a victim of anti-Muslim discrimination was positively related to support for suicide bombing (Victoroff et al., 2012). Analyses conducted on a database of violent (e.g., murder, assault, kidnapping) and non-violent (e.g., laundering money for or providing weapons to terrorists) terrorist acts on U.S. soil revealed that those who experienced abuse, rejection, or failures at work were more likely to resort to violence (Jasko et al., 2015). Likewise, data collected in Spain, Sri Lanka, and the Philippines revealed that the endorsement of extreme viewpoints (e.g., Islamic extremism, support of violent struggle for a separate state) was positively correlated with the degree to which respondents self-reported feelings of insignificance and humiliation (Webber et al., 2015). Moreover, experimental manipulations of significance loss in the form of vignettes detailing ethnic discrimination (Lemieux & Asal, 2010), vitriolic statements about the prestige of one's in-group (Webber et al., 2015), the experience of social rejection (Twenge et al., 2001; Warburton et al., 2006), and reminders of one's impending death (Pyszczynski et al., 2006) were found to increase the justification of violent political action, endorsement of an extreme political stance, aggression, and support for suicide bombing, respectively.

Significance Gain

Humiliating experiences of significance loss are not the only mechanisms that can activate the significance motive. Rather, some individuals are merely drawn by the allure of significance gain, independent of loss circumstances. This appeared to be the primary motivation for a slew of terrorists (e.g., bin Laden, Muhammed Atta, etc.) who have been identified as "megalomaniac hyper terrorists" striving for larger-than-life status within the extremist community (Sprinzak, 2009). Interviews conducted with former right-wing extremists in Germany likewise found that these individuals were often motivated by the belief that by joining the extreme movement they could collectively "exist for a thing" (Koehler, 2014).

Analyses of a database of suicide attackers also revealed how compelling the significance gain motive can be for motivating violent behavior (Webber et al., 2015). Open-source information was used to identify the presence of significance loss and significance gain circumstances of more than 200 suicide bombers. Significance gain, measured using indicators of seeking life purpose, monetary reward, or martyrdom, was the most prominent motivation among these individuals. Furthermore, the significance gain motive was three times more likely among Palestinian suicide attackers, which may be attributed to the emphasis placed on the benefits of martyrdom within the indoctrination process of young recruits (Post, 2006). What is telling in these findings, however, is that the presence of the significance gain motive had clear implications for the outcome of the attack; individuals motivated by significance gain were responsible for attacks with greater casualties (Webber et al., 2015).

Narratives

Once the significance motive has been activated, violence will only be chosen as the means if there is an available narrative or cultural ideology that depicts violence as a valid and sustainable mechanism for earning significance. Would-be extremists may face countless alternative means for earning significance that are neither counter-normative nor require the compromise of other goals. As such, one could instead strive for excellence, and hence significance, within a socially valued domain, such as work, entertainment, or sport. One could even become extreme in ways that are lauded by the mainstream, and instead of turning to violence, turn to self-sacrificial humanitarianism, for example. It is the function of the violence-justifying narrative to present violence as not only morally acceptable but also as a superior avenue for significance gain, more effective and direct than all others.

Specifically, the violence-justifying ideologies portray violence as necessary for the group's survival, and as an act that will be rewarded with glory and praise (Zartman & Anstey, 2012). These narratives typically identify a grievance that has been perpetrated against the in-group, and then identify the entity, or *culprit*, responsible for causing this grievance. Finally, the ideology identifies violence as an appropriate response toward the culprit responsible for the grievance. Essentially, the ideology provides its adherents with a justification that a specific instance of violence, say, detonating a suicide bomb in a busy Parisian cafe, is not only permissible from the moral standpoint, but necessary and laudable. The resulting destruction and loss of lives is no longer likened to murder and assault (Archer & Gartner, 1992), but rather an act of heroism and self-sacrifice that allows individuals to act, not only without feeling guilty or immoral, but to the contrary, feeling extremely proud of their actions (Bandura, 1999).

All else being equal, there is reason to believe that the nature of extreme ideological narratives makes them preferable to moderate narratives for fulfilling the significance motive. That is so because instances that trigger the significance motive operate by inducing inconsistencies and self-uncertainty (McGregor et al., 2001). A humiliating instance of significance loss forces one to confront an inconsistency between the positive way they wish to perceive themselves, and the negative way they must view themselves in light of the humiliation. Likewise, the allure of significance gain earned through future action makes apparent an inconsistency between the current state and some better future state. These inconsistencies create feelings of anxiety that motivate behavior designed to reducing the discrepancy and restore certainty (e.g., Festinger, 1957).

Extreme ideologies tend to be of a dichotomous "black and white" nature: they are clear-cut and low in ambiguity, which makes them highly appealing to those in search for certainty (Hogg et al., 2013). Clarity also characterizes the organizational structure of extreme groups, which are defined by closed boundaries, hierarchical leadership structures, and internal homogeneity, all features conducive to uncertainty reduction (Hogg & Adelman, 2013). Thus, moving toward the extreme is often perceived as the more viable option when one is motivated by instances of significance loss or gain.

Recent empirical evidence supports this notion. Previously, we reviewed evidence linking feelings of insignificance and humiliation to the endorsement of extreme ideologies (Webber et al., 2015). This relationship, however, was mediated by participants' self-reported need for closure. The need for closure represents a mindset whereby an individual has a low tolerance for ambiguity or uncertainty, and instead prefers to see things in a structured, clear-cut manner (Kruglanski & Webster, 1996). As such, the findings revealed that one of the mechanisms by which the activation of the significance motive can induce extremism is via uncertainty reduction afforded by extreme ideologies. Thus, loss or lack of significance appears to induce a self-uncertainty that is reduced by extreme ideologies that tell one precisely what to do in order to regain significance.

Networks

The social network to which one belongs—one's social ties and close relationships to individuals who embrace an extreme ideology—constitute the conduit whereby the radicalization process takes place. In this vein, a loose collective of friends and family espousing an extreme ideology can be crucial in the radicalization process of jihadists (Sageman, 2004, 2008). Likewise, over 90% of Sunni terrorists in the United States were found to have radicalized through social networks (Kleinmann, 2012), and, within a database of domestic U.S. terrorist attacks, having a close radical friend was related to a higher likelihood of ideologically motivated violence (Jasko et al., 2015).

For one, the presence of like-minded individuals can help a would-be violent extremist muster the fortitude to deviate from normative behavior. In the classic line studies on conformity, 75% of participants conformed to normative pressure within the group, but when those participants had an ally, an individual who shared in their beliefs, conformity rates decreased significantly (Asch, 1955). Similar effects were found in Milgram's (1974) studies on obedience, wherein 65% of participants blindly followed the instructions of an authority member and administered what they believed to be extreme levels of electric shock to a fellow participant. In a follow-up study, participants no longer had to follow instruction alone, but decisions were made by a committee of three individuals, two of whom were confederates instructed to refuse the orders. Under these conditions, full obedience rates dropped to 10%. The same is likely to be true among would-be extremists who need an ally to ease their walk down the pathway to terrorism.

Secondly, the presence of an extremist social network serves to validate the extreme ideology. Maintaining any ideology requires consensual validation (e.g., Berger & Luckmann, 1966); we evaluate the correctness and appropriateness of our own actions by looking to the actions, beliefs, and responses of others

(Festinger, 1954). This notion was tested in a unique laboratory paradigm that examined killing behavior (Webber et al., 2013). Participants were induced into believing that they had killed a series of live insects, and afterwards, a series of experimental manipulations were employed to manipulate perceived consensus. Some participants were led to believe that their peers approved of the killing, whereas others were led to believe their peers disapproved and refused to perform the killing task. In the absence of consensus, participants experienced significantly greater distress. That is, without their peers to validate their actions, participants were unable to perceive killing as morally justified, and were thus distressed. The same would be true of extremists who, on finding that others aren't entranced by the justification narrative, may question the accuracy of their own beliefs. Perhaps that is why leaders of extreme organizations often isolate their members from individuals on the outside with differing opinions. Palestinian suicide attacks, for instance, are carried out in isolated cells of three to five strongly committed volunteers. The purpose of this isolation is to prevent the would-be attacker from changing his mind in the face of individuals who may be unsupportive of the mission (Merari, 2004).

Finally, the nature of the social ties with other extremists also matters. Often, one's comrades come to be a second family to the individual—they become a "band of brothers" or "brothers in arms." In these cases, one's personal identity has become fused with one's group identity, and there is no differentiation between personal and group goals (Swann et al., 2012). Consider a recent survey conducted with Libyan revolutionaries; 96% of them reported being fused with their battalion, and roughly half of these reported that the bonds with their battalion members were stronger than the bonds with their own family (Whitehouse et al., 2014). Under conditions of fusion, individuals become significantly more willing to sacrifice themselves for the group and perpetrate violence in defense of the group (e.g., Atran et al., 2014; Swann et al., 2009).

Conclusion

The picture that emerges when we combine the three Ns—Needs, Narratives, and Networks—is an empirically informed depiction of how the confluence of psychological forces can lead normal individuals down a deviant path of radicalization. The various triggering events activate the significance motive and leave people searching for a means by which they can earn significance and certainty. Although extreme ideologies are particularly suited to this task, it is the pathway rarely chosen, as so doing requires forgoing other important concerns and disregarding social norms. Ideological narratives that legitimize violence and social network ties to likeminded others ease overcoming these hurdles, and thus facilitate movement toward violent extremism. This analysis is rather distinct from early approaches toward a psychology of terrorism focused on internal attributions to psychological flaws. Instead, it depicts a general process in which motivational, cognitive (ideological), and social influences combine into a field of forces that may push a wide variety of completely normal individuals into the arms of a terrorist organization. Understanding the circumstances in which such radicalization may occur may constitute a necessary first step that may afford the conceptual platform for planning programs and intervention aimed at preventing and/or reversing this pernicious and destabilizing phenomenon, the scourge of our age.

References

Agnew, R. (2010). A general strain theory of terrorism. *Theoretical Criminology, 14,* 131–153.

Archer, D., & Gartner, R. (1992). Peacetime casualties: The effects of war on the violent behaviour of noncombatants. In Aronson, E. (Ed.), *Readings about the social animal* (pp. 327–338). New York: W.H. Freeman and Co.

Asch, S. E. (1955). Opinions and social pressure. In J. Aronson & E. Aronson (Eds.), *Readings about the social animal* (11th ed., pp. 17–26). New York: Worth.

Atran, S., Sheikh, H., & Gomez, A. (2014). Devoted actors sacrifice for close comrades and sacred cause. *Proceedings of the National Academy of Sciences of the United States of America, 111,* 17702–17703.

Bandura, A. (1999). Moral disengagement in the perpetration of inhumanities. *Personality and Social Psychology Review, 3,* 193–209.

Berger, P. L., & Luckmann, T. (1966). *The social construction of reality: A treatise in the sociology of knowledge.* New York: Anchor.

Bloom, M. M. (2004). Palestinian suicide bombing: Public support, market share, and outbidding. *Political Science Quarterly, 119,* 61–88.

Bubolz, B. F., & Simi, P. (2015). Leaving the world of hate life-course transitions and self-change. *American Behavioral Scientist, 59,* 1588–1608.

Bueno de Mesquita, E. (2005). The quality of terror. *American Journal of Political Science, 49,* 515–530.

Cohen, S. J., Kruglanski, A. W., Gelfand, M. J., Webber, D., Gunaratna, R., & Katz, R. (2015). *Al-Qaeda's propaganda decoded: A psycholinguistic system for analyzing terrorist ideology.* Unpublished manuscript. John Jay College of Criminal Justice, CUNY.

Cooper, H. H. A. (1977). What is a terrorist: A psychological perspective. *Legal Medical Quarterly, 1,* 16–32.

Corner, E., & Gill, P. (2015). A false dichotomy? Mental illness and lone-actor terrorism. *Law and Human Behavior, 39,* 23.

Crenshaw, M. (1981). The causes of terrorism. *Comparative Politics, 13,* 379–399.

de Hoog, N., Stroebe, W., & de Wit, J. B. (2005). The impact of fear appeals on processing and acceptance of action recommendations. *Personality and Social Psychology Bulletin, 31,* 24–33.

Ferguson, N., Burgess, M., & Hollywood, I. (2008). Crossing the Rubicon: Deciding to become a paramilitary in Northern Ireland. *International Journal of Conflict and Violence, 2,* 130–137.

Festinger, L. (1954). A theory of social comparison processes. *Human Relationships, 1,* 117–140.

Festinger, L. (1957). *A theory of cognitive dissonance.* Evanston, IL: Row, Peterson.

Gambetta, G. (2005). *Making sense of suicide missions.* New York: Oxford University Press.

Gawronski, B. (2004). Theory-based bias correction in dispositional inference: The fundamental attribution error is dead, long live the correspondence bias. *European Review of Social Psychology, 15,* 183–217.

Gill, P., Horgan, J., & Deckert, P. (2014). Bombing alone: Tracking the motivations and antecedents behaviors of lone-actor terrorists. *Journal of Forensic Sciences, 59,* 425–435.

Greenberg, J., Pyszczynski, T., & Solomon, S. (1986). The causes and consequences of a need for self-esteem: A terror management theory. In R. F. Baumeister (Ed.), *Public self and private self* (pp. 189–212). New York: Springer-Verlag.

Gruenewald, J., Chermak, S., & Freilich, J. D. (2013). Distinguishing "loner" attacks from other domestic extremist violence. *Criminology and Public Policy, 12,* 65–91.

Heskin, K. (1984). The psychology of terrorism in Northern Ireland. In Y. Alexander & A. O'day (Eds.), *Terrorism in Ireland.* New York: St. Martins.

Hewitt, C. (2003). *Understanding terrorism in America: From the Klan to al Qaeda.* New York: Routledge.

Hogg, M. A., & Adelman, J. (2013). Uncertainty-identity theory: Extreme groups, radical behavior, and authoritarian leadership. *Journal of Social Issues, 69,* 436–454.

Hogg, M. A., Kruglanski, A. W., & van den Bos, K. (2013). Uncertainty and the roots of extremism. *Journal of Social Issues, 69,* 407–418.

Horgan, J. (2008). From profiles to pathways and roots to routes: Perspectives from psychology on radicalization into terrorism. *The ANNALS of the American Academy of Political and Social Science, 618,* 80–94.

Horgan, J. (2014). *The psychology of terrorism* (2nd ed.). New York: Routledge.

Huddy, L., Feldman, S., Taber, C., & Lahav, G. (2005). Threat, anxiety, and support of anti-terrorism policies. *American Journal of Political Science, 49,* 610–625.

Jamieson, A. (1989). *The heart attacked: Terrorism and conflict in the Italian state.* London: Marion Boyars.

Jasko, K., LaFree, G., & Kruglanski, A. W. (2015). *Quest for significance and violent extremism: The case of domestic radicalization.* Unpublished Manuscript. University of Maryland, College Park.

Jones, E. E., & Harris, V. A. (1967). The attribution of attitudes. *Journal of Experimental Social Psychology, 3,* 1–24.

Jones, E. E., & Nisbett, R. E. (1971). The actor and the observer: Divergent perceptions of the causes of behavior. In E. E. Jones, D. E. Kanouse, H. H. Kelley, R. E. Nisbett, S. Valins, & B. Weiner (Eds.), *Attribution: Perceiving the causes of behavior* (pp. 79–94). Morristown, NJ: General Learning.

Katz, R. (2014, September 16). The State Department's Twitter war with ISIS is embarrassing. *Time.* Retrieved from http://time.com/3387065/isis-twitter-war-state-department/

Kleinmann, S. E. (2012). Radicalization of homegrown Sunni militants in the United States: Comparing converts and non-converts. *Studies in Conflict & Terrorism, 35*(4), 278–297.

Koehler, D. (2014). Right-wing extremist radicalization processes: The formers' perspective. *Journal Exit-Deutschland. Zeitschrift für Deradikalisierung und demokratische Kultur, 1,* 307–377.

Kruglanski, A. W., Bélanger, J. J., Gelfand, M., Gunaratna, R., Hettiarachchi, M., Reinares, F., . . . & Sharvit, K. (2013). Terrorism—A (self) love story: Redirecting the significance quest can end violence. *American Psychologist, 68*(7), 559.

Kruglanski, A. W., Chen, X., Dechesne, M., Fishman, S., & Orehek, E. (2009). Fully committed: Suicide bombers' motivation and the quest for personal significance. *Political Psychology, 30,* 331–557.

Kruglanski, A. W., Chernikova, M., Jasko, K., Webber, D., & Dugas, M. (2015). *To the fringe and back: Violent extremism and the psychology of deviance.* Unpublished manuscript. University of Maryland, College Park.

Kruglanski, A. W., Chernikova, M., Rosenzweig, E., & Kopetz, C. (2014). On motivational readiness. *Psychological Review, 121,* 367–388.

Kruglanski, A. W., & Fishman, S. (2006). The psychology of terrorism: "Syndrome" versus "tool" perspectives. *Terrorism and Political Violence, 18,* 193–215.

Kruglanski, A. W., Gelfand, M. J., Bélanger, J. J., Sheveland, A., Hetiarachchi, M., & Gunaratna, R. (2014). The psychology of radicalization and deradicalization: How significance quest impacts violent extremism. *Political Psychology, 35*(S1), 69–93.

Kruglanski, A. W., & Thompson, E. P. (1999). Persuasion by a single route: A view from the unimodel. *Psychological Inquiry, 10,* 83–109.

Kruglanski, A. W., & Webster, D. M. (1996). Motivated closing of the mind: "Seizing" and "freezing." *Psychological Review, 103,* 263.

Landau, M. J., Solomon, S., Greenberg, J., Cohen, F., Pyszczynski, T., Arndt, J., . . . & Cook, A. (2004). Deliver us from evil: The effects of mortality salience and reminders of 9/11 on support for President George W. Bush. *Personality and Social Psychology Bulletin, 30,* 1136–1150.

Lemieux, A. F., & Asal, V. H. (2010). Grievance, social dominance orientation, and authoritarianism in the choice and justification of terror versus protest. *Dynamics of Asymmetric Conflict, 3,* 194–207.

Ligon, G. S., Harms, M., & Derrick, D. C. (2015). Lethal Brands: How VEOs Build Reputations. *Journal of Strategic Security, 8,* 3.

McAlister, A. L., Bandura, A., & Owen, S. V. (2006). Mechanisms of moral disengagement in support of military force: The impact of Sept. 11. *Journal of Social and Clinical Psychology, 25,* 141–165.

McCauley, C., & Moskalenko, S. (2008). Mechanisms of political radicalization: Pathways toward terrorism. *Terrorism and Political Violence, 20,* 415–433.

McGregor, I., Zanna, M. P., Holmes, J. G., & Spencer, S. J. (2001). Compensatory conviction in the face of personal uncertainty: Going to extremes and being oneself. *Journal of Personality and Social Psychology, 80,* 472.

Merari, A. (1998). The readiness to kill and die: Suicidal Terrorism in the Middle East. In W. Reich (Ed.), *Origins of terrorism: Psychologies, ideologies, theologies, states of mind* (pp. 192–207). Washington, DC: Woodrow Wilson Center and Johns Hopkins University Press.

Merari, A. (2004). Suicide terrorism. In R. I. Yuit & D. Lester (Eds.), *Assessment, treatment, and prevention of suicidal* behavior (pp. 431–454). Hoboken, NJ: Wiley and Sons.

Merari, A., Diamant, I., Bibi, A., Broshi, Y., & Zakin, G. (2009). Personality characteristics of "self martyrs" / "suicide bombers" and organizers of suicide attacks. *Terrorism and Political Violence, 22,* 87–101.

Merriam-Webster. (1986). *Webster's ninth new collegiate dictionary.* Springfield, MA: Merriam-Webster.

Milgram, S. (1974). *Obedience to authority: An experimental view.* New York: HarperCollins.

Morf, G. (1970). *Terror in Quebec: Case studies of the FLQ.* Toronto: Clarke Irwin.

Pape, R. (2005). *Dying to win: The strategic logic of suicide terrorism.* New York: Random House LLC.

Pedahzur, A. (2005). *Suicide terrorism.* Cambridge, UK: Polity Press.

Pearce, K. I. (1977). Police negotiations. *Canadian Psychiatric Association Journal, 22,* 171–174.

Petty, R. E., & Cacioppo, J. T. (1986). The elaboration likelihood model of persuasion. *Advances in Experimental Social Psychology, 19,* 123–205.

Post, J. (2006). *The mind of the terrorist: The psychology of terrorism from the IRA to Al Qaeda.* New York: Palgrave Macmillan.

Post, J. M., Ruby, K. G., & Shaw, E. D. (2002). The radical group in context: 1. An integrated framework for the analysis of group risk for terrorism. *Studies in Conflict and Terrorism, 25,* 73–100.

Post, J., Sprinzak, E., & Denny, L. (2003). The terrorists in their own words: Interviews with 35 incarcerated Middle Eastern terrorists. *Terrorism and Political Violence, 15,* 171–184.

Pyszczynski, T., Abdollahi, A., Solomon, S., Greenberg, J., Cohen, F., & Weise, D. (2006). Mortality salience, martyrdom, and military might: The great Satan versus the axis of evil. *Personality and Social Psychology Bulletin, 32,* 525–537.

Pyszczynski, T., Solomon, S., & Greenberg, J. (2003). *In the wake of 9/11: Rising above the terror.* Washington, DC: American Psychological Association.

Rasch, W. (1979). Psychological dimensions of political terrorism in the Federal Republic of Germany. *International Journal of Law and Psychiatry, 2,* 79–85.

Ross, L. (1977). The intuitive psychologist and his shortcomings: Distortions in the attribution process. In L. Berkowitz (Ed.), *Advances in experimental social psychology* (pp. 173–220). New York: Academic Press.

Sageman, M. (2004). *Understanding terror networks.* Philadelphia: University of Pennsylvania Press.

Sageman, M. (2008). *Leaderless Jihad: Terror networks in the twenty-first century.* Philadelphia: University of Pennsylvania Press.

Sherif, M. (1936). *The psychology of social norms.* Oxford, England: Harper.

Silke, A. (1998). Cheshire-cat logic: The recurring theme of terrorist abnormality in psychological research. *Psychology, Crime and Law, 4,* 51–69.

Smith, H. J., Pettigrew, T. F., Pippin, G. M., & Bialosiewics, S. (2012). Relative deprivation: A theoretical and meta-analytic review. *Personality and Social Psychology Review, 16,* 203–232.

Spaaij, R. (2010). The enigma of lone wolf terrorism: An assessment. *Studies in Conflict & Terrorism, 33,* 854–870.

Speckhard, A., & Paz, R. (2012). *Talking to terrorists: Understanding the psycho-social motivations of militant Jihadi terrorists, mass hostage takers, suicide bombers and martyrs to combat terrorism in prison and community rehabilitation.* McLean, VA: Advances Press.

Sprinzak, E. (2009, November 17). The lone gunman: The global war on terrorism faces a new brand of enemy. *Foreign Policy.* Retrieved from foreignpolicy.com

Stern, J. (2004). *Terror in the name of God.* New York: Ecco.

Substance Abuse & Mental Health Services Administration. (2014). Results from the 2013 national survey on drug use and health: Mental health findings. *NSDUH Series H-49, HHS Publication No. (SMA) 14–4887.* Rockville, MD.

Swann, W. B., Gomez, A., Seyle, D. C., Morales, J. F., & Huici, C. (2009). Identity fusion: The interplay of personal and social identities in extreme group behavior. *Journal of Personality and Social Psychology, 96,* 995–1011.

Swann, W. B., Jetten, J., Gomez, A., Whitehouse, H., & Bastian, B. (2012). When group membership gets personal: A theory of identity fusion. *Psychological Review, 119,* 441–456.

Taylor, M. (1988). *The terrorist.* London: Brassey's Defence Publishers.

Twenge, J. M., Baumeister, R. F., Tice, D. M., & Stucke, T. S. (2001). If you can't join them, beat them: Effects of social exclusion on aggressive behavior. *Journal of Personality and Social Psychology, 81,* 1058.

Victoroff, J. (2005). The mind of the terrorist: A review and critique of psychological approaches. *Journal of Conflict Resolution, 49*, 3–42.

Victoroff, J., Adelman, J. R., & Matthews, M. (2012). Psychological factors associated with support for suicide bombing in the Muslim diaspora. *Political Psychology, 33*, 791–809.

Warburton, W. A., Williams, K. D., & Cairns, D. R. (2006). When ostracism leads to aggression: The moderating effects of control deprivation. *Journal of Experimental Social Psychology, 42*, 213–220.

Webber, D., Babush, M., Schori-Eyal, N., Moyano, M., Hetiarachchi, M., Belanger, J. J., . . . Gelfand, M. J. (2015). *The road to extremism: How significance loss-based uncertainty fosters extremism.* Unpublished manuscript. University of Maryland, College Park.

Webber, D., Klein, K., Sheveland, A., Kruglanski, A. W., Gelfand, M. J., Brizi, A., & Merari, A. (2015). Divergent paths to martyrdom and significance among suicide attackers. *Terrorism and Political Violence.* doi:10.1080/09546553.2015.1075979

Webber, D., Schimel, J., Martens, A., Hayes, J., & Faucher E. H. (2013). Using a bug-killing paradigm to understand how social validation and invalidation affect the distress of killing. *Personality and Social Psychology Bulletin, 39*, 470–471.

Whitehouse, H., McQuinn, B., Buhrmester, M., & Swann, W. B. (2014). Brothers in arms: Libyan revolutionaries bond like family. *Proceedings of the National Academy of Sciences of the United States of America, 111*, 17783–17785.

Witte, K. (1992). Putting the fear back into fear appeals: The extended parallel process model. *Communications Monographs, 59*, 329–349.

Zarif, J. (2015). The imperative of a comprehensive strategy to fight violent extremism. *Harvard International Review.* Retrieved from http://hir.harvard.edu/archives/11547

Zartman, W. I., & Anstey, M. (2012). The problem: Preventing identity conflicts and genocide. In I. W. Zartman, M. Ansteys, & P. Meerts (Eds.), *The slippery slope to genocide: Reducing identity conflicts and preventing mass murder* (pp. 3–34). New York: Oxford University Press.

PART V

Making the World a More Peaceful Place

19

REDUCING AGGRESSION AND VIOLENCE

Farida Anwar, Douglas P. Fry, and Ingrida Grigaitytė

Psychological and social science research shows that there are numerous ways to prevent and reduce violence within and among societies (Fry, 2004; Fry & Björkqvist, 1997; Gelles & Straus, 1988; Straus, 2001). For the most part, different approaches can be seen as complementary and sometimes additive in their effects. Within schools, for example, peer mediation, anti-bullying programs, and the teaching of conflict resolution skills can be effective (see Olweus, this volume; Fry & Björkqvist, 1997). Domestic violence rehabilitation can prove beneficial as well (Gelles & Straus, 1988). Community involvement in the upbringing of youth has been shown to reduce criminality (Sampson et al., 1997). Empirical studies have demonstrated the link between receiving and witnessing corporal punishment as a child and acting aggressively as an adult (Straus, 2001), and in light of such findings a growing number of countries have passed laws prohibiting the physical punishment of children (End Corporal Punishment, n.d.). Creating cross-cutting ties among groups and highlighting a larger common identity help to reduce bias and hostilities and simultaneously enhance intergroup cooperation and positive perceptions of others (Dovidio et al., 2009; see also Densley & Peterson, this volume). Data suggest that economic and social disparities within a society correlate positively with violence (Institute for Economics and Peace, n.d.). A prescription, therefore, for reducing violence is to enhance the equitable distribution of resources across the members of society, a process that the Nordic countries have demonstrated is possible (Eisler, 2007). At the regional and global levels, research on existing nonwarring peace systems suggests that the chance of war can be reduced in various ways through recognizing and augmenting mutual interdependence, building an overarching socio-political identity, strengthening ties among subunits, promoting peace values such as appreciation for diversity, tolerance, and respect, reinforcing unity and peace through symbolic culture, developing institutions for the effective resolution of conflicts and the delivery of justice, and creating supranational organizations, norms, and legal mechanisms to address common security and economic and ecological concerns (Fry, 2012).

An expanded consideration of the plethora of violence prevention and reduction methods goes beyond the scope of one chapter, and thus with the acknowledgement that a great diversity of approaches exists, we have chosen in this chapter to highlight three interconnected areas. We will consider values and norms, socialization of the young, and nonviolence, both in terms of a philosophy and as a pragmatic mechanism for bringing about positive social change. These three thematic areas offer many insights for preventing and reducing aggression and violence, from the interpersonal to the global. The take-home message is that multiple ways to prevent and reduce violence exist, some of which have been mentioned in passing in this brief introduction and some of which we will now consider in detail. It may not be as difficult to prevent and reduce violence as commonly assumed. There are many approaches that can be adopted to produce a cumulative effect.

Peace-Promoting Values and Norms

Values—essential beliefs, ideas, or ideals shared by the members of a culture—constitute the principles that guide one's life (Triandes, 1994). Any given culture has core values that are particularly important within that social group. Core values are first learned and internalized during childhood socialization processes, and then regularly reinforced through social interaction over the course of an individual's life. Psychological research has demonstrated that values influence behavior (e.g., Bardi & Schwartz, 2003; Schultz et al., 2005). Values can become codified as norms—widely shared standards of behavior—as they come to define appropriate actions. Values and norms emphasize which behaviors are socially desired and which are not, the former being praised and applauded, the latter being met with disapproval through criticism, ridicule, shaming, and other social sanctions. For example, in a given society generosity may be rewarded over greediness, kindness praised in contrast to callousness, courage rewarded over cowardliness, or perhaps contrariwise, timidity favored over bravery, as occurs among the Buid of the Philippines (Bonta & Fry, 2006; Gibson, 1989). Values are simultaneously reflected in and validated by a society's customs and institutions as they are referenced in daily speech, myths, rituals, drama, and narratives. Literally, "the moral of the story" of many such cultural communications is to remind people to act in accordance with core values and norms.

Some societies have nonviolent values and norms, and, correspondingly, very low levels of expressed aggression (Bonta, 1996; Bonta & Fry, 2006). To give some examples, the Trio of South America back away from disputes; they "lack tolerance for conflict and the tendency is always to move in order to avoid confrontation" (Rivière, 1994, p. 336). Among the Kuikuru, also from South America, aggression is practically nonexistent and concern over "being thought stingy, quarrelsome, or aggressive keeps village life running smoothly" (Carneiro, 1994, p. 208). Among the Pacific atoll-dwelling Ifaluk, "the culture is particularly notable for its ethic of non-aggression, and its emphasis on helpfulness, sharing, and cooperation" (Spiro, 1952, p. 497). Cultural examples such as these suggest that one path to reduce aggression is to develop and promote, through a variety of social mechanisms and customs, nonviolent core values and corresponding societal norms.

The Hopi of the southwestern United States value harmony, humility, and holding "good thoughts" as core values that help to keep the peace in Hopi society. For the Hopi, respect is a central value: "Anger and violence have no part in the life of a humble person who respects the autonomy of others" (Schlegel, 2004, p. 32). Disagreements and disputes exist in Hopi society, but for the most part they do not lead to violence (Schlegel, 2004). The value placed on harmony and nonviolence contributes to peace. In 1906, a conflictual rift developed in one Hopi village. The leaders of two rival groups agreed to resolve the dispute through a contest, the outcome of which would determine which faction would move out of the village peacefully. The two unarmed groups faced off across a line drawn on the ground and began to push. Eventually, the members of one faction managed to push their rivals back and swarmed over the line. The defeated group "accepted their loss and sadly left the village. This says a great deal about the success with which the value on nonviolence was internalized and put into practice" (Schlegel, 2004, p. 33).

A given society's core values may be conducive to violence and war or to nonviolence and peace—or at times reflect inherent contradictions. Core values may favor, for example, confrontation or avoidance, assertiveness or humility, cooperation or competition, and vary on other dimensions as well, which synergistically affect the ways that people in a given society approach conflict situations.

Core values also relate to perceptions of peace. Peace is often defined only in negative terms as the absence of violence and war, but peace can also be conceptualized in positive, more robust ways (Galtung, 1975; 1985). *Positive peace* can entail protection of human rights, social justice, social equity, sustainability, mechanisms for conflict resolution, and human security. The core values of Norway, for instance, are largely geared toward the concept of positive peace, not simply the reduction of aggression, as can be seen in Norwegian political and social policies as well as public and private discourse. Concrete manifestations of Norwegian peace values and norms are clearly visible in the country's social institutions and foreign policy. Over the last decades, Norway has maintained some of the lowest homicide rates worldwide (Fry, 2006). Domestically, youth mediation mechanisms exist in every municipality nationwide, and internationally, Norway has an established track record of active peace mediation (Dobinson, 2004; Fry, 2006). "The point is not only that peace is highly valued in Norwegian society and a central element in Norwegians' self-understanding, but also that dominant discourses reinforce this self-image of Norwegians as essentially peace loving" (Dobinson, 2004, p. 160). Core values as culturally promoted, life-guiding principles reinforce normative behaviors and are manifested in social institutions and customary practices. Research findings from anthropology and psychology converge on the conclusion that core values and norms are foundational in the maintenance of peace and prevention of violence.

Socialization for Peace and Prosociality

A peaceful society has "an extremely low level of physical aggression among its members as well as shared beliefs that devalue aggression and/or positively value harmonious interpersonal relationships" (Baszarkiewicz & Fry, 2008, p. 1557). The members of peaceful societies value harmony, gentleness, kindness, and positive relationships (Peaceful Societies, n.d.). More than 80 peaceful societies from various parts of the world and with various types of social organization have been documented (Fry, 2006; Howell & Willis, 1989; Sponsel & Gregor, 1994). Nonviolent attitudes within peaceful societies are actualized in nonpunitive childrearing practices (Fry, 2006; Montagu, 1978). The predominance of nonviolent educational and socialization practices, such as ignoring a young child's aggressive tantrums or shunning physical punishment as a disciplinary method, shape children into nonviolent adults (Montagu, 1978). Nonviolent childrearing is based on instructional rather than power-assertive discipline, providing children opportunities to strengthen their prosocial behaviors and to develop empathy toward others (Santa Barbara, 2008). Children also may be taught to show respect toward others and to deal with conflicts nonviolently (Kurtz, 2008). A consideration of nonviolent patterns of socialization among the Semai and Batek of Malaysia and Bosnian Muslims of Närpes, Finland, will illustrate some of these childrearing methods that prevent aggression as they promote the learning of prosocial values, norms, and behavior.

The Semai hold an image of themselves as a nonviolent people. They value equality, peacefulness, integration of villages, and interdependence among the band members (Robarchek, 1980). Both mothers and fathers actively participate in childrearing. They rarely intervene in children's activities and do not force their children do something against their will. Parents only intervene if a child becomes angry, loses self-control, or attacks another, which seldom happens. Semai parents rely on verbal education and persuasion instead of physical coercion (Dentan, 2010; Dentan & Edo, 2008). The Semai believe that corporal punishment is harmful to a child, since it damages a child's soul, leaving the child vulnerable to disease: "if a child were spanked, he or she might die" (Peaceful Societies, n.d.).

Semai childrearing practices can be seen as a crucial dimension in the prevention of violence and the promotion of prosocial behavior (Robarchek, 1980). Semai adults do not fight, fathers do not beat mothers, and parents do not hit their children, and as a consequence children lack aggressive models within Semai society (Robarchek, 1980; Robarchek & Robarchek, 1998). Already at an early age, a child learns that aggression disrupts the harmony and serenity of the community. Semai children observe how adults use such strategies as separation, gossip, or shaming instead of physical violence. Children also witness a formal conflict resolution assembly known as *becharaa'*. *Becharaa'* is a method for dealing with conflict in a nonviolent way. During this procedure, conflicting parties have a chance to express their viewpoints, and the group discussion continues until no one has anything left to say. The headman then recaps the discussion and concludes the *becharaa'* by giving a speech that emphasizes correct behavior and the importance of maintaining harmony within the group.

Another society from Malaysia, the Batek, also possesses peaceful values and nonviolent socialization methods. Batek culture highlights such values as autonomy, helping, sharing, respect, nonviolence, and noncompetitiveness (Endicott & Endicott, 2008, 2014). Batek childrearing practices generally produce children who are happy, emotionally secure, and self-confident individuals (Endicott & Endicott, 2014). From birth to 18 months, infants are actively taken care of by their mothers, fathers, or any adult or child nearby who cuddles, carries, and holds them (Peaceful Societies, n.d.).

Normally children are expected to learn skills and mature socially on their own by observation and practice (Endicott & Endicott, 2008). If very young children direct aggression at someone, they are simply picked up and moved elsewhere. As among the Semai, Batek parents avoid striking their children (Endicott & Endicott, 2014). In case of a dispute, people have public discussions, and if conflict resolution fails, people will simply leave the group to let their feelings of anger fade away. Children, of course, witness these approaches to conflict as they are growing up and come to act in accordance with these nonviolent culturally practiced ways of responding to conflict.

Närpes is a small coastal town in Finland with a population of 9,398 (Harald, 2012; Närpes Stad, 2014), where an anthropological study of community life is currently being conducted by one of the authors (Grigaitytė). The first 28 Bosnians came to Närpes as refugees in 1992, and today the Bosnian community numbers approximately 600 (Harald, 2012; Syd-Österbotten, 2012). Bosnian families live in the traditional settings where woman are seen as the moral and cultural guardians of a Muslim society. Child socialization practices are mainly nonviolent.

Parents teach girls and boys that it is very important to behave well and always consider "what others might think about you and your behavior." Parents explain that children are taught to be good to friends, have good thoughts, be honest, and always think about the consequences of their own behavior. Parents are not supposed to set strict rules for the children because there should always be mutual trust between them. The rare cases of a parent treating a teenager harshly have been met with community disapproval. Fathers are not as active in childrearing as mothers, and are usually more gentle and mild.

From a very early age, children are introduced to the core value—respect. Respect within the Närpes Bosnian community forms a foundation for social life.

First, respect is reflected toward oneself, which means people should behave in a manner that does not result in feelings of shame over their own conduct. Second, respect is shown through a set of prosocial attitudes and behaviors that include tolerance and acceptance of others, altruistic helping and sharing—that is, giving without expectations of being paid back—and frequent social involvement with family, friends, and community through visiting, attending social gatherings, and maintaining strong interpersonal and interfamilial bonds. Third, respect is exhibited through avoidance of alcohol, since consuming alcohol is known to result in disrespectful actions toward oneself and others. People believe that drinkers are aggressive, hurt other people's feelings, and behave in ways that make others angry. In an effort to instill respectful conduct in the young, the Bosnians of Närpes frequently point out the negative consequences of excessive alcohol drinking to their teenage kids.

Bosnian parents say that it is normal for children to test the rules while growing up: "In this way they learn what is accepted or not." In most cases parents ignore a child's misbehavior. If the irritation becomes overwhelming, a parent might scold a child or send the child to his or her room to cool down. Descriptions of interviewees and field observations suggest that most of the time parents employ nonviolent methods in raising their children. Bosnian parents only rarely attempt to spank a child. A 24-year-old woman, in a joking manner, said that here in Finland the Bosnian parents are afraid to hit their children because corporal punishment is illegal. Corporal punishment is prohibited in all settings and situations in Finland (End Corporal Punishment, n.d.). Bosnian parents who have lived in Finland for some years have taken up some of the common Finnish methods of dealing with children's misdemeanors: They might "ground" a child for an interval of time within the home, forbid Internet use, or take away the child's cell phone for some days.

The Bosnians of Närpes view physical fighting as the option of last resort, and in the course of growing up Bosnian children rarely witness physical aggression in their community. Instead, the children observe how their parents engage in prolonged discussion (when conflict occurs at home) or practice avoidance (if troubles arise among strangers). Gradually children internalize the community values and norms and adopt the community-favored approaches to conflict that do not involve physical aggression. Moreover, the Bosnians of Närpes think that it is shameful to show one's frustration or anger in public. Therefore they use body language and facial expressions more than speech in public situations; they fear "what the others might think about you and your family if you quarrel in public." For instance, if Bosnian children misbehave around other people, their parents typically just give them a look to convey to the children that they should behave themselves.

It is clear that physical punishment within the Bosnian community in Närpes is not the preferred option for socializing children. Instead, Bosnian parents tend to employ positive verbal means of discipline; they laugh and joke at children's misdemeanors, they cuddle and play with their children, provide children with guidelines for correct behavior, offer advice about how to handle a situation, and explain to their children how nonconfrontational and nonviolent behaviors are rooted in Bosnian culture and custom. Values favoring nonviolence, nonconfrontation, and respect are reflected in cultural and religious adages that are sometimes directed at children: "avoid kids that are aggressive," "if somebody pushes you in school, just walk away," "do not confront angry or drunk people," "always be good and do only good to your friends," "be glad and genuine when talking with your friends," "if you say or do something bad, you will not be able to sleep well at night," "bad things happen to people that are angry," "take care of your friends and respect your elders," "Allah watches you all the time," "have only good and happy thoughts because Allah knows what is in your mind."

Shift to Nonviolence in Principle and Practice

We are living in a world where violence is so rampant that some thinkers consider it to be an "innate trait" and that "might makes right." However, just as humans are capable of learning to hate and commit atrocities, they also can learn to love, forgive, and resolve differences without aggression, as occurs in some of the societies we have considered. The moral tenets of the nonviolence hinge upon love, forgiveness, and patience.

Nonviolence is not merely a utopian ideal; the seed of nonviolence lies in the soil of our own existence, awaiting nurturance to flourish (Nagler, 2004). Every human being has the ability to remain nonviolent by maintaining control over negative feelings of hatred and anger, and channel anger in positive directions rather than through violence. The fact that peaceful societies exist demonstrates that nonviolent social life is possible.

In terms of bringing about positive peace, nonviolence is a powerful force that has been shown to shake even the most brutal regimes and crumble the foundations of social injustice. The power of nonviolence is evident over the course of history, for example, as citizens saved Jews from Nazi brutality (Krieger, 2001). In the 1980s, Poland's nonviolent Solidarity movement resulted in the recognition of free trade unions, increases in wages, the right to strike, and ultimately the expulsion of communist rule (Senser, 1989). Similarly, the nonviolent Velvet Revolution led to the collapse of communism in former Czechoslovakia (Klicperova et al., 1997; Wolchik, 1990), and very recently the Egyptian resistance overthrew 30 years of dictatorship in 18 days of nonviolent struggle. These examples bear witness to the fact that nonviolence is one of the most powerful tools for reducing direct and indirect violence at the societal level. Recent research also demonstrates that nonviolent revolutions are twice as likely to succeed as violent ones (Chenoweth & Stephan, 2011).

Mohandas Gandhi, who coined the term nonviolence, claimed that it is universally applicable for overcoming socioeconomic and political injustice. Gandhi was the first to conduct well-planned, multifaceted nonviolent resistance campaigns to attain long-term goals (Irwin & Faison, 1984). Whereas nonviolence can entail the use of coercive tactics and the application of pressure of various sorts on an opponent, force is never exerted through physical violence (Cortright, 2006; Sharp, 2005). Patiently practicing nonviolence instead of initiating or retaliating with physical force does not mean that nonviolent resistance is a passive act. As one scholar noted, "nonviolent action is not passive. It is not inaction. It is action that is nonviolent" (Sharp, 2013, p. 18). Nonviolence is an act of rejecting physical violence even in the most difficult situations of self-defense or protection of the innocent (Howes, 2013). Through nonviolent tactics the activists mobilize the public to oppose or support certain policies. Nonviolent methods can serve to express the needs and sentiments of the people. As illustrated in Table 19.1, about 200 different nonviolent methods have been classified under the three categories of protests, noncooperation, and intervention, which people around the world have employed to voice their opposition to unjust laws, policies, and oppression (Chenoweth & Stephan, 2011; Dudouet, 2013; Sharp, 2005).

TABLE 19.1 Examples of Methods of Nonviolence Derived from Global Nonviolent Action Database (2015)

Category	Method	Examples
Protest & Persuasion		
	Processions	Save the Judiciary Movement (2007–2009) Pakistan
	Drama and Music	Saffron Revolution (2007) Burma
	Symbolic Public Acts	Thai Red Shirts protest against the Thai government (2010) Thailand
Noncooperation		
	Economic Noncooperation	Asian immigrant garment workers campaign for economic justice, San Francisco (1992–1996) USA
	Social Noncooperation	Danish citizens resist the Nazis (1940–1945)
	Political Noncooperation	Asian Democracy Campaigns (1980s) China
Intervention		
	Psychological Intervention	Journalists campaign against censorship in Moldova (2004)
	Political Intervention	Women form peace camp to protest housing of cruise missiles at Greenham Common (1981–1993) England
	Economic Intervention	Danilo Dolci leads fast and reverse strike for employment (1956) Italy

Political authority, even in repressive regimes, depends on the tacit consent and cooperation of the civilian population (Chenoweth & Stephan, 2011). However, the civilian population may not challenge a regime's authority even when their rights are violated. Moreover, some citizens such as soldiers and police may commit horrendous acts of violence against their fellow citizens by carrying out the orders of brutal leaders (Muller, 2014). Reflecting on this phenomenon, Gandhi once observed, "non-cooperation with evil is as much a duty as is cooperation with good" (O'Brien & O'Brien, 2009, pp. 13–14).

It is a matter of courage to say "no" to the ones in power using only the "weapon" of nonviolence. The nonviolent resisters, like well-trained soldiers, demonstrate discipline and bravery, but they strive to win over their opponents rather than harm them and to forgive the oppressors for their violence and other forms of abuse. Forgiveness is a difficult duty and a willful decision made by brave, nonviolent people (Muller, 2014).

Whereas armed insurgents rely on torture, massacres of civilians, bombings, rape, and destruction of property (Chenoweth & Stephan, 2011), participants in nonviolent movements rely on creative and effective methods such as sit-ins, work slowdowns, demonstrations, boycotts, satirical street theatre, nonpayment of rent, and so on to bring about positive change without harming anyone (Global Nonviolence Action Database, 2015; McCarthy & Sharp, 2013; Sharp 2005). Nonviolent campaigns also make their activities visible through the use of silent vigils, music, drama, symbols, colors, and prayers. Civil rights activists faced arrest, church and home bombings, flaming crosses, police dogs and fire hoses, and economic hardships of various sorts. However, they relied on the nonviolent methods of boycotts, sit-ins, marches, and gatherings at churches. The Reverend Martin Luther King, Jr., moved the hearts of millions with his 1963 "I Have a Dream" speech in which he explicitly advocated nonviolence. The persistent nonviolent struggle under the leadership of King and others resulted in the end of racial segregation, the passage of civil rights and voting rights legislation, and reduced discrimination against African Americans (Levy, 1998). Yet more remains to be done. Similarly, during the second civil war in Liberia many houses were burnt, people displaced, women raped, citizens maimed, tortured, and killed, and boys recruited as rebel soldiers (Disney & Gbowee, 2012). Under the leadership of social activists such as Leymah Gbowee, Christian and Muslim women of Liberia joined hands to fight for peace nonviolently. Wearing white shirts, holding posters with slogans of "we want peace," dancing and singing as a mark of solidarity, and always diligent in their sit-ins and protests, the women pressured ex-president Charles Taylor and the opposing rebel warlords to attend peace talks in Ghana, which resulted in a negotiated peace settlement for Liberia (Global Nonviolent Action Database, 2015).

Unity of the participants is a prominent element in successful nonviolent movements (Gregg, 1960). Additionally, discipline is crucial (Gandhi, 2001). Careful planning, strict discipline, and steadfast commitment also may be necessary for the success of a nonviolent campaign (Sharp & Jenkins, 1990). Support from third parties may be important (Cortright, 2006). An examination of successful nonviolent movements indicates that deliberate efforts to attract media attention in order to get third-party support were important (Baylor, 1996). The Velvet Revolution in former Czechoslovakia made use of the international media to foster support (Klicperova et al., 1997). In Chile, magazines, radio, TV, and newspapers played an important role in the ousting of General Pinochet and the restoration of democracy (Gunther & Mughan, 2000). The Pakistani media, through positive coverage of the Lawyer's Movement, played a vital role in mobilizing millions of citizens to join the nonviolent movement against the military dictator Pervez Musharraf for his unconstitutional sacking of the chief justice of Pakistan (Mezzera & Sial, 2010).

Worldwide, people regularly employ nonviolent methods and tactics to protest against social injustice, terrorist attacks, religious intolerance, unemployment, government corruption, and other problems. However, due to a paucity of media coverage, such movements suffer from the lack of broader visibility and support. Mass media need to report nonviolent activities as news that is worthy of coverage. As mentioned, nonviolent revolutions actually have about twice the success rate of violent rebellions, yet receive far less media attention than violent revolutions (Chenoweth & Stephan, 2011). The avoidance of coverage of nonviolence by the mainstream media has left it up to citizen journalists to report events on Facebook, Twitter, YouTube, blogs, and other social media, as occurred in Egypt during the Arab Spring (Eltantawy & Wiest, 2011). The citizen journalists prompted the mainstream media to pay attention to unarmed activists engaged in nonviolent struggle. In terms of reducing aggression, appropriate media coverage of nonviolent movements could raise public awareness that alternatives to violence exist and are more successful and less costly than violent resistance for bringing about desired social, economic, and political change (Bacha, 2011; Fry, 2006; Krieger, 2001). As a historical case in point, Gandhi made good use of the media during the "Salt Satyagraha" against the British salt tax policies through a publicity wave that inspired millions to participate (Golson, 2008). However, lack of knowledge and awareness about the effectiveness of nonviolence hinders its application. Mass media can educate people regarding the efficacy of nonviolence by showing more clearly when and how it is effective.

Making a commitment to nonviolence helps one to live at peace with oneself and others. Adopting and promoting nonviolent values, norms, and practices that are at the psychological and social foundation of the virtues of love, compassion, empathy, forgiveness, an awareness of common humanity, courage, and patience can help to win over the hearts and minds of opponents, reduce aggression, and bring about positive social change. This assessment is not merely utopian, in the dual sense first that nonviolence has triumphed over violence and contributed to positive peace in South Africa, Poland, former Czechoslovakia, India, the United States, the Philippines, Chile, Argentina, and many other locations where nonviolent social struggles have succeeded, and second that the very existence of peaceful societies such as the Hopi, Batek, Semai, Norway, and many more send a parallel message that nonviolent social life is indeed possible. Making personal and societal shifts to a nonviolent orientation may be challenging but, as many actual cases from recent world history conclusively show, it is not impossible.

Conclusions

In sum, the first lesson we can derive for the reduction of violence and the promotion of peaceful social life is that values and norms matter. They have an important role to play in preventing and reducing aggression. Once values are internalized, the social actors speak and behave with nonviolent core values as guiding principles (Triandes, 1994). Core values that promote nonviolence directly, as among some of the societies we have considered—the Ifaluk, Semai, Batek, Bosnians of Närpes, and Norwegians—can be seen as one ingredient in the social recipe for peace. Core values that are incompatible with aggression such as social harmony, respect for others, and humility, as illustrated among the Hopi, Semai, and Batek, suggest another less direct manner in which societal values and norms can play a role in preventing aggression. Clearly societies can develop norms that promote peace based on core values such as nonviolence and respect. A second lesson entails learning from peaceful societies and engaging in nonviolent childrearing practices. Nonviolent childrearing practices not only teach children to deal with everyday conflicts nonviolently but also can teach children creative responses to conflict. A third lesson entails the power of nonviolence. Well-disciplined nonviolent resistance can win rights with less bloodshed than violence. We suggest that both the mainstream media and citizen journalists can inform the world about the effectiveness and power of nonviolence to make this alternative to violence better known.

References

Bacha, J. (2011). Pay attention to nonviolence. Retrieved from: www.ted.com/talks/julia_bacha.

Bardi, A., & Schwartz, S. H. (2003). Values and behavior: Strength and structure of relations. *Personality and Social Psychology Bulletin, 29*, 1207–1220.

Baszarkiewicz, K., & Fry, D. P. (2008). Peaceful societies. In L. Kurtz (Eds.), *Encyclopedia of violence, peace, & conflict* (2nd ed., pp. 1557–1570). San Diego: Elsevier.

Baylor, T. (1996). Media framing of movement protest: The case of American Indian protest. *The Social Science Journal, 33*, 241–255.

Bonta, B. (1996). Conflict resolution among peaceful societies: The culture of peacefulness. *Journal of Peace Research, 33*, 403–420.

Bonta, B., & Fry, D. P. (2006). Lessons for the rest of us: Learning from peaceful societies. In M. Fitzduff & C. Stout (Eds.), *The psychology of resolving global conflicts: From war to peace, volume 1* (pp. 175–210). Westport, CT: Praeger Security International.

Carneiro, R. (1994). Kuikuru. In J. Wilbert (Ed.), *Encyclopedia of world cultures, volume VII, South America* (pp. 206–209). Boston: G. K. Hall.

Chenoweth, E., & Stephan, J. M. (2011). *Why civil resistance works: The strategic logic of nonviolent conflict.* New York: Columbia University Press.

Cortright, D. (2006). *Gandhi and beyond: Nonviolence for an age of terrorism.* London: Paradigm Publishers.

Dentan, R. K. (2010). Nonkilling social arrangements. In J. Evans Pim (Ed.), *Nonkilling societies* (pp. 101–130). Honolulu: Center for Global Nonkilling.

Dentan, R. K., & Edo, J. (2008). Schooling vs. education, hidden vs. overt curricula: Ways of thinking about schools, economic development, and putting the children of the poor to work—a west Malaysian example. *Moussons: Recherche en sciences humaines sur l'Asie du Sud-Est, 12,* 3–34. Retrieved from: http://moussons.revues.org/1533.

Disney, A., & Gbowee, L. (2012). Gender and sustainable peace. In P. Coleman & M. Deutsch (Eds.), *Psychological components of sustainable peace* (pp. 197–203). New York: Springer.

Dobinson, K. (2004). A model of peacefulness: Rethinking peace and conflict in Norway. In G. Kemp & D. P. Fry (Eds.), *Keeping the peace* (pp. 149–166). New York: Routledge.

Dovidio, J., Gaertner, S., & Saguy, T. (2009). Commonality and the complexity of "we": Social attitudes and social change. *Personality and Social Psychology Review, 13,* 3–20.

Dudouet, V. (2013). Dynamics and factors of transition from armed struggle to nonviolent resistance. *Journal of Peace Research, 50,* 401–413.

Eisler, R. (2007). *The real wealth of nations: Creating a caring economics.* San Francisco, CA: Berrett-Koehler Publishers.

Eltantawy, N., & Wiest, J. B. (2011). Social media in the Egyptian revolution: Reconsidering resource mobilization theory. *International Journal of Communication, 5,* 1207–1224.

End Corporal Punishment (n.d.). End corporal punishment: States with full abolition. Retrieved from: www.endcorporalpunishment.org.

Endicott, K. M., & Endicott, K. L. (2008). *The headman was a woman.* Long Grove, IL: Waveland Press.

Endicott, K. M., & Endicott, K. L. (2014). Batek child rearing and morality. In D. Narvaez, K. Valentino, A. Fuentes, J. McKenna, & P. Gray (Eds.), *Ancestral landscapes of human evolution* (pp. 108–125). New York: Oxford University Press.

Fry, D. P. (2004). Conclusion: Learning from peaceful societies. In G. Kemp & D. P. Fry (Eds.), *Keeping the peace* (pp. 185–204). New York: Routledge.

Fry, D. P. (2006). *The human potential for peace.* New York: Oxford University Press.

Fry, D. P. (2012). Life without war. *Science, 336,* 879–884.

Fry, D. P., & Björkqvist, K. (1997). *Cultural variation in conflict resolution: Alternatives to violence.* Mahwah, NJ: Erlbaum.

Galtung, J. (1975). *Essays in peace research,* volume 1. Copenhagen: Eljers.

Galtung, J. (1985). Twenty-five years of peace research: Ten challenges and some responses. *Journal of Peace Research, 22,* 141–158.

Gandhi. K. M. (2001). *Non-violent resistance.* New York: Dover Publications.

Gelles, R., & Straus, M. (1988). *Intimate violence.* New York: Simon & Schuster.

Gibson, T. (1989). Symbolic representations of tranquility and aggression among the Buid. In S. Howell & R. Willis (Eds.), *Societies at peace* (pp. 60–78). New York: Routledge.

Global Nonviolent Action Database (2015). Liberian women act to end civil war, 2003. Retrieved from: http://nvdatabase.swarthmore.edu/content/liberian-women-act-end-civil-war-2003.

Golson, M. (2008). A grain of salt can shake an empire. *Journal of Leadership and Service at Birmingham Southern College, 1*, 14–19.

Gregg, R. B. (1960). *The power of non-violence.* Canton, ME: Greenleaf.

Gunther, R., & Mughan, A. (Eds.). (2000). *Democracy and the media: A comparative perspective.* Cambridge: Cambridge University Press.

Harald, E. (2012, February 26). En del av Bosnien finns I Yttermark. *Vasbladet*, p. 15.

Howell, S., & Willis, R. (1989). *Societies at peace.* London: Routledge.

Howes, D. E. (2013). The failure of pacifism and the success of nonviolence. *Perspectives on Politics, 11*, 427–446.

Institute for Economics and Peace (n.d.). *Pillars of peace: Understanding the key attitudes and institutions that underpin peaceful societies*, IPE Report 22. Sydney: IPE.

Irwin, B., & Faison, G., (1984). Why Nonviolence? Introduction to nonviolence theory and strategy. In D. Albert (Ed.), *People power: Applying nonviolence theory* (pp. 2–10). Philadelphia: New Society Publishers.

Klicperova, M., Feierabend, K. I., & Hofstetter, R. C. (1997). Nonviolent conflict resolution and civic culture: The case of Czechoslovakia. In D. P. Fry & K. Björkqvist (Eds.), *Cultural variation in conflict resolution: Alternatives to violence* (pp. 173–182). Mahwah, NJ: Erlbaum.

Krieger, J. (Ed.). (2001). *The Oxford companion to politics of the world.* New York: Oxford University Press.

Kurtz, L. (2008). Preface. In L. Kurtz (Ed.), *Encyclopedia of violence, peace, & conflict* (2nd ed., pp. xix–xxv). San Diego: Elsevier.

Levy, P. B. (1998). *The civil rights movement.* Westport, CT: Greenwood.

McCarthy, R. M., & Sharp, G. (2013). *Nonviolent action: A research guide.* New York: Routledge.

Mezzera, M., & Sial, S. (2010). *Media and governance in Pakistan: A controversial yet essential relationship.* Technical report, IFP Democratization and Transitional Justice Cluster (Country Case Study: Pakistan). Retrieved from: www.initiativeforpeacebuilding.eu/pdf/pakistanOct.pdf.

Montagu, A. (1978). *Learning nonaggression.* New York: Oxford University Press.

Muller, J. M. (2014). *The principle of nonviolence: A philosophical path.* Honolulu: Center for Global Nonkilling.

Nagler, N. M. (2004). *The search for a nonviolent future: A promise of peace for ourselves, our families, and our world.* Novato, CA: New World Library

Närpes Stad (2014). *Närpes stad: Invånare.* Retrieved from: http://narpes.fi/.

O'Brien, A. S., & O'Brien, E. P. (2009). *After Gandhi: One hundred years of nonviolent resistance.* Watertown, MA: Charlesbridge.

Peaceful Societies (n.d.). Retrieved from: http://peacefulsocieties.org.

Rivière, P. (1994). Trio. In J. Wilbert (Ed.), *Encyclopedia of world cultures, volume VII, South America* (pp. 334–337). Boston: G. K. Hall.

Robarchek, C. A. (1980). The image of nonviolence: World view of the Semai Senoi. *Federation Museums Journal, 25*, 103–117.

Robarchek, C. A., & Robarchek, C. J., (1998). Reciprocities and realities: World views, peacefulness, and violence among Semai and Waorani. *Aggressive Behavior, 24*, 123–133.

Sampson, R., Raudenbush, S., & Earis, F. (1997). Neighborhoods and violent crime: A multilevel study of collective efficacy. *Science, 277*, 918–924.

Santa Barbara, J. (2008). Childrearing, violent and nonviolent. In L. Kurtz (Ed.), *Encyclopedia of violence, peace, & conflict* (2nd ed., pp. 211–228). San Diego: Elsevier.

Schlegel, A. (2004). Contentious but not violent: The Hopi of northern Arizona. In G. Kemp & D. P. Fry (Eds.), *Keeping the peace* (pp. 19–33). New York: Routledge.

Schultz, P.W., Gouveia, V.V., Cameron, L.D., Tankha, G., Schmuck, P., & Franek, M. (2005). Values and their relationship to environmental concern and conservation behavior. *Journal of Cross-Cultural Psychology, 36*, 457–475.

Senser, R. A. (1989). How Poland's Solidarity won freedom of association. *Monthly Lab Review, 112*, 34–38.

Sharp, G. (2005). *Waging nonviolent struggle: 20th century practice and 21st century potential.* Boston, MA: Porter Sargent Publishers.

Sharp, G. (2013). *How nonviolent struggle works.* Boston, MA: The Albert Einstein Institution.

Sharp, G., & Jenkins, B. (1990). *Civilian-based defense: A post-military weapons system.* Princeton: Princeton University Press.

Spiro, M. (1952). Ghosts, Ifaluk, and teleological functionalism. *American Anthropologist, 54*, 497–503.

Sponsel, L. E. (1994). The mutual relevance of anthropology and peace studies. In L. E. Sponsel & T. Gregor (Eds.), *The anthropology of peace and nonviolence* (pp. 1–20). Boulder: Lynne Rienner.

Sponsel, L.E., & Gregor, T. (1994). *The anthropology of peace and nonviolence.* Boulder: Lynne Rienner.

Straus, M. (2001). Physical aggression in the family: Prevalence rates, links to non-family violence, and implications for primary prevention of societal violence. In M. Martinez (Ed.), *Prevention and control of aggression and the impact on its victims* (pp. 181–200). New York: Kluwar Academic/Plenum.

Syd-Österbotten (2012, October 11). Bosnier får bidrag för fest. *Syd-Österbotten,* p. 14.

Triandes, H. (1994). *Culture and social behavior.* New York: McGraw Hill.

Wolchik, S. L. (1990). Czechoslovakia's "Velvet Revolution." *Current History, 89*, 413–416, 435–437.

INDEX

Note: Page numbers in italics indicate figures and tables.